Lecture Notes in Computer Sci

T0250659

Commenced Publication in 1973
Founding and Former Series Editors:
Gerhard Goos, Juris Hartmanis, and Jan van Leeuw

Frank Stajano   Catherine Meadows
Srdjan Capkun   Tyler Moore (Eds.)

Security and Privacy in Ad-hoc and Sensor Networks

4th European Workshop, ESAS 2007
Cambridge, UK, July 2-3, 2007
Proceedings

 Springer

Volume Editors

Frank Stajano
Tyler Moore
Computer Laboratory
University of Cambridge
Cambridge, UK
E-mail: Frank.Stajano,Tyler.Moore@cl.cam.ac.uk

Catherine Meadows
Center for High Assurance Computer Systems
Naval Research Laboratory
Washington, DC, USA
E-mail: meadows@itd.nrl.navy.mil

Srdjan Capkun
System Security Group
ETH Zurich, Switzerland
E-mail: capkuns@inf.ethz.ch

Library of Congress Control Number: 2007929079

CR Subject Classification (1998): E.3, C.2, F.2, H.4, D.4.6, K.6.5

LNCS Sublibrary: SL 5 – Computer Communication Networks
and Telecommunications

ISSN   0302-9743
ISBN-10   3-540-73274-8 Springer Berlin Heidelberg New York
ISBN-13   978-3-540-73274-7 Springer Berlin Heidelberg New York

Springer is a part of Springer Science+Business Media

springer.com

© Springer-Verlag Berlin Heidelberg 2007
Printed in Germany

Typesetting: Camera-ready by author, data conversion by Scientific Publishing Services, Chennai, India
Printed on acid-free paper   SPIN: 12082339   06/3180   5 4 3 2 1 0

Preface

You hold in your hands the proceedings of ESAS 2007, the Fourth European Workshop on Security and Privacy in Ad hoc and Sensor Networks. The workshop took place in Cambridge, UK, on the 2nd and 3rd of July 2007.

The workshop was European in name and location but it was definitely transatlantic in scope. We had a program chair from Europe and one from the USA, and membership of our program committee was almost evenly split between those two regions. When looking at participation, the workshop was even more global than that: the submitted papers came from 25 countries in 6 continents.

We received 87 submissions. After quick-rejecting 5 papers deemed to be out of scope, the remaining 82 papers were each reviewed by at least three PC members. The two program chairs, who did not submit any works, had sole authority to decide which papers to accept and reject, based only on the directive that quality had to be the primary criterion, in order to form a proceedings volume of high international relevance. The number of papers to be accepted was not set in advance: it was selected a posteriori so as to include only solid, innovative and insightful papers. The resulting acceptance rate of about 20%, very strict for a workshop, is a testimonial of how selective we chose to be in accepting only high quality papers. Congratulations to the authors published in this volume!

We arranged the accepted papers in the following sessions:

- Device Pairing
- Key Management
  Location Verification and Location Privacy
- Secure Routing and Forwarding
- Physical Security
- Detection of Compromise, and Revocation

As well as the 17 talks corresponding to the peer-reviewed papers, the workshop program also comprised a keynote talk by Paul Wilson and closed with a rump session in which attendees reported on late-breaking results. Since we went to press well ahead of the event, none of these additional talks are written up in this volume of workshop proceedings.

We are extremely grateful to many people and institutions who helped us make ESAS 2007 a reality. First and foremost, thank you to all the authors who submitted papers to the workshop and to everyone who attended, whether as a presenter or just a member of the audience. Special thanks to our keynote speaker Paul Wilson for giving us a wider perspective on the topics discussed at the workshop. Thanks to our sponsors, Microsoft Research, whose contribution allowed us among other things to endow some student bursaries. Thanks to the program committee members and to the additional reviewers for providing insightful comments about all the submitted papers. On the organizational side, thanks to publicity chair João Girão for attracting so many submissions and for managing the workshop Web site, to Kasper Bonne Rasmussen for managing the submission server and to Carol Speed at Cambridge for helping with the back-end of the payment system.

In closing, we note that this fourth one in Cambridge was the last ESAS workshop under this name. If you share our feelings, you will have noticed that there are really too many security workshops and conferences nowadays: it's impossible to follow them all and it gets harder and harder to put together a quality program. So we encourage our community to take part in a global spring cleaning effort to reduce the number of events; from our side, we (or more precisely our steering committee) have merged ESAS with ACM SASN (Workshop on Security of Ad Hoc and Sensor Networks) and ACM WiSe (Workshop on Wireless Security) to become **WiSec**, the ACM Wireless Security Conference. Joining forces and avoiding duplication makes sense: having fewer but higher-profile events will raise the quality of the submitted papers by avoiding dilution and will make us all more likely to meet the key people in our community whenever we attend. WiSec will alternate between the US and Europe, starting in the US in 2008. See you there!

April 2007

Frank Stajano
Cathy Meadows
Srdjan Capkun
Tyler Moore

Organization

ESAS 2007 was hosted by the Security Group of the Computer Laboratory of the University of Cambridge and took place in Sidney Sussex College, Cambridge.

General Chair

Frank Stajano — University of Cambridge, UK

Program Co-chairs

Catherine Meadows — Naval Research Laboratory, USA
Srdjan Capkun — ETH Zurich, Switzerland

Local Arrangements Chair

Tyler Moore — University of Cambridge, UK

Publicity Chair

João Girã — NEC Europe Network Lab, Germany

Steering Committee

Levente Buttyán — Budapest University of Technology and Economics, Hungary
Claude Castelluccia — INRIA, France
Dirk Westhoff — NEC Europe Network Lab, Germany

Webmasters

João Girão — NEC Europe Network Lab, Germany
Kasper Bonne Rasmussen — ETH Zurich, Switzerland
Tyler Moore — University of Cambridge, UK

Program Committee

Imad Aad — DoCoMo Lab Europe, Germany
Tansu Alpcan — Deutsche Telekom Laboratories/TU Berlin, Germany
Farooq Anjum — Telcordia Research, USA
N. Asokan — Nokia, Finland
Gildas Avoine — MIT, USA

Lejla Batina	ESAT SCD/COSIC, Belgium
Levente Buttyn	Budapest University of Technology and Economics, Hungary
Mario Cagalj	University of Split, Croatia
Claude Castelluccia	INRIA, France
Xuhua Ding	Singapore Management University, Singapore
Saurabh Ganeriwal	Google, USA
Virgil Gligor	University of Maryland, College Park, USA
Christian D. Jensen	Technical University of Denmark, Denmark
Markus Kuhn	University of Cambridge, UK
Loukas Lazos	University of Washington, USA
Wenke Lee	Georgia Institute of Technology, USA
Mingyan Li	Boeing, USA
Donggang Liu	University of Texas at Arlington, USA
Refik Molva	Institute Eurocom, France
Peng Ning	NC State, USA
Kaisa Nyberg	Helsinki University of Technology, Finland
Radha Poovendran	University of Washington, USA
Michael Roe	Microsoft Research, Cambridge, UK
Mani Srivastava	UCLA, USA
Dirk Westhoff	NEC Europe Network Lab, Germany
Susanne Wetzel	Stevens Institute of Technology, USA

Additional Referees

Gergely Ács	Aurélien Francillon	Dave Singelée
Frederik Armknecht	Alban Hessler	Claudio Soriente
Farshad Bahari	Maarit Hietalahti	Gelareh Taban
Aldar Chan	Tamás Holczer	Patrick Tague
Jared Cordasco	Sotiris Ioannidis	Slim Trabelsi
László Csik	Frank Kargl	Liu Yang
Christophe De Cannière	Nitesh Saxena	Yanjiang Yang
Qi Dong	Stefaan Seys	Fan Zhang
László Dóra	Abdullatif Shikfa	

Sponsoring Institutions

Gold Sponsor

Microsoft Research Cambridge, UK

Table of Contents

Physical Security

Detection of Compromise, and Revocation

The Candidate Key Protocol for Generating Secret Shared Keys from Similar Sensor Data Streams

Rene Mayrhofer

Lancaster University, Computing Department, South Drive, Lancaster LA1 4WA, UK
rene@comp.lancs.ac.uk
http://www.comp.lancs.ac.uk/

Abstract. Secure communication over wireless channels necessitates authentication of communication partners to prevent man-in-the-middle attacks. For spontaneous interaction between independent, mobile devices, no a priori information is available for authentication purposes. However, traditional approaches based on manual password input or verification of key fingerprints do not scale to tens to hundreds of interactions a day, as envisioned by future ubiquitous computing environments. One possibility to solve this problem is authentication based on similar sensor data: when two (or multiple) devices are in the same situation, and thus experience the same sensor readings, this constitutes shared, (weakly) secret information. This paper introduces the *Candidate Key Protocol* (CKP) to interactively generate secret shared keys from similar sensor data streams. It is suitable for two-party and multi-party authentication, and supports opportunistic authentication.

Keywords: context authentication, sensor data, cryptographic hash.

1 Introduction

Secure communication over a wireless channel is a difficult problem, especially for spontaneous interaction. Spontaneous interaction in the sense of ad-hoc communication between devices is often aimed for in ubiquitous computing [1], following its vision of seamlessly interacting with whatever services are currently available and useful. Moreover, many of these proposed devices are small, need to cope with limited resources such as memory, computational power and battery life, and do not have any conventional user interfaces such as key pads or displays. Communication is assumed to happen over shared wireless channels that are open to any device, which is necessary to enable transparent interoperability.

It is difficult to secure such interactions because we can not assume the involved devices to have any a priori information about each other. Creating a secure channel depends on an authentication step. If Alice (A) wants to interact with Bob (B)[1] and does not know anything about Bob a priori, then she will

---

[1] In the context of this paper, we use A, B, and E for describing the devices that interact with each other interchangeably with the established names Alice, Bob,

F. Stajano et al. (Eds.): ESAS 2007, LNCS 4572, pp. 1–15, 2007.

be unable to distinguish a legitimate interaction with Bob from malicious behavior by Eve (E) — Eve can simply perform a valid protocol run with Alice. Currently, there is no globally trusted public key infrastructure (PKI), and it is doubtful if there will be any. Even if there was one that would be able to sign trusted devices, it would not solve the problem of authenticating spontaneous interaction: Eve could just set up a trusted device E of her own and intercept the communication by getting A to communicate with her device instead of B. We therefore need to individually authenticate the interaction between each communicating pair of devices. Such authentication essentially aims at secret key agreement between A and B.

This problem is amplified as ubiquitous computing is expected to generate far more frequent spontaneous interactions. When using hundreds of different devices each day, conventional authentication methods like passwords or PINs fail to scale. Examples of devices that communicate wirelessly with each other are mobile phones, Bluetooth headsets, networked cameras, printers, in the near future goggles with integrated displays, and many more. We use the practical example of establishing a secure channel between a mobile phone and a Bluetooth headset without loss of generality.

Our approach is to authenticate devices based on shared context, which is manifested by similar sensor readings. Whenever two devices are in the same situation, e.g. being worn by the same person, capturing the same audio environment, or just being close to the same object, their sensors will experience similar time series. These time series can be used to implicitly authenticate a secure channel between the devices. There are multiple possibilities for authentication based on similar time series. The more conventional approach is to perform an unauthenticated (anonymous) key agreement like Diffie-Hellman [2], exchange the time series using the secret shared key via some commitment scheme, and compare if they are similar enough with an appropriate metric to prevent manin-the-middle (MITM) attacks. However, this approach is computationally expensive and consists of two phases, which introduces an additional delay. We present an authentication protocol, the *Candidate Key Protocol* (*CKP*), which derives cryptographic key material directly from sensor data streams and utilizes only hash functions as cryptographic primitives.

In Section 2, we discuss related work and motivate the need for an authentication protocol based on conventional primitives in spite of more recent research on information theoretic security. After defining the threat scenarios that CKP is designed to deal with in section 3, we explain the approach and detailed specification of CKP in section 4. A first practical implementation using UDP multicast and initial experimental results are described in sections 5 and 6, respectively. We finish with discussing the security properties and possibilities for extending the protocol in section 7.

---

and Eve of the respective users. The reason is that one of the devices might be an infrastructure device, such as a printer or a display, that does not belong to any single user.

2   Related Work

Results from two research areas are relevant to the present paper: information theoretical work in cryptography with influences from quantum cryptography, and authentication protocols inspired by practical issues, mostly from ubiquitous computing research.

Generating keys from noisy channels, or more generally, from (random) correlated information, received some attention in theoretical cryptography research, e.g. [3][4][5][6]. For a good introduction into the topic and for results for public, non-authenticated channels, we refer to [7,8,9]. These publications give interesting information theoretical results on key agreement, which no longer assume the intractability of some computational problem like the discrete logarithm problem, but provide what is often called "unconditional security". The basic concept is that, when two legitimate communication partners either have a noisy communication channel or when they have access to correlated information, then it is possible for them to agree to a secret key even when an adversary has access to their noisy channel or partial knowledge of their shared information. There are two classes of such authentication protocols: interactive, e.g. [7,8,9], and non-interactive, e.g. [6]. Non-interactive protocols have the obvious advantage that they can be used to establish a shared secret when only one-way communication is available. This has additional practical consequences. Even when two-way communication is possible, issues like time delays, packet loss, etc. can be handled more easily with non-interactive protocols. On the other hand, interactive protocols are necessary under the assumption of active adversaries (see e.g. [7, section III.D]). Our proposed protocol is interactive.

Other results [10] seem particularly promising because they describe an authentication protocol based on a weak secret key, which closely matches our real world problem of using sensor time series as a weak secret key.

However, these theoretical results do not yet seem to have been implemented, and practical applicability is therefore still limited. Another problem is that, although the shared secrets may be weak, large secrets are required to guarantee the security properties of these protocols. For small and embedded devices, it is difficult to process large strings of secret data, and it is difficult to find good sources of large secret strings in the first place.

In contrast, we use conventional, i.e. computational, cryptographic primitives based on intractability assumptions which are still assumed to hold. With possible future availability of quantum computers, these assumption may need to be revised. In this paper, we use the terminology of information theoretical cryptography as far as appropriate because of the similar aims and assumptions. When adding the assumption of non-reversibility of cryptographic hash functions, then our proposed Candidate Key Protocol can be seen as an instance of a secret key agreement based on correlated random variables.

It is not obvious how the calculus introduced in [8] for noisy channels could be applied to the case of similar sensor time series that A and B have access to and which E can get some knowledge about. Future work may use this or a similar calculus to analyze the security of CKP more analytically.

A large number of interactive protocols based on authenticated Diffie-Hellman (*DH*) key exchange [11] have recently been suggested, mostly inspired by practical problems of authentication in real world applications. This is assumed to be computationally, instead of unconditionally secure. The classical interlock protocol [12] can be seen as a predecessor of these, but it already used the notion of committing to values before revealing them. Newer protocols are mostly based on commitment schemes, e.g. the MANA family of protocols for manual string input or verification [13], optimized in [14].

While the "resurrecting duckling protocol" [15] aims at long-lived pairings, Hoepman introduced pairing protocols for short-lived interactions based on manual exchange of secrets [16][17], which scales poorly from a user point of view. The protocol proposed in [16] is very similar to MANA III [13] and seems to have been developed independently. Vaudenay claims [18] that Hoepman's protocol can not be implemented securely due to the lack of known hash functions with properties required by the protocol, and presents a protocol called SAS, which provides the same level of security with shorter shared secrets.

Creese et al. introduce a formal model for verifying authentication protocols that work with empirical verification [19]. They present the analysis of three related pairing protocols and show proofs of their security under their model.

Čagalj et al. describe three other pairing protocols with similar aims, based on short string comparison, distance bounding, and integrity codes [20]. Their second protocol is based on distance measurement, but we suggest that their scheme might be applicable to an interactive challenge-response scheme based on sensor data.

CKP is related to all these protocols because it shares similar aims, but differs in the approach. Instead of authenticating ephemeral session keys or long-term pairings created with DH, CKP creates shared keys by using sensor streams as input.

3   Threat Scenarios

In this section, we briefly outline the threat scenarios that are relevant to a device authentication protocol and to CKP in particular. Typical threats for a communication channel are *eavesdropping*, *replaying* of messages, and *deletion*, *insertion* and *modification* of messages. All of these threats are subsumed in the so-called man-in-the-middle (*MITM*) attack, where E is assumed to be "in between" A and B and have complete control over their communication channel. When an unauthenticated key agreement like Diffie-Hellman is used between A and B, E can delete all messages between A and B and instead perform two independent key agreements, one with A and one with B. In this paper, we explicitly assume an active adversary, and CKP is designed to detect when a MITM attack is being performed and fail to authenticate in this case. However, in the general case, it is not possible to distinguish between a *benign* authentication failure when the sensor values experienced by A and B are not similar enough and a *malign* authentication failure caused by an attack.

Another typical threat is *denial of service* (DoS). This refers to E making communication, and in the scope of this paper, authentication impossible between A and B. When assuming an active adversary, DoS is easily possible and will therefore not be discussed further. However, the protocol should provide indication to the user when it can not complete, either due to benign communication error or due to a DoS attack. Distinguishing between these two cases is, again, not possible in the general case and we therefore treat them equally.

We also point out that attacks on the involved devices themselves are out of the scope of this paper and assume that the two devices A and B are trusted for the purpose of the interaction. If A trusts B with some document, but B (intentionally or due to an attack) forwards it to E, then authentication between A and B can not prevent this.

To summarize, our main threat scenario is an active attack on the (wireless) channel including full MITM capabilities. We assume that there is some sensor data which both A and B can get with better accuracy than E. Here we use the same argument as applied in [7, Theorem 5]: if Alice and Bob do not share any correlated information, then "from Bob's point of view, Alice has no advantage compared to Eve. If Eve performs the same protocol as Alice would, pretending to be Alice, Bob accepts with the same probability as he would accept a protocol execution with Alice". Assuming an experiment where Alice, Bob, and Eve can receive the same bit string over independent noisy channels, [7] concludes that "secret-key agreement against *active* adversaries is only possible if Alice's and Bob's channels are both less noisy than Eve's channel". This is to be intuitively expected, but in contrast to the results for passive adversaries [3].

We argue that this assumption is justified because, when A and B are in a similar context, their sensor time series should be more similar to each other than to the sensor time series perceived by E, even if only slightly. This can be achieved by measuring *local* physical phenomena which an adversary can not reasonably influence to obtain measurements with higher accuracy than A and B. Examples for appropriate phenomena are acceleration, sound, light, or radio frequency signal strength.

4 The Candidate Key Protocol

The candidate key protocol interactively generates secret shared keys from sensor streams between two (or multiple) devices. Figure 1 shows the relations between A, B and E. All devices are assumed to have full access to a wireless communication channel, and we explicitly assume E to be capable of deleting, inserting, and modifying messages between A and B without them being able to notice at this level. Additionally, A and B are assumed to share aspects of their context and have sensors that can capture these aspects. E is assumed not to share the same context, but be able to access it with (similar or different) sensors with inferior accuracy.

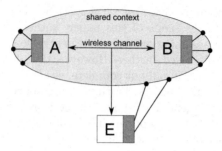

Fig. 1. Assumptions of CKP: A, B, and E share complete access to a wireless channel, and restricted access to the context in which interaction is taking place

4.1 Approach

Our approach to generating secret shared keys from similar, but not equal, sensor time series is based on the concept of *candidates*. When sampling sensor time series, raw samples are typically not used directly, but more meaningful *features* are extracted based on domain specific knowledge. We note that this step is critical for any use of sensor data, although the respective requirements depend on the application. For authentication, i.e. generating cryptographic key material, it is important for the extracted features to have high entropy from an adversary's point of view. In the terms typically used for feature extraction and context-aware systems, high entropy implies that the chosen features must clearly distinguish devices being in the same context from devices being in different contexts. The reverse, however, does not necessarily hold. Good separation in this sense does not imply high entropy, because an adversary is free to choose different features. Therefore, features should be chosen such that an adversary can learn the least amount of information about their specific values. We can not give generally valid recommendations because features are highly application specific. For the scope of this paper, we assume feature vectors to be available as input for authentication.

Even with features that perform well for a given application, there is still room for errors. To generate key material from feature vectors, we need to convert to integer values at some point; simple quantization errors can then lead to different keys even when the feature vectors are very similar. That is, quantization can increase noise. Generally, extracting and comparing feature vectors is a classification problem with the usual trade-off between separation and recall. Making features more distinctive to generate higher entropy will generate more errors in comparing feature vectors from devices in the same context, i.e. *false negatives*. Tuning the features for more robustness will make it easier for an adversary to estimate their values, i.e. generate *false positives*. For the purpose of authentication, false positives must be strictly avoided, but when the false negatives rate is too high, the authentication method may become unusable in practice. Therefore, our approach is to allow the feature extraction step to yield multiple (parallel) feature vectors in each time step. We then use these multiple

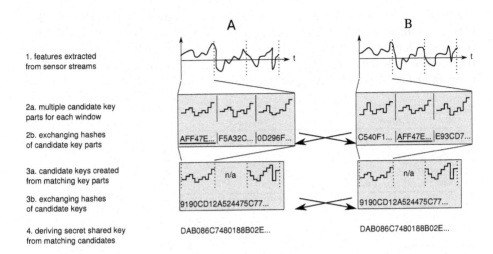

Fig. 2. Approach to generating a secret shared key: candidate key parts are time windows over extracted features from sensor time series and are concatenated to candidate keys

different candidates in a way that does not leak additional information to an adversary, and thereby provide a partial solution to this trade-off.

In Fig. 2 we show an overview of CKP, starting with the extracted features. The generation of multiple candidates for each feature vector is again application specific, but there exist general methods. One example is that different offsets for quantization can be used to alleviate the problem of quantization errors and thus solve a large class of false negatives. This method is depicted in Fig. 2. Every feature vector becomes a *candidate key part*. That is, it is a candidate for inclusion in the shared secret, subject to matching with the remote device. We then compute hashes of all candidate key parts for the current time step, which we abstract to a strictly monotonically increasing round number. These hashes are exchanged between A and B to verify which of the candidate key parts, if any, match. Note that transmitting their cryptographic hash values does not reveal any useful information about the candidate key parts themselves, because secure hash functions are assumed to be one-way functions. After a sufficient number of matching key parts, i.e. after accumulating enough entropy, the matching key parts are concatenated to a *candidate key*. With the possibility of multiple matches in each round, there are different ways to concatenate this key. Therefore, hashes of the candidate keys are again exchanged between A and B. When they match, A and B have successfully agreed to a shared secret.

4.2 Specification

After introducing the concepts of candidate key parts and candidate keys, we now present the detailed specification of CKP. Figure 3 defines the steps of the protocol.

For the formal description, we use the following notation: $H(m)$ describes the hashing of message m with some secure hash algorithm, and $m|n$ describes the concatenation of strings m and n. The symbol $\oplus$ describes bit-wise XOR and $|S|$ the number of elements in a set S. When a message M is transmitted over an insecure channel, we denote the received message $\widetilde{M}$ to point out that it may have been

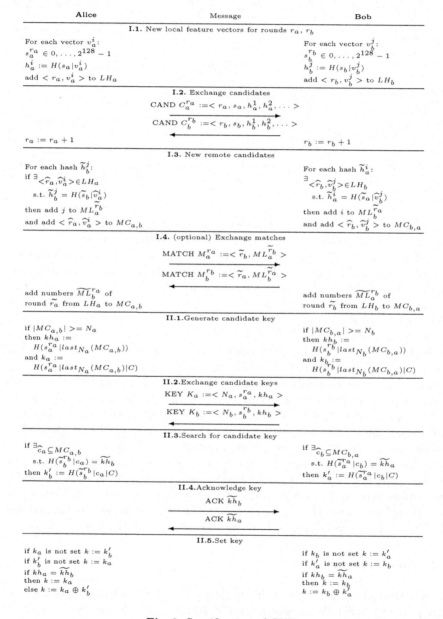

Fig. 3. Specification of CKP

modified in transit, by noise or attack. Subscripts denote the different sides (a or b for an authentication between A and B), while superscripts denote specific vectors in a set of vectors. The syntax $\hat{x}$ denotes the (open) result of a search for matches in a set. When a hash is computed from a set of vectors, we mean the concatenation of all vectors in some pre-defined order, typically by their round number.

v denotes raw feature vectors without cryptographic key properties, i.e. they do not need to be distributed uniformly. h denotes cryptographic hashes of feature vectors and r denotes round numbers. Each host keeps a set LH as a history of recently added local feature vectors and one set MC for each remote host to store the matching candidates as reported by this host. Any of the SHA family of hashes seems appropriate to implement H, and we currently use SHA-256 as a secure hash.

CKP consists of two phases:

I *Collecting entropy from feature vectors and determining matching candidate key parts*: In step I.1, locally generated feature vectors are stored in a local history for future reference. This history LH may be implemented as a circular buffer, overwriting oldest feature vectors. By computing the secure hash, *candidate key parts* are created from these feature vectors and sent to the remote device in step I.2. Note that each round r uses a unique salt value s^r that is prepended before hashing to make attacks with lookup tables more expensive.

In step I.3, received candidate key parts are compared with feature vectors in the local history LH. All matching vectors are advanced to the status of *matching key parts* by adding them to the set of matching candidates MC, which is specific to each remote host that CKP is run with.

Step I.4 is optional, and should only be used in asymmetrical settings. In an asymmetrical setting, only one host broadcasts candidate key parts. Any host receiving the candidate key parts and recognizing matching key parts acknowledges these matches, which enables the broadcasting host to keep track of matching key parts.

II *Generating the secret shared key*: Each host can check locally if enough matching key parts have been collected, and/or if the associated feature vectors accumulate enough entropy for a secret shared key. When the local criteria are fulfilled, a *candidate key* k and an associated *candidate key identifier* kh are generated in step II.1 by concatenating the feature vectors that belong to the last N matching key parts and, again, computing secure hashes over the concatenated string with prepended salt values. To decouple the actual key and its identifier, a public padding string C is appended before hashing for the generation of k. The candidate key identifiers are exchanged in step II.2.

In step II.3, the hosts then try to locally generate a key that matches a received candidate key identifier. This may be computationally expensive, depending on the number of matching key parts in MC, the number of matching key parts N used for the generation of kh, and the number of duplicate matches in each round. The reason is that, for example, host B has no knowledge about the exact set of matching key parts chosen by host A to generate its kh_a. Because hosts A and B may be out of sync with their round counters, it is unknown which rounds contributed matching key parts. And because A and B most probably generate candidate key parts in different order even within the same round, it is unknown which of the matches in a specific round was chosen when there were multiple. B therefore needs to try all possible combinations of N_a elements of $MC_{b,a}$, which has potentially a run time complexity of $O(A^H)$ where A is the maximum number of different candidate feature vectors generated in each round, and $H > N$ is the maximum size of the history MC. However, in practice we expect only few duplicates, and the search can be further optimized by starting with the most likely, i.e. the most recent, round numbers recorded in MC. Another possible optimization is to transmit the round and vector numbers with candidate key messages to uniquely identify the set of parts. This trade-off between message size and computational cost depends on application-specific cost models, but does not influence the security level of the protocol.

If a matching key could be generated, it is acknowledged in step II.4. After receipt of a *key acknowledge*, the hosts can start to use the generated key k that matches the acknowledged key identifier kh.

Note that at this stage, there is the possibility that the generated keys at hosts A and B are different. This can happen when hosts A and B independently generate and exchange candidate keys in steps II.1 and II.2 and the respective KEY messages overlap during transmission. Then, in steps II.3 and II.4, both hosts may find and acknowledge the respective remote host's key, again with overlapping ACK messages. That is, when host A generated a key k_1 and B a key k_2 in step II.1, then after step II.4, host A may have found and acknowledged k_2 while B may have found and acknowledged k_1. By concurrently reacting to overlapping messages, A and B have effectively swapped their keys, but are still left with different k_1 and k_2. To solve this synchronization problem locally, the hosts remember the originally generated keys and check if the received key acknowledge is different. If yes, they can simply compute the final secret shared key as the XOR of the two different keys.

In this form, CKP does not assume the communication channel to have any specific properties, because our basic assumption is a MITM with full control over this channel.

5 Implementing CKP with Lossy Channels

In a practical implementation, the communication channel may be lossy. That is, packet delivery is not guaranteed even when no MITM attack is taking place. This is the case for most broadcast radio frequency (RF) channels such as IEEE 802.11 WLAN or IEEE 802.15.4 ZigBee.

Our first implementation of CKP uses UDP as a lossy communication protocol. This has three advantages: a) UDP can be used directly between any hosts connected via an IP based network. b) UDP allows to broad- or multicast packets and can therefore be used for group authentication or spontaneous authentication as described in more detail below. c) UDP offers guarantees comparable to many low-level broadcast RF channels, thus porting our implementation e.g. to TinyOS [21], should be straightforward.

The protocol specification presented in section 4 lends itself to implementation on lossy channels, because it is robust against packet loss. When candidate key parts get lost, there will simply be no matches for the respective round. When candidate keys get lost, they can not be used to generate secret shared keys, but new candidate keys will be generated in subsequent rounds. However, issues arising from asynchronism and overlapping messages need to be dealt with at the implementation level.

There are various possibilities for asynchronism in CKP. Here we concentrate on the case where a remote message arrives for a round before the respective local action has been processed. This includes many special cases like a disparity between the system clocks or delayed processing due to multi-tasking. To cope with such asynchronism, we introduce message buffers to keep a history of recently received messages. Then, when local operations such as adding new feature vectors are processed, this history is replayed to simulate a new arrival of messages using the updated local state. This method allows to cope with asynchronism while considering limited resources in terms of memory and CPU capabilities.

Note that, among others, [7, Theorem 8] states that "perfect synchronization is impossible", i.e. that there are always some cases in which the decisions of Alice and Bob about generating a common key are different. Our implementation of CKP using UDP can only safeguard against Alice and Bob agreeing to a different shared key (i.e. a MITM attack). But, under the assumption of a completely insecure communication channel without any guarantees, it will always be possible for one host to finish the protocol with success, while the other finishes with failure. In this case, further secure communication is not possible, and the hosts can use time-outs to detect it.

6   First Experimental Results

CKP has already been applied to one specific device pairing method: implicit authentication by shaking devices together for a few seconds [22]. This method uses 3D accelerometers as input to two alternative authentication protocols, one of them being CKP. When shaking two devices with integrated accelerometers together, their sensor time series are similar enough to create a secret shared key, but an adversary can not obtain these time series with sufficient accuracy. The lower bound of the entropy rate has been estimated at about 7 bits per second [22], which means that around 20 s of shaking are sufficient to generate over 128 bits of entropy. Experiments on "human man-in-the-middle" attacks, where adversaries try to duplicate the shaking patterns of victims to produce similar sensor time series, show that people are unable to reproduce these patterns even when we allow for cooperation between adversary and victim (which would not be possible during a real attack). It remains to be shown if high-speed cameras could be used to estimate the local acceleration values and thus lower the candidate key parts entropy from an adversary's point of view.

7   Security Analysis and Discussion

When generating cryptographic key material, the most important point is to achieve high entropy with regards to a possible adversary's knowledge. A key can only remain secret if Eve is sufficiently uncertain about it. It is important to note that, principally, CKP can not increase the entropy of a secret key compared to the total entropy of all feature vectors it has been created from. Instead, any public communication between Alice and Bob must reveal something about the key — CKP can only try to make this additional information useless to Eve. Note that feature extraction and estimation of entropy are entirely application specific. We can only assume the locally added feature vectors to carry sufficient entropy, and leave it to the specific implementation to guarantee this.

Hashing the sensor time series to generate candidate key parts and candidate keys serves to reduce an adversary's usable information about them. This is often termed "privacy amplification". When we assume the SHA family of hash functions to be universal as defined in [23] and reproduced in [24], then an upper bound for the information that Eve can obtain about the secret key has been shown in [24, Corollary 5]: if Eve has access to t bits of the (weak) secret W with n bits, then her expected knowledge about a key $K = H(W)$ with a length of $r = n - t - s$ bits for some safety parameter $s < n - t$ is restricted to a maximum of $2^{-s}/\ln 2$. This assumes that W is uniformly distributed. For our application to sensor time series, W is not uniformly distributed, and a significant part of its distribution function may be known to Eve. We can only conjecture that the above corollary may be applicable to those components of the sensor time series that are completely unknown to Eve and thus uniformly distributed from her point of view, but can not currently provide a proof. This conjecture suggests that, if we intend to extract a secret shared key with a size of $r = 128$ bits, then the difference between the length of the sensor time series W and Eve's information about it, i.e. $n - t$ bits, must be larger then 128. Intuitively, this requirement is trivial. But the theoretical analysis indicates that by hashing the input, all the entropy of the weakly secret sensor time series should be retained in K. This means that transmitting the candidate key parts, which are hashes over the sensor time series, should not reveal more about them than an adversary already knew. It is currently unclear if more information about the final secret key is revealed when MATCH messages are transmitted to acknowledge matching candidate key parts, but we do not expect this to be the case. Nonetheless, the normal mutual authentication mode seems more conservative, because only the candidate key part hashes and the candidate key hashes are transmitted, but no more information about which of the candidate key parts have been used to construct the secret key.

It is important to note that there is a possibility for brute-force attack. The problem arises when parts that are extracted from sensor time series only have a small entropy from Eve's point of view. In this situation, even when reversing the hash function is impossible, she could just generate lookup tables of all possible time series parts and compare their hashes with the CAND messages. This is slightly mitigated by our use of salting, but only makes the attack more computationally expensive, and not less likely to be successful. Eve only needs to keep a small amount of possibly matching key parts in a history to try and create keys that match the transmitted KEY messages, in much the same way that is also used in the legitimate protocol run. For this reason, it is better to use less candidate key parts to construct a key. When the sensor time series parts that can be extracted naturally using domain specific knowledge only have a small entropy, then multiple such parts should be buffered and bundled into one candidate key part. Guessing a candidate key part and verifying that it matches its received hash value has an average complexity of $O\left(2^{e-1}\right)$ when the feature vector has e bits of entropy from Eve's point of view. Thus, two concatenated feature vectors would need $O\left(2^{2e-1}\right)$ steps to guess. This entropy level directly defines the security level of the whole CKP run. It has been shown in [24] that adding random material can in principle increase the length of K that can be extracted from the weak secret W, but we currently do not see a method to apply this to CKP.

Finally, there are two additional advantages of CKP over more traditional authentication protocols, e.g. ones based on public key infrastructures. First, the continuous broadcasting of candidate key parts and, after detecting matches, of candidate keys, allows remote hosts to "tune in to" another host's authentication stream. This allows to easily construct applications with *opportunistic authentication*, where hosts automatically authenticate with each other as soon as they enter a shared context: when a host picks up broadcasts from another and is able to generate matching key parts, they are guaranteed to record similar sensor readings.

Second, CKP can be trivially generalized to group authentication. In the specification in Fig. 3, only steps II.4 and II.5 need to be adapted. All hosts can continue to generate candidate key parts and candidate keys, and to search for candidate keys as for two-host authentication. However, keys can only be acknowledged and used in steps II.4 and II.5, respectively, after all hosts that should be members of the authenticated group were able to generate matching keys. A possible solution is to split step II.4 into a *tentative acknowledge* and a *group acknowledge* message, where the latter is only sent after the tentative acknowledge has been received from all group members.

8   Conclusions

Our proposed Candidate Key Protocol (CKP) is one approach to solving the problem of device-to-device authentication for spontaneous interactions. Replacing *explicit* means of authentication like manual password input or string verification with an *implicit* authentication based on similar sensor data streams offers significant advantages from a user point of view: wireless communication can be made secure by default instead of relying on a separate authentication step.

Context-based authentication is in fact a classification problem, with the known problems of false positives, which need to be strictly avoided for security reasons, and false negatives, which hinder seamless and unobtrusive user interaction. One main novelty of CKP is that multiple candidate key parts in each step can be used to address the problem of false negatives. Its advantages over other proposed approaches to the same problem and based on Diffie-Hellman key agreement authenticated by short, or weak, shared secrets are threefold: it is less computationally expensive and thus well suited for implementation with limited resources, it provides opportunistic authentication, and it is trivially extensible to group authentication. The major disadvantage is that the generated secret shared key is only as secure as the entropy of the candidate key parts and that it does not provide forward secrecy. Newer results on information theoretically secure key agreement are very promising for authentication based on sensor data streams, but have not yet been implemented in practice. Relying on conventional secure hashes allows us to implement and test CKP in real-world settings like the authentication method based on shaking devices together.

Complete source code of our current Java implementation is available at http://www.openuat.org, as part of the open source ubiquitous authentication toolkit.

Acknowledgments

We gratefully acknowledge support by the Commission of the European Union under the FP6 Marie Curie Intra-European Fellowship program contract MEIF-CT-2006-042194 "CAPER".

References

1. Weiser, M.: The computer of the twenty-first century. Scientific American 1496, 94–100 (September 1991)
2. Diffie, W., Hellman, M.E.: New directions in cryptography. IEEE Trans. on Information Theory IT-22(6), 644–654 (1976)
3. Maurer, U.M.: Perfect cryptographic security from partially independent channels. In: Proc. STOC '91: 23rd ACM Symp. on Theory of Computing, May 1991, pp. 561–571. ACM Press, New York (1991)
4. Juels, A., Wattenberg, M.: A fuzzy commitment scheme. In: Proc. 6th ACM Conf. on Computer and Communications Security, pp. 28–36. ACM Press, New York (1999)
5. Juels, A., Sudan, M.: A fuzzy vault scheme. Cryptology ePrint Archive, Report 2002/093 (July 2002)
6. Dodis, Y., Smith, A.: Correcting errors without leaking partial information. In: Proc. STOC '05: 37th ACM Symp. on Theory of Computing, May 2005, pp. 654–663. ACM Press, New York (2005)

7. Maurer, U., Wolf, S.: Secret-key agreement over unauthenticated public channels — part i: Definitions and a completeness result. IEEE Trans. on Information Theory 49(4), 822–831 (2003)
8. Maurer, U., Wolf, S.: Secret-key agreement over unauthenticated public channels — part ii: The simulatability condition. IEEE Trans. on Information Theory 49(4), 832–838 (2003)
9. Maurer, U., Wolf, S.: Secret-key agreement over unauthenticated public channels — part iii: Privacy amplification. IEEE Trans. on Information Theory 49(4), 839–851 (2003)
10. Renner, R., Wolf, S.: Unconditional authenticity and privacy from an arbitrarily weak secret. In: Boneh, D. (ed.) CRYPTO 2003. LNCS, vol. 2729, pp. 78–95. Springer, Heidelberg (2003)
11. Boyko, V.M.P., Patel, S.: Provably secure password-authenticated key exchange using Diffie-Hellman. Cryptology ePrint Archive, Report 2000/044 (2000)
12. Rivest, R.L., Shamir, A.: How to expose an eavesdropper. Commununications of ACM 27(4), 393–394 (1984)
13. Gehrmann, C., Mitchell, C.J., Nyberg, K.: Manual authentication for wireless devices. RSA Cryptobytes 7(1), 29–37 (2004)
14. Pasini, S., Vaudenay, S.: An optimal non-interactive message authentication protocol. In: Pointcheval, D. (ed.) CT-RSA 2006. LNCS, vol. 3860, pp. 280–294. Springer, Heidelberg (2006)
15. Stajano, F., Anderson, R.: The resurrecting duckling: Security issues for ad-hoc wireless networks. In: Proc. 7th Int. Workshop on Security Protocols, April 1999, pp. 172–194. Springer, Heidelberg (1999)
16. Hoepman, J.H.: The emphemeral pairing problem. In: Proc. 8th Int. Conf. Financial Cryptography, February 2004, pp. 212–226. Springer, Heidelberg (2004)
17. Hoepman, J.H.: Ephemeral pairing on anonymous networks. In: Hutter, D., Ullmann, M. (eds.) SPC 2005. LNCS, vol. 3450, pp. 101–116. Springer, Heidelberg (2005)
18. Vaudenay, S.: Secure communications over insecure channels based on short authenticated strings. In: Shoup, V. (ed.) CRYPTO 2005. LNCS, vol. 3621, Springer, Heidelberg (2005)
19. Creese, S., Goldsmith, M., Harrison, R., Roscoe, B., Whittaker, P., Zakiuddin, I.: Exploiting empirical engagement in authenticated protocol design. In: Hutter, D., Ullmann, M. (eds.) SPC 2005. LNCS, vol. 3450, pp. 119–133. Springer, Heidelberg (2005)
20. Čagalj, M., Čapkun, S., Hubaux, J.P.: Key agreement in peer-to-peer wireless networks. IEEE (Special Issue on Cryptography and Security) 94, 467–478 (2006)
21. TinyOS Alliance: TinyOS web page (2006) http://www.tinyos.net
22. Mayrhofer, R., Gellersen, H.: Shake well before use: Authentication based on accelerometer data. In: Proc. Pervasive 2007: 5th International Conference on Pervasive Computing, May 2007, Springer, Heidelberg (to appear, 2007)
23. Carter, L., Wegman, M.: Universal classes of hash functions. Journal of Computer and System Science 18, 143–154 (1979)
24. Bennett, C.H., Brassard, G., Crépeau, C., Maurer, U.: Generalized privacy amplification. IEEE Transaction on Information Theory 41(6), 1915–1923 (1995)

The Martini Synch: Joint Fuzzy Hashing
Via Error Correction

Darko Kirovski, Michael Sinclair, and David Wilson

Microsoft Research

Abstract. Device pairing is a significant problem for a large class of increasingly popular resource-constrained wireless protocols such as Bluetooth. The objective of pairing is to establish a secure wireless communication channel between two specific devices without a public-key infrastructure, a secure near-field communication channel, or electrical contact. We use a surprising user-device interaction as a solution to this problem. By adding an accelerometer, a device can sense its motion in a Cartesian space relative to the inertial space. The idea is to have two devices in a fixed, relative position to each other. Then, the joint object is moved randomly in 3D for several seconds. The unique motion generates approximately the same distinct signal at the accelerometers. The difference between the signals in the two inertially conjoined sensors should be relatively small under normal motion induced manually. The objective is to derive a deterministic key at both sides with maximized entropy that will be used as a private key for symmetric encryption. Currently, our prototype produces between 10–15 bits of entropy per second of usual manual motion using off-the-shelf components.

Keywords: device pairing, key exchange, secret generation, fuzzy hashing, error correction.

1 Introduction

Establishing a secure session is one of the least efficiently resolved problems with modern low-cost wireless protocols such as Bluetooth [1]. The key challenge is that such protocols do not assume the existence of a trusted authority that can certify public-keys; hence one cannot build a standard public-key infrastructure (PKI) [2]. In a PKI, the public key of the trusted authority would be hardwired into all devices. Each device or user would have a single public-private key-pair along with a certificate that vouches the authenticity of the public key. Key exchange using an underlying public-key cryptosystem such as RSA [5], would involve authentication followed by generation of a common secret, i.e., session key [6]. Using a system of certificates, the central authority could manage the trust in the world-wide network [7]. Unfortunately, this class of solutions is prohibitively expensive for most applications of mobile ad-hoc wireless protocols.

We introduce the first protocol that derives a common secret between two devices based on kinetic user-device interaction. The idea is simple: two devices

F. Stajano et al. (Eds.): ESAS 2007, LNCS 4572, pp. 16–30, 2007.

equipped with 3-axis accelerometers and moved along the same trajectory, should produce approximately similar output from each of the sensors. While similar ideas have been proposed earlier for device notification (e.g., [3,4]), our protocol is the first to derive a common secret from two fuzzy replicas of a common source. We show that in our scenario the difficulty of the traditional fuzzy hashing problem can be successfully overcome as the participants in the protocol **can communicate** while deriving the common secret. Although the replicas are only probabilistically equivalent to the source, our algorithm uses error correcting codes to produce two equivalent keys on both devices with a certain probability of failure. In the protocol, Alice computes a syndrome based upon a mutually agreed error correcting code and sends it to Bob. Based upon the syndrome, Bob can correct the errors in his sensor readings, i.e., adjust them to equal Alice's sensor readings. The error corrected sensor readings are then used on both sides to set up a private mutually-agreed session key. As high entropy of the session key stems only from the random motion of the two devices, much like shaking a drink of Martini, we have named our protocol The Martini Synch.

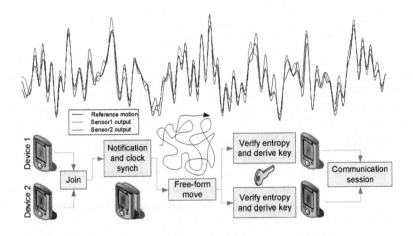

Fig. 1. (top) Sensor output for two devices compared to the acceleration for the reference motion. (bottom) Basic steps of The Martini Synch protocol.

The Martini Synch is power-efficient; the amount of data exchanged between devices is lower compared to traditional key exchange protocols specified in standards such as the IEEE P1363 [8]. Cost-wise 3D accelerometers should not increase the device price by more than US$1 per axis [9], however, we stress that there exist design proposals that could lower this price at least one order of magnitude. As we impose only relative measurement consistency across different sensors, not their absolute accuracy, we believe that such sensors can be built at low cost. To evaluate the platform, we built two prototype devices based upon off-the-shelf accelerometers and Bluetooth transceivers. The devices resulted in key generation rates of 10–15 bits per second under normal manual motion.

2   Related Work

2.1   Bluetooth Security

Bluetooth uses the SAFER+ algorithm for authentication and key generation [10] and the E0 stream cipher is used for encrypting packets [11,12,13]. Frequency hopping makes eavesdropping on Bluetooth-enabled devices more difficult [1]. Still, there are a number of security concerns reported for Bluetooth. Some of the first concerns were raised with respect to certain poor implementations [14] – the security flaw would lead to disclosure of certain personal data. First reverse engineering of the security PIN used for device pairing was revealed in [15]. Since then both passive [16] and active attacks [17] have been realized. The essence of the problem is in the fact that wireless communication occurs over a public channel, therefore key exchange is prone to the man-in-the-middle attack [18]. Typically, inexpensive protocols do not assume a trusted authority, therefore it is difficult to build a PKI in the system. According to our research, the work proposed in this paper is the first that relies on device motion, not traditional cryptography, to establish a shared secret between two devices.

2.2   Gesture-Based Device Notification

Several gesture-based techniques have been proposed to date for device notification. In this context, two devices use a gesture to signal demand for mutual communication. Bumping devices as a gesture has been proposed by Hinckley for aligning multiple-screen images [3]. Holmquist et al. have proposed shaking conjoined devices as means of establishing communication. Their system, "Smart-Its Friends," does not incorporate a communication protocol to derive a shared secret [4]. In "Smart-Its Friends" two devices exchange their sensed motion patterns in plain-text as a request for communication. Lester et al. used motion sensors to identify that in a cloud of mobile devices, two or more are worn by the same person by analyzing the stress patterns due to walking and other activities [19]. Patel et al. proposed a gesture-based communication initiation between a mobile device augmented with accelerometers and a public terminal [20]. Castelluccia and Mutaf proposed shaking devices together in order to filter out the radio frequency noise stemming from the environment while the relative signal energy between the two devices would stay the same [21]. With the exception of the last technique, none of the previous efforts aimed at generating a shared secret key between the communicating parties: the essential ingredient of private communication. To that extent, our proposal is the first to establish such a secret in accelerometer-equipped devices using a fuzzy hashing protocol.

2.3   Fuzzy Hashing

Hashing of fuzzy data has been addressed for several different types of sources: images [22,23,24], audio [25,26], biometrics [27], and graphics and protein matching [28]. In most of the related work, hashing diverse similar structures is efficient if the resulting hashes are within a certain minimal distance. In our application we have an additional relaxation that the encoder and decoder can communicate while agreeing on a mutually equivalent secret. This relaxation greatly simplifies this otherwise difficult task. For that reason we do not review in detail the fuzzy hashing techniques deployed in the referenced previous work.

3   The Martini Synch Protocol

The steps of the proposed protocol are illustrated in Figure 1. The hardware requirements include a 3-axis accelerometer in the participating devices and a reliable wireless communication stack such as Bluetooth. Hardware platforms that contain a hard-drive are typically equipped with accelerometers to detect shock or free fall for data protection – hence, a large class of existing devices already satisfies the hardware requirements. We review the protocol steps:

- **Notification.** In order to launch the protocol, the two participating devices are initially notified by their users that they should establish a session key. This can be done in several ways including: a physical *push-button* (unless it already exists, an action-specific push-button can be prohibitively expensive), a *proximity test* performed by measuring the energy of a received radio beacon or by detecting a source of near-field communication such as an RFID, or by *bumping the devices* and detecting the bumps in the accelerometers' output [3].
- **Synchronization.** Upon initial discovery, the devices synchronize their internal clocks. Since sensor output is typically sampled at rates lower than 1kHz, millisecond accuracy is both sufficient and inexpensive to establish.
- **The Martini shake.** Next, the devices are mechanically confined to a single object (i.e., held together) and then randomly moved in free-space. The motion is induced manually. While moving, the devices internally estimate the resulting entropy of the collected sensor measurements. When one or both of the devices reaches a desired minimal entropy, they signal to each other the end of the data collection process.
- **Joint fuzzy hashing.** If the entropy of the collected signals is sufficient on both sides, the devices finalize the key generation phase by exchanging a set of messages whose purpose is to perform the joint fuzzy hashing of the sensor outputs while securing the integrity of the derived deterministic secret. The protocol for joint fuzzy hashing is detailed in the subsequent section.
- **Secret verification.** Finally, the devices verify that they have derived the same key by exchanging the ciphertext of a known plaintext. If the ciphertexts match, the devices proceed with the secure session.

The key characteristic of the protocol is that it establishes a common secret on two devices based upon an activity in the physical world. Thus, private keys are established on both sides without the assistance from public-key cryptography. Assuming a secure symmetric encryption scheme,[1] the only remaining

---

[1] Unfortunately this is not the case with Bluetooth currently [11,12,13].

tool for the adversary is video-taping the motion using high-speed cameras and then deploying 3D computer vision techniques to estimate the motion [29]. Suspecting that, users can take certain straightforward precautions in case they are concerned about this type of attack.

4   Joint Fuzzy Hashing

In this section we propose a solution to the joint fuzzy hashing problem. First Alice and Bob convert their sensor measurements into a sequence of 0's and 1's which they will largely agree upon, with possibly some errors. This sequence of 0's and 1's is the "preliminary secret". Then Alice and Bob communicate a small number of bits of information about this preliminary secret, enough bits to figure out where the discrepancies are, but without leaking too many bits about their preliminary secret to an eavesdropper. This is the error correction phase. When Alice and Bob estimate that they have enough entropy in their secrets which was not leaked during the error correction phase, they then hash their corrected preliminary secrets down to a common secret key. The Martini Synch protocol is illustrated in Figure 2.

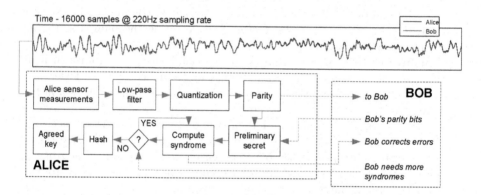

Fig. 2. Block diagram of the Martini Synch protocol. An example of sensor measurements taken from two devices during a 72.7 second Martini Synch at a sampling rate of 220Hz.

4.1   Preliminary Secret

After the signals are passed through a low-pass filter to reduce noise, Alice and Bob quantize their respective signals by dividing by a quantization step size Q and rounding the result to the nearest integer. Next Alice and Bob tell each other the parities of each of these quantized values. If the quantization step size Q is large enough, and Alice and Bob agree on the parity of the quantized value, then it is likely that they agree upon the quantized value itself.

Figure 3 shows one possible stream of quantized values that Alice and Bob might measure, and the corresponding parity bits that they would then communicate to

Alice measures:	5	5	5	5	4	4	3	2	2	5	4	5	6	6	7	8	5	5	5	3	2
Bob measures:	5	4	4	5	4	4	2	2	2	3	5	5	5	6	7	8	6	5	5	3	2
Alice transmits:	1	1	1	1	0	0	1	0	0	1	0	1	0	0	1	0	1	1	1	1	0
Bob transmits:	1	0	0	1	0	0	0	0	0	1	1	1	1	0	1	0	0	1	1	1	0
Alice records:				D					U					U	U	U			D		D
Bob records:				D					D					U	U	U			D		D

Fig. 3. An example sequence of quantized measurements that Alice and Bob might make, with the parity bits that they would communicate to each other. Shown in gray are those times for which Alice and Bob agree on the parity, and for which the parity is different than for the previous time that Alice and Bob agreed on the parity. At each time shown in gray, Alice and Bob record an "up vs. down" bit which indicates whether their quantized signals went up or down since the last time shown in gray. Since an eavesdropper learns essentially nothing about the "up vs. down" bits from the parity bits, and most of the time Alice and Bob agree on the "up vs. down" bits, we use they bits to form the preliminary secret.

each other. An eavesdropper can of course listen to these parity bits. Since the sampling rate is relatively high (220 Hz) and the signals have gone through a low-pass filter, an eavesdropper might reasonably infer that if the parity bits of either Alice or Bob have not changed, then it is likely that the quantized values have not changed either (see e.g. the first 4 measurements in Figure 3). If a secret is made out of all the quantized values, then the parity bits leak some partial information about this secret. Therefore we extract a preliminary from the agreed-upon quantized values in a different manner, as described in the caption of Figure 3.

Devices with three accelerometers will produce three data streams, while it is only necessary to produce one secret key, so we splice these three streams of "up vs. down" bits into one preliminary secret.

There are two issues with Alice and Bob's preliminary secret. Due to inertia, the bits within the secret are correlated with one another, so there are fewer bits of entropy than the length of the preliminary secret would indicate. We will need to estimate the entropy. A second issue is that unless Q is rather large, Alice and Bob will disagree on some fraction of the bits in their "common" preliminary secret — these bits are errors. For practical purposes, if any bits are in error, then the mutual secret has no value. But if Q is taken to be so large as to ensure that there are likely no errors, then this significantly reduces the entropy of the mutual secret that Alice and Bob can obtain from their measurements. We deal with this second issue first.

4.2 Error Correction

In the interest of increasing the bits of entropy per second of the Martini Synch, one would like to sample the signals more frequently, and make the quantization intervals correspondingly smaller. Reducing the quantization intervals will necessarily increase the likelihood that the two devices measure a different value. We now describe how Alice and Bob may correct the resulting discrepancies in their preliminary secrets.

The idea is for Alice and Bob to use a parity-check error-correcting code to correct the errors in their measurements. This use of an error-correcting code is somewhat unusual in that the encoding procedure is skipped, the participants only perform the decoding part. To explain, we introduce some notation. Let a be a column vector of size n containing Alice's preliminary secret, and let b be a column vector containing Bob's preliminary secret. Let e denote the column vector of errors — $e = a \oplus b$. Let H denote the $k \times n$ parity-check matrix of a binary error-correcting code.

In the normal use of an error-correcting code, a message of $m = n - k$ bits is expanded into a vector v of n bits satisfying the property that $Hv = 0$. Upon transmitting v over a noisy channel, some of the bits are corrupted, so that the received message is $r = v + e$, where e denotes the errors. The receiver then computes $Hr = H(v \oplus e) = He$, and from this infers where the errors were, and corrects them. Most decoders correct the errors using only He, but sometimes the receiving device outputs not just r but also a vector of reliability estimates that the decoder may make use of when correcting errors [30].

In our application, Alice computes Ha and sends the resulting k bits to Bob. Bob computes Hb and takes the exclusive-or of the result with what Alice sent — $Hb \oplus Ha = H(b \oplus a) = He$. At this point Bob is in the same position as the receiver of an encoded message that was corrupted by a noisy channel, and can determine which bits of his measurements b he needs to flip for them to agree with Alice's measurements a.

4.3   Progressive Error Correction

Rather than use an error correcting code with a fixed number of checksum bits, Alice and Bob are at liberty to transmit checksum bits until they decide that they have corrected all the errors. In the event that there is a small number of errors, they may stop communicating checksum bits early so as to avoid leaking data to an eavesdropper. In the event that there are many errors, Alice and Bob many continue to communicate checksum bits until they are satisfied that all the errors have been corrected.

To illustrate this "progressive error correction", where the number of checksum bits depends on the errors that occur, it is instructive to consider a concrete example, such as the scheme that we adopted. For our application we use BCH codes on blocks of length 63 bits [30,31]. The preliminary secret is partitioned into blocks of length 63 which are corrected separately. In a BCH code, the bit positions are indexed by the non-zero elements of a finite field, in our case the field is $\mathbb{F}_{64}$, represented as binary polynomials in $\mathbb{F}_2[x]$ modulo $x^6 + x + 1$. The element x generates the multiplicative subgroup of $\mathbb{F}_{64}$. So for integers p, Alice can transmit $S_p^A := \sum_{i=1}^{63} a_i x^{pi} \bmod x^6 + x + 1$ in six bits, whereupon Bob can compute $S_p^B := \sum_{i=1}^{63} b_i x^{pi} \bmod x^6 + x + 1$ and determine

$$S_p := S_p^A \oplus S_p^B = \sum_{i=1}^{63} e_i \alpha^{pi} \bmod x^6 + x + 1.$$

In the event that there are t errors, knowing S_p for the first t odd positive integers p ($S_1, S_3, \ldots, S_{2t-1}$) is enough to determine the locations of the t errors using the Berlekamp-Massey algorithm [30], which would allow Bob to change his copy of the preliminary secret to agree with Alice's. Of course Alice and Bob do not know beforehand how many errors there will be. But if the first t odd power-sums $S_1, S_3, \ldots, S_{2t-1}$ are consistent with there being significantly fewer than t errors, then Bob can infer that there are in fact fewer than t errors, and that it is not necessary for Alice to transmit additional checksum bits. When t is large, in the event that there are more than t errors, it becomes increasingly likely that the decoding procedure will detect this. Thus for large t there is less need for Alice to send Bob extra checksum bits for Bob to be confident that there are not extra errors. To better take advantage of the fact that the decoding procedure can often detect the presence of too many (random) errors, and to offset the fact that errors are frequently clumped together (not randomly located), we picked and fixed a random permutation on 63 items, and permuted the input bits according to this permutation before doing the error correction. To run the protocol we need to specify a function $f(t) \leq t$ such that, when $S_1, \ldots, S_{2t-1}$ are consistent with $\leq f(t)$ errors, Bob is satisfied that he knows Alice's preliminary secret. We used the function:

$$f(t) = \begin{cases} t-2, & t \leq 4 \\ t-1, & 5 \leq t \leq 10 \\ t, & t \geq 11 \end{cases} \tag{1}$$

An eavesdropper listening to Bob's communications will learn about the number of discrepancies between the two preliminary secrets, but Bob's communications do not reveal anything about Alice's version of the preliminary secret, which is the one that will be hashed to form a secret key. Each time that Alice sends a S_p^A she reveals at most six bits about her preliminary secret. It turns out that sending $S_1^A, S_3^A, \ldots, S_{2t-1}^A$ will in general reveal fewer than $6t$ bits about the preliminary secret, since there are some linear relations between the transmitted bits. The number of bits revealed is the rank of the associated checksum matrix, and is fairly well understood [31, Chapt. 9, sec. 3 & 4]. For the BCH code over $\mathbb{F}_{64}$ we summarize the number of leaked bits in Table 1.

4.4 Dealing with Information Leakage

When Alice transmits the k bits of $H\boldsymbol{a}$ to Bob, an outside observer gains some information about Alice's measurements $\boldsymbol{a}$, so Alice and Bob would not want

Table 1. Number of bits leaked when t syndrome packets are sent from Alice to Bob

t:	1	2	3	4	5	6	7	8	9	10	11	12	13	14	15	16–31	32–63
# leaked bits:	6	12	18	24	27	33	39	45	45	45	47	53	53	56	56	62	63

to simply use $\boldsymbol{a}$ itself as their common secret. This problem is easy enough to deal with when all 2^n possible values of $\boldsymbol{a}$ are equally likely. In this case Alice and Bob can simply agree beforehand upon a maximal rank submatrix A of H, and discard the bits of $\boldsymbol{a}$ whose positions correspond to the columns of A. Let us assume that H has rank k, since otherwise the bits of $H\boldsymbol{a}$ corresponding to dependent rows of H give no extra information to either Bob or the outside observer. Regardless of the values of the remaining $n-k$ bits that Alice and Bob keep, since the k discarded bits are uniformly random, and since their positions correspond to a full-rank submatrix of H, the message $H\boldsymbol{a}$ is uniformly random, and thus contains no information about the $n-k$ bits that Alice and Bob keep.

When the measured values $\boldsymbol{a}$ are not completely independent of one another, more care is needed to ensure that $H\boldsymbol{a}$ does not leak much information about the secret that Alice and Bob derive from $\boldsymbol{a}$. We shall assume that for some $r < 1$, no set of measurements $\boldsymbol{a}$ occurs with probability greater than r^n. Under these circumstances we might hope to extract $n \log_2 r^{-1} - k - O(1)$ nearly uniformly random bits from $\boldsymbol{a}$ which are nearly independent of $H\boldsymbol{a}$, since conditional on the transmitted syndrome, no measurement occurs with probability more than $2^k r^n$. Alice and Bob can do this making use of a random hash function which may be public and known to the outside observer. Let M be a $s \times n$ uniformly random matrix of 0's and 1's which may be public, where $s = n \log_2 r^{-1} - k - O(1)$. The common secret of Alice and Bob is $M\boldsymbol{a}$.

The probability that two different measured values $\boldsymbol{a}_1$ and $\boldsymbol{a}_2$ get hashed to to the same secret $M\boldsymbol{a}_1 = M\boldsymbol{a}_2$ is precisely 2^{-s}. Conditional upon the values of $H\boldsymbol{a}$, no value of $\boldsymbol{a}$ occurs with probability greater than $2^k r^n$. It can be shown using the second-moment method, that even after an observer has learned $H\boldsymbol{a}$, the expected total variation distance between the secret $M\boldsymbol{a}$ and uniformly random set of s bits, is no more than $2^{k+s} r^n$ (e.g., see [32] for further explanation). When s is chosen to be $n \log r - k - O(1)$, the outside observer learns essentially nothing about Alice and Bob's common secret $M\boldsymbol{a}$.

4.5 Entropy Estimate

Empirically estimating the entropy of a process is generally difficult, but we need estimates of the entropy to judge the strength of the common secret that Alice and Bob distill from their measurements. As mentioned above, the length of the preliminary secret consisting of "up vs. down" bits is a poor estimate of the entropy, since there tend to be alternating strings of 1's and 0's whose length is longer than what one would find in a uniformly random string. To better estimate the entropy, for each of the three data streams from the three coordinate axes, we let r_i denote the number of runs of 0's and 1's there are of length r_i, and estimate the entropy for a given data stream to be:

$$\sum_i r_i \log_2 \frac{\sum_i r_i}{r_i}.$$

When the sum of the three entropy estimates, minus the number of leaked bits, exceeds a specific security requirement, e.g., 60 bits, Alice and Bob determine that they have enough entropy in the corrected preliminary secret to hash down to form a common secret key.

4.6 Additional Remarks

Since a crucial part of the Martini Synch protocol occurs in the physical world, it is important to stress the constraints related to this process. The difference in **x** and **y** is influenced by two components:

  i noise in the sensors stemming from calibration and other physical influences, and
 ii the actual difference in the motion vectors for the two fixed points in the relative Cartesian space where device accelerometers are positioned.

In order to reduce the latter noise, the devices must be designed so that the accelerometers are positioned as closely as possible during the protocol. In our experiments, motion induced using typical manual kinetics caused negligible additional noise compared to the noise collected when both devices are still (e.g., noise type *i*). In the tests, the accelerometers were positioned at a distance of approximately one inch.

4.7 Parameters

We have found the following parameters to generally work well for the Martini Synch. For the noise filtering, we removed the DC component of the signal (to reduce the need for calibration) and convolved the signal with a binomial distribution of order 256 (whose characteristic width is around 16–32). The sensors we used generated 10-bit measurements, and for the quantization parameter Q we found $Q = 40$ to work satisfactory. The performance of the protocol depends in part on how vigorously the user accelerates the devices, but with these parameters 16000 measurements (corresponding to 72.7 seconds) generally produces a preliminary secret of about $n = 800\text{-}1400$ bits (per coordinate axis), containing about $n/3$ blocks of 0's and 1's, and about $n/10$ errors. After correcting the errors one can expect to have about 400 bits of entropy for each of the three coordinate axes.

5 Empirical Evaluation

The prototypes produced for this research consist of two handheld battery operated devices, each equipped with a 3-axis accelerometer and a Bluetooth radio. The testbed is illustrated in Figure 4. For the prototype, the information

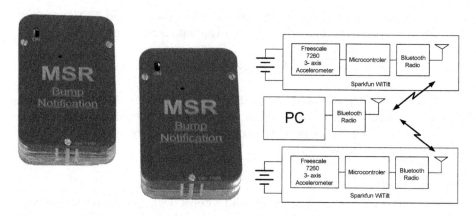

Fig. 4. (left) Encased prototype devices used in the experiments. (right) Block diagram showing two portable devices and an intermediate PC for processing.

exchanged was mediated by an intermediate Bluetooth-enabled PC. In a real-world scenario, the two devices would process the information locally as well as communicate with each other via their radios. The WiTilt 3-axis accelerometer with Bluetooth radio was purchased from Sparkfun [33]. The accelerometers are model 7260 from Freescale Semiconductors [34]. They are MEMS (micro-electromechanical systems) 3-axis accelerometers with a 1.5-6g acceleration range, 0.5mA operating current with a detection range greater than 1kHz.

5.1 Evaluation of The Martini Synch

In this subsection we quantify the key performance features of the Martini Synch protocol. We collected data for thirteen 3-axis sensor vectors of length 16K samples from a group of 5 users. The sensor vectors were sampled at 220Hz. We did not specifically calibrate the sensors prior to the experiments. The usage of the platform is sufficiently simple so that no other guidelines were issued to the users except that they should randomly move the joined objects.

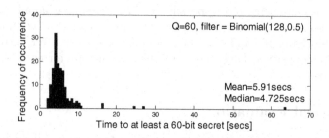

Fig. 5. Distribution of timings required to obtain a shared secret of estimated minimal 60 bits

We show the first set of results in Figure 5. We illustrate the distribution of timings required to obtain a shared secret of estimated minimal 60 bits. The subjects followed usual manual motion for 11 and severe shaking for 2 out of the 13 benchmarks. As a result, the mean and the median results are 5.9 and 4.7 seconds respectively over the acquired set of sensor measurements. Here we report results for $Q = 60$ and a binomial(128,0.5) filter. Overly energetic shaking of the devices resulted in acceleration that could not be captured accurately with our sensors – hence, in these cases users required longer times (> 10 seconds) to generate a strong secret.

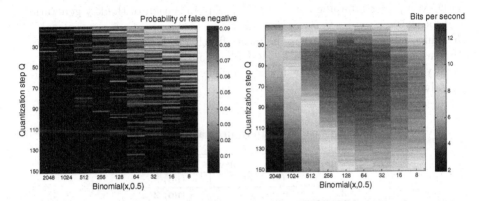

Fig. 6. (left) Color-coded plot of the probability of a false negative ε_{FN}. (right) Color-coded plot of the entropy per second for correctly resolved shared secrets.

In the second set of experiments we evaluate the probability of a false negative and false positive (i.e., produced entropy per second). The left diagram shows a color-coded plot of the probability of a false negative ε_{FN} for various quantization step values and binomial(x, 0.5) filters. One can observe that in a large part of the region of interest we have $\varepsilon_{FN} < 0.02$. For example, this type of performance corresponds to the false negatives produced while typing a textual password. Similarly on the right side we present in a color-coded diagram the achieved entropy per second for correctly resolved shared secrets. We computed the entropy according to the algorithm presented in Subsection 4.5. One can observe that a relatively large area in the tested parameter set, corresponded to bit-rates in excess of 12 bits per second. Thus, we point to a particular parameter selection $Q = 50$ and a binomial(128,0.5) filter as a good design solution for the experimental platform we developed. For the selected design parameters, individual five second Martini Synch's produced entropies commonly in the range between 10 to 15 bits per second.

6   A User-Study

The simplicity of the proposed user-device interface points to a few unknowns with respect to user acceptance of the Martini Synch. During a demonstration fair we asked 47 persons, most of them with technical background, about the convenience of using the Martini Synch. We conducted the following survey:

1 Is shaking a pair of devices convenient for generating a shared secret?
2 For a given device, no other mechanism is available for generating a shared secret. Would you perform the Martini Synch to accomplish this task or you would deem the device unusable?
3 In your opinion, how many seconds of shaking devices results in a good balance between usability and security?
4 Are you likely to hide the device motion for fear of computer vision attacks?
5 Do you prefer bumping devices vs. software initiation of the key generation protocol?
6 Which mechanical feature is the most effective to lock two devices in place?
7 Is usage of the Martini Synch self-explanatory?
8 In your opinion, is the user-device interface appealing to the following individual age groups?

Table 2. Results of a small user study. In total, 47 persons were surveyed.

Question	Answers				
1	(yes) 39			(no) 8	
2	(yes) 45			(no) 2	
3	< 2s	2-3s	3-4s	4-5s	> 5s
	3	3	18	17	3
4	(yes) 2			(no) 45	
5	(yes) 36			(no) 11	
6	magnet	velcro	joints	hi-friction surf.	
	25	2	1	19	
7	(yes) 45			(no) 2	
8	10-20	21-40	41-60	61+	
(yes)	43	35	20	45	

Responses to the survey are tabulated in Table 2. In summary, the technology was well accepted. All but two participants acknowledged that they would use the technology if available on a low-cost device. A majority recognized the need for shaking the device over a longer period – most of them targeting the 3-5 second period as convenient. Similarly most participants preferred bumping devices to initiate a key generation session as opposed to a software-only user interface. Almost all users found the protocol easy to comprehend. The participants estimated that the 40-60 age group is least likely to accept the new user-device interface while its appeal is the strongest to the youngest and elderly. We conclude the report on this informal user study with a disclaimer that the sample of users was not statistically large as well as broad in terms of technical background and acceptance of modern technology. To that extent, we point to a likely discrepancy of the presented results with respect to ground truth.

7 Summary

The Martini Synch protocol establishes a secure wireless communication channel between two specific devices without a PKI, a secure near-field communication channel, or electrical contact. It relies on a surprising user-device interaction to achieve its objective. Using an accelerometer, a device can sense its motion in a Cartesian space relative to inertial space. The idea is to have two devices in a fixed, relative position to each other. The joint object is moved randomly in 3D for several seconds. The unique motion generates approximately the same distinct signal at corresponding devices' accelerometers. The protocol uses a novel distributed fuzzy hashing algorithm based upon exchanging error correction syndromes that derives probabilistically the same secret key in both devices based upon the observed joint motion. We developed a prototype platform using off-the-shelf components to show that even in a simple implementation, our protocol generates between 10 and 15 bits of entropy per second of manual motion.

Acknowledgments

We would like to thank Kris Andersen, Tom Blank, and Gideon Yuval for insightful discussions that have improved the contents of this manuscript.

References

1. Haartsen, J., et al.: Bluetooth: Vision, goals, and architecture. Mobile Computing and Communications Review 2, 38–45 (1998)
2. IETF PKIX workgroup. Public-Key Infrastructure X.509
3. Hinckley, K.: Synchronous Gestures for Multiple Users and Computers. ACM UIST Symposium on User Interface Software & Technology, pp. 149–158 (2003)
4. Holmquist, L.E., et al.: Smart-its friends: a technique for users to easily establish connections between smart artefacts. In: Abowd, G.D., Brumitt, B., Shafer, S. (eds.) Ubicomp 2001: Ubiquitous Computing. LNCS, vol. 2201, pp. 116–122. Springer, Heidelberg (2001)
5. Rivest, R.L., et al.: A method for obtaining digital signatures and public-key cryptosystems. Communications of ACM 21(2), 120–126 (1978)
6. IETF TLS workgroup. Transport Layer Security
7. Naor, M., Nissim, K.: Certificate revocation and certificate update. USENIX Security Symposium (1998)
8. IEEE 1363-2000: Standard Specifications for Public Key Cryptography.
9. Analog Devices Corp. ADXL330. Available on-line at http://www.analog.com.
10. Massey, J., Khachatrian, G., Kuregian, M.: Nomination of SAFER+ as Candidate Algorithm for the Advanced Encryption Standard. NIST AES Proposal (1998)
11. Fluhrer, S., Lucks, S.: Analysis of the E0 Encryption System. In: Vaudenay, S., Youssef, A.M. (eds.) SAC 2001. LNCS, vol. 2259, Springer, Heidelberg (2001)
12. Lu, Y., Vaudenay, S.: Faster correlation attack on Bluetooth keystream generator E0. In: Franklin, M. (ed.) CRYPTO 2004. LNCS, vol. 3152, pp. 407–425. Springer, Heidelberg (2004)

13. Armknecht, F.: A linearization attack on the Bluetooth key stream generator. Cryptology ePrint Archive, report 2002/191 (2002) available from http://eprint.iacr.org/2002/191

14. Laurie, A., Herfurt, M., Holtmann, M.: Hacking Bluetooth enabled mobile phones and beyond. 21st Chaos Communication Congress (2003)

15. Whitehouse, O.: War nibbling: Bluetooth insecurity. @Stake, research report (2003)

16. Wong, F.-L., Stajano, F.: Repairing the Bluetooth pairing protocol. In: Proceedings of Security Protocols Workshop (2005)

17. Shaked, Y., Wool, A.: Cracking the Bluetooth PIN. International Conference on Mobile Systems, Applications, and Services, pp. 39–50 (2005)

18. Menezes, A.J., et al.: Handbook of applied cryptography. CRC Press, Boca Raton, FL (1997)

19. Lester, J., et al.: Are You with Me? – Using Accelerometers to Determine If Two Devices Are Carried by the Same Person. Pervasive Computing, pp. 33–50 (2004)

20. Patel, S.N., et al.: A gesture-based authentication scheme for untrusted public terminals. ACM User. Interface Software and Technology, pp. 157–160 (2004)

21. Castelluccia, C., Mutaf, P.: Shake Them Up!: a movement-based pairing protocol for CPU-constrained devices. MobiSys, 2005 (2005)

22. Monga, V., et al.: A Clustering Based Approach to Perceptual Image Hashing. IEEE Transactions on Information Forensics and Security 1(1), 68–79 (2006)

23. Johnson, M., Ramchandran, K.: Dither-Based Secure Image Hashing Using Distributed Coding. IEEE International Conference on Image Processing (2003)

24. Swaminathan, A., Mao, Y., Wu, M.: Robust and Secure Hashing for Images. IEEE Transactions on Information Forensics and Security (2006)

25. Kalker, T., Haitsma, J., Oostveen, J.: Robust audio hashing for content identification. International Workshop on Content Based Multimedia Indexing (2001)

26. Burges, C.J., et al.: Distortion discriminant analysis for audio fingerprinting. IEEE Transactions on Speech and Audio Processing 11(3), 165–174 (2003)

27. Dodis, Y., Reyzin, L., Smith, A.: Fuzzy Extractors: How to Generate Strong Keys from Biometrics and Other Noisy Data. In: Cachin, C., Camenisch, J.L. (eds.) EUROCRYPT 2004. LNCS, vol. 3027, pp. 523–540. Springer, Heidelberg (2004)

28. Wolfson, H.J., Rigoutsos, I.: Geometric Hashing: An Overview. IEEE Computational Science and Engineering 4(4), 10–21 (1997)

29. Neumann, J., et al.: Polydioptric camera design and 3d motion estimation. IEEE Conference on Computer Vision and Pattern Recognition II, 294–301 (2003)

30. Berlekamp, E.R.: Algebraic coding theory, pp. xiv+466. McGraw-Hill Book, New York (1968)

31. MacWilliams, F.J., Sloane, N.J.A.: The theory of error-correcting codes. I. North-Holland Mathematical Library 16, xv+369 (1977)

32. Wilson, D.B.: Random random walks on $\mathbb{Z}_2^d$. Probability Theory and Related Fields 108(4), 441–457 (1997)

33. Sparkfun, Inc. Available on-line at http://www.sparkfun.com

34. Freescale Semiconductors, Corp. Available on-line at http://www.freescale.com

Private Handshakes*

Jaap-Henk Hoepman

TNO Information and Communication Technology
P.O. Box 1416, 9701 BK Groningen, The Netherlands
`jaap-henk.hoepman@tno.nl`
Institute for Computing and Information Sciences
Radboud University Nijmegen
P.O. Box 9010, 6500 GL Nijmegen, the Netherlands
`jhh@cs.ru.nl`

Abstract. Private handshaking allows pairs of users to determine which (secret) groups they are both a member of. Group membership is kept secret to everybody else. Private handshaking is a more private form of secret handshaking [BRS+03], because it does not allow the group administrator to trace users. We extend the original definition of a handshaking protocol to allow and test for membership of multiple groups simultaneously. We present simple and efficient protocols for both the single group and multiple group membership case.

Private handshaking is a useful tool for mutual authentication, demanded by many pervasive applications (including RFID) for privacy. Our implementations are efficient enough to support such usually resource constrained scenarios.

Keywords: secret handshakes, group membership, authentication, pervasive security.

1 Introduction

A secret handshake allows members of a (secret) group to identify each other, without revealing their membership to potential eavesdroppers or malicious impostors. As an informal example taken from the real world, it would allow FBI agents attending a hacker convention to recognise each other without giving away their presence to the rest of the audience[1].

Several years ago, Balfanz *et al.* [BRS+03] revived interest (e.g., [CJT05]) in the development of secure (cryptographic) protocols to implement such secret handshakes. According to them, secret handshakes are fundamentally different from *one-way accumulators* [BF01] and *private matchmaking* [BG85, Mea86, ZN] (not

---

* Id: secret-handshakes.tex,v 1.5 2007/04/03 21:53:25 jhh Exp.
[1] This, of course, is not withstanding the use of any other distinctive features to 'spot' a typical FBI agent. Moreover, in this scenario, where all people present belong essentially to just two groups, non-membership of one group 'proves' membership of the other...

F. Stajano et al. (Eds.): ESAS 2007, LNCS 4572, pp. 31–42, 2007.

to be confused with distributed match making [MV88]). We show that this distinction is only superficial (depending on a particular notion of traitor tracing), and that much simpler protocols, derived from the literature on matchmaking (and pretty much equivalent to one-way accumulators) serve equally well as secret handshake protocols. We call these protocols *private* handshaking protocols.

Such private handshaking protocols (that, unlike secret handshaking, do not implement traceability) are quite suitable to resource constrained environments, like low-end smart card, RFID or NFC-based[2] systems [RE03, Fin03]. Moreover, they implement a form of mutual authentication that is sorely needed in many pervasive systems [WSRE03, HHJ+06]. For instance, the privacy of a holder of an RFID tag is better protected if the reader must authenticate to the tag before the tag releases any information. A private handshaking protocol could ensure that the tag would only grant access if the reader and the tag belong to the same group.

1.1 State of the Art

Private matchmaking protocols, originally studied by Baldwin and Gramlich [BG85] (and followed up upon by Zhang and Needham [ZN]), allow users that share the same 'wish' to locate and identify each other securely and privately. The canonical example used in both papers is that of matching job openings at big corporations with high-ranked managers looking for their next job opportunity. In this example a corporation will not want to publicly announce availability of a position, and similarly, a high-ranked manager will not want to reveal his or her job aspirations to everybody. The protocol of Baldwin and Gramlich [BG85] requires the presence of an on-line trusted third party. Zhang and Needham [ZN] improve on this by not using a trusted third party at all, and not using public-key cryptography either (making their protocol very light-weight).

Secret handshaking protocols, as studied by Balfanz *et al.* [BRS+03] consider membership of a secret group instead, and allow members of such groups to reliably identify fellow group members without giving away their group membership to non-members and eavesdroppers. An example of this problem was given in the introduction. Balfanz *et al.* also pose the additional requirement that a group member can choose to authenticate to other group members that have a certain *role* within that group. Furthermore, they require that group membership is revocable, and that the protocols are forward repudiable, traceable and collusion resistant (see section 2.2 for details). Their protocols are secure under the Bilinear Diffie-Hellman assumption [BF01] and the random oracle model [BR93b]. They require that each user periodically obtains fresh pseudonyms from the group administrator, for use in a handshake protocol run.

Their results were later improved by Castelluccia *et al.* [CJT05] with protocols based on CA-Oblivious encryption secure under the random oracle model and either the Computational Diffie Hellman assumption or the RSA assumption [MOV96]. Like Balfanz *et al.* , unlinkability in their protocols is achieved at

---

[2] RFID stands for Radio Frequency IDentification. NFC stands for Near Field Communication. See the references for more information.

the cost of an ample supply of fresh pseudonyms used one by one in every protocol run. Also, both protocols assume the existence of a group administrator that distributes group secrets to group members, and that can discover any traitors. Unfortunately, this also implies that the administrator can discover all instances of a protocol run in which a particular user participated[3]. This is clearly a strong breach of privacy.

Tsudik and Xu [TX05] extend the secret handshaking problem to more than 2 participants (but still determining shared membership of a *single* group), and present protocols solving this generalisation with reusable credentials. This removes the main drawback found in previous protocols. Xu and Yung [XY04] previously achieved a similar reusability of credentials.

Meadows [Mea86] built a matchmaking protocol without relying on an on-line trusted third party (but using public key cryptography, cf. [ZN]). Interestingly, she studied the matchmaking problem in the secret handshake setting: i.e., she considered secret group membership instead of communicating wishes. The difference between both is subtle, but important (see [BRS+03]): if the wish can be guessed, then (by definition of the matchmaking problem that any pair of users sharing the same wish can identify each other) the owner of that wish can be identified. Similarly, if 'secret' group names are used as input to matchmaking protocols, then anybody able to guess the group name can locate the other, real, group members, and moreover can impersonate a group member.

In a similar vain, set intersection protocols [FNP04, KS05] are subtly different from private handshaking protocols as well. Typically, the domains of the sets over which the intersection has to be computed is much smaller, and in any case, any element in the domain is a possible member. For private handshaking protocols, however, group membership is encoded by a secret value from a much larger, sparsely occupied, domain. Moreover, not all set intersection protocols require the outcome of the computation to be secret. A more thorough discussion of the relationship between secret handshaking, oblivious encryption/signatures and hidden credentials can be found in [Hol05].

1.2 Our Results

We define the *private handshaking* problem as a more private form of secret handshaking [BRS+03], that does not allow a group administrator (or anyone else) to trace users running the protocol. This makes private handshaking a more private form of secret handshaking. Our model and definitions are described in Sect. 2. The main contribution of this paper is the conclusion that, when dropping traceability, much more efficient implementations of handshaking are possible. This makes such protocols viable for resource constrained environments, like RFID or NFC-based systems.

---

[3] In the current implementations of these protocols, this is trivial because the parties exchange pseudonyms initially distributed by the group administrator. More fundamentally, this could be achieved in full generality by running the traitor tracing protocol on a normal protocol run. By definition, this this would reveal the parties involved (provided they were members of the group).

We extend the definition of handshake protocols to handle the (much more common) case where people are members of several groups. Using existing, single-group, handshaking protocols Alice and Bob (member of a and b groups respectively) can do no better than running $a \times b$ handshake protocols in parallel to determine all the groups that they share membership of. We show that, in fact, $O(a + b)$ type protocols exist.

We then present two protocols for private handshaking, one for the case where Alice and Bob are members of a single group (Sect. 3), and another where Alice and Bob are a member of any number of groups each (Sect. 4). Both use a single Diffie-Hellman key exchange [DH76] and exchange as many hashes as the largest number of allowed group membership per user[4]. Security of the protocols relies on the Diffie-Hellman assumption [MOV96] and the random oracle assumption [BM93].

2   Model and Notation

2.1   System and Adversary Model

We assume a distributed system of n nodes, connected by asynchronous message passing. Nodes can be members of zero, one or more groups $G \in \mathcal{G}$. There are m different groups. We write $i \in G$ if node i belongs to group G, and $\mathcal{G}_i$ for the set of all groups to which node i belongs. We assume group membership is fixed and part of the initialisation of the system. We will discuss the ramifications of this assumption later on in Sect. 5.

The system is controlled by a Dolev and Yao [DY81] style adversary $\mathcal{A}$ that may block, delay, relay, delete, insert or modify messages. This allows him to force nodes to participate in a protocol run together with other nodes specified by the adversary[5]. The adversary may also corrupt any number of nodes in the system, read all data stored by such nodes, and participate in protocol runs "being within" such nodes. Nodes and the adversary are modelled as probabilistic polynomial-time Turing machines. We write $\mathcal{A} \in G$ if the adversary corrupted a member of group G, and $\mathcal{G}_\mathcal{A}$ for the set of all groups for which the adversary corrupted a node. If a node i is corrupted we write $i \in \mathcal{A}$. In this case $\mathcal{G}_i$ is assumed to be equal to $\mathcal{G}_\mathcal{A}$.

Uncorrupted nodes are honest.

In other words, the adversary induces a sequence of message exchanges and protocol steps called a *run*. At the start of each run, all nodes are initialised. In this phase, nodes may be given long term secret data needed to securely run the protocol. However, the adversary may subvert any number of nodes and retrieve this secret information stored by them. Finally, the adversary may force

---

[4] Balfanz *et al.* [BRS+03] argue that a Diffie-Hellman key exchange cannot be used to implement secret handshaking. Their argument however depends on the requirement that individual members of a group need to be traceable, and hence does not apply to *private* handshaking protocols.

[5] Bellare *et al.* [BR93b, BR93a] model the same adversarial power by allowing the adversary to query an infinite supply of protocol oracles.

any node to reveal any secret information resulting from a particular protocol exchange. Typically, this involves a session key established by the protocol.

2.2   The Private Handshake Problem

We have the following set of requirements (cf. [BRS+03, TX05]) for a private handshake protocol run between two nodes i and j, belonging to groups $\mathcal{G}_i$ and $\mathcal{G}_j$ that returns output $\mathcal{O}_i$ to i and $\mathcal{O}_j$ to j. All statements below hold with overwhelming probability, for arbitrary adversary $\mathcal{A}$, for an arbitrary group G and nodes i, j.

correctness/safety. $\mathcal{O}_i, \mathcal{O}_j \subseteq \mathcal{G}_i \cap \mathcal{G}_j$.
progress. If i and j are honest and all messages exchanged between them during the run are delivered unaltered, $\mathcal{O}_i = \mathcal{O}_j = \mathcal{G}_i \cap \mathcal{G}_j$.
resistance to detection. Let $j \in \mathcal{A}$ but $\mathcal{A} \notin G$. Then the adversary $\mathcal{A}$ cannot distinguish a protocol run in which it interacts with a node $i \in G$ from a run involving a simulator[6].
indistinguishability to eavesdroppers. Let $i, j \notin \mathcal{A}$. Then the adversary $\mathcal{A}$ cannot determine whether $i \in G$ or $i \notin G$. This holds even if $\mathcal{A} \in G$. Note that both participants in the run need to be uncorrupted, and that the adversary does not modify[7]. messages exchanged between i and j.
unlinkability. Adversary $\mathcal{A}$ is unable to distinguish a protocol run involving node i from a protocol run involving a node $j \neq i$ with $\mathcal{G}_j = \mathcal{G}_i$, even when $\mathcal{G}_\mathcal{A} = \mathcal{G}_i$ and $\mathcal{A}$ participates in the protocol runs[8].
forward repudiability. After the run, node i cannot convince another node k whether $j \in G$ or not. In other words, a run between i and j is indistinguishable from a run between i and i, for anyone except i.

Traditionally, the following two requirements are listed as well.

resistance to impersonation. Let $j \in \mathcal{A}$ but $\mathcal{A} \notin G$. Then the adversary is not able to convince a node $i \in G$ that $\mathcal{A} \in G$.
non traceability. The group administrator of group G is unable to link two different protocol runs involving the same node $i \in G$.

However, resistance to impersonation is actually implied by correctness and the definition of $\mathcal{G}_i$ when i is corrupted. And non-traceability is equivalent to unlinkability if the group administrator is missing (or considered to be a normal, corruptible, node). We therefore omit these requirements from the list.

---

[6] Note how this requirement subtly circumvents the problem that the adversary *does* learn non-membership of i of the groups it is itself a member of (by corruption or otherwise).

[7] The powers of the adversary are limited to eavesdropping in this case. Clearly, an active adversary belonging to the same group as i can stage a man-in-the-middle attack and determine membership of G for i just like a legitimate node j could.

[8] The statement of this requirement is a bit involved because technically, an adversary can distinguish different nodes from the groups they are a member of, if the adversary itself is a member of those groups and if it participates in the runs. Intuitively, the requirement simply says that protocol runs do not carry node identifiers or similar.

We refrain from imposing a fairness requirement (cf. [BRS+03]) which would require $\mathcal{O}_i = \mathcal{O}_j$ always. Fairness can be guaranteed, but at the expense of running a complex fair exchange type protocol.

Similarly, we do not require the protocol participants to set up a shared session key to be used whenever mutual authentication was successful. The protocols we present, however, do establish such a shared key.

Finally, we note that Meadows [Mea86] stipulates that an adversary that has stolen a secret from a group member cannot find out membership of the someone else without at least revealing group membership. This is similar to the resistance to impersonation requirement, when fairness is guaranteed. Otherwise, it will only hold when the adversary initiates the handshake.

3 Single Membership Protocols

We first present a protocol to determine shared membership of a single group. This protocol is basically a Diffie Hellman key exchange using a secret generator s as the group secret, and using the key validation phase as group membership test. The validated key can be discarded or used for secure communication between the authenticated parties. In fact, the protocol is very similar to SPEKE [Jab96], and Meadows [Mea86] basic protocol idea (but without exchanging the secret session key in the clear, instead using a key verification round as in [BR93a]).

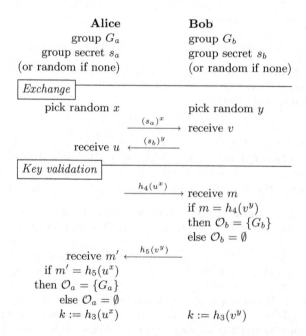

Fig. 1. Message flow of the single membership private handshaking protocol

3.1 Security Proof

The following lemmas prove that protocol 1 implements private handshaking. We only sketch the proofs. Consider an arbitrary run between two nodes i and j, belonging to groups $\mathcal{G}_i = \{G_a\}$ and $\mathcal{G}_j = \{G_b\}$ where i returns output $\mathcal{O}_i$ and j returns output $\mathcal{O}_j$. Let $\mathcal{A}$ be an arbitrary adversary, and let G be an arbitrary group. A property holds with overwhelming probability if it holds with probability larger than $1 - 1/2^\sigma$, where σ is the security parameter. It holds with negligible probability if the probability is less than $1/2^\sigma$.

Lemma 3.1 (correctness/safety). *$\mathcal{O}_i, \mathcal{O}_j \subseteq \mathcal{G}_i \cap \mathcal{G}_j$ with overwhelming probability.*

Proof. Clearly the protocol ensures $\mathcal{O}_i \subseteq \mathcal{G}_i$. We have $G_a \in \mathcal{O}_i$ when $h_5(u^x) = h_5(v^y)$. This happens only, with overwhelming probability, when $u^x = v^y$, in other words $(s_b^y)^x = (s_a^x)^y$. This holds only with overwhelming probability when $s_a = s_b$. □

Lemma 3.2 (progress). *If i and j are honest and all messages exchanged between them during the run are delivered unaltered, then $\mathcal{O}_i = \mathcal{O}_j = \mathcal{G}_i \cap \mathcal{G}_j$.*

Proof. This is easily verified by case analysis. □

Lemma 3.3 (resistance to detection). *Let $j \in \mathcal{A}$ but $\mathcal{A} \notin G$. Then the adversary $\mathcal{A}$ cannot distinguish a protocol run in which it interacts with a node $i \in G$ from a run involving a simulator with non-negligible probability.*

Proof. The adversary has to distinguish s_a^x from g^z given f^x for f known to the adversary, where x is fresh, random and unknown to the adversary. Moreover, s_a is unknown to the adversary (but it may know many s_a^y, for fresh and unknown y, from previous protocol runs). Distinguishing this would violate the Diffie-Hellman assumption. □

Lemma 3.4 (indistinguishability to eavesdroppers). *Let $i, j \notin \mathcal{A}$. Then the adversary $\mathcal{A}$ cannot determine whether $i \in G$ or $i \notin G$ with non-negligible probability. This holds even if $\mathcal{A} \in G$.*

Proof. Similar to the proof of the previous lemma. □

Lemma 3.5 (unlinkability). *Adversary $\mathcal{A}$ is unable to distinguish a protocol run involving node i from a protocol run involving a node $j \neq i$ with $\mathcal{G}_j = \mathcal{G}_i$, even when $\mathcal{G}_\mathcal{A} = \mathcal{G}_i$ and $\mathcal{A}$ participates in the protocol runs.*

Proof. Nodes i and j share the same state. Hence all messages sent by i could have been sent by j as well. □

Lemma 3.6 (forward repudiability). *After the run, node i cannot convince another node k whether $j \in G$ or not.*

Proof. Because i is a member of G, it can construct a valid protocol run between i and j all by himself, without j participating at all. □

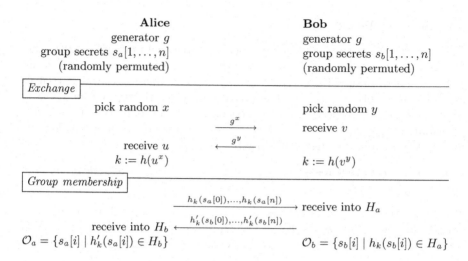

Fig. 2. Message flow of the generalised private handshaking protocol

4   Arbitrary Membership Protocols

It is possible to use the single membership protocol to determine all groups of which both Alice and Bob are a member, by running the previous protocol for all candidate pairs separately. However, if Alice is a member of a groups and Bob is a member of b groups, this requires $a \times b$ message exchanges (and more if the number of groups one is a member of should not be revealed). In this section we describe a more efficient protocol (see Protocol 2), which does *not* provide traitor tracing.

Suppose each user can be a member of at most n groups. Each group is identified by a group secret (which, essentially, is a random value). Each user A that is a member of a group stores its group secret in an array $s_A[]$. Any remaining cells in the array are filled with random values (not corresponding to groups). The array is randomly permuted after initialisation[9]. After establishing a shared secret session key k using a Diffie-Hellman key exchange, Alice and Bob exchange keyed hashes h_k and h'_k of each group secret. Real implementations should use HMAC [BCK96]. Alice stores the hashes it receives in a set H_B, looks for entries in $s_A[]$ whose hash occurs in H_B, and adds those as common group members to G_A.

Note that Alice needs to use a hash function different from the one used by Bob, in order to avoid detection of shared membership by eavesdroppers. If Alice wishes not to reveal membership of certain groups, she can replace the corresponding group secret with a random value. However, Bob cannot avoid revealing his membership of those groups (unless he decides to do so independently from Alice).

---

[9] If not, Bob might be able to infer the number of groups of which Alice is a member from the fact that the x-th token happens to coincide with a group he himself is a member of.

4.1 Security Proof

The following lemmas prove that protocol 2 implements private handshaking for multiple group. We sketch the proofs of the lemmas. Consider an arbitrary run between two nodes i and j, belonging to groups $\mathcal{G}_i$ and $\mathcal{G}_j$ where i returns output $\mathcal{O}_i$ and j returns output $\mathcal{O}_j$ (where we treat the group secrets $s_i[x]$ to represent their respective groups). Let $\mathcal{A}$ be an arbitrary adversary, and let G be an arbitrary group. A property holds with overwhelming probability if it holds with probability larger than $1 - 1/2^\sigma$, where σ is the security parameter. It holds with negligible probability if the probability is less than $1/2^\sigma$.

Lemma 4.1 (correctness/safety). $\mathcal{O}_i, \mathcal{O}_j \subseteq \mathcal{G}_i \cap \mathcal{G}_j$ *with overwhelming probability.*

Proof. Clearly $\mathcal{O}_i \subseteq \mathcal{G}_i$. If $x \in \mathcal{O}_i$ then also $h'_k[x] \in H_j$. Hence $h'_k(x) = z$ for some z received in the second phase of the protocol. If z is not sent by j, then k is unknown to the adversary. Hence the chances that $h'_k(x) = z$ are negligible. If z is sent by j then $z = h'_k(s_j[y])$ for some y. This happens with overwhelming probability if $x = s_j[y]$ and hence $x \in \mathcal{G}_j$. $\square$

Lemma 4.2 (progress). *If i and j are honest and all messages exchanged between them during the run are delivered unaltered, then $\mathcal{O}_i = \mathcal{O}_j = \mathcal{G}_i \cap \mathcal{G}_j$.*

Proof. This is easily verified by case analysis. $\square$

Lemma 4.3 (resistance to detection). *Let $j \in \mathcal{A}$ but $\mathcal{A} \notin G$. Then the adversary $\mathcal{A}$ cannot distinguish a protocol run in which it interacts with a node $i \in G$ from a run involving a simulator with non-negligible probability.*

Proof. Since $j \in \mathcal{A}$, the adversary does know the shared session key k derived using the Diffie-Hellman key exchange. However, since $\mathcal{A} \notin G$, it does not know the secret $s_i[x]$ for group G. Hence it cannot tell whether $h_k(s_i[x])$ and $h_{k'}(s_i[r])$ are hashes for the same group exchanged during different sessions, or if these hashes correspond to different groups. This holds even if the adversary knows k' for the other session as well. $\square$

Lemma 4.4 (indistinguishability to eavesdroppers). *Let $i, j \notin \mathcal{A}$. Then the adversary $\mathcal{A}$ cannot determine whether $i \in G$ or $i \notin G$ with non-negligible probability. This holds even if $\mathcal{A} \in G$.*

Proof. If $i, j \notin \mathcal{A}$, then the adversary does not know the shared session key k derived using the Diffie-Hellman key exchange. With a fresh, unknown, random key k, the keyed hash value $h_k(s_i[x])$ corresponding to the secret for group G is indistinguishable from a random value, even if the adversary knows $s_i[x]$. $\square$

Lemma 4.5 (unlinkability). *Adversary $\mathcal{A}$ is unable to distinguish a protocol run involving node i from a protocol run involving a node $j \neq i$ with $\mathcal{G}_j = \mathcal{G}_i$, even when $\mathcal{G}_{\mathcal{A}} = \mathcal{G}_i$ and $\mathcal{A}$ participates in the protocol runs.*

Proof. Nodes i and j share the same state. Hence all messages sent by i could have been sent by j as well.   □

Lemma 4.6 (forward repudiability). *After the run, node i cannot convince another node k whether $j \in G$ or not.*

Proof. Because i is a member of G, it can construct a valid protocol run between i and j all by himself, without j participating at all.   □

5   Conclusions

We have presented two efficient protocols for secret handshaking. The second protocol efficiently supports membership of more than one group. The focus in this work is the efficiency of the protocols. They use only a few, quite simple, operations. This may allow the implementation of these protocols on resource constrained devices, like perhaps higher-end RFID tags. It is especially in these kinds of environments that a form of mutual authentication is required to provide a certain level of security and/or privacy.

Our protocols do not allow for easy revocation of group membership: all remaining members need to be given a new, fresh, group secret. More efficient ways to support group membership revocation are an interesting topic for further research, especially given the requirement that the resulting protocols should still be efficient and should not allow a group adminstrator to trace users. We also wish to develop more formal proofs for the security of our protocols.

Two other possible extensions of the basic pairwise private handshake are left for further investigation. First of all, one could consider a private group handshake where a subgroup of a secret group can recognise membership of the same group simultaneously (e.g., when setting up a meeting). Secondly, one could create password based private handshakes by using the original idea of Jablon [Jab96] based on a passkey shared by the members of the group.

We thank Flavio D. Garcia, David Galindo and Berry Schoenmakers for fruitful discussions on this topic, and the anonymous referees for their very insightful comments and suggestions.

References

[BG85]   Baldwin, R.W., Gramlich, W.C.: Cryptographic protocol for trustable match making. In: IEEE Security & Privacy IEEE Symp. on Security and Privacy, Oakland, CA, April 22–24, 1985, pp. 92–100. IEEE, New York (1985)

[BRS+03]   Balfanz, D., Durfee, G., Shankar, N., Smetters, D.K., Staddon, J., Wong, H.C.: Secret handshakes from pairing-based key agreements. In: IEEE Security & Privacy IEEE Symp. on Security and Privacy, Oakland, CA, pp. 180–196. IEEE, New York (2003)

[BCK96]   Bellare, M., Canetti, R., Krawczyk, H.: Keying hash functions for message authentication. In: Koblitz, N. (ed.) CRYPTO 1996. LNCS, vol. 1109, pp. 1–15. Springer, Heidelberg (1996)

[BPR00]   Bellare, M., Pointcheval, D., Rogaway, P.: Authenticated key exchange
           secure against dictionary attacks. In: Preneel, B. (ed.) EUROCRYPT 2000.
           LNCS, vol. 1807, pp. 139–155. Springer, Heidelberg (2000)
[BR93a]   Bellare, M., Rogaway, P.: Entity authentication and key distribution. In:
           Stinson, D.R. (ed.) CRYPTO 1993. LNCS, vol. 773, pp. 232–249. Springer,
           Heidelberg (1994)
[BR93b]   Bellare, M., Rogaway, P.: Random oracles are practical: A paradigm for
           designing efficient protocols. In: 1st CCS Int. Conf. on Computer and Com-
           munications Security, Fairfax, VA, November 1993, pp. 62–73. ACM, New
           York (1993)
[BM93]   Benaloh, J., de Mare, M.: One-way accumulators: A decentralized alter-
           native to digital signatures. In: Helleseth, T. (ed.) EUROCRYPT 1993.
           LNCS, vol. 765, pp. 274–285. Springer, Heidelberg (1994)
[BF01]   Boneh, D., Franklin, M.: Identity-based encryption from the weil pairing.
           In: Kilian, J. (ed.) CRYPTO 2001. LNCS, vol. 2139, pp. 213–229. Springer,
           Heidelberg (2001)
[CJT05]   Castelluccia, C., Jarecki, S., Tsudik, G.: Secret handshakes from ca-
           oblivious encryption. In: Lee, P. (ed.) ASIACRYPT 2005. LNCS, vol. 3788,
           pp. 293–307. Springer, Heidelberg (2005)
[DH76]   Diffie, W., Hellman, M.E.: New directions in cryptography. IEEE Trans.
           Inf. Theory IT-11, 644–654 (1976)
[DY81]   Dolev, D., Yao, A.: On the security of public-key protocols. In: 22nd FOCS
           Symp. on Foundations of Computer Science, Nashville, TN, October 18-30,
           1981, pp. 350–357. IEEE Comp. Soc. Press, Los Alamitos, CA (1981)
[Fin03]   Finkenzeller, K.: RFID-Handbook, 2nd edn. Wiley & Sons, Chichester
           (2003)
[FNP04]   Freedman, M., Nissim, K., Pinkas, B.: Efficient private matching and set
           intersection. In: Cachin, C., Camenisch, J.L. (eds.) EUROCRYPT 2004.
           LNCS, vol. 3027, pp. 1–19. Springer, Heidelberg (2004)
[HHJ+06]   Hoepman, J.-H., Hubbers, E., Jacobs, B., Oostdijk, M., Wichers Schreur,
           R.: Crossing borders: Security and privacy issues of the european e-
           passport. In: Yoshiura, H., Sakurai, K., Rannenberg, K., Murayama, Y.,
           Kawamura, S. (eds.) IWSEC 2006. LNCS, vol. 4266, pp. 152–167. Springer,
           Heidelberg (2006)
[Hol05]   Holt, J.E.: Reconciling ca-oblivious encryption, hidden credentials, osbe
           and secret handshakes. Cryptology ePrint Archive, Report 2005/215 (2005)
           http://eprint.iacr.org/
[Jab96]   Jablon, D.P.: Strong password-only authenticated key exchange,
           Comput. Comm. Rev. Computer Communications Review (1996)
           www.integritysciences.com and http://www.std.com/~dpj.
[KS05]   Kissner, L., Song, D.: Privacy-preserving set operations. In: Wang, L.,
           Chen, K., Ong, Y.S. (eds.) ICNC 2005. LNCS, vol. 3612, pp. 241–257.
           Springer, Heidelberg (2005)
[Mea86]   Meadows, C.: A more efficient cryptographic matchmaking protocol for use
           in the absence of a continuously available third party. In: IEEE Security
           & Privacy IEEE Symp. on Security and Privacy, Oakland, CA, April 7–9,
           1986, pp. 134–137. IEEE, New York (1986)
[MOV96]   Menezes, A.J., van Oorschot, P.C., Vanstone, S.A.: Handbook of Applied
           Cryptography. CRC Press, Boca Raton, FL (1996)
[MV88]   Mullender, S.J., Vitányi, P.M.B.: Distributed match-making. Algorithmica
           Algorithmica 3, 367–391 (1988)

[RE03]   Rankl, W., Effing, W.: Smart Card Handbook, 3rd edn. Wiley & Sons, Chichester (2003)

[TX05]   Tsudik, G., Xu, S.: Flexible framework for secret handshakes (multi-party anonymous and un-observable authentication). Cryptology ePrint Archive, Report 2005/034 (2005) http://eprint.iacr.org/

[WSRE03] Weis, S.A., Sarma, S.E., Rivest, R.L., Engels, D.W.: Security and privacy aspects of low-cost radio frequency identification systems. In: Hutter, D., Müller, G., Stephan, W., Ullmann, M. (eds.) Security in Pervasive Computing. LNCS, vol. 2802, pp. 201–212. Springer, Heidelberg (2004)

[XY04]   Xu, S., Yung, M.: k-anonymous secret handshakes with reusable credentials. In: Atluri, V., Pfitzmann, B., McDaniel, P.D. (eds.) 11th CCS Int. Conf. on Computer and Communications Security, Washington DC, October 25–29, 2004, pp. 158–167. ACM, New York (2004)

[ZN]   Zhang, K., Needham, R.: A private matchmaking protocol. http://citeseer.nj.nec.com/71955.html

Security Associations in Personal Networks: A Comparative Analysis*

Jani Suomalainen[1], Jukka Valkonen[2,3], and N. Asokan[2,3]

[1] VTT Technical Research Centre of Finland
Jani.Suomalainen@vtt.fi
[2] Helsinki University of Technology
Jukka.Valkonen@tkk.fi
[3] Nokia Research Center
N.Asokan@nokia.com

Abstract. Introducing a new device to a network or to another device is one of the most security critical phases of communication in personal networks. There have been several different proposals to make this process of *associating* devices both easy-to-use and secure. Some of them have been adapted by emerging standard specifications. In this paper, we first present a taxonomy of protocols for creating security associations in personal networks. We then make use of this taxonomy in surveying and comparing association models proposed in several emerging standards. We also identify new potential attack scenarios.

Keywords: Personal networks, security association, survey.

1 Introduction

Short-range communication standards have brought a large number of new services to the reach of common users. For instance, standards for personal networking technologies such as Bluetooth, Wi-Fi, Wireless Universal Serial Bus (WUSB), and HomePlugAV enable users to easily introduce, access, and control services and devices both in home and mobile environments.

The initial process of introducing a new device to another device or to a network is called an *association*. Association consists of the participating devices finding each other, and possibly setting up a *security association*, such as a shared secret key, between them. The part of the association procedure that is visible to the user is called an *association model*.

Association models in today's personal networks such as those based on Wi-Fi or Bluetooth, typically consist of the user scanning the neighborhood from one device, selecting the other device or network to associate with, and then typing in a shared passkey. These current association procedures have several usability and security drawbacks arising primarily from the fact that they are used by ordinary non-expert users.

To address these concerns, various new ideas have been proposed with the intent of providing a secure yet usable association model. For instance, there have

---

* The full version of this paper is a Nokia Research Center technical report [14].

F. Stajano et al. (Eds.): ESAS 2007, LNCS 4572, pp. 43–57, 2007.

been proposals for schemes utilizing short passwords/checksums [5,7,15,16] or out-of-band channels . In reality, it is impractical to mandate a single association model for all kinds of devices because different devices have different hardware capabilities. Also, different users and application contexts have different usability and security requirements. Because of this, forthcoming standards are adopting multiple association models. Although low-end devices like headsets and wireless access points may be limited to one association model, richer devices like mobile phones and personal computers will naturally support several. The security of individual association models has been studied widely. But new kinds of threats may emerge when several models are supported in personal devices and several standards, both new and old, are in use simultaneously.

In this paper, we make a comparative analysis of proposed association models in different standards from a practical point of view. The surveyed standards are Bluetooth Secure Simple Pairing [13], Wi-Fi Protected Setup [17], Wireless USB Association Models [18], and HomePlugAV security modes [9].

The standards have some similarities. All of the them can address the problem of finding the right peer device usually by supporting some variation of the notion of *user-conditioning*: a device participates in the association only when it is in a special association mode; typically a device enters the association mode in response to an explicit user action, such as pressing a button. All of them are targeted for personal networks and support multiple association models. Also, all of them utilize some sort of key establishment procedure for agreeing on a shared secret key between the devices.

The rest of the paper is organized as follows. Section 2 provides a systematic taxonomy of different protocols for key establishment. Section 3 describes how and which key establishment protocols and related association models are used in the surveyed standards. Section 4 presents a comparative analysis on the security of these standards. Section 5 describes novel attack scenarios where attackers utilize simultaneous availability of different association models.

2 Association Protocols

All of the association models we will survey in Section 3 are based on one or more protocols for human mediated establishment of a shared key between two devices. The shared key is typically used to protect subsequent communication and, possibly, in authentication for other access control decisions. We show that the same basic protocols are used in different standard specifications, even though the exact instantiations naturally differ.

As a prelude to identifying and comparing these different instantiations, we present a systematic classification of human-mediated key establishment protocols that can be used in personal networks. Figure 1 provides an overview of this classification.

At a high level, key establishment may be a simple *key transport* or involve running a *key agreement* protocol.

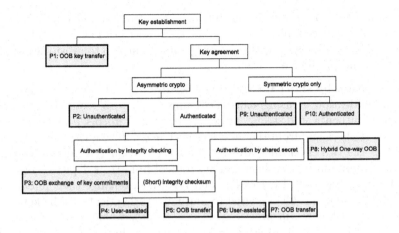

Fig. 1. Classification of Key Agreement Protocols

Key transport: In key transport, one device chooses the key and transmits it directly to the second device using an out-of-band communication channel (**P1**). Typical out-of-band channels used for key transport include a direct USB cable connection or the use of flash drives. The security of key transport depends on the out-of-band channel being secret and unspoofable: a man-in-the-middle (MitM) must not be able to modify the data transmitted between the devices.

Key Agreement: Key agreement protocols may be based purely on symmetric key cryptography, or may be based on asymmetric key cryptography as well. In the latter case, the typical protocol is Diffie-Hellman key exchange [4].

Key agreement may be *unauthenticated* or *authenticated*. Unauthenticated symmetric key agreement (**P9**) is vulnerable even to passive eavesdroppers. Unauthenticated asymmetric key agreement (**P2**) is secure against passive eavesdroppers but is vulnerable to active MitM.

Key agreement based on symmetric key cryptography is authenticated by using a sufficiently long *pre-shared secret* (**P10**). The security of such protocols depend on the length of the pre-shared secret. Authentication of asymmetric key agreement can be performed using some form of *integrity checking*, or by using a pre-shared secret or using a combination of these two. There are two ways to authenticate by integrity-checking: by exchanging commitments to public keys, or by verifying a short integrity checksum. Now we take a closer look at the protocols involved in the different ways of authenticating key agreement based on asymmetric key cryptography.

Authentication by exchanging key commitments: Balfanz, et al., propose in [1] to exchange commitments to public keys using an out-of-band channel (**P3**). The commitments can be the public keys of the devices or their hashes. When the devices exchange public keys via the in-band channel, they can validate the authenticity of these public keys by using the information exchanged via the out-of-band channel.

The security of the protocols depends on the out-of-band channel being unspoofable. Also, the commitments of public keys must be strong enough (e.g., a cryptographic hash function with at least 80 bits of output) to resist the attacker finding a second pre-image to the commitment.

Authentication by short integrity checksum: Several researchers have proposed authentication by using short checksums [11,7,16,15], sometimes referred to as "short authenticated string" protocols. In such protocols, each device computes a short checksum from the messages exchanged during the key agreement protocol. If the two checksums are the same, the exchange is authenticated. A basic three round mutual authentication protocol from [7] is depicted, in a simplified form, in Figure 2. Devices D_1 and D_2 first exchange their public keys PK_1 and PK_2. The protocol is used to mutually authenticate public keys. The notations are as follows: in practice, $h()$ is a cryptographic hash function like SHA-256; $f()$ is also a cryptographic hash function, but with a short output mapped to a human-readable string of digits. The hat ('ˆ') symbol is used to denote the receiver's view of a value sent in protocol message.

The check in the last step can be done in many different ways. One way is to ask the user to do the comparison **(P4)**. An alternative way is to do the check using a physical out-of-band channel **(P5)** as in [12].

To succeed, a MitM attacker has to choose random mumbers R'_1, R'_2 and public keys PK'_1, PK'_2 so that $f(PK'_1, PK_2, R'_1, R_2)$ equals $f(PK_1, PK'_2, R_1, R'_2)$ The security of the protocol depends on the quality of the functions $h()$ and $f()$. If $h()$ is collision-resistant, attacker has to choose R'_1 without knowing anything about R_2. If $h()$ is one-way, attacker has to choose R'_2 without knowing about R_1. If the output of $f()$ is a uniformly distributed n-bit value, then the chance of a MitM attacker succeeding is 2^{-n} because the attacker cannot influence the outcome of $f()$. This success probability does not depend on any additional assumptions about the computational capabilities of the attacker beyond that he cannot break $h()$ in real time. See [8] for a formal proof.

Authentication by (short) shared secret: Key exchange can also be authenticated using a short pre-shared secret passkey. A number of different methods

---

1. D_1 generates a long random value R_1, computes commitment $h = h(R_1)$ and sends it to D_2
$$D_1 \rightarrow D_2: h$$
2. D_2 generates a long random value R_2 and sends it to D_1
$$D_1 \leftarrow D_2: R_2$$
3. D_1 opens its commitment by sending R_1 to D_2
$$D_1 \rightarrow D_2: R_1$$
4. D_2 checks if $\hat{h} \stackrel{?}{=} h(\hat{R}_1)$. If equality holds, D_2 computes $v_2 = f(P\hat{K}_1, PK_2, \hat{R}_1, R_2)$, otherwise it aborts.
D_1 computes $v_1 = f(PK_1, P\hat{K}_2, R_1, \hat{R}_2)$.
5. Both devices check if v_1 equals v_2.

Fig. 2. Authentication by Short Integrity Checksum

1. D_1 generates a long random value R_{i1}, computes commitment $h_{i1} = h(1, PK_1, P\hat{K}_2, P_i, R_{i1})$ and sends it to D_2
   $$D_1 \rightarrow D_2: h_{i1}$$
2. D_2 generates a long random value R_2, computes commitment $h_{i2} = h(2, PK_2, P\hat{K}_1, P_i, R_{i2})$ and sends it to D_1
   $$D_1 \leftarrow D_2: h_{i2}$$
3. D_1 responds by opening its commitment and sending R_{i1} to D_2
   $$D_1 \rightarrow D_2: R_{i1}$$
   D_2 checks if $\hat{h}_{i1} \stackrel{?}{=} h(1, P\hat{K}_1, PK_2, P_i, \hat{R}_{i1})$ and aborts if it does not hold.
4. D_2 responds by opening its commitment and sending R_{i2} to D_1
   $$D_1 \leftarrow D_2: R_{i2}$$
   D_1 checks if $\hat{h}_{i2} \stackrel{?}{=} h(2, PK_1, P\hat{K}_2, P_i, \hat{R}_{i2})$ and aborts if it does not hold.

Fig. 3. Round i of Authentication by (Short) Shared Secret

have been proposed for password-authenticated key exchange since Bellovin and Merrit introduced the idea in [3]. In Figure 3 we describe a variant of the MANA III protocol by Gehrmann, et al., originally described in [5]. It uses a one-time passkey P to authenticate PK_1 and PK_2. P is split into k pieces, labelled $P_1 \dots P_k$. The steps in the protocol are repeated k times. The figure shows the exchanges in the ith round.

In each round, each party demonstrates its knowledge of P_i. A MitM can easily learn P_1 by sending garbage in message 2, and figuring out P_1 by exhaustive search once D_1 reveals R_1 in message 3. However, without knowing $P_i, i = 2 \dots n$, the attacker cannot successfully complete the protocol run (recall that P is a *one-time* passkey). With n-bit passkey and k rounds the probability for a successful MitM attack is $2^{-(n-\frac{n}{k})}$. As in the case of short authentication string, the MitM success probabilities do not depend on additional assumptions about the attacker's computational capabilities.

There are many different ways for arranging for both devices to know the same P. One way is to have the user as the intermediary **(P6)**: the user may choose P and enter it into both devices, or one device may show a value for P which the user is asked to enter into the second device. Alternatively, P may be transported from one device to another using an out-of-band channel **(P7)**.

Hybrid authentication: Hybrid authentication protocols are used to achieve mutual authentication when only a one-way out-band-channel is available **(P8)**. The one-way channel is used to transmit the shared secret value and a hash of the public key from the first device to the second. The second device authenticates the first based on the public key hash. The first device authenticates the second based on its knowledge of the shared secret. A basic protocol is depicted in Figure 4. The function $c(M, K)$ is a message authentication code on message M using a key K.

The security of the protocol depends on the out-of-band being secret and unspoofable, as well as on strength of the commitment function $h()$ and the message authentication code function $c()$.

1. D_1 picks a long random value R_1, computes a commitment c to public key PK_1 as $C_1 = h(PK_1, R_1)$ and sends C_1 and secret S using OOB channel
$$D_1 \Rightarrow D_2: S, C \text{ (OOB)}$$
2. D_1 sends its public key and random value using in-band channel.
$$D_1 \rightarrow D_2: PK_1, R_1$$
3. D_2 checks if $\hat{C}_1 \overset{?}{=} h(\hat{PK}_1, \hat{R}_1)$ and aborts if it does not hold. Otherwise, D_2 picks its own long random value R_2, computes $C_2 = c(\hat{PK}_1 | PK_2 | \hat{R}_1 | R_2, \hat{S})$ and sends the result to D_1 with its own public key and random value.
$$D_1 \leftarrow D_2: PK_2, R_2, C_2$$
4. D_1 checks if $\hat{C}_2 \overset{?}{=} c(PK_1 | \hat{PK}_2 | R_1 | \hat{R}_2, S)$ and aborts if it does not hold.

Fig. 4. Hybrid Authentication Protocol

3 Association Models in Standards for Personal Networks

In this section, we survey the association models proposed in four emerging standards [13,17,18,9]. We then compare them by referring to the classification presented in Section 2.

3.1 Bluetooth Secure Simple Pairing

Bluetooth Secure Simple Pairing (SSP) [13] is a standard developed by Bluetooth Special Interest Group. It is intended to provide better usability and security than the original Bluetooth pairing mechanism, and is expected to replace it. Simple pairing consists of three phases. In the first phase, the devices find each other and exchange information about their user input/output capabilities and their elliptic curve Diffie-Hellman public keys for the FIPS P-192 curve [10]. In the second phase, the public keys are authenticated and the Diffie-Hellman key is calculated. The exact authentication protocol, and hence the association model, is determined based on the device user-I/O capabilities. In the third phase, the agreed key is confirmed (in one association model, the authentication spans both the second and third phase).

SSP supports four different association models: Numeric Comparison, Passkey entry, 'Just Works' and Out-of-band models. Now we will examine each of these models and the protocols they use for authentication in phase 2.

Numeric comparison model is where the user manually compares and confirms whether the short integrity checksum displayed by both devices are identical (Figure 1: **P4**). The compared checksum is 6 digits long. The phase 2 protocol is an instantiation of the protocol in Figure 2.

Passkey entry model is targeted primarily for the case where only one device has a display but the other device has a keypad. The first device displays the 6-digit secret passkey, and the user is required to type it into the second device. The passkey is used to authenticate the Diffie-Hellman key agreement (Figure 1: **P6**). The protocol is based on user-assisted authentication by shared secret in Figure 3 with 20 rounds ($k = 20$). Devices prove knowledge of one bit of the passkey in each round.

'Just works' model is targeted for cases where at least one of the devices has neither a display nor a keypad. Therefore, unauthenticated Diffie-Hellman key agreement is used (Figure 1: **P2**) to protect against passive eavesdroppers but not against MitM attacks.

Out-of-band model is intended to be used with different out-of-band channels, in particular with Near Field Communication technology. Device D_A uses the out-of-band channel to send a 128-bit secret r_a and a commitment C_a to its public key PK_a. Similarly, D_B uses the out-of-band channel to send r_b and C_b. If out-of-band communication is bidirectional, mutual authentication is achieved by each party verifying that the peer's public key matches the commitment received via the out-of-band channel. (Figure 1: **P3**).

If the out-of-band channel is two way, then message 1 and message 2 will both be sent. Mutual authentication is complete at the end of step 2.

If the out-of-band channel is only one way, the party receiving the out-of-band message can authenticate the public key of its peer. However, the party sending the out-of-band message must wait until the third, key confirmation, phase of SSP which we now describe.

In phase 3, the same key confirmation protocol is executed in all association models to confirm successful key exchange by exchanging message authentication codes using the newly computed Diffie-Hellman key. Each device includes the random value r received from the peer in the calculation of its message authentication code. In the one-way out-of-band case, the message authentication code serves as a proof-of-knowledge of the shared secret r received out-of-band. This is the hybrid authentication protocol **P8** (Figure 4).

Peer discovery: In current Bluetooth pairing, peer discovery is left to the user: the user initiates pairing from one device which constructs a list of all other Bluetooth devices in the neighborhood that are publicly discoverable and asks the user to choose the right one to pair with. In SSP out-of-band association model, device addresses are sent via the out-of-band channel. This makes it possible to uniquely identify the peer to pair with, without requiring user selection. SSP does not contain any new mechanisms to make peer discovery easier in the other association models. Individual implementations could use existing Bluetooth modes, like the "limited discoverable mode" and "pairable mode" to support user-conditioning on the peer device. However, since such user-conditioning is not mandated by the specification, it is quite possible that the SSP implementations may still need to resort to asking the user to choose the right peer device from a list.

Model selection: The association model to be used is uniquely selected during the initialization of the session. If the association process is initiated by out-of-band interaction, and security-information is sent through the out-of-band channel, then the out-of-band model is chosen automatically. Otherwise, in phase 1, the devices exchange their input-output capabilities. The SSP specification describes how these capabilities should be used to select the association model.

3.2   Wi-Fi Protected Setup

Wi-Fi Protected Setup (WPS) is Wi-Fi alliance's specification for secure association of wireless LAN devices. Microsoft's Windows Connect Now (WCN) includes a subset of association models described in WPS. The objective of WPS is to mutually authenticate the enrolling device with the Wi-Fi network and to deliver network access keys to the enrolling device. This is done by having the enrolling device interact with a device known as the "registrar", responsible for controlling the Wi-Fi network. The registrar may be, but does not have to be, located in the Wi-Fi access point itself. WPS supports three configuration methods: In-band, out-of-band, and push-button configurations.

In-band configuration enables associations based on a shared secret passkey (Figure 1: **P6**). The user is required to enter a passkey of enrollee to the registrar. This passkey may be temporary (and displayed by the enrollee) or static (and printed on a label). 8-digit passkeys are recommended but 4-digit passkeys are allowed. The passkey is used to authenticate the Diffie-Hellman key agreement between the enrollee and the registrar. The protocol used is a variation of the modified MANA III protocol in Figure 3 with two rounds ($k = 2$).

As in MANA III (Figure 3), once a passkey is used in a protocol run, an attacker can recover the passkey by dictionary attack (although in this instantiation, the attacker needs to be active since the computation of the used commitments includes a key derived from the Diffie-Hellman key).

Out-of-band configuration is intended to be used with channels like USB-flash drives, NFC-tokens or two-way NFC interfaces. There are three different scenarios:

1. Exchange of public key commitments (Figure 1: **P3**), typically intended for two-way NFC interfaces, where the entire Diffie-Hellman exchange and the delivery of access keys takes place over the out-of-band channel.
2. Unencrypted key transfer (Figure 1: **P1**). An access key is transmitted from a registrar to enrollees in unencrypted form, either using USB-flash drives or NFC-tokens.
3. Encrypted key transfer. This is similar to the previous case, except that the key is encrypted using a key derived from the (unauthenticated) Diffie-Hellman key agreed in-band. From a security perspective, this is essentially out-of-band key transfer (Figure 1: **P1**).

Push button configuration is an optional method that provides an unauthenticated key exchange (Figure 1: **P2**). The user initiates the Push button configuration (PBC) by conditioning the enrollee (e.g., by pushing a button), and then, within 120 seconds the user has to condition the registrar as well. The enrollee will start sending out probe requests to all visible access points inquiring if they are enabled for PBC. Access points are supposed to respond affirmatively only when their registrar has been conditioned by the user for PBC. If a device or registrar sees multiple peers ready to start PBC, it is required to abort the process and inform the user.

Peer discovery: Enrollees start association in response to explicit user conditioning. They scan the neighborhood for available access points and send Probe Request messages. The Probe Response message has a "SelectedRegistrar" flag to indicate if the user has recently conditioned a registrar of that access point to accept registrations. This is mandatory for push button configuration but is optional for other models. Thus it is possible that user may have to be asked to select the correct Wi-Fi network from a list of available networks.

Model selection: The model is explicitly negotiated at the beginning.

3.3 Wireless USB Association Models

Wireless USB (WUSB) is a short-range wireless communication technology for high speed data transmission. WUSB Association Models Supplement 1.0 specification [18] supports two association models for creating trust relationships between WUSB hosts and devices:

Cable model uses out-of-band key transfer (Figure 1: **P1**) and utilizes wired USB connection to associate devices. Connecting two WUSB devices together is considered as an implicit decision and, hence, the standard does not require users to perform additional actions like accept user prompts.

Numeric model relies on the users to authenticate the Diffie-Hellman key agreement by comparing short integrity checksum values (Figure 1: **P4**). The protocol is an instantiation of the protocol in Figure 2. First D_A and D_B negotiate the length of the checksum to be used. The specification requires that WUSB hosts must support 4-digit checksums whereas WUSB devices must support either 2 or 4-digit checksums.

Peer discovery: The association is initialized by implicit or explicit user conditioning. Attaching a USB-cable is interpreted as an implicit conditioning. The user pressing a button is an example of explicit user conditioning. In the numeric model the user sets a USB device to search for hosts and a USB host to accept connections. The host advertise its willingness to accept a new association in the control messages it transmits on the WUSB control channel.

Model selection: The choice of the association model is based on the type of user conditioning done. In case a cable is plugged, the devices exchange information on whether they support cable association. If so, they use cable model. If conditioning is explicit, they use numeric model.

3.4 HomePlugAV Protection Modes

HomePlugAV is a power-line communication standard for broadband data transmission inside home and building networks. In addition to protecting deliberate attacks, association mechanisms are used to create logically separate subnetworks by distributing an 128-bit AES network encryption key (NEK) for devices in each subnetwork. As with WPS, each HomePlugAV network has a controller device. HomePlugAV supports the following association models [9]:

Simple connect mode uses unauthenticated symmetric crypto based key agreement to agree on a shared key (Figure 1: **P9**). This network membership key (NMK), is used to transport NEK to the new device. The key agreement process is as follows. To admit a new device, the user is required to first condition the controller device, and then condition the new device, e.g., by turning on its power. The devices find each other and exchange nonces. A temporary encryption key (TEK) is formed by hashing the two nonces together. The controller encrypts the NMK using the TEK and sends it to the new device.

Secure mode allows new devices to have a secret passkey, of at least 12 alphanumeric characters long, typically printed on a label. The user is required to type in this passkey to the controller device. The controller device uses it to construct an encryption of NMK and send it to the new device. The keys for devices joining in secure mode is different from the keys for devices joining in simple connect mode. This is an example of authenticated symmetric crypto key agreement (Figure 1: **P10**).

Optional modes enable alternative use of alternative models for distributing NMKs or NEKs between devices. These include "manufacturer keying" where a group of devices have a factory installed shared secret, and external keying, where trust is bootstrapped from other methods.

MitM attacks are prevented in simple connect mode by utilizing characteristics of powerline medium. Before two nodes can communicate, they must negotiate tone maps, which enable devices to compensate disturbances caused by powerline channel. This negotiation is done in a reliable, narrow-band broadcast channel. Thus a MitM trying to negotiate tone maps with the legitimate endpoints will be detected.

Passive eavesdropping in the point-to-point channel is difficult since an attacker, even with the knowledge of the tone maps used between the legitimate endpoints, will not be able to extract the signal from the channel because the signal-to-noise ratio will be too poor at different locations, particularly, when the attacker is outside a building and the legitimate end points are inside. Also, licensees of HomePlugAV technology do not provide devices that can extract signal without negotiating tone maps. Hence, attackers must be able to build expensive devices for eavesdropping.

Peer discovery: In simple connect mode the peer discovery is performed by the user conditioning the devices into a suitable modes, and the new device scanning the network to find a controller that is willing to accept new devices.

Model Selection: The model is selected by user conditioning. There is no automatic negotiation.

4   Comparison of Proposed Association Models

In this section, we summarize and compare the security levels provided by the different association models discussed in Section 3. A comparative summary of models' security characteristics are presented in Table 1.

Table 1. Comparison of Security Characteristics of Association Models

Association Model	Offline Attacks		Online Active Attacks		
	Protection	Work[1]	Protection	Success Probability	Work[2]
Bluetooth Simple Pairing					
Numeric Comparison	DH	2^{80} [2]	6 digit checksum	10^{-6}	2^{128}
Just Works	DH	2^{80} [2]	-	1	0
Passkey Entry	DH	2^{80} [2]	6 digit passkey	10^{-6}	2^{128}
Out-of-band	DH	2^{80} [2]	OOB security	-	2^{128}
Wi-Fi Protected Setup					
In-band	DH	2^{90} [6]	8 digit passkey	10^{-4}	2^{256}
In-band + OOB [3]	DH	2^{90} [6]	OOB security	2^{-128}	2^{256}
Out-of-band	OOB	2^{90} [6]	OOB security	-	-
PushButton	DH	2^{90} [6]	-	1	0
WUSB Association Models					
Numeric Model	DH	2^{128} [2]	2/4 digit checksum	10^{-2} or 10^{-4}	2^{256}
Cable Model	OOB	2^{128} [2]	OOB	-	-
HomePlugAV Protection Modes					
Simple Connect	SNR	Assumed high	Traffic monitoring	Assumed low	Assumed high
Secure Mode	AES	2^{72}	passkey	2^{-72}	2^{72}

[1] Rough work effort estimates based on Table 2 of [2] and Section 8 of [6].
[2] Work effort to break commitments exchanged.
[3] OOB passkey + checksum.

4.1 Offline Attacks

The out-of-band association models rely on the secrecy of out-of-band communication to protect against passive attacks against key agreement. The in-band and hybrid models in all of the standards except HomePlugAV use Diffie-Hellman key agreement to protect against passive attacks. The level of protection depends on the strength of the algorithms and the length of the keys used. In the "Work" subcolumn under the "Offline Attacks" column of Table 1, we use some recent sources [6,2] to estimate the amount of work an attacker has to do in order to be successful. The figures correspond to approximate lower bounds, and should be treated as rough ballbark estimates only. Offline attack protection in HomePlugAV relies on the characteristics of the power-line communications: namely the signal-to-noise ratio (SNR) make it difficult for an attacker to eavesdrop. The HomePlugAV Secure Mode uses symmetric key encryption as protection.

4.2 Online Active Attacks

Mounting an online active attack as a man-in-the-middle against key agreement is significantly more difficult than passive eavesdropping. Several of the models ('Just Works', 'Push Button', and 'Simple Connect') trade off protection against man-in-the-middle attacks, in return for increased ease-of-use.

Other in-band association models rely on authentication as the means to protect against online active attacks. The probability of success for an online active attack depends on the length of the key as well as the protocol. Bluetooth Simple Pairing numeric comparison model uses 6-digit checksums leading to a success probability of $\frac{1}{1000000}$. WUSB numeric model allows a success probability of $\frac{1}{100}$ when two digit checksum is used, and $\frac{1}{10000}$ when four digit checksum is used. These probabilities do not rely on any assumptions about the computational capabilities of the man-in-the-middle. All of these use hash functions with 128-bit outputs to compute commitments. In principle, a man-in-the-middle who can find a second pre-image of a hash commitment, *during* the key agreement process can also succeed. We show this in Table 1, in the "Work" subcolumn under the "Online Active Attacks" column by indicating the amount of *on-line* work the attacker has to perform in order to succeed. In this case, assuming that the hash function is strong, and requires exhaustive search to find a second pre-image we use the figure 2^{128}.

Recall from Section 2 that with n bit passkeys and k rounds the success probability for an online active attack against the passkey protocols is $2^{-(n-\frac{n}{k})}$. Bluetooth Simple Pairing passkey entry model uses 6-digit ($n \approx 20$) one-time passwords in $k = 20$ rounds. This leads to approximately $\frac{1}{1000000}$ success probability. WPS network uses essentially the same protocol, but in two rounds only. This leads to success probabilities of $\frac{1}{100}$ when 4-digit passkeys are used, and $\frac{1}{10000}$ when 8-digit passkeys are used. In both cases, the passkey must be single-use. If the passkey is re-used, the success probability of man-in-the-middle rises dramatically, reaching 1 after the kth re-use, where k is the number of rounds in the original protocol. In other words, if the same fixed passkey in WPS network model is re-used even *once*, the man-in-the-middle can succeed in the next attempt with certainty. As before, we can estimate the on-line work effort the attacker has to do to break the hash commitments. HomePlugAV secure mode uses a 12 character passkey which is used to generate a key for AES encryption, leading to a probability of 2^{-72} and the amount of on-line work effort is 2^{72}.

The hybrid models using a one-directional out-of-band channel, the random secret transferred using the out-of-band channel is 128 bits long leading to a computational security of 2^{-128}.

An interesting implication of Table 1 is that in all the systems (except Home-Plug AV), the work factor for online active attack *far exceeds* the work factor for offline attack. This reflects the difficulties in comparing the relative security of cryptographic hash functions with that of public key algorithms.

4.3   Associations with Wrong Peers

Unauthenticated association models face the risk of a device being associated with a wrong peer. For instance, in WPS push button model, the user may condition first the enrollee to search for registrars before conditioning the registrar. If the attacker sets a bogus registrar to accept connections before the users does it with the legitimate registrar, the enrollee associates with the attacker's registrar. Only in the case when both registrars, the bogus and the legitimate one, are simultaneously accepting connections, is the procedure aborted.

In HomePlugAV Simple Connect mode, the user sets the control device to accept connections before starting the joining device up. This could be used to reduce the probability for an attacker to successfully masquerading as a bogus control device because since, if the new device sees multiple control points, it can abort association. However, the mode is potentially vulnerable for fatal errors where the user is slow to switch power to the new device. In this case an attacker may connect to user's control point and get the network encryption key.

5   Attacks Against Multiple Association Models

Simultaneous support for multiple association models may be utilized in different attacks. In this section, we examine such threats.

Consider specifications that support an unauthenticated association model as well as user-assisted comparison of integrity checksums. An example is a Bluetooth Simple Pairing device that supports the numeric association model and the 'just works' model. Figure 5 illustrates a MitM attacker who can intercept messages exchanged during an association. The first associated device has a display and the second may or may not have a display. The attacker changes device capability information so that the first device will be using the numeric comparison model and that the second device will be using 'just works' model. This leads to a situation where the first device shows a 6-digit checksum and the second device, using 'just works' model, does not display a checksum, even if it would have a display. The user may have been educated to detect a mismatch in checksums. But now, when only one device displays a checksum, the user is likely to be confused and may just go ahead and accept the association.

To get an idea about whether such user confusion is likely, we included the situation depicted in Figure 5 as a test scenario in one round of an on-going series of usability testing. Out of 40 test users, 6 accepted the pairing on both

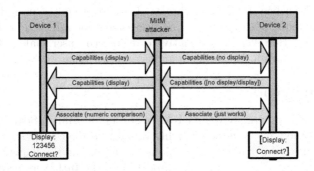

Fig. 5. Man-in-the-middle between Different Association Models

devices, 11 noticed the problem and rejected the pairing on both devices, and the rest rejected pairing on Device 1 but accepted it on Device 2.

This attack has two implications. Firstly, when the second device has a display, it is a bidding down attack against this device. The second device will know that the association is unauthenticated. However, the user may still allow the association to happen. Secondly, it is a bidding up attack against the first device since it believes that the association is made using a secure protocol resistant to MitM attacks. Consequently, the first device may choose to trust this security association more than it would trust a 'just works' security association. For instance, it may have a policy rule, which allows more trustworthy devices to initiate connections without user confirmations.

A scenario related to the attack on Figure 5 arises with devices that are willing to participate in setting up a security association without immediate user conditioning. Public printers and access points are examples of devices that may be permanently conditioned for association. Suppose a user starts associating Device 1 with Device 2 using an association model that does not require any user dialog (e.g., WUSB cable model, or HomePlugAV Simple Connect mode) and that Device 2 is permanently conditioned to accept incoming association requests. If an attacker now initiates association with Device 2, say using Bluetooth Simple Pairing numeric association, a user dialog will pop up on Device 2. Since the user is in the middle of associating Device 1 and Device 2, he might answer the dialog thinking that it is a query about Device 1. Depending on the nature of the dialog, the attacker may end up gaining unintended privileges on Device 2.

6   Conclusions

New standards for associating devices in personal networks are emerging. The objective of the new standards is to make the association process more user-friendly while improving the security at the same time. We surveyed the protocols and association models used in different standards specifications. We presented a systematic classification of protocols for human-mediated establishment of session keys. We showed how the different protocols in standard specifications are related by using our classification.

The flexibility of the new proposals also introduce potential for some new attacks. We described some such threats. Careful design of user dialogs may reduce the likelihood of these attacks, as discussed in the full version of this paper ([14] Section 6). However, how exactly to design the user dialogs to preserve security without harming usability remains an open issue.

Acknowledgments

We thank Dan Forsberg, Kristiina Karvonen, Janne Marin, Seamus Moloney, Kaisa Nyberg and Gene Tsudik for highly valuable feedback. We are particularly grateful to Kaisa for her many suggestions for improving the paper.

The work of the second author is supported by the InHoNets project funded by TEKES.

References

1. Balfanz, D. et al.: Talking to strangers: authentication in ad-hoc wireless networks. In: Proceedings of the Network and Distributed System Security Symposium (2002)
2. Barker, E. et al.: Recommendation for key management - part 1: General (revised), (2006) http://csrc.nist.gov/CryptoToolkit/kms/SP800-57Part1_6-30-06.pdf
3. Bellovin, S.M., Merritt, M.: Encrypted key exchange: Password-based protocols secure against dictionary attacks. In: Steven, M. (ed.) Proceedings of the 1992 IEEE Symposium on Security and Privacy, pp. 72–84 (1992)
4. Diffie, W., Hellman, M.E.: New Directions In Cryptography. IEEE Transactions on Information Theory IT-22, 644–654 (1976)
5. Gehrmann, C. et al.: Manual authentication for wireless devices. RSA CryptoBytes (2004)
6. Kivinen, T., Kojo, M.: RFC3526: More Modular Exponential (MODP) Diffie-Hellman groups for Internet Key Exchange (IKE) (May 2003) http://www.ietf.org/rfc/rfc3526.txt
7. Laur, S. et al.: Efficient Mutual Data Authentication Using Manually Authenticated Strings. Cryptology ePrint Archive, Report 2005/424 (2005)
8. Laur, S., Nyberg, K.: Efficient mutual data authentication using manually authenticated strings. In: Proceedings of the 5th International Conference on Cryptology and Network Security, pp. 90–107 (2006)
9. Newman, R., et al.: Protecting domestic power-line communications. In: Proc. of The Second Symposium on Usable Privacy and Security, pp. 122–132 (2006)
10. NIST: National Institute of Standards and Technology. Digital Signature Standard (DSS). U.S. Department of Commerce (January 2000)
11. Pasini, S., Vaudenay, S.: SAS-based Authenticated Key Agreement. In: Proceedings of The 9th International Workshop on Theory and Practice in Public Key Cryptography, pp. 395–409 (2006)
12. Saxena, N., et al.: Secure device pairing based on a visual channel (short paper). In: Proc. of the 2006 IEEE Symposium on Security and Privacy, pp. 306–313 (2006)
13. Simple Pairing Whitepaper. Bluetooth Special Interest Group (2006) http://www.bluetooth.com/Bluetooth/Apply/Technology/Research/Simple_Pai ring.htm
14. Suomalainen, J. et al.: Security associations in personal networks: A comparative analysis. Technical Report NRC-TR-2007-004, Nokia Research Center (2007) http://research.nokia.com/tr/NRC-TR-2007-004.pdf
15. Vaudenay, S.: Secure communications over insecure channels based on short authenticated strings. In: Shoup, V. (ed.) CRYPTO 2005. LNCS, vol. 3621, pp. 309–326. Springer, Heidelberg (2005)
16. Čagalj, M., Čapkun, S., Hubaux, J.-P.: Key agreement in peer-to-peer wireless networks. In: Proceedings of the IEEE (Special Issue on Cryptography and Security), pp. 467–478 (2006)
17. Wi-Fi Alliance. Wi-Fi Protected Setup Specification. Wi-Fi Alliance Document (January 2007)
18. Wireless USB Specification. Association Models Supplement. Revision 1.0. USB Implementers Forum (2006) http://www.usb.org/developers/wusb/

Key Establishment in Heterogeneous Self-organized Networks

Gelareh Taban[1,*] and Rei Safavi-Naini[2,**]

[1] University of Maryland, College Park
gelareh@umd.edu
[2] University of Calgary
rei@cpsc.ucalgary.ca

Abstract. Traditional key pre-distribution schemes in sensor and ad hoc networks rely on the existence of a trusted third party to generate and distribute a key pool. The assumption of a single TTP however can be very strong in practice, especially when nodes belong to different domains and they come together in an ad hoc manner. In this work, we show the shortcomings of previous approaches [3,13] in terms of both efficiency and security. By incorporating a heterogeneous network, we show that we can dramatically reduce the load on resource constrained devices whilst also increasing their security. We also propose a new strengthened security model for self-organized ad hoc networks and evaluate the security of our protocol in this model.

Keywords: group key, key pre-distribution, self-organized networks.

1   Introduction

Traditional ad hoc and sensor network settings generally assume a trusted third party (TTP) who is trusted with the keying information and enables secure delivery of keys to the network principals and/or nodes. Security associations, such as authentication of nodes or securing communication channels, are then bootstrapped using this information. In key pre-distribution schemes, the TTP allocates keys to each node prior to deployment either randomly from a key pool [8,5], or by using a well-defined combinatorial structure such as a t-design [10] that ensures the key subsets allocated to the nodes satisfy certain properties.

---

* Research was sponsored by the U.S. Army Research Laboratory and the U.K. Ministry of Defence and was accomplished under Agreement Number W911NF-06-3-0001. The views and conclusions contained in this document are those of the author and should not be interpreted as representing the official policies, either expressed or implied, of the U.S. Army Research Laboratory, the U.S. Government, the U.K. Ministry of Defence or the U.K. Government. The U.S. and U.K. Governments are authorized to reproduce and distribute reprints for Government purposes notwithstanding any copyright notation hereon.

** This work is in part supported by Informatics Circle of Research Excellence, Alberta, Canada.

F. Stajano et al. (Eds.): ESAS 2007, LNCS 4572, pp. 58–72, 2007.
© Springer-Verlag Berlin Heidelberg 2007

However, the assumption of a single TTP can be restrictive in scenarios where the network is self-organized and formed without prior planning. In the following we list some of the immediate applications that require distribution of trust. The first example is in disaster response scenarios where a network may be formed with members belonging to different administrative domains. Furthermore, it might be impossible to access an outside authority due to the lack of preexisting infrastructure or inability to contact off-site systems [12]. In such life-threatening situations, it is not acceptable to deny data from a legitimate principal that might save someone's life. Therefore a 'best-effort' security model might be appropriate in this scenario, allowing strong guarantees when a single TTP can be established and weaker guarantees when no TTP can be assumed. Similarly in combat situations it is essential to allow members of a coalition to join and form collaborative groups. In such dynamic coalitions there is typically no single TTP prior to or during deployment.

Existence of a TTP is also in immediate conflict with privacy enhancing applications. As sensor and ad hoc testbeds have been deployed, it has become clear that user privacy can be easily compromised as a side effect to seemingly innocuous applications [4]. For example a humidity sensing network can also be used to monitor activity in a room as the human body effectively alters the room humidity. Therefore by removing the presence of an all knowing authority (i.e. the TTP), communication can be made private to the restricted user set.

Finally, to allow the wide adoption of sensor and ad hoc networks in everyday scenarios, it is desirable to reduce the required knowledge base of network owners. Customers should be able to purchase a set of nodes that are usable upon purchase without requiring the presence of a network administrator. Therefore the node manufacturer can install public data in the nodes that can bootstrap future security associations.

In the following we focus on the problem of group key distribution in self-organized ad hoc and sensor networks where no single point of trust exists. A group key allows nodes to securely communicate with each other and participate in collaborative tasks. The dynamic property of the network allow new nodes to join or exiting nodes to leave the group. This is an essential mechanism in the first two applications listed above. We consider heterogeneous networks consisting of two types of nodes: typical low performance sensor nodes and more powerful nodes with more computation and communication resources. It has been recently shown [7,1] that networks that consist of homogeneous nodes cannot scale well and also have lower performance compared to networks that include a number of more powerful nodes. Introducing more powerful nodes also improves reliability and lifetime of the network [1]. Furthermore [15] showed that pairwise communication security in the presence of a TTP is not necessarily sacrificed if a key distribution scheme leverages the existence of more capable nodes.

1.1   Related Work

The first work on key pre-distribution in ad hoc network without a TTP is due to Chan [3]. In this construction each group member individually selects her keys from a common *public* key pool in a specified way. The aim of the protocol is to probabilistically construct a *Cover Free Family (CFF)* that will ensure shared keys between nodes. Chan showed that his scheme allows any two nodes to communicate securely with a high probability and the system provides security against collusion attack. However, [16] showed that the probability that the constructed structure is a CFF is very low and so the protocol cannot achieve its stated goal.

The closest work to our scheme is Luo et. al [13] who proposes a probabilistic group key management protocol (referred to as LSBS) for ad hoc homogeneous networks. The objective of LSBS is to establish a common shared key for the whole group. The protocol consists of three phases. In the setup phase, each node randomly selects a set of keys from the key pool and performs a shared key discovery (SKD) protocol with each neighboring node to discover shared keys. The group key is generated by special subsets of nodes called initiating groups (IG), and is distributed by flooding the network. Although LSBS protocol achieves its stated goal, in practice there are challenges that if not addressed makes the protocol impractical. In particular, our simulation of LSBS in [14] show the following shortcomings in the protocol.

Firstly, LSBS implicitly assumes that a single IG is formed where in practice many IGs may simultaneously exist. In fact our simulation results show that in a network of 1000 nodes, where each node has a key ring of size 150 keys, we can form up to 100 IGs. To obtain a single group key for all nodes some mechanism for negotiation and/or cooperation among IGs is required, which substantially increases the communication and computation cost which is very undesirable in a resource constrained network. The solutions also needs to be carefully designed to prevent security compromise. The communication cost of the shared key discovery (SSD) phase of the protocol is $\mathcal{O}(l)$ where l is the size of the key ring. LSBS requires a node u to execute the SSD protocol with all of its neighboring nodes. If on average a node is in the neighborhood of d other nodes, a communication cost of $\mathcal{O}(d \cdot l)$ per node is incurred. For networks with battery powered nodes it is essential to reduce this cost in order to prolong network lifetime. Finally, LSBS is analyzed using a simple threat model that does not take into account real life threats in a wide range of application scenarios. The adversary is considered passive and can only eavesdrop on the communications. Given that the key pool is public, the adversary's objective is to either determine the node key or the link key that secures the link between two nodes. In sensor networks it is common to assume that the adversary can compromise a subset of nodes and obtain the secret information of the nodes. Such information includes the key rings of the node and the keys that the nodes share with their neighbors. This latter information will reduce the effort required for finding the key rings of uncompromised nodes, and/or the link keys for links between the compromised node and its neighbor nodes.

1.2   Our Contribution

In this paper, we propose a Layered Key Pre-Distribution (LKD) Scheme for networks of heterogenous nodes: resource constrained nodes and a small number of high performance nodes (level 1) which have more resources and are possibly better protected (e.g. use tamper proof hardware). LKD uses an unbalanced distribution of keys, where high performance nodes are allocated a larger key ring. The level 1-centric clusters that are formed around result in more efficient generation of group keys.

We give a probabilistic analysis of the protocol and show that the inclusion of a small number of more powerful nodes in the network results in constant communication and computation cost, independent of the neighborhood size of a node. We support our analysis via simulation results. We next evaluate the security of the protocol in a strengthened security model. We argue that with a public key pool and without a TTP, previous proposed threat models and security metrics such as network resiliency [5,8], which assumed secret key pool and a TTP, are no longer valid. We update these definitions for our new system and trust model and define a new security metric called neighbor resiliency. We analyze the security of both LKD and LSBS under this new threat model. Our analysis shows that LKD achieves better security than LSBS against node compromising adversaries because sensing nodes in LKD learn much less information about the nodes in their neighborhood.

The paper is organized as follows: Section 2 describes our network and trust model; Section 3 introduces the LKD protocol; Sections 4, 5 provide the correctness and the security analysis of the LKD protocol; Section 6 supports the theoretical analysis with simulation results. We provide concluding remarks and future directions in Section 7.

2   System Model

We consider the network to be fully self-organized, meaning that there is no infrastructure (hence no public key (PK) infrastructure). Traditional network models considered for sensor models not only assume a homogeneous network but also assume either a grid or a random graph [8,5] model where all neighboring nodes are in communication contact. A more realistic model takes into consideration the various signal-blocking barriers and interference sources such as hills and buildings that exist in the deployed environment. In practice, deployed nodes are often segregated into exclusive neighborhoods due to the features of the landscape [15]. Our model accounts for this by considering a cluster based network, where sensor nodes form ad hoc groups around more powerful nodes which act as the backbone of the network. Therefore the sensor nodes connect to the rest of the network through the powerful 'gateway' nodes.

We assume a heterogeneous sensor network of size n consisting of two types of nodes: sensing or level 2 (L2) nodes which are resource constrained and have limited storage and energy capabilities and level 1 (L1) nodes which are more capable, with larger memory, more powerful transceivers and energy source. As a result L1 nodes can store larger key rings and other state data as well as communicate with a larger neighborhood of nodes. The network consists of c L1 nodes and $(n - c)$ L2 nodes. Example L2 nodes are small Berkeley Mica2 motes with 8-bit 4MHz processors and 128 KB memories [2]. L1 nodes can be more powerful nodes such as laptops or other portable devices. Such devices have better physical protection against compromise, such as the use of tamper resistance hardware. However for simplicity, we assume the same type of protection for L1 and L2 nodes. We also assume that each node u_i has a unique identifier i.

Trust Model. We assume that the network has no central authority or a single TTP. Each node essentially acts as its own domain authority. Public information (e.g. the key pool) is available to all, including malicious parties.

Authentication. Since we do not assume any TTP, it is impossible to establish strong authentication and identification amongst network nodes. We weaken our requirements such that to control the join of malicious nodes to the group, we assume some auxiliary identification mechanism for nodes (e.g. node hardware). Details of such a mechanism is outside the realm of our work.

3   Layered Key Pre-Distribution (LKD) Scheme

In this section we describe the LKD scheme to establish both pairwise and group keys in a self-organized network that does not have a TTP. The heterogenous network consists of resource constrained nodes (L2) and more capable nodes (L1) that contain a larger portion of the key pool than L2 nodes. It follows that L1 nodes are able to establish secure links with a larger portion of the nodes. In each neighborhood, local (l, r)-secure groups are established where l denotes the security level and r is the minimum number of nodes in the group. We will show later that r does not effect the security of the protocol and is used for efficiency purposes. Local groups in a neighborhood together generate a cluster group key which are exchanged to contributively generate a network group key. We ensure that the key generated in each layer (i.e. local, cluster or network) is independent. The overall algorithm consists of the following phases: initial setup, neighborhood discovery, cluster and group key generation, join and leave.

In the initial setup phase nodes agree on parameters used in the protocol. The system parameters include a public key pool and its partition into κ blocks of size m each. The security parameter is l which defines the level of link security by specifying the minimum number of keys two nodes need to share to establish a secure communication channel. The size of the key rings of L1 and L2 nodes are also set to k_A and k_B. We note that these parameters can either be set by the node manufacturers or during an initial setup phase prior to deployment.

A node u_i randomly selects one key from each key block to form a key ring $\{K_j^i\}_{j=1}^k$, where $k = k_A$ or k_B. Let $k_B = \kappa$. Thus an L1 node needs to choose multiple keys from each block. Let $k_A = t k_B + s$, where $t, s \in \mathbb{Z}$. Node selects t keys from block 1 to $(k - s)$ and select $(t + 1)$ keys from blocks $(k - s) + 1$ to block k (in total s key blocks).

Neighborhood Discovery Phase. In this phase, L1 nodes initially send beacons identifying themselves to their neighborhood nodes. The beacon message for L1 node u_i can take the simple syntax of $< i, L1 >$ where i is the node identifier.

An L2 node 'discovers' an L1 node when it hears its beacon message. To establish a secure channel with the L1 and help populate L1's incidence matrix, it runs a secure shared key discovery (SSKD) protocol, reminiscent of [3,13]. This SSKD protocol is essentially a privacy preserving set intersection protocol that allows the two participating parties to discover their shared keys from their individual key sets.

For L1 node v_i, the incidence matrix I^i has k columns labeled by the node keys $\{K_j^i\}_{j=1}^k$, and one row for each neighbor. $I^i(j, t) = 1$ if K_t^i is shared with node u_j in the neighborhood of v_i, and zero otherwise. The incidence matrix of v_i can be used to keep an account of the keys shared by the nodes in L1's neighborhood, *given that the keys are shared with v_i*. This property is important as it maintains the optimal privacy for the neighboring L2 nodes. Specifically v_i does not learn any information about the key ring of its neighboring nodes other than the shared key information it learns during the execution of the SSKD protocol.

If an L2 node is not directly connected to an L1 node (i.e. it is isolated from an L2), it simply waits and performs the join protocol after the key establishment protocol is complete. In this step, L1 nodes also discover each other and establish an l-secure channel between pairs of nodes. This communication network forms the backbone of the larger network.

Secure Shared Key Discovery (SSKD). Consider the case when node u_j wants to discover the keys it shares with node u_i. Let u_i have keys $\{K_j^i\}_{i=1}^l$ and u_j have $\{K_j^i\}_{i=1}^m$, where $l, m \in \mathbb{Z}$. Assume the existence of a homomorphic encryption scheme, where $E_k(m)$ denotes encrypting message m using key k. The SSD protocol is as follows:

1. u_i forms $f_i(x) = \prod_{j=1}^l (x - K_j^i)$ and send to u_j the encrypted coefficients, $E_{K_i}(\cdot)$.
2. u_j computes $z_g = E_{K_i}(r f_i(K_g^j))$ using the homomorphic property of the encryption scheme, where r is a random number. u_j returns z_g to u_i.
3. u_i decrypts z_g to obtain $r f_i(K_g^j)$. If value is zero, then they have a common key.
4. u_i returns to u_j an m-bit bitmap with 1 at bits where $r f_i(K_g^j) = 0$ and 0 elsewhere.

In contrast to LSBS, our SSKD protocol requires the nodes to exchange an m-bit bitmap indicating the shared keys of the participating nodes (step 4). The main reason for this inclusion is that L1 nodes in LKD can select more than one key from each block and so nodes must indicate which key in the block is shared or not, using the bitmap.

Securing Bitmap Transmission. A potential security leakage is the bitmap exchange step of the SSD, which identifies to an eavesdropper the number of keys shared by two nodes. A smart adversary can then compromise a neighboring node which shares the most keys with a target node, as well as reducing the search space for the channel securing key.

The following protocol takes advantage of the privacy preserving characteristics of a homomorphic encryption scheme such as El Gamal [9]. Assume node u_i wants to privately send a k-bit bitmap b to node u_j. We use the *multiplicative homomorphic properties* of the El Gamal [9] encryption scheme for u_i to send b to u_j. Specifically this property is defined as: $E_K(m_1 m_2) = E_K(m_1) \times E_K(m_2)$ where $E_K(m)$ is the encryption of m using key K.

Let the El Gamal public key of u_j be (g, h) and the secret key be $(x = log_g h)$.

$\mathbf{u_j} \rightarrow \mathbf{u_i}$: $r, d \leftarrow \{0,1\}^*$; Send $< C_1, C_2 > = < g^r, h^r \cdot d >$, (g, h)
$\mathbf{u_i} \rightarrow \mathbf{u_j}$: $r' \leftarrow \{0,1\}^*$; Send $< C_3, C_4 > = < C_1 g^{r'}, C_2 h^{r'} \cdot m >$
$\mathbf{u_j}$: bitmap $b = \frac{C_4}{C_3^x \cdot d}$

Node u_j encrypts a dummy message d and sends to u_i the ciphertext and its PK. u_i multiplies the bitmap with the ciphertext and randomizes the message using r'. Using its private key, u_j can decrypt the processed ciphertext and obtain the bitmap. This protocol ensures that the bitmap remains private to u_i, u_j assuming the El Gamal encryption scheme is secure.

By loading nodes with a set of random r values and associated g^r, h^r during the setup phase it is possible to reduce computation to one exponentiation and two multiplications per node. Furthermore we note that although we are using PK cryptography, we do not rely on the existence of a PKI and therefore we preserve the distributed nature of the network. Finally, we point out that this step is only performed once or twice by sensing nodes through out their lifetime. [14] shows further techniques to reduce energy consumption during this step.

Cluster and Group Key Generation. In this phase, L1 nodes v_i use their incidence matrix I^i to assist the nodes in their neighborhoods to initiate local (l, r) groups where a minimum of r nodes share l keys. This is done by finding a set of r rows $\mathcal{R}$ and at least l columns $\mathcal{L}$ in the incidence matrix for which an (l, r)-secure subset can be formed. The formation of the local groups allow v_i to communicate to a group of nodes via multicast thus reducing communication. Also nodes in local groups contribute to the formation of the cluster keys thus preventing the selection of weak keys. Once a local (l, r) group is formed, v_i informs the group members of their group membership using secure channels. Local group members now can communicate securely using their secret group key K_L, which is the XOR of the group shared keys. Each local group L_i in cluster C contributively generate a partial cluster key $K_C^{L_i}$ in order to democratically agree on a cluster key $K_C = \oplus_i K_C^{L_i}$.

Potentially two L2 nodes which are not in direct communication can belong to the same local group. In this case, the L1 node can be used as an intermediate routing point to forward messages. Also if L1 nodes use directed antennas, L1 node can group an (l, r) subset together iff they are in the same vicinity.

The group key can be generated similar to the cluster key by requiring nodes to select a key share for the group key along with the cluster key share. L1 nodes then exchange the partial group key generated in their neighborhoods to arrive at the final group key.

Join and Leave. A newly deployed node u_i can join the network by establishing an l-secure channel to a node u_j which already belongs to the secure group. u_j essentially acts for u_i as the 'gateway' to the network. In the case of an L2 node u_i leaving the group, the neighborhood L1 node uses its incidence matrix to determine the effected keys and purging them. Thus the departing node has no information regarding the key rings of the nodes in its neighborhood. Due to space constraint, we refer the reader to [14] for more details of these protocols.

4   Correctness Analysis

In this section we show the correctness of the LKD protocol. We say that LKD is *correct* if the protocol allows the 'backbone' L1-network as well as the cluster of L2 nodes around an L1 node, to be connected and thus functioning with a high probability. Later we verify our results by simulation.

In our theoretical analysis we limit the key ring size of L1 nodes $k_A = t \cdot k_B + s$ as follows (k_B is the key ring size of L2 nodes): $t = 1$, $s = [0..k_B]$. We analyze the general case when s can be assigned any value from $[0..k_B]$. We refer the reader to [14] for the special case when $s = k_B$. To establish an l-secure link, two nodes share at least l keys. For readability purposes, in the rest of the paper we use the notation A and B to refer to L1 and L2 nodes respectively.

Let set S consist of the s key blocks from which an L1 node selects two keys and let $\bar{S}$ consist of the remaining $k - s$ key blocks. Let $P_{A,B}(r, l)$ be the probability of r nodes (one L1 node and $(r-1)$ L2 nodes) sharing at least l keys. Let Z_x be the event that r nodes share a key in a given block x. The probability that Z_x occurs, is equal to p_s for blocks $x \in S$, and $p_{\bar{s}}$ for $x \in \bar{S}$. Key collisions for each block can be modeled as independent Bernoulli trials. The generating function for probabilities $P_{A,B}(r, l)$ is calculated as the product of two binomials with success probabilities of p_s and $p_{\bar{s}}$:

$$f(x) = (p_s x + (1 - p_s))^s (p_{\bar{s}} x + (1 - p_{\bar{s}}))^{k-s} \tag{1}$$

Proposition 1. *The probability that the r nodes share exactly l keys is equal to the coefficient C_l of the x^l term in polynomial Equation 1, and $P_{A,B}(r, l) = \sum_{i=l}^{k_B} C_i$, where C_i is the coefficient of the x^i term in $f(x)$ and k_B denotes the size of the key ring of L2 nodes.*[1]

Proposition 2. *Let $P_{A,A}(2, l)$ be the probability of two L1 nodes sharing at least l keys. Let α, β, γ be non-negative integers satisfying $2\alpha + \beta + \gamma = l$. Let p_i be the probability of sharing i keys for the first s blocks and $\tilde{p}_i$ be the probability of sharing i keys for the remaining $k - s$ blocks. Then:*

$$P_{A,A}(2, l) = \sum_{\substack{\alpha, \beta, \gamma \\ 2\alpha+\beta+\gamma=l}} \binom{s}{\alpha}\binom{s-\alpha}{\beta} p_2^\alpha \, p_1^\beta \, p_0^{s-\alpha-\beta} + \binom{k-s}{\gamma} \tilde{p}_1^\gamma \, \tilde{p}_0^{k-s-\gamma} \tag{2}$$

---

[1] Examples to illustrate how the above proposition can be used are provided in [14].

This proposition is based on the fact that the first s blocks can contribute 0, 1 or 2 shared keys per block, and the last $(k-s)$ blocks can contribute 0 or 1 shared keys per block. In the above formulae, α represents blocks that share 2 keys and β and γ represent blocks that share only 1 key in S and $\bar{S}$ respectively. For a more detailed proof, refer to [14].

Fig. 1(a) compares the probabilities of two nodes establishing an l-secure channel for different node types, when the key pool is made up of 200 blocks, with a block size of five keys. We can see a rapid transition in the probability of establishing an l-secure channel for different l. Fig. 1(b) generalizes the node pair to groups of r nodes. It is intuitive that establishing an l-secure channel becomes less probable as the group size increases. We also note that when there is a high probability for l-secure channel among r nodes, the probability of establishing a secure channel between two L1 nodes will be an even higher value. It is also interesting to note that the phase transition becomes slower as the number of nodes in the group increases. Fig. 1(c) graphs the probability of establishing an

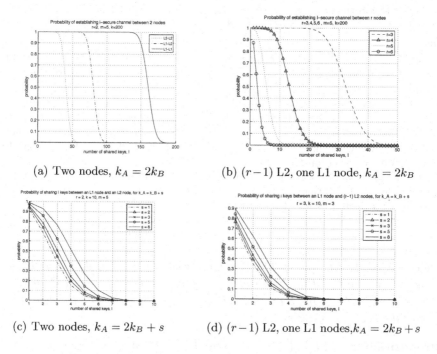

(a) Two nodes, $k_A = 2k_B$

(b) $(r-1)$ L2, one L1 node, $k_A = 2k_B$

(c) Two nodes, $k_A = 2k_B + s$

(d) $(r-1)$ L2, one L1 nodes, $k_A = 2k_B + s$

Fig. 1. Probability of establishing an l-secure channel

l-secure channel between an L1 node and an L2 node for different values of s. The results confirm intuition by showing that as the key ring of an L1 node becomes larger, the probability of a secure connection with a L2 node increases. A similar result is verified in Fig. 1(d) when we consider r nodes, consisting of one L1 node and $(r-1)$ L2 nodes.

In a more general version of this problem, a node can select extra keys from any block of its choosing, rather than the first s blocks. It is intuitive that in this version of the problem, the probabilities of establishing an l-secure channel do not increase to the same extent as the more special case presented above. We leave the analysis of this problem as a future exercise.

The graphs presented in this section allow a network administrator to choose appropriate values for the system parameters. In the following section, we show how an increased key ring not only increases the probability of establishing a secure channel (as shown), but also decreases the security of the system. It is therefore important to achieve the proper balance between connectivity and security. Section 6 gives simulation results to confirm the theoretical results.

5   Security Model and Analysis

We analyze the security of LKD against two types of adversaries: (i) *Passive* adversary with only access to public data, protocol description and transcript of node communications; (ii) *Node Capturing* (NC) adversary with access to all the information available to a passive adversary, and also the private data of nodes that it has captured. We do not allow a NC adversary to interact with the nodes. That is we only consider the case when the adversary uses its information to eavesdrop on others' communication. The goal of both adversaries therefore, is to learn the secret keys between nodes that are used to secure their links.

The security of traditional key pre-distribution schemes that assume the existence of a TTP [8,5,6,11] are based on the facts that (i) the keys in the key pool are exclusively secret to the TTP, (ii) nodes key ring are private, and (iii) the link communication is confidential. In this model an adversary cannot introduce a 'new' device into the network because even if there is no authentication mechanism, it does not have access to the key pool. However by compromising legitimate nodes and obtaining their key rings and/or identities, an adversary can gain entrance into the secure network. The more nodes an adversary compromises, the more it learns of the key pool and the more effective an attack it can launch against a target secure channel. This notion is captured by the *resiliency* of the protocol against node compromise, where resiliency metric is defined to be "the fraction of links in the network a node-compromising adversary is able to eavesdrop on, as a result of recovering keys from captured nodes" [5]. A protocol has stronger security if the adversary is forced to compromise a larger percentage of the nodes to eavesdrop on a target channel. Also, in [8,5] information that an NC adversary obtains from captured devices combined with the key indices allows him to gain information about the keys belonging to other network nodes.

The security of the self-organized (SO) protocols do not rest on the secrecy of the key pool; in fact, the key pool is considered to be public information and can be accessed by the adversary. This means that if there are no auxiliary means of authentication, the adversary can introduce a malicious node v with the aim of extracting key information from a victim node u: v can choose a key ring and run SKD with u to find out a subset of keys of u (that they share). It can then select a new key ring and repeat the protocol. After sufficient runs of this, v can learn all the keys of u. This means that it is crucial to assume a method of node authentication that prevents the adversary from introducing nodes of its choice. Since this is not the focus of our paper, we do not consider this scenario and leave it for future work.

The security of the SO protocols is based exclusively on (i) the size of the key pool and (ii) the security of link keys. In LKD, a NC adversary gains only local information from a compromised node; that is, it learns only the key ring of the node and potentially any information it shares with nodes it associates with. In the case of LKD, a node u_i associates only with its neighboring nodes $\mathcal{N}_i$; by compromising u_i an adversary learns not only the key ring of u_i but also the keys it shares with its neighboring nodes. Thus by compromising u_i, the adversary can tighten its search space when attacking (i) a link between two nodes where at least one is neighbor to u_i or (ii) the key ring of a node neighbor to u_i. We capture this notion in the following security parameter for the SO model: *Neighbor resiliency* is defined as the fraction of the key pool the adversary can discard in its exhaustive key search to attack a target secure channel, as a result of recovering keys from neighboring captured nodes. Another security metric we consider is the advantage the adversary gains in determining the key ring of a node when it is in the neighborhood of a compromised node.

In the following, we analyze LKD against first a passive and then a NC adversary. An eavesdropping adversary cannot obtain any information about the keys except to exhaustively guess at the final shared key between nodes. This is because in the course of the key establishment protocol, no information about the key ring of the nodes is leaked. The adversary knows that there are $N = mk$ possible keys and at least l keys from k different possible blocks are used to secure a link. Thus, the search space for the attacker is equal to $\sum_{t=l}^{k} \binom{k}{t} m^l$. Similarly, to determine the key ring of a node of size k, the adversary must exhaustively search $\binom{k}{t} m^l$ possibilities. Due to space constraints, we refer the reader to [14] for the detailed analysis of LSBS.

Because L2 nodes in LKD do not compute an incidence matrix, a compromised L2 node u_c does not leak any keying information about its neighboring nodes. However the adversary does learn (i) The keys that u_c has in common with the L1 node in its cluster, or if it is not connected to an L1 node, the connecting L2 node; (ii) If it is part of an (l, r)-secure local group, only the keys it shares with *all* of them.

Consider three nodes u_i, u_j and u_c. Assume $u_i \in \mathcal{N}_c$, $u_i \in \mathcal{N}_j$, and u_c is a compromised node. Let k be the size of the key rings of u_c, u_i, u_j respectively. The goal of the adversary is to break the secret link between u_i, u_j. By compromising u_c, the adversary obtained the following information: u_c and u_i share b keys and do not share $(k_c - b)$. To guess the key ring of u_i, the adversaries' search space is reduced from m^k to m^{k-b}. The search space to exhaustively guess l shared keys between u_i and u_j is reduced from $\binom{k}{l} m^l$ to $\sum_{\alpha=0}^{l} \binom{k-b}{\alpha} \binom{b}{l-\alpha} m^\alpha$. We can easily see that the search space has been reduced because:

$$\sum_{\alpha=0}^{l} \binom{k-b}{\alpha}\binom{b}{l-\alpha} m^{\alpha} \leq \sum_{\alpha=0}^{l} \binom{k-b}{\alpha}\binom{b}{l-\alpha} m^{l} = \binom{k}{l} m^{l} \qquad (3)$$

Thus the search space to break an l-secure link between u_i and u_j is equal to:

$$\sum_{t=l}^{k}\sum_{\alpha=0}^{t} \binom{k-b}{\alpha}\binom{b}{t-\alpha} m^{\alpha} \qquad (4)$$

However the number of links and nodes to which these reduced probabilities can be applied to has been decreased dramatically. This is primarily because LKD does not require an L2 node to connect to every node in its neighborhood. Instead the number of secure connections an L2 node needs to establish as well as the keys it shares with neighboring nodes has been reduced to only those that are necessary.

In the event that an adversary compromises an L1 node and the L1 node does not have any tamper resistant hardware, the adversary gains keying information about all the nodes in its neighborhood. In this case the adversary gains as much information as in the LSBS protocol. Since the majority of the nodes in the network are L2 nodes, we can conclude that on average the advantage that an adversary gains by compromising nodes in LKD has been reduced and therefore LKD is more secure than LSBS.

6   Simulation and Discussion

The simulation assumes a static network of $n = 1060$ nodes, consisting of 60 L1 nodes and 1000 L2 nodes. This is a reasonable assumption in a dense static network or a highly dynamic network when nodes move around but in a bounded region (e.g a group of rescuers in an emergency situation or troops in a battle-field). We assume that L1 nodes have twice the transmission range R_A of L2 nodes R_B. To guarantee network connectivity and thus allow a large portion of the nodes to participate in the secure group communication, we use the system parameter relationships derived by [8] based on the phase transition theory of Erdös and Rényi for connected random graphs. For network connectivity, we require that the neighborhood of each L2 node include 40 other nodes. This is a reasonable assumption used by [8,5,15]. We also need to guarantee that the L1-network (the network of L1 nodes) is connected. Using the area needed for 1000 L2 nodes where the neighborhood of each L2 node has on average 40 nodes, we use 60 L1 nodes where each L1 node is neighbor to 10–15 L1 nodes. At the beginning of the simulation, each node randomly selects a key ring of size $k_A = 300$ for L1 nodes and $k_B = 150$ for L2 nodes. Nodes can establish an l-secure connection by sharing at least l keys.

We simulated LSBS using the above configuration in [14] by excluding the L1 nodes. Our results highlighted the shortcomings of LSBS and various practical issues regarding IG formation that were not dealt with in [13]. We summarize these as follows: (1) As the number of shared keys needed to establish a secure channel decreases, a larger number of initiator groups get created. This leads to high network communication due to the respective network floods and higher computation load due to the subsequent encryption and decryption of flooded messages; (2) There is a sharp transition rate for the number of IGs formed for different key block sizes m. Fig. 2(a) shows the jump from very small number of IGs (e.g. $m = 5$) to almost 50 IGs when $m = 4$. However we know that the larger the number of keys shared between two neighbors, the less resilient the protocol is against neighbor-compromise. It is thus important to select network parameters such that allow us to minimize the number of IGs that get created but to also achieve a high degree of security against both an active and a passive adversary. By introducing hierarchy in the LSBS scheme, we are able to better control

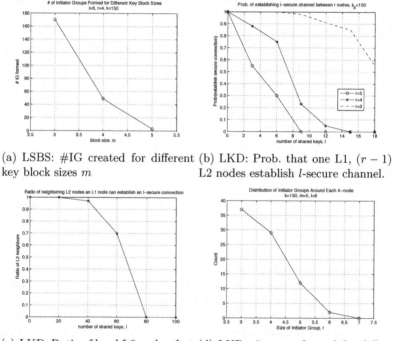

(a) LSBS: #IG created for different key block sizes m

(b) LKD: Prob. that one L1, $(r - 1)$ L2 nodes establish l-secure channel.

(c) LKD: Ratio of local L2 nodes that an L1 can establish l-secure channel.

(d) LKD: #groups formed for different security parameters l.

Fig. 2.

not only the formation of the local and cluster groups but also the distribution of the group keys. Fig. 2(b) and (c) show the probabilities of connection for different local group sizes as well how much of the neighborhood can establish a pairwise l-secure connection with an L1 node. Our results show that with very high probability, we can achieve a connected network. In particular, an L2 node can establish a secure connection with an L1 node with very high probability. Fig. 2(d) graphs the distribution of the size of the (l, r)-groups centering around each L1 node. Each group on average is made up of one L1 node and three L2 nodes. We emphasize that the size of a group has no influence on the security of the group key, rather it ensures a more democratic process since more nodes contribute to the calculation of the group key.

Comparing the performance of LKD and LSBS protocols, the necessary resources of a sensing node is reduced in LKD as:

Reduced communication load. The L2-network is no longer flooded with all the partial group keys due to the clustering of the nodes and the management of the local (l, r) groups by the L1 nodes. In particular, each L2 node, with a high probability, needs to only connect to the neighboring L1 node. Furthermore if it falls in an (l, r) group, it needs to exchange $\mathcal{O}(r)$ number of messages to generate a partial cluster and group key. Therefore the number of messages that a sensing node receives and transmits is no longer a function of the neighborhood size.

Reduced computation load. LKD avoids the need for each sensing node to perform multiple decryption and re-encryptions when transporting the group key. In addition the management and decision making required for IG formation has been avoided and made a responsibility of the powerful L1 nodes. In particular in LKD with a high probability, each sensing node performs the SSKD protocol once with the neighboring L1 node. In contrast in LSBS nodes executed the SSKD protocol with every node in their neighborhood (e.g. in our simulation, this would be 40 times).

Reduced storage space. In LKD sensing nodes do not store the incidence matrix which is of the order $\mathcal{O}(k \cdot d)$ where k is the key ring size and d is the size of the neighborhood. Nodes also do not need to keep an account of the different local groups or IGs they belong to.

Finally we note that in LKD, the load on each L1 node is at most equal to the load on *every* node in LSBS. Also, the number of times LKD floods the network of L1 nodes is in the same order as the number of floods of the *whole* network for LSBS.

7   Concluding Remarks

Traditional solutions for key pre-distribution assume the existence of a single TTP. This assumption however can be very strong in practice, especially when nodes belong to different domain and they come together in an ad hoc manner, as in disaster response scenarios. In this work we showed the shortcomings of previous works [3,13] in this area using both theoretical analysis as well as simulation. We propose a new scheme that incorporates heterogeneous nodes to ameliorate the previous shortcomings, whereby the load on resource limited nodes is reduced dramatically while in fact improving their security against node-compromising adversaries. In the course of our security analysis we pointed out a lack of security model for self-organized networks and thus presented a security model of key distribution protocols in a self-organized ad hoc network.

Our theoretical and simulation analysis pointed to a number of future research directions. The adversary model can be analyzed further, providing simulation results to compare with the theoretical results presented in this paper. We need to also come up with a good communication model to ensure that we do not end up with a disconnected graph. Finally, it is interesting to see how mobility of nodes can help ameliorate the lack of connectivity in the network.

References

1. http://www.intel.com/research/exploratory/heterogeneous.htm
2. Mica motes. http://www.xbow.com
3. Chan, A.: Distributed symmetric key management for mobile ad hoc networks. In: Proc. of Annual Joint Conference of IEEE Computer and Communication Societies, INFOCOM, March 2004, vol. 4, pp. 2414–2424 (2004)
4. Chan, H., Perrig, A.: Security and privacy in sensor networks. In: IEEE Computer, October 2003, vol. 36, pp. 103–105 (2003)
5. Chan, H., Perrig, A., Song, D.: Random key predistribution schemes for sensor networks. In: Proc. of Symposium on Security and Privacy, May 2003, pp. 11–14 (2003)
6. Du, W., Deng, J., Han, Y., Varshney, P., Katz, J., Khalili, A.: A pariwise key predistribution scheme for wireless sensor networks. ACM Transactions on Information and Systems Security 8(2), 228–258 (2005)
7. Du, X., Lin, F.: Improving routing in sensor networks with heterogeneous sensor nodes. IEEE Vehicular Technology Conference, pp. 2528–2532 (2005)
8. Eschenauer, L., Gligor, V.: A key management scheme for distributed sensor networks. In: Proc. of 9th ACM Conference on Computer and Communications Security, Washington, DC, pp. 41–47 (2002)
9. Gamal, T.E.: A public-key cryptosystem and a signature scheme based on discrete logarithms. IEEE Transactions on Information Theory 31(4), 469–472 (1985)
10. Lee, J., Stinson, D.R.: A combinatorial approach to key predistribution for distributed sensor networks. In: Proc. of IEEE Wireless Communications and Networking Conference, March 2005, vol. 2, pp. 1200–1205 (2005)
11. Liu, D., Ning, P.: Location-based pairwise key establishments for static sensor networks. In: Proc. of 1st ACM Workshop on Security of Ad hoc and Sensor Networks, Fairfax, Virginia, pp. 72–82 (2003)
12. Lorincz, K., Malan, D.J., Fulford-Jones, T.R.F., Nawoj, A., Clavel, A., Shnayder, V., Mainland, G., Welsh, M., Moulton, S.: Sensor networks for emergency response: Challenges and opportunities. IEEE Pervasive Computing, pp. 16–23 (October 2004)
13. Luo, L., Safavi-Naini, R., Baek, J., Susilo, W.: Self-organized group key management for ad-hoc networks. In: Proc. of ACM Symposium on Information, Computer and Communications Security (AsiaCCS) (2006)
14. Taban, G., Safavi-Naini, R.: Key establishment in heterogeneous self-organized networks. ISR Tech. Report TR2007-6, University Of Maryland, College Park (2007)
15. Traynor, P., Choi, H., Cao, G., Zhu, S., La Porta, T.: Establishing pair-wise keys in heterogeneous sensor networks. In: Proc. of Annual Joint Conference of IEEE Computer and Communication Societies, INFOCOM, vol. 4, pp. 2414–2424 (2006)
16. Wu, J., Wei, R.: Comments on Distributed Symmetric Key Management for Mobile Ad hoc Networks from INFOCOM'04. Cryptology ePrint Archive, Report 2005/008 (2005) http://eprint.iacr.org/

Enabling Full-Size Public-Key Algorithms on 8-Bit Sensor Nodes

Leif Uhsadel, Axel Poschmann, and Christof Paar

Horst Görtz Institute for IT Security
Communication Security Group (COSY)
Ruhr-Universität Bochum, Germany
Universitätsstrasse 150
44780 Bochum, Germany
{uhsadel,poschmann,cpaar}@crypto.rub.de
www.crypto.rub.de

Abstract. In this article we present the fastest known implementation of a modular multiplication for a 160-bit standard compliant elliptic curve (secp160r1) for 8-bit micro controller which are typically used in WSNs. The major part (77%) of the processing time for an elliptic curve operation such as ECDSA or EC Diffie-Hellman is spent on modular multiplication. We present an optimized arithmetic algorithm which significantly speed up ECC schemes. The reduced processing time also yields a significantly lower energy consumption of ECC schemes. With our implementation results we can show that a 160-bit modular multiplication can be performed in 0.39 ms on an 8-bit AVR processor clocked at 7.37 MHz. This brings the vision of asymmetric cryptography in the field of WSNs with all its benefits for key-distribution and authentication a step closer to reality.

Keywords: wireless sensor network, elliptic curve cryptography, 8-bit micro controller, Micaz, secp160r1.

1 Introduction

The terms *ubiquitous* and *pervasive computing* designate the penetration of our everyday life with intelligent devices. *Wireless sensor networks* (WSN) will play a fundamental role to enable this vision. WSNs consist of many tiny and smart devices, referred to as nodes, which typically combine an 8-bit processor with memory, sensors, radio unit and power supply. The foreseen applications for WSNs range from medical scenarios to agricultural, military and environmental monitoring. Since many data may be very critical (e.g., for the health of human beings in medical scenarios or safety critical monitoring) security mechanisms are required to ensure integrity, confidentiality and authenticity of the data.

WSNs face major security problems because the communication is wirelessly and the devices are often easy to access. Therefore, an adversary can easily eavesdrop on communication or simply steal a node. Since sensor nodes are usually not tamper-resistant, an adversary can often read out any content that

F. Stajano et al. (Eds.): ESAS 2007, LNCS 4572, pp. 73–86, 2007.

is stored on the node. Furthermore, the devices are very constrained in terms of memory, computing power, and energy supply. Since battery powered devices have a limited amount of energy, the major metric in the area of WSNs is energy consumption. The lifetime of a WSN is directly proportional to its energy efficiency, i.e., the less energy is consumed by applications the longer the batteries will last.

Symmetric algorithms are generally preferable to asymmetric algorithms in the field of WSNs because they are more efficient in terms of energy consumption and memory requirements. However, when symmetric algorithms are used, two problems arise: (1) key distribution and (2) number of stored keys. When individual keys are used in a WSN with n nodes, each node has to store $(n-1)$ keys. This has good resiliency properties but obviously scales badly and is especially unsuitable for large WSNs. Moreover, perfect forward secrecy is not given after a node's key have been compromised. When one single symmetric key is used, memory requirement is greatly reduced, but at the same time this is not resilient anymore. To cope with this problem many probabilistic key distribution schemes for symmetric algorithms have been proposed [EG02, CPS03, DDHV]. In general these approaches either need pre-distributed keys, which means a higher configuration effort before deployment, or they produce much traffic, which results in higher energy consumption. Therefore, asymmetric algorithms are very valuable for key establishment and authentication in WSN.

Asymmetric cryptography has long seen as being too demanding for constrained devices such as sensor nodes with an 8-bit micro controller. However, there exist several protocols for asymmetric cryptographic algorithms for WSNs. In [WKC+04] Watro et al. describe public-key based protocols for WSNs. In particular, they present authentication and key-agreement protocols based on RSA. The so-called TinyPK was implemented in NesC for MicaZ 8-bit micro controller. However, one RSA exponentiation with a 1024-bit key needs 14.5 seconds, which is arguably not acceptable in many applications. RSA needs much longer key lengths compared to elliptic curve cryptography to achieve the same security level (1024 bit vs. 160-bit) [Res00]. Considering the limited amount of memory, computing power and energy of a typical 8-bit sensor node, it seems that ECC is a much better choice for public-key cryptography for WSN rather than RSA. Since TinyPK is based on the more demanding RSA algorithm and was implemented in NesC, it is not surprising that this is more than one order of magnitude slower than the fastest known implementation of a point multiplication for ECC in assembly. In [GPW+04] Gura et al. describe a point multiplication on a 160-bit standard curve within 0.81 seconds. The majority (77%) of the clock cycles was required by the modular multiplication. However, the source code of this implementation is not publicly available, it is rather intellectual property of Sun Microsystems. Therefore, these impressive results are not usable for the scientific community. Alternatively there is the TinyECC implementation [LN06], which may be used free of charge. TinyECC is a free software package for TinyOS that supports all SECG recommended 128-bit, 160-bit and 192-bit elliptic curve domain parameters. However, it is slower and needs more memory than the equivalent of SUN Microsystems. Therefore, our goal was to implement a prime field arithmetic for an ECC scheme for 8-bit micro controller, which is open source and at the same time faster than the aforementioned implementation of SUN.

The remainder of this work is organized as follows: In Section 2 we give an introduction to elliptic curve cryptography and constraints of the target devices. Subsequently, in Section 3 our implementation of the modular multiplication for a 160-bit standard elliptic curve is described. The results of our implementation are presented in Section 4. Finally, this paper is concluded in Section 5.

2   Preliminary Assumptions and Introduction to Elliptic Curve Cryptography

In this section, we first state the constraints of the target micro controller. Subsequently we introduce the mathematical background of ECC. Finally, we state the implementation issues that arise when trying to implement ECC for constrained devices.

2.1   Constrained Devices

For the envisioned applications of WSNs, up to tens of thousands of smart, but battery powered devices are required, which communicate wirelessly. In order to lower costs, these devices will be very constrained in terms of memory capacity, computing power and energy supply. Nowadays, the de-facto standard sensor nodes for researchers are the so-called Mica motes [xbo, HSW+00]. They comprise an 8-bit RISC ATMEL AVR ATmega128L [Atm] micro controller, 4 KB configuration EEPROM memory, 512 KB data Flash memory, 128 KB program Flash memory, various sensors, ZigBee radio interface, and two standard AA batteries. Ideally these batteries should last for several months up to years. Therefore, a small power consumption is a crucial requirement for any application running on these nodes. Sending and receiving of messages is by far the most energy consuming task on the nodes [HMV04], therefore the traffic should be minimized wherever possible. Furthermore, the energy consumption of an application is mainly determined by its execution time. Therefore, a rule-of-thumb is: the shorter the processing time of an algorithm, the lower its energy consumption.

2.2   Introduction to Elliptic Curve Cryptography

Compared with symmetric algorithms the asymmetric algorithms work very slow. In particular on low-power processors they are felt as not practical and are used only rarely or not at all. For this purpose special algorithms were developed, but they have to be cryptanalyzed and shown to be secure, which takes a long time, before they are suitable for protecting sensitive data or application. Elliptic curves represent a special case. The advantage of the Elliptic Curve

Cryptography (ECC) is that on one hand it is meanwhile quite well investigated and thus considered secure while on the other hand just a very short bit length is needed as compared to other asymmetric systems. In order to reach a security level, which is equivalent to an RSA key with a length of 1024-Bit, already 160 bits are sufficient with elliptic curves [Res00]. This is a ratio of 6.4 and will significantly reduce the consumed energy for key establishment.

Let E be an elliptic curve defined over a field K as shown in figure 1, then a set of points can be created by a *chord-and-tangent rule* (extended addition). If P and Q are two different points, which are part of the set, that intersect the elliptic curve in a straight line, there will be a third intersection on the straight line with the curve. The reflection on the x axis of the latter is called R and represents the sum of P and Q. Doubling works the same, but the straight line is given by the tangent of the curve in the according point. This set of points defined by the extended addition extended by the point ∞ forms an Abelian group. $P + P$ is referred to as $2P$. Accordingly is $P + .. + P = kP$. For every point P exist a point Q with $P = kQ$, if P is not the identity and the order of the elliptic curve is prime. Finding the appropriate k for a given set (Q, P) is considered to be hard and called the *elliptic curve discrete logarithm problem* (ECDLP). Most ECC protocols rely on the ECDLP.

There are various algorithms for the extended addition on an elliptic curve for different coordinates and different underlying fields. They can be optimized according to the used protocol and hardware. A good overview is given by [HC02] and [Bro01]. Regardless which algorithm is used, they are all based on the arithmetic of the underlying field. Especially the multiplication in the field comes at great cost in time and energy. An efficient field arithmetic is therefore the base for an efficient implementation of an elliptic curve cryptographic system.

As prime fields are potential to be implemented in software with good performance, we rely in the following on elliptic curves of the form

$$E/K : y^2 = x^3 + ax + b, char(K) \neq 2, 3 \tag{1}$$

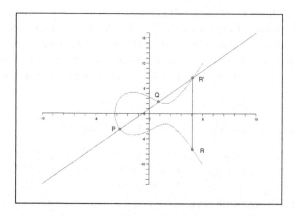

Fig. 1. Elliptic Curve, Parameters: a=-7 and b=11

2.3 Elliptic Curve Cryptography Implementation Issues

The basis for an efficient cryptographic system based on elliptic curves is a very efficient prime field arithmetic. As shown in Figure 2, a cryptographic system based on elliptic curves can be divided into three layers. The highest level actually represents the application layer. Protocols implemented here are for example ECDSA [HC02] or EC ElGamal [HC02]. Optimizations in this layer vary strongly, depending on the application (signature, coding etc.) and have to be partly or completely redone for each application. The underlying layer is the arithmetic of the elliptic curve. Most protocols are based on the multiplication of a point on the elliptic curve with an integer $(k * P)$. However, optimizations at this level usually also strongly depend on the protocol layer. Optimizations in the underlying prime field arithmetics layer will always improve the performance of the whole ECC-System, because they are layer independent. More than 77% of the computing time can be applied here. Therefore, a very efficient prime field arithmetic is crucial for ECC based systems on constrained devices and time critical systems.

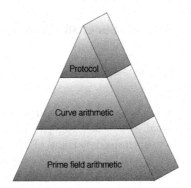

Fig. 2. Three Layers of an ECC-system

3   Implementation of Modular Multiplication

In this section, we first state criteria for an efficient implementation of an ECC system. Subsequently we will present details of our implementation of the modular multiplication, on which ECC system are based on.

3.1   Criteria for an Efficient ECC Implementation

Since optimizations in the prime fields arithmetic, contrary to other optimizations, will always improve the performance of the ECC system, the main attention goes here. Further optimization should be done depending on the application and the selected EC domain parameters. Prime field arithmetic should provide the operations multiply, add, subtract, halve and reduction. Operations with the most potential for optimization are the multiplication and the reduction. Starting point for the implementation is to choose a curve. For security reasons it

should be a standardized curve with at least 160 bit in length. To keep computations fast the bit length should be as short as possible. The curve "secp160r1"
standardized by *Standards for Efficient Cryptography (SEC2)* [Cer00] was chosen for our implementation. It has two advantages that can be used to speed up
prime field arithmetic reduction and to speed up curve arithmetic double and
add. Because its underlying prime field is based on a pseudo Mersenne prime
the reduction in the prime field can be done by several shifts and adds [Sol99]
which is much faster than any other known algorithm on constrained devices.
The curve parameter $a = -3$ can be used to reduce the effort of point doubling
and point addition when using Jacobian projective coordinates [HC02].

   To adapt the algorithms in the best possible way to the hardware the prime
field arithmetic is completely implemented in assembly. As mentioned before
the reduction can be implemented very efficiently if pseudo Mersenne primes are
used. Addition and subtraction can be done without special optimization. The
highest cost of computation lies in the 160-bit multiplication of the prime field.
When choosing an algorithm for this multiplication it is important to consider
the hardwares characteristic, such as processor word-size and number of general
purpose registers. The ATmega128L is able to perform an 8-bit multiplication
in two cycles. Loading one 8-bit word from SRAM to registers also requires two
cycles. Basically two different approaches are possible:

1. reduce the number of multiplication or
2. reduce SRAM usage.

   The first attempt would be to implement Karatzuba [MVPV96] and the
second some kind of *improved schoolbook* algorithm. The hybrid multiplication [GPW+04] is a memory optimized variant of the schoolbook algorithm.
A special characteristic of the algorithm is that the computational cost rises linearly with smaller numbers of registers and processor word size. It also is much
easier to implement than Karatzuba and hence much easier to port to different
platforms. For these reasons the hybrid multiplication was chosen.

   When doing a multiplication using the schoolbook algorithm the multiplication is divided in several parts that are accumulated to get the final result. The
summands can be sorted in two ways before the addition: adding them from
left-to-right or right-to-left[1] it is called *row wise multiplication*, see Figure 3(a).
Sorting them by bit length is called *column wise multiplication*, see Figure 3(b).
The hybrid multiplication algorithm [GPW+04] combines both methods: the
summands that are used in the column wise way are calculated by using the row
wise method, see Figure 4.

   The number of rows per column is called *column width* (d). According to
[GPW+04] the optimal column width is:

$$d = \max\{i \mid 1 \leq i \geq n, r \geq 3i + \lceil \log_2{(n/i)/k} \rceil\}, \qquad (2)$$

where n is the operand size, r are the available registers and k is the bitlength.

---

[1] This is what is taught in school when learning the multiplication the first time -
   probably giving the algorithm its name.

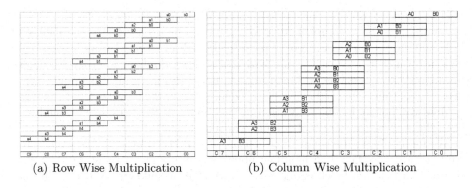

(a) Row Wise Multiplication   (b) Column Wise Multiplication

Fig. 3. Row Wise and Column Wise Multiplication

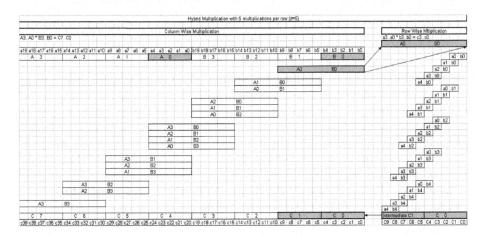

Fig. 4. 160-bit Hybrid Multiplication on ATMega128L with five Multiplications per Row

3.2   Implementation of the Modular Multiplication

According to Formula 2 the optimal d is 10 using all registers of the micro controller. In our first approach this parameter was used. The implementation benchmark showed that the implementation was about 50% slower than the benchmarks of SUN Microsystems in [GPW+04]. This overhead was mainly caused by handling carry bits. Let's have a look at the theoretic minimum effort of the algorithm. The core of the row wise part is the elemental 8 bit multiplication of the CPU followed by two additions to add the product to an intermediate result. These three operations are performed in the inner loop and will be referenced as the *elementary instruction block* in the remainder as illustrated in Figure 5(a). When using 160-bit operands this is done exact 400 times regardless of d. One multiplication and two additions equal 4 cycles. This means 1600 cycles in total plus the effort to get the operands from SRAM and write them back. This effort depends on the parameter d which depends on the machine's hardware. For the theoretic best d $(d = 10)$ on our target device the memory load and store effort would be 80 data loads and 40 stores consuming 240 cycles in total. For $d = 5$ the data load effort would double to 160 cycles while data store effort remains at 40 consuming 400 cycles in total. In summary, the theoretic optimum is 1840 cycles for d equal to 10 or 2000 cycles for d equal to 5. However, our first implementation needed about 4500 cycles, even though we used the -theoretical- optimal column width d of size 10.

We found that surprisingly, the major part of the overhead was caused by carry handling rather than handling pointers or other arbitrary effort. The elementary instruction block is one 8-bit multiplication followed by two additions as mentioned before. Since the additions are targeted to an intermediate result which is in general not zero the addition produces a carry bit in the general case. When the next iteration starts the elementary 8-bit multiplication will overwrite the carry flag in the CPU. Hence the carry bit has to be stored and restored in each *elementary instruction block*, which would result, in at least two additional cycles per elementary instruction block or an overhead of at least 66.66% only for carry handling! Note that at the end of each row and also at the end of each column additional carry handling is required. Even if an efficient carry store and restore is available, the operation "add with carry" would add the carry to the wrong register, as can be seen in Figure 5(b). The best solution we found that solves both problems requires three additional cycles per iteration of each *elementary instruction block*. Compared to the four cycles of the *elementary instruction block*, this is an overhead of 75%. Any other possible solution found needed more spare registers.

In our second implementation the column width d was chosen equal to 5. Note that in this case a 160-bit multiplication consists of 16 columns, each of them is

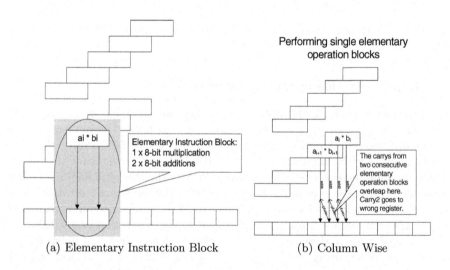

(a) Elementary Instruction Block   (b) Column Wise

Fig. 5. Carry Handling Problems with *Elementary Instruction Blocks*

comprised of five rows. Five *elementary instruction blocks* are required to calculate one row. Furthermore, by halving the column width d the number of memory loads is doubled. In other words, we trade at least 80 additional cycles for the sake of more spare registers. Storing and restoring the carry bit after each 8-bit multiplication is not efficient. Several different solutions are possible, but discussing them all would exceed the frame of this work. A solution in which the carry bit can be handled by the "add with carry" command is required. In the next subsections we will emphasize the overhead produced by carry handling within one row and within one column. Finally we will summarize the carry handling costs.

Calculating a Row: The number of consecutive *elementary instruction blocks* performed in the row wise part is set by the parameter d. In this case five iterations are done in a row. The spare registers can be used as a buffer to safe the five 16-bit products of the five 8-bit multiplications, see Figure 6. After the five multiplications are executed and buffered, eleven additions follow, which are performed in the order shown by the numbers in Figure 6. Addition number six is represented by the -carryadd- arrow. It represents a normal "add with carry" instruction, that adds a zero to the register holding the high significant byte of the result of an 8-bit multiplication, thus adding the carry bit. We call this carry add "secure" because it cannot produce another carry. This is due to the fact that the maximal product $0xFF * 0xFF = 0xFE01$. Hence, adding a carry bit to the high significant byte of $0xFE01$ results in $0xFF01$ and does not produce another carry bit. This *serialization/pipelining* of *elementary instruction blocks* reduces the carry handling within a row to four move instructions (the last multiplication does not need to be buffered) and one addition instruction or, respectively, one clock cycle per *elementary instruction block*. Note that the previous approach required three cycles per *elementary instruction block* for carry handling. In other words the overhead is reduced from 75% in the first approach to now 25%. However, again additional handling is needed for carry bits occurring at the end of each row and column.

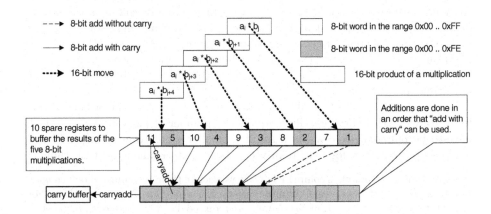

Fig. 6. Carry Handling in one Row

Calculating a Column: Recall that a column is comprised of five rows, i.e. five rows have to be processed to calculate a column. The last addition done in a row produces a carry bit which has to be processed in one of the upcoming rows, as we will see below. Figure 6 shows the carry handling within columns. A white box denotes an 8-bit register holding a value smaller than 0xFE, i.e. a "secure" carry add is possible with this register, whereas a gray box denotes an 8-bit register with an arbitrary value. As mentioned before, the carry bit which occurs at the end of each row needs to be processed later on, therefore it is buffered either in "carry buffer 1" or in "carry buffer 2". The correct position where this carry bit has to be added is displayed by the position of the carry buffer holding it. Figure 6 shows furthermore, that in two successive rows the latter one has no register in which the carry bit of the former could be "securely" added. In the subsequent row this is possible, hence a second carry buffer is required. The two buffers are used alternating to safe the carry bits, which occur after the calculation of each row. Therefore, two additional cycles overhead are required for carry handling for each column.

The carry bit occurring at the end of the column is stored in a third buffer. Since more than one row may be calculated using the same accumulator bytes, more than one carry bit is accumulated in the third carry buffer. If the next column starts with new accumulator bytes the carry buffer has to be processed. Figure 7 shows the correct position. In this case two additions are done, whereby the latter is "secure". This is because the carry buffer may exceed the value 0x01 making a single "secure" carry add impossible. Therefore, three additional cycles for carry handling are required if columns start with a new accumulator.

Summary of Carry Handling Costs: This way the total carry handling results in:

- 5 cycles for 5 elementary instruction blocks (equals 1 row)
- 2 cycles for each column
- 3 cycles for each column starting with new accumulator

Altogether $\frac{400+32+15}{400} = 1.1175$ additional cycles[2] per *elementary instruction block* are required for the carry handling, which is equivalent to an overhead of 28%. Note that this calculation includes all carry handling for the entire multiplication, whereas in the estimation of our first approach (75% overhead) additional carry handling at the end of each row and column was required. Since the *elementary instruction block* is repeated 400 times the benefits in saving both time and energy is enormous.

Two more aspects shall be mentioned here: First, the amount of needed registers to apply this carry handling equals the number of partial product which have to be buffered per row. As a result a smaller d has to be applied. Choosing the optimum size for d in reality can be a quite challenging task though.

---

[2] Recall that each column is comprised of 5 rows, each of them is comprised of 5 *elementary instruction blocks*, i.e. each column consists of 25 *elementary instruction blocks*. For a 160-bit point multiplication 16 columns are required, i.e. 400 *elementary instruction blocks*. Five columns starting with a new accumulator require additional cycles.

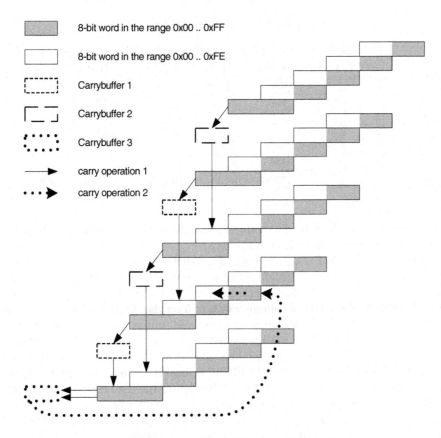

Fig. 7. Carry Handling in Columns

Second, the additional effort for handling carry bits in the way presented here can be divided in a static and a dynamic part. The effort of one clock cycle per *elementary instruction block* is static, while the remainder is supposed to grow with smaller column width.

4   Results

The basic requirement for a fast and thus energy efficient implementation of ECC is a very fast multiplication in the prime field. The fastest known implementation was implemented by SUN Microsystems. In [GPW+04] they provide a benchmark for the micro controller that we used as well, hence a direct comparison is possible. A 160-bit multiplication from SUN Microsystems' implementation requires 3106 cycles, which is at a clock rate of 7.37 MHz equivalent to 0.42 ms.

The implementation presented in this work needs 2881 cycles for a 160-bit multiplication, which is equivalent to 0.39 ms at 7.37 MHz. In fact, this represents a time saving of 7.2%. To the best of our knowledge this is the fastest

Table 1. Overview of instructions used

Instr.	#C/I	This work		SUN Microsystems		Theoretical Min.	
		Instr.	Cycles	Instr.	Cycles	Instr.	Cycles
add/adc	1	986	986	1360	1360	800	800
mul	2	400	800	400	800	400	800
ld/lds	2	238	476	167	334	160	320
st/sts	2	40	80	40	80	40	80
mov/movw	1	355	355	335	335		
other			184		197		
Sum			**2881**		**3106**		**2000**

implementation world wide of a modular multiplication of a 160-bit standardized elliptic curve for an 8-bit micro controller.

In Table 1 we present a detailed list of instructions used by our and SUN Microsystems' implementation as published in [GPW+04]. A third column contains the theoretical minimum amount of the appropriate instruction, as required by the hybrid multiplication with a column width of 5 on the ATMega128L micro controller. However, this number cannot be achieved, but is mentioned to show the limit and the overhead. Each row represents an instruction or a set of instructions, which are very similar. The first row represents the 8-bit addition with and without carry. In the next row the number of 8-bit multiplications can be seen. In the following row all used data loads are combined. Thereafter the used commands to write back to SRAM are listed. The underlying row shows all 8-bit and 16-bit register moves. Finally all other instructions are combined. In this row only the number of used cycles is given while the number of instructions is missing, because different instructions may consume different number of cycles to be executed.

As one can see, the main differences between our implementation and SUN Microsystems' lie in the number of used additions and data loads. Note that data loads require two cycles contrary to the addition, which only requires one cycle. Although SUN Microsystems' implementation executes less data load instructions, in total it requires more cycles than our implementation. The time saving results from the improved carry handling reducing the number of needed additions close to the minimum. In SUN Microsystems' implementation the number of data loads is close to the minimum number of 160 data loads for a column width of 5. The additional data loads in our implementation result from pointer handling. Pointers have to be restored from SRAM very often, because the carry handling needs all spare registers.

Comparison with TinyECC is cumbersome for two reasons: on the one hand neither time tables for curve nor modular arithmetic for TinyECC are available. On the other hand we did not implement a full ECDSA protocol. Therefore we estimate the execution time of an ECDSA signature based on our modular multiplication. [GPW+04] state that 77% of the execution time of one point multiplication are required for modular multiplication. Assuming our multiplication to be used here would result in 0.76s. Note that this curve arithmetic includes some well applied algorithmic optimizations which are best fitted to hardware, because they are done in assembly. On the other hand no special optimization for ECDSA were included, e.g. the y-coordinate is calculated but not used at all for the ECDSA protocol. A signature requires one inversion, two modular multiplication, and one modular addition. In addition one SHA-1 has to be executed to hash the message. Generally SHA-1 and a modular multiplication are both roughly three orders of magnitude faster than a point multiplication. The execution time of an inversion is in the range of several modular multiplications. The execution time of the modular addition is roughly four orders of magnitude faster than the execution of a point multiplication. Therefore, we estimate that all required operations for an ECDSA signature, including the SHA-1, can most probably be performed in less than one second. A TinyECC ECDSA signature generation takes slightly less than two seconds, including the time for the SHA-1 execution. Furthermore, once a precomputation time of a 3.5s is required.

5   Conclusion and Future Work

We presented the fastest implementation of a modular multiplication for a 160-bit standardized elliptic curve for 8-bit micro controller in Section 3 and compared the results in Section 4. We also highlighted the criteria for efficient implementations of ECC schemes for 8-bit micro controller and pointed out the problems that arise when implementing

Since modular multiplications take up the major part of the computing time of point multiplications over an elliptic curve, our results can be used to significantly increase the efficiency of point multiplications over an elliptic curve. Many ECC schemes such as EC ElGamal or ECDSA are based on modular multiplication and will therefore directly benefit from our results. Our results bring the vision of asymmetric cryptography in the field of WSNs with all its benefits for key-distribution and authentication a step closer to reality.

Next steps are the efficient implementation of point multiplication over the elliptic curve and some ECC schemes such as EC ElGamal and ECDSA. Furthermore an integration into existing ECC modules for TinyOS is thinkable.

Acknowledgments

The authors would like to thank Bodo Möller and André Weimerskirch for their insights and comments on various aspects of this work. The work presented in this paper was supported in part by the European Commission within the STREP UbiSec&Sens of the EU Framework Programme 6 for Research and Development (www.ist-ubisecsens.org). The views and conclusions contained herein are those of the authors and should not be interpreted as necessarily representing the official policies or endorsements, either expressed or implied, of the UbiSec&Sens project or the European Commission.

References

[Atm]   Atmel. 8-bit Microcontroller with 128K Bytes In-System Programmable
           Flash http://www.atmel.com/
[Bro01]   Brown, M., Hankerson, D., López, J., Menezes, A.: Software Implemen-
           tation of the NIST Elliptic Curves Over Prime Fields. In: Naccache, D.
           (ed.) Topics in Cryptology - CT-RSA 2001. LNCS, vol. 2020, p. 250.
           Springer, Heidelberg (2001)
[Cer00]   Certicom Research. SEC 2: Recommended Elliptic Curve Domain Pa-
           rameters. Standards for Efficient Cryptography Version 1.0 (September
           2000)
[CPS03]   Chan, H., Perrig, A., Song, D.: Random Key Predistribution Schemes
           for Sensor Networks. In: Proceedings of the IEEE Security and Privacy
           Symposium 2003 (2003)
[DDHV]   Du, W., Deng, J., Han, Y., Varshney, P.: A Pairwise Key Pre-distribution
           Scheme for Wireless Sensor Networks. In: CCS '03: Proceedings of the
           10th ACM Conference on Computer and Communications Security
[EG02]   Eschenauer, L., Gligor, V.: A Key Management Scheme for Distributed
           Sensor Networks. In: CCS '02: Proceedings of the 9th ACM Confer-
           ence on Computer and Communications Security, ACM Press, New York
           (2002)
[GPW+04]   Gura, N., Patel, A., Wander, A., Eberle, H., Shantz, S.C.: Compar-
           ing Elliptic Curve Cryptography and RSA on 8-bit CPUs. In: Joye,
           M., Quisquater, J.-J. (eds.) CHES 2004. LNCS, vol. 3156, pp. 119–132.
           Springer, Heidelberg (2004)
[HC02]   Hankerson, D., Menezes, A.J., Vanstone, S.: Guide to Elliptic Curve
           Cryptography. Springer, Heidelberg (2004)
[HMV04]   Hill, J., Szewczyk, R., Woo, A., Hollar, S., Culler, D., Pister, K.: Sys-
           tem Architecture Directions for Networked Sensors. SIGOPS Oper. Syst.
           Rev. 34(5), 93–104 (2000)
[HSW+00]   Hill, J.L., Culler, D.: Mica: a Wireless Platform for Deeply Embedded
           Networks. Micro, IEEE 22(6), 12–24 (2002)
[LN06]   Liu, A., Ning, P.: TinyECC: Elliptic Curve Cryptography for Sensor
           Networks. available for download at (September 2006)
           http://discovery.csc.ncsu.edu/software/TinyECC
[MVPV96]   Menezes, A.J., Van, O., Paul, C., Vanstone, S.A. (eds.): Handbook of
           Applied Cryptography. CRC Press, Boca Raton, FL (1996)
[Res00]   Certicom Research. SEC 1: Elliptic Curve Cryptography, Version 1.0
           (September 2000)
[Sol99]   Solinas, J.: Generalized Mersenne Numbers. Technical report CORR-39,
           Dept. of C&O, University of Waterloo (1999) Available from
           http://www.cacr.math.uwaterloo.ca
[WKC+04]   Watro, R., Kong, D., Cuti, S.F., Gardiner, C., Lynn, C., Kruus, P.:
           TinyPK: Securing Sensor Networks with Public Key Technology. In:
           SASN '04: Proceedings of the 2nd ACM Workshop on Security of Ad
           Hoc and Sensor Networks, pp. 59–64. ACM Press, New York (2004)
[xbo]   Crossbow Technology, Inc., http://www.xbow.com

Key Distribution in Mobile Ad Hoc Networks Based on Message Relaying⋆

Johann van der Merwe, Dawoud Dawoud, and Stephen McDonald

University of KwaZulu-Natal, School of Electrical, Electronic and Computer
Engineering, South Africa
{vdmerwe,dawoudd,mcdonalds}@ukzn.ac.za

Abstract. Securing wireless mobile ad hoc networks (MANETs) is challenging due to the lack of centralized authority and poor connectivity. A key distribution mechanism is central to any public key management scheme. We propose a novel key distribution scheme for MANETs that exploits the routing infrastructure to effectively chain peer nodes together. Keying material propagates along these virtual chains via a message relaying mechanism. We show that the proposed approach results in a key distribution scheme with low implementation complexity, ideally suited for stationary ad hoc networks and MANETs with low to high mobility. The proposed scheme uses mobility as an aid to fuel the rate of bootstrapping the routing security, but in contrast to existing schemes does not become dependent on mobility. The key dissemination occurs completely on-demand; security associations are only established as needed by the routing protocol. We show through simulations that the scheme's communication and computational overhead has negligible impact on network performance.

Keywords: Mobile ad hoc networks, wireless network security, key management, network level key distribution, trust establishment, data dissemination.

1 Introduction

Protecting the network infrastructure in mobile ad hoc networks (MANETs) is an important research topic in wireless security. Key management is central to MANET security [1] [2] [3]; most secure routing schemes ([4] [5] [6] [7] [8]) neglect the crucial task of secure key management and assume pre-existence and pre-sharing of secret and/or public/private key pairs [1]. One of the primary objectives of any key management scheme is the efficient and secure dissemination of keying material. *Key distribution* in MANETs is more difficult than in conventional wireline networks due to poor connectivity. Furthermore, using conventional methods such as an online key distribution center (KDC), results in a single point of vulnerability. Issuing all the nodes in the network with their

---

⋆ This work was supported by ARMSCOR, the Armaments Corporation of South Africa.

F. Stajano et al. (Eds.): ESAS 2007, LNCS 4572, pp. 87–100, 2007.
© Springer-Verlag Berlin Heidelberg 2007

own keying material *and* with the keying material of all other potential network participants, *prior* to network formation, makes the network nonscalable and introduces a tedious, inefficient, offline initialization phase. This approach may be impractical for a large group of MANET applications [9] [10] and does not allow for 'ad hoc' network formation.

There are two main approaches in the area of key management for MANETs. Most schemes either make use of a distributed trusted authority [1] [11] [12] or take on a fully self-organized nature [3] [9] [10].

Existing self-organized key management schemes, such as [3] [9] [10], allow nodes to generate their own keying material. Each node thus acts as its own authority domain and generates its own public key certificate or establishes symmetric keying material on a peer-to-peer basis. In [3], as an alternative to the fully self-organized setting, an *offline* trusted authority can also issue each node with its own certificate and a universal set of system parameters. Nodes exchange certificates when they come into transmission range. This *authority-based* approach allows for strong access control while eliminating any form of online trusted authority. We look more closely at key distribution in an authority-based setting and therefore do not explicitly consider the fully self-organized case.

The key management scheme in [9] [10] [7] distributes public keys by including them in the routing control packets. A similar approach is taken in [13]. With the large number of route requests sent by on-demand routing protocols, inflating the control packets (specifically route request messages) wastes valuable bandwidth, which is a limited commodity in ad hoc networks. Adding keying material in routing control packets is therefore not an ideal solution.

The key establishment mechanisms proposed in [3] break the *routing-security interdependence cycle* as defined in [13], but rely on node mobility to bring nodes within transmission range (or a "secure range") to set up bi-directional security associations. The dependence on mobility introduces a time delay in bootstrapping of the routing security. Furthermore, the key establishment mechanisms of [3] is not designed for a stationary (or low mobility) network, but are well suited for establishing keying material on the application layer in a fully self-organized setting.

Informal Problem Statement. In the light of the above discussion on the existing key management schemes, we identify a new problem within the area of key management; the challenge is to design a straightforward *key distribution* scheme that can issue all the nodes in *authority-based* MANETs with the minimum amount of required keying material (e.g. certificates), while satisfying the following constraints:

- The key distribution mechanism must exploit mobility as originally shown by Capkun et al. [3], but in contrast to existing solutions [3] avoid relying on node mobility in any way; the key dissemination mechanism must therefore be fully functional in a stationary or low mobility ad hoc network and perform even better in a high mobility scenario. If the scheme is dependent on node mobility the key distribution mechanism will fail in low mobility or stationary settings.
- The scheme should be *fully distributed* and therefore equally share the responsibility of setting up security associations between all nodes forming the

network. This is to ensure reliable security services that place the same burden on the computational, memory and energy resources of *all* nodes [1] [2].

- The key dissemination mechanism should break the *routing-security interdependence cycle* [13], while ensuring network scalability. Pre-distributing keying material to all the nodes, such that security associations between all nodes will be *guaranteed*, trivially mitigates the routing-security interdependence cycle. This however makes the network nonscalable; the offline trusted third party needs to engage with all nodes before the network can be formed. The key distribution mechanism should thus only require each node to be issued with its own keying material prior to network formation and not with the keying material of other nodes, that is, the key distribution scheme should allow for 'ad hoc' network formation.
- The scheme should avoid introducing any noticeable delay in the set up of security associations; the routing must be secure from the start of network formation, hence leave no window of opportunity for an attacker during security bootstrapping.
- The key distribution scheme should reduce communication and computational overhead to have negligible impact on network performance under realistic traffic and mobility scenarios.
- The scheme should avoid inflating the routing protocol control packets in order not to waste bandwidth.
- The key dissemination mechanism should introduce minimal changes in the underlying secure MANET routing protocol and integrate seamlessly with existing secure routing protocols.
- Certificates must be distributed (on-demand) as needed on the network (routing) layer and be transparent to the network participants, that is, the scheme should require no user involvement. Unnecessary user involvement makes the scheme prone to attacks that exploit human error.

In this paper we contribute a new *key distribution* mechanism in support of secure routing that satisfies all the constraints given above. We will not focus on a complete key management solution, but concentrate our efforts on the described key distribution problem. The proposed scheme is designed specifically to have a low implementation complexity and to allow for easy integration into most secure MANET routing protocols. The proposed scheme, called Certificate Dissemination based on Message Relaying (CertRelay), is derived from the following straightforward procedure, illustrated in Fig. 1:

When a node (RN) receives a routing control packet it checks in its certificate database if it has the certificates of the packet originator (ON) and the previous-hop node (PN) on the forward route. If RN has both the certificates of ON and PN ($Cert_{ON}$ and $Cert_{PN}$), it can process the control packet as normal. If not, it requests both the certificates from PN. If RN does not have the certificate of PN it also sends its own certificate with the request to the previous-hop. Note that if RN is the first-hop on the route, then the previous-hop node and the control packet originator node will be the same entity. The routing messages thus effectively chain nodes together and allow them to relay all keying material, as required, along the virtual chains.

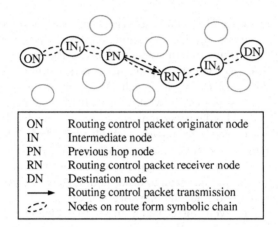

Fig. 1. CertRelay certificate distribution main procedure

The paper is organized as follows: in Sect. 2 we propose the new key distribution mechanism, called Certificate Dissemination based on Message Relaying (CertRelay). Section 3 discusses the security, performance and features of the proposed certificate distribution scheme. Some conclusions are provided in Sect. 4.

2   Proposed Certificate Distribution Mechanism

The discussion commences by giving an overview of CertRelay's system model followed by an abstract explanation of the proposed scheme.

2.1   System Model

Similar to [3], we consider a fully distributed network of wireless nodes with generic medium access control (such as IEEE 802.11) and secure on-demand routing mechanisms (such as *endairA* [8]). Nodes can be stationary or move with low to high mobility speeds $(0m/s - 20m/s)$. We assume that there are no pre-existing infrastructure and no form of *online* trusted authority to assist the key distribution mechanism. Since we are considering *authority-based* MANETs as defined in [3], there exists an *offline* authority to bootstrap the system; before users join the network they have to acquire a certificate from the *offline* trusted authority. The trusted authority thus only issues each node with their own certificate and not with the certificates of any other nodes. This requirement is fundamental to ensuring scalability and on-demand network formation. Each node is also issued with the authentic public key of the trusted authority and a universal set of system parameters. The certificate must contain the offline authority's identity, the node's public key and identity/network address, a unique sequence number, certificate generation date and expiry date.

We are now ready to discuss our key distribution mechanism, called Certificate Dissemination based on Message Relaying (CertRelay).

2.2   Proposed Key Distribution Scheme

While reading the explanation of the proposed key relaying mechanism below, it will be useful to keep in mind an existing MANET routing protocol. Being familiar with the operation of, for example, *endairA* [8], one of the latest *provably* secure MANET routing protocols, will help to visualize how the proposed protocol will integrate into an existing routing protocol. We point out that any other secure routing protocol will also suffice. For example, SAODV [14] [7] can also help to place the functionality of CertRelay into context.

Table 1. Message exchange decision table for receiver node (RN)

Case 1: ON IP address = PN IP address		
Case# ON cert stored PN cert stored		Messages exchanged with PN
1a no no		Peer-to-Peer certificate exchange $Cert_{RN} \longrightarrow ON$,[a] $Cert_{ON} \longrightarrow RN$
1b yes yes		No action, process routing packet as normal
Case 2: Originator IP address $\neq$ PN IP address		
Case# ON cert stored PN cert stored		Messages exchanged with PN
2a no no		Peer-to-Peer certificate exchange $[Cert_{RN} \parallel CertQ \longrightarrow PN]$,[b] $[Cert_{PN} \parallel Cert_{ON} \longrightarrow RN]$
2b yes no		Peer-to-Peer certificate exchange $Cert_{RN} \longrightarrow PN$, $Cert_{PN} \longrightarrow RN$
2c no yes		$CertQ \longrightarrow PN$, $Cert_{ON} \longrightarrow RN$
2d yes yes		No action, process routing packet as normal

[a] RN = Receiver node, ON = Originator node, $Cert_X$ = certificate of X.
[b] PN = Previous-hop node, $CertQ$ = certificate query (RN uses this message to request $Cert_{ON}$ from PN, $A \parallel B$ = concatenation of messages A and B.

The proposed key distribution scheme, CertRelay, is mainly based on the straightforward procedure introduced in Sect. 1. Table 1 explains CertRelay's core procedure in more detail from the routing control packet (RCP) receiver node's perspective (see Fig. 1). Table 1 can alternatively be seen as a summary of the conditions under which the RCP receiver node (RN) will request certificates from and relay certificates to the previous-hop node (PN) in the virtual chain. We briefly discuss Table-1:

– When any node in the network receives a RCP it first determines if the originator of the message (ON) has the same network address as the previous-hop node (PN) on the forward route, that is, RN has to determine if ON is the first-hop. Assume the addresses of ON and PN are equivalent as shown in Table 1, Case 1. RN consults its certificate repository and searches for the certificate corresponding to ON.

- In Case 1a the search produces no result and the RN sends the ON its own certificate, $Cert_{RN}$. The ON replies with $Cert_{ON}$. After $Cert_{ON}$ is verified by RN the RCP can be processed as specified by the routing protocol.
- If the search yields a positive result the routing message can be processed without RN requesting $Cert_{ON}$ (Case 1b).

- If the ON address and the previous-hop node (PN) address are not equal (Case 2, Table 1), the RN will search its certificate repository for $Cert_{ON}$ and $Cert_{PN}$.

- In Case 2a the search yields a negative result. RN concatenates its own certificate $Cert_{RN}$ with a certificate query (CertQ) and relays (unicasts) the message to the previous-hop[1]. PN responds with a concatenation of its own certificate and the certificate of ON ($Cert_{PN} \parallel Cert_{ON}$). Node RN should verify both certificates before continuing to process the RCP as defined by the routing protocol.
- If RN already has $Cert_{ON}$, but not $Cert_{PN}$, it initiates a peer-to-peer certificate exchange by sending its own certificate to PN (Case 2b). PN will respond with $Cert_{PN}$, which should be verified by RN before proceeding.
- Case 2c is applicable if RN has $Cert_{PN}$, but not $Cert_{ON}$. This case will be the most probable since PN is within RN's local neighborhood (transmission range). RN sends PN a CertQ message. PN responds with $Cert_{ON}$. Again RN verifies $Cert_{ON}$ before processing the RCP.
- The routing message can be processed as normal in Case 2d, since $Cert_{ON}$ and $Cert_{PN}$ are already stored in the node's certificate repository.

We have discussed how the proposed key distribution scheme can be integrated into most secure MANET routing protocols. In summary, any routing message that is received by a node acts as a trigger for the node to request from the previous hop, the relaying of required keying material. The conditions that warrant the requests and format of the requests are defined by the rules in Table 1. In the following section we will analyze CertRelay in terms of efficiency and security.

3   Discussion on the Security and Features of CertRelay

3.1   On the Security of CertRelay

To ensure the integrity of all messages sent by CertRelay we require that messages are signed using a secure digital signature scheme (for example RSA). Ideally CertRelay should use the same signature scheme as deployed by the

---

[1] RN sends its own certificate to PN, since PN may require $Cert_{RN}$ when routing control messages are sent back via the established route. In addition, since RN and PN are neighbors they will most probably require each others certificates during future route discovery procedures. We show in Sect. 3.3 that the success rate of localized peer-to-peer certificates exchanges are high, thus if RN does not have $Cert_{PN}$ then PN will also not have $Cert_{RN}$ with high probability.

underlying routing protocol. A unique sequence number or random number (to guarantee the uniqueness of each message) must also be included in the messages to avoid replay attacks.

In the remainder of the section we will analyze the security of CertRelay in the authenticated-links adversarial model (AM) of Bellare, Canetti, and Krawczyk [15]. Cagalj, Capkun and Hubaux [16] also uses AM to prove the security of their scheme, which supports our use of AM. As formally proven in [15] and further explained in [16], a strong security argument in the AM model (or ideal world model) will also apply in the unauthenticated links model (UM) by correctly applying a signature-based *message transmission* (MT)-authenticator to each message sent. The security of the protocol, if provably secure in an *authenticated* network, can then be conveniently reduced to the security of the digital signature scheme in an *unauthenticated* network [15]. The goal is thus to show that CertRelay is secure in AM, which will imply equivalence in UM. Without losing credence in the security argument we will keep our treatment informal, but firmly rooted in the formal foundations of the AM adversarial model defined by [15].

Consider Case 1a in Table 1, which portrays a generic communication scenario in CertRelay. The discussion also applies with minor modifications to any of the other cases (Case 1b to 2d). Let ON be party A and RN party B [2]. Note that in Case 1a the originator node is the same entity as the previous-hop node (ON = PN). An AM adversary ($\mathcal{M}$) models the authentication protocol executed by party A and party B (from A's perspective) as an oracle $\prod_{A,B}^{s}$ with session ID $s \in \mathbb{N}$ [17]. In the same way, queries sent to B from $\mathcal{M}$ and the corresponding responses are modelled by oracle $\prod_{B,A}^{t}$, where session ID $t \in \mathbb{N}$. Using the notation of [16], the timely messages sent to and received from $\prod_{A,B}^{s}$ are denoted by conversation $conv_A$ and $conv_B$ for $\prod_{B,A}^{t}$. Oracles $\prod_{A,B}^{s}$ and $\prod_{B,A}^{t}$ have *matching conversations* (as defined in [17] and further explained in [16]) if message m sent out by $\prod_{A,B}^{s}$ at time τ_i is received by $\prod_{B,A}^{t}$ at time τ_{i+1}.

In the AM model the adversary $\mathcal{M}$ has full control, that is, $\mathcal{M}$ can activate or corrupt parties at random, but cannot forge or replay messages to impersonate uncorrupted parties and is also bound to deliver sent messages faithfully [15]. The CertRelay protocol commences by $\mathcal{M}$ activating $\prod_{A,B}^{s}$ at time τ_0. The outgoing routing control message R_{msg} of $\prod_{A,B}^{s}$ contains the identity (or network address) of A [3]. The AM adversary cannot modify the network address (identity) in the AM model by definition (see [15]) and has to deliver the message to $\prod_{B,A}^{t}$, modelling an arbitrary party B of $\mathcal{M}$'s choice[4]. Incoming message R_{msg} activates $\prod_{B,A}^{t}$ to respond with B's certificate $Cert_B$ at time τ_1 (any other activation will not comply with CertRelay). $Cert_B$ (containing the identity of B) is appended to

---

[2] We assume that both A and B can be trusted to behave as specified by CertRelay, otherwise there is not much to discuss.

[3] Once $\mathcal{M}$ has activated $\prod_{A,B}^{s}$ for an arbitrary party A, $\mathcal{M}$ cannot alter the identity of A anymore without violating CertRelay or the rules of AM.

[4] Party B does not necessarily know the identity of A a priori and does not need to until B receives R_{msg} from A. If B receives the R_{msg}, $\mathcal{M}$ cannot alter the identity of B anymore without violating CertRelay or AM.

A's identity and delivered to $\prod_{A,B}^{s}$ as required of $\mathcal{M}$. Up to this point there is not much the adversary can do to attack the protocol; according to the definition of AM, $\mathcal{M}$ can activate any of the oracles (in an appropriate manner in compliance with the CertRelay protocol), but cannot forge messages coming from the oracles that simulate uncorrupted parties (A and B) and has to deliver the outgoing messages after activation to the oracles. In the next round the AM adversary has no option but to activate $\prod_{A,B}^{s}$ which will respond to $\prod_{B,A}^{t}$ with $Cert_A$ (containing the identity of A, appended with the identity of B) at time τ_2. Since $\tau_0 < \tau_1 < \tau_2 < \tau_3$ and $conv_A$ and $conv_B$ are matching conversations, as illustrated below, both oracles will output "Accept" [5].

$$conv_A = (\tau_0, \bot, R_{msg}), (\tau_2, CertB, CertA);$$
$$conv_B = (\tau_1, R_{msg}, CertB), (\tau_3, CertA, \bot);$$

As described above the AM adversary cannot attack CertRelay in the AM model without breaking the rules of AM or modifying the oracles not to comply with CertRelay. Considering the communication model of [15] and the security argument above, it is clear that CertRelay is a *message driven protocol* (as defined in [15]) that forces *matching conversations* between parties that engage via CertRelay. CertRelay is therefore a secure mutual authentication protocol (with authenticated data as described by [17]) in the AM model.

As mentioned above CertRelay can be transformed from a secure AM protocol to a secure UM protocol using a signature-based MT-authenticator [15]; each unique message m (containing the identity of the sender) is signed with the private key of the sender. The signatures are verified with the sender's corresponding public key. Each public key is bound to the identity of the corresponding private key holder by an offline authority to form a certificate. As assumed in the system model (see Sect. 2.1) each network participant has the authentic public key of the offline authority readily available to verify the authenticity of the received certificates. Successful verification convinces the receiver of the binding between the public key and the user's identity (network address). Since the certificates are included in the exchanged messages, it is therefore clear that CertRelay is a mutual authentication protocol in the UM model with an exchange of *implicitly* authenticated data. As a final observation we note that the probability of *No-Matching*, as defined in [17], between $conv_A$ and $conv_B$ (in the UM model) is given by the probability that the adversary can break the underlying signature scheme, which should be negligible if the signature scheme is carefully chosen and securely implemented.

3.2   On the Efficiency of CertRelay

The efficiency analysis of CertRelay on the network layer in an ideal setting, i.e. assuming guaranteed connectivity, is rather easy. Certificate exchanges all take place on a peer-to-peer basis. From Table 1 it can be seen that all the exchanges

---

[5] To remain compatible with [16] we also use $\bot$ to denote that a party receives/sends no message in the corresponding time τ_i.

take at most two asynchronous rounds with one unicast message from each node. Each node pair only exchanges their certificates once on a need-to-know basis.

In the following section we evaluate CertRelay in a more realistic setting.

3.3   Performance Evaluation of CertRelay

The performance of CertRelay was evaluated in a simulation study, as commonly done in the validation of MANET protocols, where factors such as poor connectivity and route failures (due to the error-prone wireless channel, node mobility, congestion, packet collisions etc.) have an impact on performance. The ease of coding CertRelay in the ns-2 simulator (release 2.28) [18] confirmed the low implementation complexity of the proposed key distribution scheme.

Simulation Model. In the simulation of CertRelay we used the IEEE 802.11b physical layer and medium access control (MAC) protocols included in the ns-2 simulator. The radio-model was set to a nominal bit-rate of 11Mb/s and a transmission range of 250m. The network area for all simulations was set to 2000m x 2000m. The ns-2 constant bit-rate (CBR) traffic generator was used to set up the connection patterns. For all simulations a 512byte CBR packet size was used and the traffic loading was varied between 1 CBR packet/sec and 7 CBR packets/sec. The size of certificates was also set to 512bytes. The total of 50 nodes in the network each had one CBR traffic connection with a single unique destination, with an average path length of approximately 4 hops between connected nodes. The traffic sources were started within the first 60sec of each 1000sec simulation. We note that this is unlikely to occur in practice, but it is an effective strategy to force as much certificate distribution activity as possible from the start of network formation.

The choice of an appropriate mobility model is a problem and it is unlikely that everybody will agree with any specific choice. Although mobility models for MANETs have received much attention lately [19], a widely used, realistic mobility model is not available and it is unlikely to appear due to the application specific nature of mobility patterns. To be consistent with most literature the random waypoint model was chosen to simulate node mobility. The *mobgen-ss* [20] mobility scenario generator was used to produce random mobility patterns. It is pointed out that the *setdest* mobility generator included in the ns-2 distribution is flawed [20]. The initial probability distribution of *setdest* differs at a later point in time as it converges to a "steady-state distribution" [20]. All simulation results were averaged over 10 random seeds (runs).

We wanted to observe the effectiveness of CertRelay in very low (almost stationary), moderate and high node mobility settings. In the simulations the mean speed was set to 0.1m/sec, 5m/sec and 20m/sec for each traffic scenario. These mobility speeds are widely used in MANET simulations based on the random waypoint model. Since a pause time greater than zero reduces the relative node speed, the pause time was set to zero. The Ad Hoc On-demand Distance Vector (AODV) routing protocol [21] was chosen for the simulations. The implementation of CertRelay in ns-2 *closely* followed the discussions in Sect. 2 and will not be explained here in order to avoid repetition.

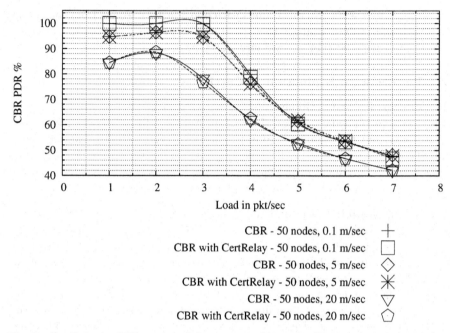

Fig. 2. CertRelay's CBR packet delivery ratio % vs. load in pkt/sec for 0.1m/sec, 5m/sec and 20m/sec mobility

Simulation Results. In this section the simulation results of CertRelay are presented. The aim is to make an assessment of CertRelay's impact on network performance. The following two metrics are observed: 1) Constant bit-rate (CBR) packet delivery ratio (PDR) as a function of mobility and load. 2) CBR packet end-to-end delay as a function of mobility and load.

The primary function of any communication network is to deliver data packets between end points with an acceptable success rate and tolerable delay. It is therefore important to establish if the proposed key distribution mechanism degrades the performance of the network. We limit our scope to the routing and upper layers; to save space we do not consider message overhead occurred on the lower layers.

In Fig. 3, it can be seen that the PDR of the "CBR reference" simulation corresponds closely with that of the "CBR with CertRelay" (CBRwC) simulation[6]. We claim that the impact on network performance is negligible for 0.1m/sec, 5m/sec and 20m/sec mobility. As per design specification, CertRelay exploits mobility; as the mobility increases the CBR and CBRwC simulations become even more correlated (see Fig. 2). The mobility characteristic of MANETs is widely regarded as a limiting factor, as it is a major contribution to route failures. The close relation between the CBR and CBRwC at 0.1m/sec indicates that CertRelay not only

---

[6] Note that the "CBR reference" simulation was performed with a standard ns-2 installation with no modifications. The implementation of such a simulation in ns-2 is straightforward and widely accepted as a suitable benchmark.

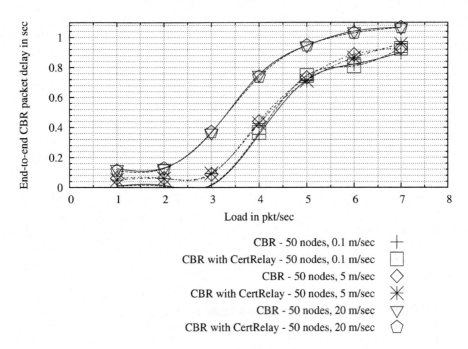

Fig. 3. CertRelay's CBR packet end-to-end delay vs. load in pkt/sec for 0.1m/sec, 5m/sec and 20m/sec mobility

turns mobility around as an aid, but in contrast to previous efforts [3] does not rely on mobility. We believe that [3] mainly indicates that mobility can aid security on the application layer. We thus make a novel contribution and show that mobility can aid security in MANETS on the routing layer, but *without* forcing security to become dependent on mobility.

To place the PDR vs. load results into context, the average CBR packet end-to-end delay is shown in Fig. 3. The figure confirms that CertRelay does not add any significant delay to the delivery of CBR packets for 0.1m/sec, 5m/sec and 20m/sec mobility.

CertRelay avoids dependence on mobility by using only localized (one-hop) communication. The certificates of nodes not within transmission range are re-layed along the virtual chain formed by intermediate nodes. The effectiveness of this mechanism relies on the node's channel access success rate, which is MAC protocol specific. Figure 4 shows that this form of communication with the IEEE 802.11b MAC protocol is very effective. As the load increases one would expect a significant decrease in the certificate delivery ratio. What we can see from Fig. 4 is that the average certificate delivery ratio does decrease with an increase in mobility, but does not deteriorate significantly as the load increases. Between 86% and 97% of the certificates sent between nodes on a one-hop basis are delivered. This explains why RN includes its own certificate $Cert_{RN}$ with the request for the certificate of PN in Case 1a, 2a and 2b defined in Table 1; if RN does not have the certificate of PN, then PN most probably does not have the certificate of RN.

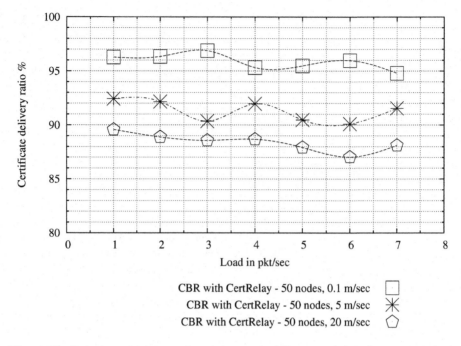

Fig. 4. CertRelay's certificate one-hop delivery ratio % vs. load in pkt/sec for 0.1m/sec, 5m/sec and 20m/sec mobility

PN may also require $Cert_{RN}$ when a packet transverses the reverse route or during a future route discovery process. The proposed certificate scheme exploits the successful localized communication to avoid becoming dependent on the routing infrastructure's performance and thus overcomes one of the main problems of ensuring the availability of the key distribution mechanism in MANETs.

4   Conclusion

The paper identifies a new key distribution problem within the area of key management for MANETs. We propose a novel, key distribution scheme, called Certificate Dissemination based on Message Relaying (CertRelay), as an effective solution to the problem. CertRelay helps nodes to set up security associations in a fully distributed manner without the assistance of an online trusted authority. CertRelay is based on a straightforward procedure to establish security associations in support of the routing infrastructure. The proposed scheme allows nodes to form a virtual chain (by exploiting the routing control messages) along which keying material can be relayed, as required, using only reliable one-hop communication. CertRelay breaks the classic routing-security interdependence cycle and during its entire operation eliminates any explicit dependence on the routing infrastructure for certificate delivery; keying material is relayed along the chain without setting up and maintaining a route. This is an important feature since it implies that CertRelay does not suffer from poor connectivity, aggravated by route failures which are caused by node mobility and error-prone wireless connectivity. In fact, we have shown through simulations that as mobility increases, and the number of route failures increases, the performance of CertRelay improves. The proposed scheme does not introduce any noticeable delay in the set up of security associations, that is, the routing can be secured from the start of network formation leaving no window of opportunity for an attacker.

Capkun et al. [3] have shown that mobility can aid key distribution, but their scheme relies on the temporary proximity of users to exchange certificates. As a result users will experience a delay in the bootstrap of the routing security with evident failure in a stationary setting. Their proposal is however ideal for key establishment on the application layer in a fully self-organized MANET. In this paper we make a novel contribution: to the best of our knowledge, the fact that mobility can be exploited to aid security in MANETs (on the routing layer), *without* depending on mobility, has not been demonstrated prior to this submission.

The simplicity of CertRelay allows for a strong security argument in a widely accepted, formal adversarial model. The nodes of CertRelay exchange only authenticated information on a peer-to-peer basis, which provides provable protection against forgery and undetected modification. The fully distributed scheme preserves the symmetric relationship between the nodes and provides an adversary with no convenient point of attack.

The effectiveness of CertRelay, its low implementation complexity and ease of integration into existing secure routing protocols were verified through coding and simulating the scheme in ns-2. We have shown that CertRelay has negligible impact on the network performance. It was concluded that the message relay mechanism provides an efficient way to distribute keying material. The one-hop certificate exchange success rate varied between 86 % and 97 % which highlighted the effectiveness of localized communication in MANETs.

References

1. Zhou, L., Haas, Z.J.: Securing Ad Hoc Networks. IEEE Network: Special Issue on Network Security 13(6), 24–30 (1999)
2. Capkun, S., Buttyan, L., Hubaux, J.P: Self-Organized Public-Key Management for Mobile Ad Hoc Networks. IEEE Trans. on Mobile Computing 2(1), 52–64 (2003)
3. Capkun, S., Hubaux, J., Buttyan, L.: Mobility Helps Peer-to-Peer Security. IEEE Trans. on Mobile Computing 5(1), 43–51 (2006)
4. Hu, Y.C., Johnson, D.B., Perrig, A.: Ariadne: A Secure OnDemand Routing Protocol for Ad Hoc Networks. In: Proc. Eighth ACM International Conf. on Mobile Computing and Networking (Mobicom) (2002)
5. Hu, Y.C., Johnson, D.B., Perrig, A.: SEAD: Secure Efficient Distance Vector Routing for Mobile Wireless Ad Hoc Networks. In: IEEE Workshop on Mobile Computing Systems and Applications (2002)

6. Papadimitratos, P., Haas, Z.J.: Secure Routing for Mobile Ad Hoc Networks. In: Proc. SCS Communication Network and Distributed System Modeling and Simulation Conf. (2002)
7. Guerrero Zapata, M.: Secure Ad Hoc On-demand Distance Vector (SAODV) Routing (September, 15 2005) INTERNET-DRAFT draft-guerrero-manet-saodv-04.txt
8. Acs, G., Buttyan, L., Vajda, I.: Provably Secure On-demand Source Routing in Mobile Ad Hoc Networks. IEEE Trans. on Mobile Computing 5(11), 1533–1546 (2006)
9. Guerrero Zapata, M.: Key Management and Delayed Verification for Ad Hoc Networks. In: Proc. International Conference on High Performance Computing (HiPC): 3rd International Trusted Internet Workshop (TIW) (2004)
10. Guerrero Zapata, M.: Key management and Delayed Verification for Ad hoc networks. Journal of High Speed Networks 15(1), 93–109 (2006)
11. Luo, H., Zerfos, P., Kong, J., Lu, S., Zhang, L.: Self-securing Ad Hoc Wireless Networks. In: Proc. Seventh International Symposium on Computers and Communications (ISCC) (2002)
12. Yi, S., Kravets, R.: MOCA: Mobile certificate authority for wireless ad hoc networks. In: Proc. of the 2nd Annual PKI Research Workshop (PKI) (2003)
13. Bobba, R.B., Eschenauer, L., Gligor, V.D., Arbaugh, W.: Bootstrapping Security Associations for Routing in Mobile Ad-Hoc Networks. In: Proc. IEEE Global Telecommunications Conf. (2003)
14. Guerrero Zapata, M.: Secure Ad Hoc On-demand Distance Vector (SAODV) Routing. ACM Mobile Computing and Communications Review (MC2R) 6(3), 106–107 (2002)
15. Bellare, M., Canetti, R., Krawczyk, H.: A Modular Approach to the Design and Analysis of Authentication and Key Exchange Protocols. In: 30th Annual ACM Symposium on the Theory of Computing, pp. 419–428 (1998)
16. Cagalj, M., Capkun, S., Hubaux, J.: Key agreement in peer-to-peer wireless networks. Proceedings of the IEEE (Special Issue on Cryptography and Security) 94(2), 467–478 (2005)
17. Bellare, M., Rogaway, P.: Entity Authentication and Key Distribution. In: Stinson, D.R. (ed.) CRYPTO '93. LNCS, vol. 773, Springer, Heidelberg (1994)
18. The Network Simulator - ns-2, Available at http://www.isi.edu/nsnam/ns or http://nsnam.isi.edu/nsnam/index.php/User_Information
19. Boundec Le, J.Y., Vojnovic, M.: Perfect Simulation and Stationarity of a Class of Mobility Models. In: Proc. IEEE INFOCOM (2005)
20. Navidi, W., Camp, T.: Stationary Distributions for the Random Waypoint Mobility Model. IEEE Trans. on Mobile Computing 3(1), 99–108 (2004)
21. Perkins, C.E., Belding-Royer, E.M.: Ad-hoc On-demand Distance Vector Routing. In: Proc. The Second IEEE Workshop on Mobile Computing Systems and Applications (WMCSA) (1999)

Distance Bounding in Noisy Environments

Dave Singelée and Bart Preneel

ESAT-COSIC, K.U.Leuven,
Kasteelpark Arenberg 10, 3001 Heverlee-Leuven, Belgium
{Dave.Singelee,Bart.Preneel}@esat.kuleuven.be

Abstract. Location information can be used to enhance mutual entity authentication protocols in wireless ad-hoc networks. More specifically, distance bounding protocols have been introduced by Brands and Chaum at Eurocrypt'93 to preclude distance fraud and mafia fraud attacks, in which a local impersonator exploits a remote honest user. Hancke and Kuhn have proposed a solution to cope with noisy channels. This paper presents an improved distance bounding protocol for noisy channels that offers a substantial reduction (about 50%) in the number of communication rounds compared to the Hancke and Kuhn protocol. The main idea is to use binary codes to correct bit errors occurring during the fast bit exchanges. Our protocol is perfectly suitable to be employed in low-cost, noisy wireless environments.

Keywords: secure localization, distance bounding, wireless sensor networks, entity authentication.

1 Introduction

1.1 Proximity Based Authentication

In mobile networks, location information can be used to enhance mutual entity authentication protocols. Entities which are in a specific location or within a certain range of a device (*"the verifier"*) are granted some privileges, in contrast to all other entities. In most scenarios, one would like to determine an upper bound on the distance to another entity. For instance, one could conduct a cryptographic identification protocol at the entrance to a building. Only entities with the correct credentials and who are not more than a few meters away are granted access to the building.

The concept of *proximity based authentication* is graphically depicted in Fig. 1. Authentication requests originating from devices that are located within the range d of the verifier V are accepted, all other requests are rejected. So in Fig. 1, authentication requests originating from device A are accepted (and as a consequence, A is granted some privileges), while the requests of B are rejected. Contactless smart cards and RFID tokens are often used for proximity-based authentication (see Bardram et al. [1]). Such mobile devices have very limited processing power. Therefore, one has to employ low-cost cryptographic

F. Stajano et al. (Eds.): ESAS 2007, LNCS 4572, pp. 101–115, 2007.
© Springer-Verlag Berlin Heidelberg 2007

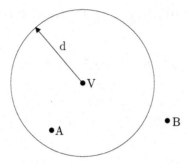

Fig. 1. Proximity based authentication

primitives to authenticate the mobile devices, and verify the distance between both parties.

How can one securely verify if a certain device is within a specific range? There are several methods to accomplish this; one of them is to apply *distance bounding protocols*. These protocols enable the verifying party to determine an upper bound on the distance between itself and a prover, who claims to be within a certain range. Distance bounding protocols combine physical and cryptographic properties to determine an upper bound on the distance between verifier and prover. They allow the prover to authenticate itself to the verifier, and in the same time enable the verifying party to check if the prover is located within a certain range. Distance bounding techniques can measure the received signal strength (RSS) [2], the angle of arrival (AoA), or the time of flight (ToF) to estimate an upper bound on the distance. The first two techniques (RSS and AoA) are typically discarded because of security reasons: e.g., an attacker can construct a directional antenna to substantially increase the sending or receiving range [3]. This only leaves measuring the time of flight as a possible technique for secure distance bounding protocols.

1.2   Organization of the Paper

This paper is organized as follows. In the introduction, we briefly discussed the idea of proximity based authentication in mobile ad-hoc networks. We put forward the idea of employing distance bounding protocols. The general principles of these protocols are discussed more in detail in Sect. 2. Section 3 and 4 describe two important distance bounding protocols: the protocol of Brands and Chaum protocol, and the protocol of Hancke and Kuhn protocol respectively. In Sect. 5, we show how to adapt the Mutual Authentication with Distance Bounding (MAD) protocol of Čapkun et al. (extended version of the Brands and Chaum protocol) to make it noise resilient. This protocol requires about half of the number of communication rounds compared to other noise resilient distance bounding protocols, as will be shown in Sect. 6. Section 7 concludes the paper.

2   Background

2.1   How Do Distance Bounding Protocols Work?

Secure distance bounding protocols measure the time of flight to determine an upper bound on the distance between prover and verifier. This measurement is typically performed during a challenge-response protocol, the main building block of the distance bounding protocol. During n fast bit exchanges, the time between sending a challenge and receiving the response is measured. Multiplying the time of flight with the propagation speed of the communication medium gives the distance between prover and verifier.

One should however take into account some important details. It should be impossible for the prover to send the response before receiving the challenge [4]. This implies that the response should be dependent on the (random) challenge. A second remark is that a challenge-response protocol is not sufficient. After execution of this protocol, the verifier only knows that some party is close. But how does one know that this entity is the prover? This problem arises for example in the Echo protocol [5]. That is why the prover has to identify itself somewhere in the scheme (not necessarily in the challenge-response protocol itself). Finally, one should notice that the round trip time is not equal to the propagation time. It takes some time to compute and transmit the response. This processing delay should be as small as possible compared to the propagation time, because we are only interested in the latter. We consider two communication technologies: (ultra-)sound and electromagnetic signals.

Ultra-sound: (Ultra-)sound is interesting to measure distances because it is relatively slow. The processing delay can hence be neglected compared to the propagation time and the accuracy of the measurements is not very critical. An example of a protocol using this technique is described by Kindberg and Zhang [6]. There are however some security problems. (Ultra-)sound is not resistant to physically present attackers. Such an attacker can modify the medium (e.g., sound travels faster through metal than through the air) or use wormholes (e.g., by retransmitting the signal using electromagnetic waves) to claim that he is closer than he really is. By delaying the response, he can also claim to be further away.

Electromagnetic signals: An active attacker can not use wormholes since the signals travel with the speed of light and nothing propagates faster. This means that an attacker can only claim to be further away than he really is (by delaying the response). There are however some practical issues. The verifier has to be able to measure the round trip time with very high precision. A small deviation of the time of flight has a strong influence on the estimated distance. A similar problem is estimating the processing delay. One has to design the distance bounding protocol in such a way that the processing delay can be neglected to the (very small) time of flight.

2.2   Attack Scenarios

By employing the principle of distance bounding attacks in a clever way, one can preclude one or more fundamental attacks.

One wants to prevent a dishonest prover claiming to be closer than he really is. This attack is called **distance fraud attack**. It is relatively easy to design a distance bounding protocol which prevents this type of attack. Bussard presents in [7] an overview of location mechanisms that are resistant or partially resistant to distance fraud attacks.

Mafia fraud attacks, also called *relay attacks*, were first described by Desmedt [8]. In this attack scenario, both prover and verifier are honest, but a malicious intruder is performing the fraud. It is a man-in-the-middle attack where the intruder I is modeled as a malicious prover $\bar{P}$ and verifier $\bar{V}$ that cooperate, as shown in Fig. 2. The malicious verifier $\bar{V}$ interacts with the honest prover P and the malicious prover $\bar{P}$ interacts with the honest verifier V. The physical distance between the intruder and the verifier is small. This attack enables the intruder to identify itself to V as P being close to V, without any of P and V noticing the attack.

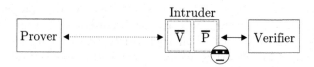

Fig. 2. Mafia fraud attack

Terrorist fraud attacks [8] are an interesting extension of the mafia fraud attack. The intruder and the prover will collaborate in this attack. This implies that a protocol which is resistant to terrorist fraud attacks, also prevents mafia fraud attacks. The terrorist fraud attack is shown in Fig. 3. The dishonest prover uses the intruder to convince the honest verifier that he is close, while in fact he is located at a large distance. The intruder does not know the private or secret key. This certainly has to be emphasized: if the intruder would know this private key, then it is impossible to make a distinction between the intruder and the prover, since distance bounding protocols only check if a party which knows the private key is close to the verifier. Several distance bounding protocols are resistant to terrorist fraud attacks [7, 9, 10].

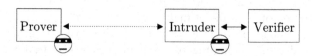

Fig. 3. Terrorist fraud attack

2.3   Design Principles for Secure Distance Bounding Protocols

Without going in too many details, one can formulate the following (simplified) cryptographic design principles of distance bounding protocols:

- In at least one of the messages of the distance bounding protocol, the prover has to "identify" itself (e.g., by proving knowledge of a shared secret key).
- To prevent mafia fraud attacks, the distance bounding protocol should contain a challenge-response protocol that consists of a series of rapid bit exchanges (n rounds in total) [4]. By measuring the round trip time in each of the n rounds, the verifier can determine an upper bound on the distance between verifier and prover. To prevent the prover sending the response too soon, the challenge has to be random and unpredictable, and the response has to depend on this challenge.
- To avoid terrorist fraud attacks, one has to make sure that the fast bit exchanges and the phase in which the prover identifies itself, are intermingled in a cryptographic way. It has to be impossible to split the distance bounding protocol into these two distinct phases. There are at least two ways to accomplish this: either one uses the private (or symmetric) key during the fast bit exchanges, or one uses trusted hardware. For more details, we refer to [9].

The design principles described above are not sufficient. Clulow et al. show that one has to optimize the choice of communication medium and transmission format according to the following four principles [11], if one wants to prevent certain "physical" attacks:

- Use a communication medium with a propagation speed as close as possible to the physical limit for propagating information through space-time.
- Use a communication format in which the recipient can instantly react on each single transmitted bit.
- Minimize the length of the symbol used to represent this single bit.
- Design the distance bounding protocol to cope with bit errors taking place during the rapid bit exchanges.

3   The Distance Bounding Protocol of Brands and Chaum

In 1993, Brands and Chaum presented their distance bounding protocol [4]. This clever protocol prevents mafia fraud attacks and embodies a series of n rounds (n is a security parameter). Each round consists of a single bit challenge and a rapid single bit response. The delay time for receiving the responses enables the verifier to compute an upper bound on the distance. After **correct** execution of the distance bounding protocol, the verifier knows that an entity in possession of a certain secret is in the vicinity.

The protocol is carried out as follows. It contains three phases. First, the prover sends out a commitment to n random bits m_i. Next, a series of n fast bit exchanges is performed. The verifier sends a random challenge α_i to the prover.

This challenge is XOR'ed with the bit m_i and the result (β_i) is sent back to the verifier. After the n fast bit exchanges, the prover opens the commitment and signs the string y, which embodies the concatenation of the challenges α_i and the responses β_i. If the signature is correct, the protocol is successful. In each of the n rounds, an attacker has a probability of $\frac{1}{2}$ to send a correct response [4]. Note that in every of the n rounds, the prover has to compute the XOR of two bits. This can be done very efficiently in hardware.

Čapkun et al. extended the protocol to MAD, a mutual authentication protocol using distance bounding [12]. This protocol has the advantage that both parties can estimate an upper bound on the distance between themselves, and learn each other's identity, which is not the case in the original protocol of Brands and Chaum. From all other points of view, both protocols are very similar. In the rest of this paper, we will assume that mutual entity authentication is required, and use the MAD protocol.

4 The RFID Protocol of Hancke and Kuhn

Both the distance bounding protocol of Brands and Chaum [4] and the MAD protocol [12] were not designed to cope with bit errors during the fast bit exchanges. A single bit error causes the protocol to fail. This can be an important problem in noisy environments such RFID. That is why Hancke and Kuhn proposed a distance bounding protocol [13] that can easily be extended to deal with bit errors.

The protocol is carried out as follows. First, prover and verifier exchange a random nonce (N_P and N_V respectively). Both parties then use a pseudorandom function (typically a MAC algorithm such as CBC-MAC and HMAC is used since these have been shown to be pseudo-random functions [14]) to compute two n-bit sequences $v^{(0)}$ and $v^{(1)}$ (more in detail: $MAC_K(N_V, N_P) = v^{(0)}|v^{(1)})$. Next, a series of n fast bit exchanges is performed. In each round, the verifier sends a random single bit challenge C_i to the prover. If this challenge equals 0, then the prover responds with the i-th bit of $v^{(0)}$. If the challenge equals 1, then the prover sends the i-th bit of $v^{(1)}$. If all responses are correct, the protocol succeeds. In each round, an attacker has a probability of $\frac{3}{4}$ to send a correct response. After **correct** execution of the distance bounding protocol, the verifier knows that with probability $1 - \left(\frac{3}{4}\right)^n$ an entity in possession of the secret key K is in the vicinity.

If we compare the Hancke and Kuhn distance bounding protocol with the Brands and Chaum protocol, we notice that the latter requires a signature to be sent at the end of the protocol, while the former stops after the execution of the n fast bit exchanges. So the Brands and Chaum protocol requires more bits to be interchanged on the slower communication channel, while the Hancke and Kuhn protocol needs more rounds of rapid single-bit exchanges. Munilla et al. proposed to use *"void challenges"* in the Hancke and Kuhn protocol [15] to improve the security. However the disadvantage of their solution is that is requires three (physical) states: 0, 1 and *void*.

The Hancke and Kuhn protocol can easily be adapted to make it noise resilient. First one has to select a security parameter x. This parameter denotes the number of bit errors that are allowed during the n fast bit exchanges; it depends on the bit error rate. The distance bounding protocol succeeds if at least $(n - x)$ of the responses sent by the prover are correct. The security parameter x has to be chosen very carefully. Incrementing the number of allowed errors x increases the false acceptance ratio dramatically. A more detailed discussion on the influence of the different security parameters will be presented in Sect. 6.

5 Noise Resilient Mutual Authentication with Distance Bounding

As discussed in Sect. 3, the MAD protocol of Čapkun et al. has the nice property that in each of the n rounds of the fast bit exchanges, an attacker only has a $\frac{1}{2}$ probability of replying to the verifier with a correct response. It also offers mutual entity authentication. On the other hand, the distance bounding protocol of Hancke and Kuhn can be easily made resilient to bit errors during the fast bit exchanges, which is a very desirable feature. It would be ideal to combine the good properties of both distance bounding protocols.

A trivial way of making the MAD protocol noise resilient, is exchanging all challenges and responses again on a slower communication channel with error correction (of course, this has to be done after the fast bit exchanges). However, this is not very efficient. We will now present an efficient modification of the MAD protocol, which is also resilient to some bit errors (we allow x bit errors in total) during the fast bit exchanges. Our protocol, in which the two parties (denoted by *Alice* and *Bob*) will authenticate each other, is shown in Fig. 4.

The protocol is carried out as follows. First, both parties agree on an (n, k) *Error Correcting Code (ECC)*. In order to correct at least x bit errors during the fast bit exchanges, this binary code should have a minimal Hamming distance d_{min} such that $x = \lfloor \frac{d_{min} - 1}{2} \rfloor$. More information on which (n, k) error correcting code to use for a given distance d_{min} can be found in [16, 17, 18, 19]. Note that we consider both linear and non-linear codes.

Next, *Alice* and *Bob* generate k random bits ($r_1, \ldots, r_k$ and $s_1, \ldots, s_k$ respectively). These k bits are extended to n-bit strings ($r_1, \ldots, r_n$ and $s_1, \ldots, s_n$) by applying the error correcting code described above and a commitment to this string is sent to the other party. Several secure commitment schemes can be used in our distance bounding protocol. E.g., one could first generate a 128-bit random string, then concatenate it with the n-bit string $r_1, \ldots, r_n$ or $s_1, \ldots, s_n$ and apply a cryptographic hash function to the resulting string of bitlength $128 + n$. The output of this function is sent to the other party. To open the commitment, one should reveal the 128-bit random string. This commitment scheme is unconditionally hiding and conditionally binding. More information can be found in [20].

During the n fast bit exchanges, the following two steps are repeated n times:

- *Alice* sends the bit α_i to *Bob* where $\alpha_1 = r_1$ and $\alpha_i = r_i \oplus \beta_{i-1}$.
- *Bob* sends the bit β_i to *Alice* where $\beta_i = s_i \oplus \alpha_i$.

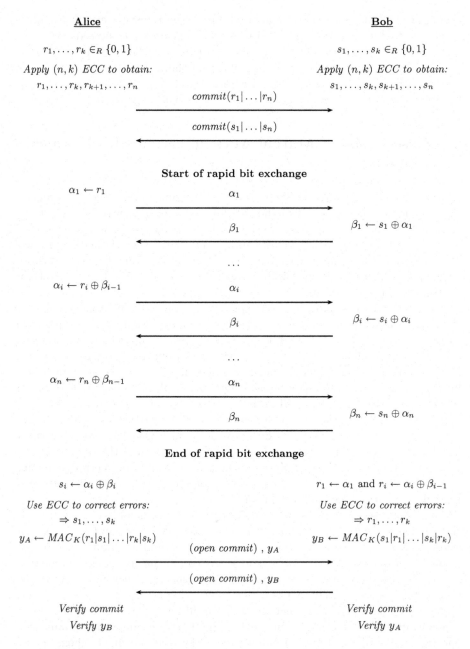

Fig. 4. Noise resilient mutual entity authentication with distance bounding protocol

In each round, the time between sending α_i and receiving β_i (or sending β_i and receiving α_{i+1}) is measured. The maximum round trip time is selected and this measurement determines an upper bound on the estimation of the distance between *Alice* and *Bob*. After the fast bit exchanges, both parties use the (n, k) ECC to correct bit errors (each party can correct a maximum of x bit failures) and this way recover the bits $s_1, \ldots, s_k$ and $r_1, \ldots, r_k$ respectively. Finally, Alice (and Bob) compute a *MAC* on the concatenation of r_i and s_i (or s_i and r_i) and open the commitment sent in the beginning of the protocol. If the *MAC* and the commitment are correct, the protocol is successful. In each of the first k rounds, an attacker has a $\frac{1}{2}$ probability of sending a correct response. Note that our protocol only requires low-cost cryptographic primitives, and hence is perfectly suitable to be employed in resource constrained wireless networks.

6   Performance Analysis

6.1   False Rejection and False Acceptance Ratio

In our analysis, we assume that the fast communication channel used during the rapid bit exchanges is symmetric. So a bit error is as likely to occur in a challenge as in a response. We also assume that a bit error is independent of previous bit errors. The bit error rate is denoted by P_b.

Before numerically analyzing and deriving the statistical properties of our distance bounding protocol, let us first clearly define the notion of a *round* (during the fast bit exchanges). This definition depends on the distance bounding protocol that is being used. In the Hancke and Kuhn protocol, we define a **round** as a challenge and the corresponding response. In our noise resilient MAD protocol, a **round** are two consecutive messages (so α_i and β_i, or β_i and α_{i+1}).

Some of the challenges and/or responses will be corrupted by noise. The probability that a round fails is denoted by ε. A **round fails** if the verifying party receives an incorrect response, or if one of the parties in our noise resilient MAD protocol gets a corrupted bit $\overline{r_i}$ or $\overline{s_i}$. Let us first have a look to the Hancke and Kuhn protocol. A bit error can appear in the challenge, or in the response (both with probability P_b). We neglect the probability that a bit error occurs in both messages. If the prover receives an incorrect challenge, he still has a $\frac{1}{2}$ probability of sending the correct response (this event happens when the responses for both the challenges 0 and 1 are equal). If the verifier receives a corrupted response, the round fails certainly. So one can easily compute the probability ε_H that a round fails in the Hancke and Kuhn distance bounding protocol:

$$\varepsilon_H = \frac{3}{2} P_b . \tag{1}$$

In our noise resilient MAD protocol, a round fails by definition with 100% probability when a bit α_i or β_i is corrupted. The probability ε_{MAD} that a round fails in our noise resilient MAD protocol is equal to

$$\varepsilon_{MAD} = 2P_b . \tag{2}$$

We can now compute the false rejection and false acceptance ratio, two important parameters to evaluate (noise resilient) distance bounding protocols. An honest prover is falsely rejected if more than x bit errors occur during the fast bit exchanges (which consist out of n rounds). The false rejection ratio depends on the probability ε (equal to ε_H or ε_{MAD}) and is equal to

$$P_{FR} = \sum_{i=0}^{n-x-1} \binom{n}{i} \cdot (1-\varepsilon)^i \cdot \varepsilon^{(n-i)}. \tag{3}$$

This expression is valid for both distance bounding protocols.

An attacker can use the uncertainty of which bits are corrupted by noise, to its advantage. In the worst case, no bit errors occur, but the (honest) verifier expects a maximum of x bit errors. As a consequence, an attacker only has to guess $(n-x)$ responses right in the Hancke and Kuhn distance bounding protocol to perform a successful attack (without taking into account noise, an attacker should have to guess all n responses correctly to be successful). The false acceptance ratio of the Hancke and Kuhn protocol equals

$$P_{FA} = \sum_{i=n-x}^{n} \binom{n}{i} \cdot \left(\frac{3}{4}\right)^i \cdot \left(\frac{1}{4}\right)^{(n-i)}. \tag{4}$$

The situation is slightly different in our noise resilient MAD protocol. Since the first k bits of r_i and s_i are independent and uniformly distributed in $\{0,1\}$, the two sequences α_i and β_i are independent up to the point where the index is k (and by consequence, the first k rounds of rapid single-bit exchanges are also independent). If the commitments sent in the beginning of the protocol are (un)conditionally hiding and binding, it is infeasible for a computationally bounded attacker to determine these bits in advance. The last $(n-k)$ bits of r_i and s_i depend of the first k bits and can be easily computed by applying the (n,k) error correcting code. In the worst case scenario (no bit errors occur), the last $(n-k)$ bits of the sequences α_i and β_i can be computed in advance (from the moment the first k rounds are conducted) and do not offer extra security. To be successful, an attacker hence has to correctly guess the first k bits r_i (or s_i).[1] The false acceptance ratio of our noise resilient MAD protocol equals

$$P_{FA} = \left(\frac{1}{2}\right)^k. \tag{5}$$

6.2   Numerical Results

Both noise resilient distance bounding protocols have some interesting characteristics. We will now compare both protocols, and have a closer look at the most interesting properties.

An Attacker Has a Major Advantage When Bit Errors Due to Noise Can Appear. In the worst case scenario, an honest verifier expects to receive

---

[1] Note that the number of allowed errors x is always strictly smaller than the minimal Hamming distance d_{min} of the (n,k) error correcting code.

some corrupted bits due to noise, while in fact there is no noise at all. As a direct consequence, an attacker can obtain a major advantage. Whenever he guesses a response wrongly, he can blame it to the noise. As long as an attacker has a maximum of x wrong guesses, the Hancke and Kuhn distance bounding protocol will be successful (because the verifier believes that the incorrect bits were corrupted by noise). The more errors that are allowed, the larger the false acceptance ratio. The same property is also valid for our noise-resilient MAD protocol. For a fixed number n of rounds, the more errors x have to be corrected, the smaller the parameter k has to be [16,17,18,19]. And because only the first k rounds of the fast bit exchanges contribute to the security, the false acceptance ratio will increase with decreasing k. This property is demonstrated for both distance bounding protocols in Table 1. In this numerical example, $n = 37$ and the bit error rate P_b is 0.01. The error correcting codes for our noise resilient MAD protocol have been selected following [16]. The results in Table 1 clearly show that the false acceptance ratio increases significantly with the number x of allowed errors. One can also notice that the false acceptance ratio is remarkably smaller in our noise resilient MAD protocol (several orders of magnitude). We will discuss this observation later in this section.

Table 1. Influence of the number of allowed errors x on the false acceptance ratio P_{FR} for $n = 37$ and $P_b = 0.01$

# allowed errors	Hancke-Kuhn	Noise Resilient MAD	
x	P_{FR}	(n, k) ECC	P_{FR}
4	0.0284	(37, 16)	$1.5259 \cdot 10^{-5}$
3	0.0089	(37, 22)	$2.3842 \cdot 10^{-7}$
2	0.0021	(37, 26)	$1.4901 \cdot 10^{-8}$
1	$3.1784 \cdot 10^{-4}$	(37, 31)	$4.6566 \cdot 10^{-10}$
0	$2.3838 \cdot 10^{-5}$	(37, 37)	$7.2760 \cdot 10^{-12}$

The False Rejection Ratio Is Slightly Lower in the Hancke and Kuhn Distance Bounding Protocol. Whereas noise helps an attacker to deceive an honest verifier, it is disadvantageous for an honest prover behaving correctly. The higher the bit error rate P_b, the higher the probability that the distance bounding protocol will fail because of too many bit errors during the fast bit exchanges. If no bit errors occur during the fast bit exchange phase, an honest prover will always be able to authenticate itself successfully. To decrease the false rejection ratio, one has to allow more bit errors to take place (denoted by x) for a fixed number n of rounds, or decrease the number of rounds (without changing x). The choice of the parameter x has to be in accordance to the expected number of errors, which depends on the number n of rounds and the bit error rate P_b.

As demonstrated in (1) and (2) in Sect. 6.1, the probability ε_{MAD} of a round to fail in our noise resilient MAD protocol is higher than in the Hancke and Kuhn distance bounding protocol (ε_H). A direct consequence of this fact, is that the false rejection ratio is lower in the Hancke and Kuhn protocol (for equal number

n of rounds and allowed errors x). This property is demonstrated in Table 2. In this numerical example, $n = 37$ and $P_b = 0.01$. Note that the difference in false rejection ratio between both distance bounding protocols is relatively small. When the number n of rounds is larger (e.g., around 50), one should allow one or two more errors to occur in our MAD resilient to keep the false rejection ratio comparable in both protocols (e.g., for $n = 47$: $P_{FR}(Hancke, x = 9) = 1.7985 \cdot 10^{-9} \approx P_{FR}(MAD, x = 10) = 1.8353 \cdot 10^{-9}$).

Table 2. Comparison of the false rejection ratio for $n = 37$ and $P_b = 0.01$

# allowed errors x	Hancke-Kuhn: P_{FR}	Noise Res. MAD: P_{FR}
$x = 6$	$1.1849 \cdot 10^{-6}$	$7.7770 \cdot 10^{-6}$
$x = 5$	$1.7760 \cdot 10^{-5}$	$8.7314 \cdot 10^{-5}$
$x = 4$	$2.2184 \cdot 10^{-4}$	$8.1806 \cdot 10^{-4}$
$x = 3$	0.0023	0.0062
$x = 2$	0.0179	0.0375
$x = 1$	0.1062	0.1689
$x = 0$	0.4283	0.5265

The False Acceptance Ratio Is Significantly Higher in the Hancke and Kuhn Distance Bounding Protocol. As demonstrated above, to decrease the false acceptance ratio, one has to allow fewer bit errors (denoted by x) for a fixed number n of rounds, or increase the number of rounds (without changing x).

Table 1 shows that the false acceptance ratio is remarkably higher in the Hancke and Kuhn protocol. The main reason is that an attacker has a $\frac{3}{4}$ probability of guessing a response correctly in the Hancke and Kuhn protocol, but only a $\frac{1}{2}$ probability in our noise resilient MAD protocol. This difference is amplified exponentially, and not entirely compensated by the fact that an attacker has to guess more bits correctly in the Hancke and Kuhn protocol ($(n - x)$ bits, compared to k bits in our noise resilient MAD protocol). This property is also demonstrated in Table 3. In this numerical example, $n = 63$ and $P_b = 0.02$. The error correcting codes have been selected based on [17] (some of these codes are non-linear).

Note that the difference in false acceptance ratio is quite large: even allowing a slightly lower number of errors x in the Hancke and Kuhn protocol does not really help to remove this inequality (e.g., if we have a look at Table 3: $P_{FA}(Hancke, x = 1) = 2.9599 \cdot 10^{-7} > P_{FA}(MAD, x = 7) = 3.7253 \cdot 10^{-9}$). One could also fix the number of allowed errors x, but perform more fast bit exchanges in the Hancke and Kuhn protocol (or in other words, increase the number n of rounds). This would however make the distance bounding protocol more expensive, as the cost is directly related to the number n of fast bit exchanges. Figure 5 shows the relation between the false acceptance ratio and the number of rounds n, for a fixed number of allowed errors x. In this example, we fixed the number x of allowed errors to 5, the bit error rate P_b is 0.005, and the information on which error correcting code to use (in our noise

Table 3. Comparison of the false acceptance ratio for $n = 63$ and $P_b = 0.02$

# allowed errors	Hancke-Kuhn	Noise Resilient MAD	
x	P_{FR}	(n, k) ECC	P_{FR}
13	0.2611	$(63, 12)$	$2.4414 \cdot 10^{-4}$
10	0.0584	$(63, 18)$	$3.8147 \cdot 10^{-6}$
7	0.0052	$(63, 28)$	$3.7253 \cdot 10^{-9}$
5	$5.1111 \cdot 10^{-4}$	$(63, 37)$	$7.2760 \cdot 10^{-12}$
3	$2.3004 \cdot 10^{-5}$	$(63, 47)$	$7.1054 \cdot 10^{-15}$
1	$2.9599 \cdot 10^{-7}$	$(63, 57)$	$6.9389 \cdot 10^{-18}$

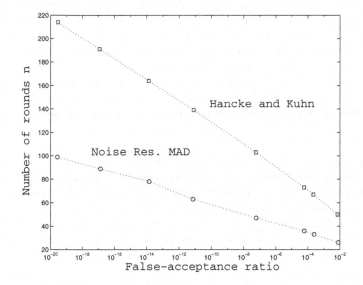

Fig. 5. Relation between the number n of rounds and the false acceptance ratio P_{FA} for $x = 5$ and $P_b = 0.005$

resilient MAD protocol) is based on [17]. Figure 5 demonstrates that the Hancke and Kuhn protocol needs about twice as many rounds n to obtain the same false acceptance ratio. This largely increases the cost, and also causes the false rejection ratio to rise several orders of magnitude. If mutual autentication is required, the number of fast bit exchanges n even needs to be doubled (and becomes the quadruple of the number of rounds needed in our noise resilient MAD protocol).

7   Conclusion

Location information can be used to enhance mutual entity authentication protocols in wireless ad-hoc networks. Distance bounding protocols, which have been introduced by Brands and Chaum at Eurocrypt'93 to preclude distance fraud and mafia fraud attacks, can be employed in proximity based authentication schemes to determine an upper bound on the distance to another entity. Hancke and Kuhn have presented a solution to cope with noisy channels, which is important in mobile environments.

In this paper, we have extended the mutual authentication distance bounding (MAD) protocol of Čapkun et al. to make it tolerant to bit errors. This is accomplished by employing binary codes to correct bit errors occurring during the fast bit exchanges, the main building block of the distance bounding protocol. The protocol is best used for radio frequency communications, which is more suited for secure applications than ultrasonic. Our noise resilient MAD protocol requires about half of the number of communication rounds to obtain the same false acceptance ratio as the Hancke and Kuhn protocol. It also provides mutual entity authentication and can be made robust to terrorist fraud attacks by executing the protocol in trusted hardware. Compared to the Hancke and Kuhn protocol, our noise resilient MAD protocol requires slightly more bits to be exchanged on the slower communication channel. The exact total cost depends on the technical characteristics of the communication medium and the required level of security. Our distance bounding protocol is perfectly suitable to be employed in low-cost, noisy wireless environments.

Acknowledgments. Dave Singelée is funded by a research grant of the Katholieke Universiteit Leuven. This work was supported in part by the Concerted Research Action (GOA) Ambiorics 2005/11 of the Flemish Government and by the IAP Programme P6/26 BCRYPT of the Belgian State (Belgian Science Policy). The authors would like to thank Markus G. Kuhn for the valuable comments and interesting discussions on distance bounding protocols.

References

1. Bardram, J., Kjær, R., Pedersen, M.: Context-Aware User Authentication – Supporting Proximity-Based Login in Pervasive Computing. In: Dey, A.K., Schmidt, A., McCarthy, J.F. (eds.) UbiComp 2003: Ubiquitous Computing. LNCS, vol. 2864, pp. 107–123. Springer, Heidelberg (2003)
2. Bahl, P., Padmanabhan, V.: RADAR: An In-Building RF-based User Location and Tracking System. In: Proceedings of the 19th annual conference on Computer Communications (INFOCOM '00), vol. 2, pp. 775–784. IEEE, Los Alamitos (2000)
3. Cheung, H.: The Bluesniper Rifle (2004)
   http://www.tomsnetworking.com/Sections-article106.php
4. Brands, S., Chaum, D.: Distance-Bounding Protocols. In: Helleseth, T. (ed.) EUROCRYPT '93. LNCS, vol. 765, pp. 344–359. Springer, Heidelberg (1994)
5. Sastry, N., Shankar, U., Wagner, D.: Secure Verification of Location Claims (2003)
   http://www.cs.berkeley.edu/~nks/locprove/csd-03-1245.pdf
6. Kindberg, T., Zhang, K.: Validating and Securing Spontaneous Associations between Wireless Devices. In: Boyd, C., Mao, W. (eds.) ISC 2003. LNCS, vol. 2851, pp. 44–53. Springer, Heidelberg (2003)

7. Bussard, L.: Trust Establishment Protocols for Communicating Devices. PhD thesis, ENST Paris, p. 233 (2004)
8. Desmedt, Y.: Major Security Problems with the Unforgeable (Feige)-Fiat-Shamir Proofs of Identity and how to overcome them. In: Proceedings of SecuriCom '88, pp. 15–17 (1988)
9. Singelée, D., Preneel, B.: Location Verification using Secure Distance Bounding Protocols. In: Proceedings of the 2nd IEEE International Conference on Mobile, Ad Hoc and Sensor Systems (MASS '05), pp. 834–840 (2005)
10. Waters, B., Felten, E.: Proving the Location of Tamper-Resistant Devices (2003)
    http://www.cs.princeton.edu/bwaters/research/location_proving.ps
11. Clulow, J., Hancke, G., Kuhn, M., Moore, T.: So Near and Yet So Far: Distance-Bounding Attacks in Wireless Networks. In: Buttyán, L., Gligor, V., Westhoff, D. (eds.) ESAS 2006. LNCS, vol. 4357, pp. 83–97. Springer, Heidelberg (2006)
12. Čapkun, S., Buttyán, L., Hubaux, J.: SECTOR: Secure Tracking of Node Encounters in Multi-hop Wireless Networks. In: Proceedings of the 1st ACM Workshop on Security of Ad Hoc and Sensor Networks (SASN '03), pp. 21–32 (2003)
13. Hancke, G., Kuhn, M.: An RFID Distance Bounding Protocol. In: Proceedings of the 1st International Conference on Security and Privacy for Emerging Areas in Communications Networks (SECURECOMM '05), pp. 67–73. IEEE Computer Society, Los Alamitos (2005)
14. Menezes, A.J., van Oorschot, P.C., Vanstone, S.A. (eds.): Handbook of Applied Cryptography. CRC Press, Boca Raton, FL (1996)
15. Munilla, J., Ortiz, A., Peinado, A.: Distance Bounding Protocols with void-challenges for RFID. Workshop on RFID Security – RFIDSec '06 (2006)
16. Jaffe, D.: Information about binary linear codes.
    http://www.math.unl.edu/~djaffe2/codes/webcodes/codeform.html
17. Litsyn, S.: Table of Nonlinear Binary Codes,
    http://www.eng.tau.ac.il/~litsyn/tableand/index.html
18. MacWilliams, F., Sloane, N.: The Theory of Error-Correcting Codes. North-Holland, Amsterdam (1977)
19. Pless, V., Brualdi, R., Huffman, W.: Handbook of Coding Theory. Elsevier Science Inc, Amsterdam (1998)
20. Damgård, I.: Commitment Schemes and Zero-Knowledge Protocols. In: Damgård, I.B. (ed.) Lectures on Data Security. LNCS, vol. 1561, pp. 63–86. Springer, Heidelberg (1999)

Multiple Target Localisation in Sensor Networks with Location Privacy

Matthew Roughan[1] and Jon Arnold[2]

[1] School of Mathematical Science, University of Adelaide, SA 5005, Australia
matthew.roughan@adelaide.edu.au
[2] Defence Science and Technology Organisation, Australia
jon.arnold@dsto.defence.gov.au

Abstract. It is now well known that data-fusion from multiple sensors can improve detection and localisation of targets. Traditional data fusion requires the sharing of detailed data from multiple sources. In some cases, the various sources may not be willing to share such detailed information. For instance, current military allies may be willing to share some level of information, but only if they can do so without revealing their secrets. This situation appears relevant for modern sensor networks, which may be comprised of networks from multiple participants. It has previously been shown that localisation of a single target can be performed while preserving location privacy of the sensor nodes. Here we extend this to the case of multiple targets. The novel aspect of the problem is related to the ambiguity in target labels, and how we resolve this ambiguity.

Keywords: privacy-preservation, localization, ad-hoc networks.

1 Introduction

It is now a standard data-fusion problem to use multiple sensors to improve the localisation and subsequent tracking of targets. However, there may be cases where such co-operation is limited by the nature of the parties who wish to co-operate. For instance, consider several parties who wish to be able to detect illegal fishing, drug smuggling, or terrorist activities. In the modern context such issues apply to sensor networks, and in particular we consider the case where nodes in the sensor network wish to maintain location privacy (i.e. they wish the location of the node to remain private). There is now a substantial literature on Privacy-Preserving Data Mining (PPDM) and Secure Distributed Computing (SDC) (for examples see [1, 2, 3, 4, 9, 11, 10]) and these techniques are applicable here.

We shall consider two problems. First we consider a problem where each party has estimates of a set of targets' positions. They then wish to combine this information to provide a better estimate of the targets' locations without revealing information about their sensors. Previously this problem was solved for a single target in [6].

The second problem we consider is one where any one sensor doesn't have enough information (in itself) to localise the targets. The example we consider

F. Stajano et al. (Eds.): ESAS 2007, LNCS 4572, pp. 116–128, 2007.

here is where each sensor provides range measurements (such as might be gained from examining time of arrival of signals, or signal power). In itself, such information is inadequate to localise a target, but in combination with data from other sensors, the measurements can provide good position estimates. This type of approach appears particularly relevant in the context of ad-hoc networks where we may wish to localise some resource on the network from purely passive measurements of signal strength at a number of points [5, 8], and each node in the network could be controlled by a separate party. Again, this problem was solved for a single target in [6].

Our approach allows extensions of the solutions of these problems to multiple targets, while maintaining the privacy of the participants. That is, the participating sensors need not reveal their location, or sensor characteristics in order to participate. The method is a simple, iterative improvement scheme that attempts to resolve the ambiguity between the different sensors' labellings of the targets, and its performance is good (close to the ideal performance of co-operating sensors) for small numbers of targets (< 6) after which we find that performance degrades, though this appears to be a more fundamental problem, rather than a problem with the privacy preserving approach.

2   Problems and Assumptions

2.1   Problem 0

We first consider a simple problem where N sensors (nodes) each measure an estimate of the position of a single target. We denote the position of the target by (x, y) (relative to some arbitrarily chosen, but agreed point), and the estimate from party i by $(\hat{x}_i, \hat{y}_i)$. We assume that the position estimate has negligible bias and that the errors in position are independent between sensors, and have covariance matrix S_i. Given constant covariance $S_i = S$, we might improve our estimate of the position of the target by taking

$$\hat{x} = \frac{1}{N} \sum_{i=1}^{N} \hat{x}_i, \tag{1}$$

$$\hat{y} = \frac{1}{N} \sum_{i=1}^{N} \hat{y}_i. \tag{2}$$

The natural approach to computing the sum would be for each party in the measurement to pool values and then compute the sum. This approach reveals at least some values to other parties. An alternative would be to use a trusted third party to pool the results, and hence keep them secret. However trusted third parties are not easy to find.

The above problem was considered in [6], and the solution amounts to a Secure Distributed Summation (SDS). It is simple (see [4, 7]) to perform such a sum without leaking any information except the solution itself (even in the presence of collusion between some parties). Once we compute the sum, it is a simple matter to compute the average of the location estimates, and distribute this value to all parties. These approaches only work for $N > 2$, and in reality, where one could make meaningful guesses about some values it is only really secure for reasonable values of N, but this is the case for a sensor network.

Although the above approach hides some information — the individual position estimates — the final result is that each sensor learns a positional estimate, and so hiding the individual data seems to make little sense. However, it is simple to adapt this technique to the case where the sensors in question have different characteristics, *e.g.*, accuracy. It makes a lot more sense for a sensor operator to wish to hide their sensor's characteristics from other operators. For instance, accuracy may depend on distance, and so knowing accuracy may reveal the distance of the node from the target. This is even more important in the multi-target environment where a sensor would reveal multiple measurements at each time-step if no privacy-preserving measures were taken.

Consider the simple case where each sensor's estimate has covariance $S_i = \sigma_i^2 I$ where I is the identity matrix. We then compute a weighted mean

$$\hat{x} = \frac{1}{\sum_{i=1}^{N} w_i} \sum_{i=1}^{N} w_i \hat{x}_i, \tag{3}$$

$$\hat{y} = \frac{1}{\sum_{i=1}^{N} w_i} \sum_{i=1}^{N} w_i \hat{y}_i, \tag{4}$$

where the weights $w_i = 1/\sigma_i^2$. If an operator wants to conceal the characteristics of his sensor, they would wish to keep the weights w_i secret. This is easily accomplished by performing two SDSs (for each co-ordinate), one over the weighted position, and the other over the weights themselves.

2.2   Problem 1

As noted, Problem 0 was solved in [6]. However, it is unrealistic (in general) to assume only a single target. In the case of distributed measurements of multiple targets there is an ambiguity between measurements. For instance, consider Figure 1. In the figure, we as outside observers can uniquely associate each measured position (the arrows) with a unique target. However, the sensor nodes themselves cannot associate (unambiguously) the position estimates with targets. We refer to this issue as a labelling problem.

One approach to solve the labelling would be to assume one possible arrangement of measurements with respect to targets, and then compute the joint estimate of the targets' positions. Once the joint position estimate is obtained (and shared with each node), then these nodes could estimate a likelihood function for the set of measurements with respect to the target and their known measurement error distributions. The joint likelihood of the measurements with respect to the labelling could then be computed (again using a secure distributed summation) across the sensors. Given the likelihood for each possible arrangement of nodes and targets, we could choose the maximum likelihood arrangement, or if we wish to track these targets, we could use the likelihoods in a multiple-hypothesis tracker.

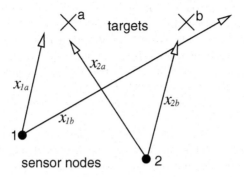

Fig. 1. Two target example: dots show sensor nodes, crosses are targets, and the arrows show the four position estimates

The problem with this simple approach to multiple targets is the number of possible hypotheses. If we have M targets, each node could have $M!$ possible labellings with respect to the targets. Given N sensor nodes there would therefore be $(M!)^N$ possible hypotheses to test. Clearly this does not scale well.

Note that this problem with ambiguity is not unique to privacy-preserving algorithms. In general, the multi-target labelling problem between a group of sensors must be solved for any distributed sensors. There are a number of approaches one could adopt to solve such a problem (e.g., probabilitistic data association, or multi-hypothesis tracking). In the following sections we will investigate a very simple approach that easily extends to become a privacy-preserving algorithm.

2.3   Problem 2

In problem 2 we allow the N sensor nodes to make only range estimates — a common case, for instance where we can only measure power of a signal from a target, and not the direction to a target. The combination of two such estimates is enough to localise a single target to two possible points, and three or more such measurements are capable of deducing the position uniquely (in a 2D plane) with some rare exceptions. It is noteworthy, however, that when the measurements contain errors, the measurements may be inconsistent, resulting in a problem in estimating the target's position precisely. We denote range estimates from party i by D_i (which is an unbiased estimate of the true range d_i), and the position of the sensor of party i by (X_i, Y_i). Again this localization problem for a single target has been solved [6], but the multiple target problem presents the same new challenges mentioned above.

2.4   Assumptions

The main privacy aim here is to hide the location of the sensor nodes, but we also wish to keep secret, information about the characteristics of these nodes.

The security model we use here is the commonly used "honest-but-curious" model. That is, we assume that the co-operating parties are honest in the sense that they follow the algorithms correctly, but they are curious and they will perform additional operations in order to attempt to discover more information than intended. The honest-but-curious assumption has been widely used, and appears applicable here. Sensor operators will benefit from participating honestly in such a scheme without revealing their private information, and there is no downside in participating honestly. Dishonest partners in computation (partners who do not follow the algorithm) will reduce their own benefits, without any obvious gain.

It is noteworthy that while we assume that participants follow the algorithm correctly, we do allow collusion. Multiple partners are allowed to collude to attempt to learn more information than they otherwise could. The protocols we present can be made resistant to such collusion in the presence of a majority of non-colluding participants. Additionally, there is now a substantial literature on PPDM (*e.g.* see [1,2,3,4,9,11,10] and the references therein), and this literature considers many variations on the type of assumptions considered here. It is therefore likely that the assumption of honest-but-curious participants can be substantially weakened. This is an important topic for future research, as the honest-but-curious assumption may well be too strong for some applications.

3   Solutions: Problem 1

The number of possible hypotheses we might have to test grows as $(M!)^N$ for M targets and N sensors. However, a quick look by eye (say at Figure 1) suggests that it will be common that many of the possible hypotheses are very unlikely, and it is our goal to eliminate the vast majority of these.

The approach proposed here is a simple iterative approach. Each of the N sensors first assigns a random set of labels $\{1, 2, \ldots, M\}$ to the targets. The joint position estimates of the targets are then calculated. Each node then calculates the likelihood of its measurements with respect to the current labelling, and the joint position estimates. Each sensor looks for a single swap of labels that improves this likelihood as much as possible (from its perspective). They then iterate. At each step, a node only swaps two labels if this increases the likelihood, and they compute how many sensor nodes performed a swap using a SDS. When zero nodes perform a swap in one iteration, we terminate the algorithm as it can make no further progress.

This approach is ideal for a privacy-preserving algorithm for a number of reasons. Its simplicity makes the information required at each step obvious, and hence it is easy to develop a privacy-preserving version of the algorithm. The computation of the joint estimate of the positions of the targets is simply the solution to problem 0 (discussed above) for a given set of labels. The computation reveals only the average of the measurements (the position estimate itself), and so performing it multiple times reveals only a series of position estimate for the targets. However, each position estimate is based on a different set of labellings, and so in theory, there may be some information revealed from the iterations, however, as we show below, generally it takes very few iterations to perform the algorithm, and the number of possible labellings is exponentially large. It therefore seems very unlikely that enough information could leak from these intermediate results to allow any useful inferences, especially as the number of sensor nodes grows. Even if such inferences were possible, the exponential number of possibilities would make the computational expense of such inferences high. The computation of likelihoods is a local operation for each node, and so requires no additional information transfers, and so creates no additional risks of leaking intermediate information.

A minor addition to this algorithm is that we can also compute the average likelihoods at each stage (using a SDS), and the algorithm can be terminated if this decreases at any point, preventing the possibility of oscillation between solutions. However, note that in the solutions below we did not have to apply this test, as the solutions always converged in relatively few iterations.

In order to test this approach we make a number of simplifying assumptions:

- location estimate errors are Gaussian, with covariance σI, where σ is a constant variance across all sensors.
- location estimates between targets are independent.

It is worth noting that these assumptions are not a prerequisite of the algorithm. All that is required of the algorithm is that the sensor nodes know their own distribution of measurement errors — these errors can be different for each sensor, and the sensors can maintain the privacy of their measurements.

Given Gaussian errors, computation of the relative likelihoods for sensor j is easily performed by computing

$$L\{(\hat{x}_i^{(j)}, \hat{y}_i^{(j)})|(\hat{x}_i(k), \hat{y}_i(k)\} \propto \exp\left(\frac{\sum_{i=1}^{M}(\hat{x}_i^{(j)} - \hat{x}_i(k))^2 + (\hat{y}_i^{(j)} - \hat{y}_i(k))^2}{2\sigma^2}\right),$$

where $(\hat{x}_i^{(j)}, \hat{y}_i^{(j)})$ is the position estimate of sensor node j for the target i given the current labelling, and $(\hat{x}_i(k), \hat{y}_i(k))$ is the joint estimate of the position of target i after k iterations of the algorithm. Note that we need not calculate the exponential function here, as we are maximizing L, and the exponential function is monotonically increasing.

Each node computes (locally) this likelihood for each possible swap of a pair of targets, resulting in $O(M^2)$ computations, and then uses the new labels in a new joint computation of the positions of the targets. Each node can alternatively declare that it cannot improve its likelihood, and we use a SDS to find how many nodes are in this situation. When all nodes are at this point, we terminate the algorithm, and say it has converged.

We simulate this algorithm where we distribute the N sensor nodes, and the M targets randomly in a unit square, and we vary M, N and σ.

Initial results for the above algorithm are shown in Figure 2 (a), which appears to show a number of problems in the algorithm. The figure shows the Root Mean Squared Error (RMSE) of estimates of the targets position for an ideal estimate (a simple average of all the measurements); independent measurements by each sensor node; and an estimate using the above algorithm. The algorithm shows worse performance than the independent estimates over a wide range of input

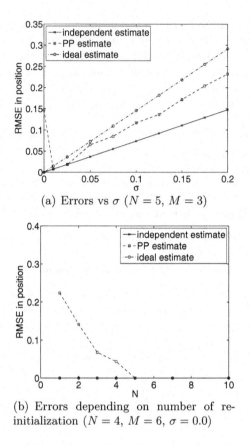

(a) Errors vs σ ($N = 5$, $M = 3$)

(b) Errors depending on number of re-initialization ($N = 4$, $M = 6$, $\sigma = 0.0$)

Fig. 2. RMSE for position estimates over 100 simulations

noise (σ). Most worrying is the non-zero value of the error for $\sigma = 0$. Investigation of the cause of this error found that in some (relatively rare cases) the initial label led to a situation where the labelling was "locked" in the sense that no change (of a single pair of labels) would improve the likelihood. This is a fairly rare occurrence (for small numbers of targets) and so an obvious solution is to re-initialize the algorithm a number of times. Figure 2 (b) shows the effect of such random initializations for $N = 4$, $M = 6$ and $\sigma = 0.0$. We can see that a relatively small number of re-initializations removes the error caused by this initial locking (the number of re-initializations can be smaller for a few targets, but we will use 5 throughout this paper).

Given 5 re-initializations we again simulate the performance of the algorithm, with results shown in Figures 2, 3 and 4. Figure 2 (a) shows the performance for $N = 4$, $M = 3$ over a range of values of σ. We can see that the algorithm performs close to the ideal value for moderate values of σ, but starts to deviate from the ideal, for large values. It should be noted that for the scenario simulated (with targets and sensors distributed across the unit square), a value of $\sigma = 0.2$ is very large — the 95th percentile confidence intervals for a measurement will

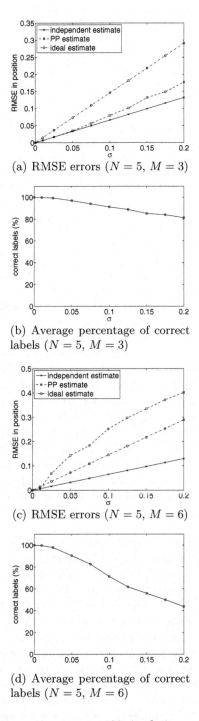

(a) RMSE errors $(N = 5,\ M = 3)$

(b) Average percentage of correct labels $(N = 5,\ M = 3)$

(c) RMSE errors $(N = 5,\ M = 6)$

(d) Average percentage of correct labels $(N = 5,\ M = 6)$

Fig. 3. RMSE for position estimates over 100 simulations, given 5 re-initializations

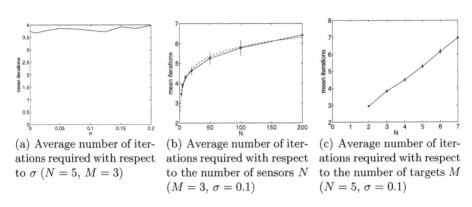

(a) Average number of iterations required with respect to σ ($N = 5$, $M = 3$)

(b) Average number of iterations required with respect to the number of sensors N ($M = 3$, $\sigma = 0.1$)

(c) Average number of iterations required with respect to the number of targets M ($N = 5$, $\sigma = 0.1$)

Fig. 4. Average number of iteration over 100 simulations, given 5 re-initializations

lie in a region approximately ± 0.4, a substantial part of the possible field. As σ increases, the number of labels that are incorrect (after convergence) increases (shown in Figure 2 (b)). This is inevitable because some measurements may lie closer to an incorrect target, and so the likelihood will be maximized by an incorrect labelling. As σ increases more measurements will fall into this category, and so more labels will be incorrect.

The problem is greatly exacerbated as the number of targets increases. The more densely packed the targets are, the more likely their measurements will overlap, and an incorrect labeling will maximize the likelihood. Figure 3 (c) and (d) show much worse performance for six targets. For larger numbers of targets, the algorithm is effective only for small values of σ. As noted, however, this seems to be a fundamental problem with labelling the measurements when there is a significant probability that incorrect labellings will look more natural than the correct labelling. In essence this seems to be a problem in multi-target localisation, and although it is no doubt possible to improve on the algorithm we present here, it is unlikely that fundamental improvements are possible without further measurements (e.g., if one had other data such as radial velocities the task might be easier).

Also of interest are the number of iterations required for these algorithms. The computational and communications cost is directly proportional to the number of iterations, and so we would like the value to be small. In fact it is, as is shown in Figure 4. The number of iterations seems to be insensitive to the value of σ (as shown in Figure 4 (a)). On the other hand, Figure 4 (b) shows that the number of iterations does depend on the number of sensors N, approximately logarithmically (see dashed line). This represents quite a win for the approach (the naive approach of testing all hypothesis is exponential in N, whereas this approach is logarithmic in N). The number of iterations is also dependent roughly linearly on the number of targets, but given that this algorithm can only be applied to moderate numbers of targets, this is not a great concern. As a result, the communications costs of this algorithm is only a few times the cost of an ideal algorithm where no ambiguity existed. Any real approach would have to pay some communications cost to resolve the ambiguity of target labels, and so this approach seems quite reasonable – certainly it is better than evaluating $(M!)^N$ hypotheses.

The figures above show illustrative results — we have simulated many other parameter values and the results above are representative.

4   Solutions: Problem 2

The iterative solution generalizes to range measurements. The approach is the same, use a random initial labelling, compute the positions (using the privacy-preserving method described in [6]), and then try to iteratively improve the labels. The only complicating factor is that in order to compute the likelihood of a measurement (with respect to a hypothetical position of a sensor node) the sensor nodes should perform a contour integral along a circular arc through the 2D Gaussian distribution function. For simplicity, we approximate this by taking a point estimate at the distance of the measurement (assuming it lies along a

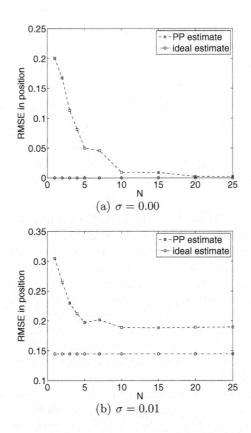

(a) $\sigma = 0.00$

(b) $\sigma = 0.01$

Fig. 5. RMSE for position estimates with respect to the number of re-initializations $N = 10$, $M = 3$

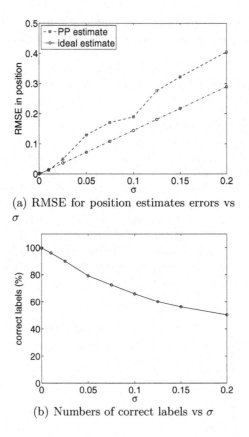

(a) RMSE for position estimates errors vs σ

(b) Numbers of correct labels vs σ

Fig. 6. Performance of range-based estimation over 100 simulations ($N = 10$, $M = 3$), and 20 re-initializations

line between sensor and node) from the hypothetical position of the node. This approximation greatly reduces the computational complexity of the algorithm.

The first result to note is that for this case, the algorithm does not always converge quickly. In most cases the algorithm converges quickly, but in 1.5% of (600) simulated cases, we observe quite a large number of iterations of the algorithm (we terminate it at 100 iterations). The failure to converge quickly could be caused by the approximation we use above, and so would perhaps be removed by replacing this with the correct likelihood. However, these cases could be simply avoided by re-initializing the algorithm after a moderate number (say 20) of iterations, though they still increase the overall average number of iterations required for the algorithm.

The second issue to consider is that we need more sensors for the range-only measurements because each sensor contributes less information in its own right (we need at least 3 to obtain a unique position estimate at all). As a result, there is more potential for locking at the initial step, and so we must re-initialize the algorithm a little more often. Figure 5 shows graphs of the performance with respect to the number of re-initializations with $M = 3$ and $N = 10$. We can see that moderate values, i.e. around 20 produce good results (though the marginal improvement over 10 is small, and so we might tradeoff performance versus communications costs if needed).

Figure 6 shows the performance of the algorithm with respect to σ (for $N = 10$ and $M = 3$). Note that there are only two curves here, as there is no possibility of independent nodes coming up with their own position estimated based on range alone. Clearly the results are not as good as those for problem 1. It will be interesting in the future to test whether we can improve the performance by improving the approximation for the likelihood function. However, at the least this demonstrates the possibility of performing this type of multi-target localization without information sharing.

5   Conclusion

This paper has demonstrated that a privacy-preserving approach can be used for multiple-target localization in sensor networks. The approach preserves location privacy of sensor nodes, as well as the performance of the individual sensors.

This paper presents work in progress. There are many questions left unanswered.

- Is it possible to prevent leakage even of the intermediate information (the series of position estimates);
- how can we weaked the honest-but-curious assumption;
- can the performance be improved for larger numbers of targets;
- how could we mesh this type of localization algorithm with tracking algorithms such as multi-hypothesis tracking;
- how should we approach the problem when not all sensors can see the same set of targets; and
- are there approaches which could further minimize the communications cost (this is important in the context of sensor networks where nodes may have a limited power budget)?

References

1. Atallah, M., Bykova, M., Li, J., Frikken, K., Topkara, M.: Private collaborative forecasting and benchmarking. In: Proc. of the ACM Workshop on Privacy in the Electronic Society (WPES'04), Washington, DC (October 2004)
2. Benaloh, J.: Secret sharing homomorphisms: Keeping shares of a secret secret. In: Odlyzko, A.M. (ed.) CRYPTO '86. LNCS, vol. 263, pp. 251–260. Springer, Heidelberg (1987)
3. Brickell, J., Shmatikov, V.: Privacy-preserving graph algorithms in the semi-honest model. In: Roy, B. (ed.) ASIACRYPT 2005. LNCS, vol. 3788, pp. 236–252. Springer, Heidelberg (2005)
4. Clifton, C., Kantarcioglu, M., Vaidya, J., Lin, X., Zhu, M.: Tools for privacy preserving distributed data mining. In: SIGKDD Explorations, vol. 4(2) (December 2002)

5. Patwari, N., Hero, A.O., Costa, J.A.: Learning Sensor Location from Signal Strength and Connectivity. Springer, Heidelberg (2006) (to appear, chapter)
6. Roughan, M., Arnold, J.: Data fusion without data fusion: localization and tracking without sharing sensitive information. In: Information, Decision and Control (IDC), Adelaide, Australia (February 2007)
7. Roughan, M., Zhang, Y.: Secure distributed data-mining and its application to large-scale network measurements. SIGCOMM Comput. Commun. Rev. 36(1), 7–14 (2006)
8. Shang, Y., Ruml, W., Zhang, Y., Fromherz, M.: Localization from mere connectivity. In: MobiHoc'03, Annapolis, Maryland (2003)
9. Verykios, V.S., Bertino, E., Fovino, I.N., Provenza, L.P., Saygin, Y., Theodoridis, Y.: State-of-the-art in privacy preserving data mining. SIGMOD Record 33(1), 50–57 (2004)
10. Yao, A.: Protocols for secure computations. In: Proc. of the 23th IEEE Symposium on Foundations of Computer Science (FOCS), pp. 160–164 (1982)
11. Yao, A.: How to generate and exchange secrets. In: Proc. of the 27th IEEE Symposium on Foundations of Computer Science (FOCS), pp. 162–167 (1986)

On the Effectiveness of Changing Pseudonyms to Provide Location Privacy in VANETs

Levente Buttyán, Tamás Holczer, and István Vajda

Laboratory of Cryptography and System Security (CrySyS)
Budapest University of Technology and Economics
{buttyan,holczer,vajda}@crysys.hu

Abstract. The promise of vehicular communications is to make road traffic safer and more efficient. However, besides the expected benefits, vehicular communications also introduce some privacy risk by making it easier to track the physical location of vehicles. One approach to solve this problem is that the vehicles use pseudonyms that they change with some frequency. In this paper, we study the effectiveness of this approach. We define a model based on the concept of the *mix zone*, characterize the tracking strategy of the adversary in this model, and introduce a metric to quantify the level of privacy enjoyed by the vehicles. We also report on the results of an extensive simulation where we used our model to determine the level of privacy achieved in realistic scenarios. In particular, in our simulation, we used a rather complex road map, generated traffic with realistic parameters, and varied the strength of the adversary by varying the number of her monitoring points. Our simulation results provide detailed information about the relationship between the strength of the adversary and the level of privacy achieved by changing pseudonyms.

Keywords: location privacy, pseudonym, vehicular ad hoc network.

1 Introduction

Recently, initiatives to create safer and more efficient driving conditions have begun to draw strong support in Europe [4], in the US [25], and in Japan [1]. Vehicular communications will play a central role in this effort, enabling a variety of applications for safety, traffic efficiency, driver assistance, and entertainment. However, besides the expected benefits, vehicular communications also have some potential drawbacks. In particular, many envisioned safety related applications require that the vehicles continuously broadcast their current position and speed in so called *heart beat* messages. This allows the vehicles to predict the movement of other nearby vehicles and to warn the drivers if a hazardous situation is about to occur. While this can certainly be advantageous, an undesirable side effect is that it makes it easier to track the physical location of the vehicles just by eavesdropping these heart beat messages.

One approach to solve this problem is that the vehicles broadcast their messages under pseudonyms that they change with some frequency [18]. The change

F. Stajano et al. (Eds.): ESAS 2007, LNCS 4572, pp. 129–141, 2007.

of a pseudonym means that the vehicle changes all of its physical and logical adresses at the same time. Indeed, in most of the applications, the important thing is to let other vehicles know that there is a vehicle at a given position moving with a given speed, but it is not really important which particular vehicle it is. Thus, using pseudonyms is just as good as using real identifiers as far as the functionality of the applications is concerned. Obviously, these pseudonyms must be generated in such a way that a new pseudonym cannot be directly linked to previously used pseudonyms of the same vehicle.

Unfortunately, changing pseudonyms is largely ineffective against a global eavesdropper that can hear all communications in the network. Such an adversary can predict the movement of the vehicles based on the position and speed information in the heart beat messages, and use this prediction to link different pseudonyms of the same vehicle together with high probability. For instance, if at time t, a given vehicle is at position p and moves with speed v, then after some short time τ, this vehicle will most probably be at position $p + \tau \cdot v$. Therefore, the adversary will know that the vehicle that reports itself at (or near to) position $p + \tau \cdot v$ at time $t + \tau$ is the same vehicle as the one that reported itself at position p at time t, even if in the meantime, the vehicle changed pseudonym.

On the other hand, the assumption that the adversary can eavesdrop all communications in the network is a very strong one. In practice, it is more reasonable to assume that the adversary can monitor the communications only at a limited number of places and only in a limited range. In this case, if a vehicle changes its pseudonym within the non-monitored area, then there is a chance that the adversary loses its trace. Our goal in this paper is to characterize this chance as a function of the strength of the adversary (i.e., its monitoring capabilities). In particular, our main contributions are the following:

- We define a model in which the effectiveness of changing pseudonyms can be studied. We emphasize that while changing pseudonyms has already been proposed in the literature as a countermeasure to track vehicles [18], to the best of our knowledge, the effectiveness of this method has never been investigated rigorously in this context. Our model is based on the concept of the *mix zone*. This concept was first introduced in [2], but again, to the best of our knowledge, it has not been used in the context of vehicular networks so far. We characterize the tracking strategy of the adversary in the mix zone model, and we introduce a metric to quantify the level of privacy provided by the mix zone.
- We report on the results of an extensive simulation where we used our model to determine the level of privacy achieved in realistic scenarios. In particular, in our simulation, we used a rather complex road map, generated traffic with realistic parameters, and varied the strength of the adversary by varying the number of her monitoring points. As expected, our simulation results confirm that the level of privacy decreases as the strength of the adversary increases. However, in addition to this, our simulation results provide detailed information about the relationship between the strength of the adversary and the level of privacy achieved by changing pseudonyms.

The organization of the paper is the following: In Section 2, we introduce the mix zone model, we define the behavior of the adversary in this model, and we introduce our privacy metric. In Section 3, we describe our simulation setting and the simulation results. Finally, we report on some related work in Section 4, and conclude the paper in Section 5.

2   Model

2.1   The Concept of the Mix Zone

We consider a continuous part of a road network, such as a whole city or a district of a city. We assume that the adversary installed some radio receivers at certain points of the road network with which she can eavesdrop the communications of the vehicles, including their heart beat messages, in a limited range. On the other hand, outside the range of her radio receivers, the adversary cannot hear the communications of the vehicles.

Thus, we divide the road network into two distinct regions: the observed zone and the unobserved zone. Physically, these zones may be scattered, possibly consisting of many observing *spots* and a large unobserved area, but logically, the scattered observing spots can be considered together as a single observed zone. This is illustrated in Part (a) of Figure 1.

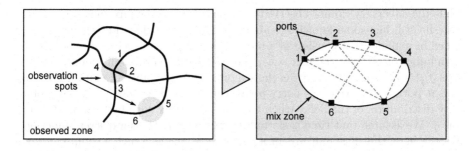

Fig. 1. Part (a) illustrates how a road network is divided into an observed and an unobserved zone in our model. In the figure, the observed zone is grey, and the unobserved zone is white. The unobserved zone functions as a *mix zone*, because the vehicles change pseudonyms and mix within this zone making it difficult for the adversary to track them. Part (b) illustrates how the road network on the left can be abstracted as single mix zone with six ports.

Note that the vehicles do not know where the adversary installed her radio receivers, or in other words, when they are in the observed zone. For this reason, we assume that the vehicles continuously change their pseudonyms[1]. In this paper,

---

[1] Otherwise, if the vehicles knew when they are in the unobserved zone, then it would be sufficient to change their pseudonyms only once while they are in the unobserved zone.

we abstract away the frequency of the pseudonym changes, and we simply assume that it is high enough so that every vehicle surely changes pseudonym while in the unobserved zone. We intend to relax this assumption in our future work.

Since the vehicles change pseudonyms while in the unobserved zone, that zone functions as a *mix zone* for vehicles (see Part (b) of Figure 1 for illustration). A mix zone [2,3] is similar to a mix node of a mix network [6], which changes the encoding and the order of messages in order to make it difficult for the adversary to link message senders and message receivers. In our case, the mix zone makes it difficult for the adversary to link the vehicles that emerge from the mix zone to those that entered it earlier. Thus, the mix zones makes it difficult to track vehicles. On the other hand, based on the observation that we made in the Introduction, we assume that the adversary can track the physical location of the vehicles while they are in the observed zone, despite the fact that they may change pseudonyms in that zone too.

Since the vehicles move on roads, they cannot cross the border between the mix zone and the observed zone at any arbitrary point. Instead, the vehicles cross the border where the roads cross it. We model this by assuming that the mix zone has *ports*, and the vehicles can enter and exit the mix zone only via these ports. For instance, in Part (b) of Figure 1, the ports are numbered from 1 to 6.

2.2   The Model of the Mix Zone

While the adversary cannot observe the vehicles within the mix zone, we assume that she still has some knowledge about the mix zone. This knowledge is subsumed in a model that consists of a matrix $Q = [q_{ij}]$ of size $M \times M$, where M is the number of ports of the mix zone, and M^2 discrete probability density functions $f_{ij}(t)$ $(1 \leq i, j \leq M)$. q_{ij} is the conditional probability of exiting the mix zone at port j given that the entry point was port i. $f_{ij}(t)$ describes the probability distribution of the delay when traversing the mix zone between port i and port j. We assume that time is slotted, that is why $f_{ij}(t)$ is a discrete function. We note here, that it is unlikely for an attacker to achieve such a comprehensive knowledge of the mix zone. However it is not impossible with comprehensive real world measurements to approximate the needed probabilities and functions. In the rest of the paper, we consider the worst case (as it is advisable in the field of security), the attacker knows the model of the mix zone.

2.3   The Operation of the Adversary

The adversary knows the model of the mix zone and she observes *events*, where an event is a pair consisting of a port (port number) and a time stamp (time slot number). There are entering events and exiting events corresponding to vehicles entering and exiting the mix zone, respectively. Naturally, an entering event consists of the port where the vehicle entered the mix zone, and the time when this happened. Similarly, an exiting event consists of the port where the vehicle left the mix zone, and the time when this happened.

The general objective of the adversary is to relate exiting events to entering events. More specifically, in our model, the adversary picks a vehicle v in the observed zone and tracks its movement until it enters the mix zone. In the following, we denote the port at which v entered the mix zone by s. Then, the adversary observes the exiting events for a time T such that the probability that v leaves the mix zone before T is close to 1 (i.e., $\Pr\{t_{out} < T\} = 1 - \epsilon$, where ϵ is a small number, typically, in the range of $0.005 - 0.01$, and t_{out} is the random variable denoting the time at which the selected vehicle v exits the mix zone). For each exiting vehicle v', the adversary determines the probability that v' is the same as v. For this purpose, she uses her observations and the model of the mix zone. Finally, she decides which exiting vehicle corresponds to the selected vehicle v.

The decision algorithm used by the adversary is intuitive and straightforward: The adversary knows that the selected vehicle v entered the mix zone at port s and in timeslot 0. For each exiting event $k = (j, t)$ that the adversary observes afterwards, she can compute the probability p_{jt} that k corresponds to the selected vehicle as $p_{jt} = q_{sj}f_{sj}(t)$ (i.e., the probability that v chooses port j as its exit port given that it entered the mix zone at port s multiplied by the probability that it covers the distance between ports s and j in time t). The adversary decides for the vehicle for which p_{jt} is maximal. The adversary is successful if the decided vehicle is indeed v.

Indeed, the above described decision algorithm realized the Bayesian decision (see the Appendix for more details). The importance of this fact is that the Bayesian decision minimizes the error probability, thus, it is in some sense the ideal decision algorithm for the adversary.

2.4   The Level of Privacy Provided by the Mix Zone

There are various metrics to quantify the level of privacy provided by the mix zone (and the fact that the vehicles continuously change pseudonyms). A natural metric in our model is the success probability of the adversary when making her decision as described above. If the success probability is large, then the mix zone and changing pseudonyms are ineffective. On the other hand, if the success probability of the adversary is small, then tracking is difficult and the system ensures location privacy.

We note that the level of privacy is often measured using the anonymity set size as the metric [5], however, in our case, this approach cannot be used. The problem is that as described above, with probability ϵ, the selected vehicle v is not in the set V of vehicles exiting the mix zone during the experiment of the adversary, and therefore, by definition, V cannot be the anonymity set for v. Although, the size of V could be used as a lower bound on the real anonymity set size, there is another problem with the anonymity set size as privacy metric. Namely, it is a an appropriate privacy metric only if each member of the set is equally likely to be the target of the observation, however, as we will see in Section 3, this is not the case in our model.

Obviously, the success probability of the adversary is very difficult to determine analytically due to the complexity of our model. Therefor, we ran simulations to determine its empirical value in realistic situations. The simulation setting and parameters, as well as the simulation results are described in the next section.

3   Simulations

The purpose of the simulation was to get an estimation of the success probability of the attacker in realistic scenarios. In this section, we first describe our simulation settings, and then, we present the simulation results.

3.1   Simulation Settings

The simulation was carried out in three main phases. In the first phase, we generated a realistic map, where the vehicles moved during the simulation. This map was generated by MOVE [15], a tool that allows the user to quickly generate realistic mobility models for vehicular network simulations. Our map is illustrated in Figure 2. In fact, it is a simplified map of Budapest, the capital of Hungary, and it contains the main roads of the city . We believe that despite of the simplifications, this map is still complex enough to get realistic traffic scenarios.

The second phase of the simulation was to generate the movement of the vehicles on the generated map. This was done by SUMO [24], which is an open source micro-traffic simulator, developed by the Center for Applied Informatics (ZAIK) and the Institute of Transport Research at the German Aerospace Center. SUMO dumps the state of the simulation in every time step into files. This state dump contains the location and the velocity of every vehicle during the simulation.

In the third phase of the simulation, we processed the state dump generated by SUMO, and simulated the adversary. This part of the simulation was written in Perl, because Perl scripts can easily process the XML files generated by SUMO. Note that for the purpose of repeatability, we made the source code available on-line at http://www.crysys.hu/~holczer/ESAS07.

We implemented the adversary as follows. First, we defined the observation spots (position and radius) of the adversary in a configuration file. Then, we let the adversary build her model of the mix zone (i.e., the complement of its observation spots) by allowing her to track the vehicles as if they do not change their pseudonyms. In effect, the adversary's knowledge is represented by a set of two dimensional tables. Each table $K^{(i)}$ corresponds to a port i of the mix zone, and contains empirical probabilities. More specifically, the entry $K_{jt}^{(i)}$ of table $K^{(i)}$ contains the empirical probability that a vehicle exits the mix zone at port j in time t given that it entered the mix zone at port i at time 0. The size of the tables is $M \times T$, where M is the number of the ports of the mix zone and T is the duration of the learning procedure defined as the time until which every observed vehicle left the mix zone. Once the adversary's knowledge is built, she could use that for making decisions as described above in Section 2. We executed several simulation runs in order to get an estimation for the success probability of the adversary.

We made experiments with adversaries of different strength, where the strength of the adversary depends on the number of her eavesdropping receivers.

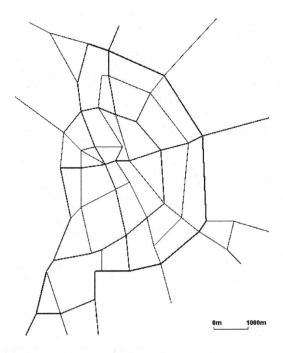

Fig. 2. Simplified map of Budapest generated for the simulation

In the simulations, all receivers were deployed in the middle of the junctions of the roads. The eavesdropping radius of the receivers was set to 50 meter. The number of the receivers varied between 5 and 59 with a step size of 5 (note that the map contains 59 junctions). Always the junctions with the highest traffic was chosen as the observation spots of the adversary (for instance, when the adversary had ten receivers, we chose the first ten junctions with the largest traffic).

In addition to the strength of the adversary, we varied the intensity of the traffic. More specifically, we simulated three types of traffic: low, medium, and high. Low traffic means that in each time step 250 vehicles are emitted into the traffic flow, medium traffic is defined as 500 vehicles are emitted into the flow, and in case of high traffic 750 vehicles are emitted.

For each simulation setting (strength of the adversary and intensity of the road traffic) we ran 100 simulations.

3.2 Simulation Results

Figure 3 contains the resulting success probabilities of the adversary as a function of her strength. The different curves belong to different traffic intensities. The results are quite intuitive: we can conclude that the stronger the adversary, the higher her success probability. Note, however, that from above a given strength, the success probability saturates at about 60 %. Higher success probabilities

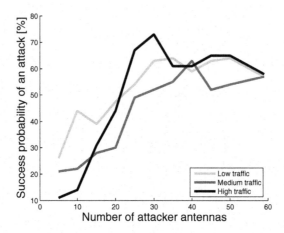

Fig. 3. Success probabilities of the adversary as a function of her strength. The three curves represent three different scenarios (the darker the line, the more intensive the traffic).

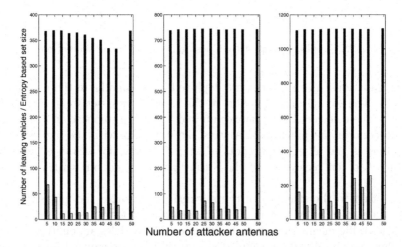

Fig. 4. The dark bars show how the size of the set V of the vehicles that exit the mix zone during the observation period varies with the strength of the adversary. The three sub-figures are related to the three different traffic situations (low traffic – left, medium traffic – middle, high traffic – right). The light bars illustrate the effective size of V. As we can see, the effective size is much smaller than the real size, which means that distribution corresponding to the members of V is highly non-uniform.

can not be achieved, because the order of the vehicles may change between junctions without the adversary being capable of tracking that. Note also that the saturation point is reached with the control of only the half of the junctions. The intensity of the traffic is much less important parameter, than the strength of the attacker. The success probability of the attacker is nearly independent from the intensity of the traffic above a given attacker strength..

The dark bars in Figure 4 show how the size of the set V of the vehicles that exit the mix zone during the observation period and from which the adversary has to decide to the selected vehicle varies with the strength of the adversary. The three sub-figures are related to the three different traffic situations (low traffic – left, medium traffic – middle, high traffic – right). While the size of V seems to be large (which seemingly makes the adversary's decision difficult), it is also interesting to examine how uniform this set V is in terms of the probabilities assigned to the vehicles in V. Recall that the adversary computes a probability p_{jt} for each vehicle v' in V, which is the probability of $v' = v$. These probabilities can be normalized to obtain a distribution, and the entropy of this distribution can be computed. From this entropy, we computed the effective size of V (i.e., the size to which V can be compressed due to the non-uniformity of the distribution over its members), and the light bars in the figure illustrate the obtained values. As we can see, the effective size of V is much smaller than its real size, which means that distribution corresponding to the members of V is highly non-uniform. This is the reason why the adversary can be successful.

4   Related Work

The privacy of VANET's is a recent topic. Many author addressed the whole problem in some papers (for example in [9,14,18,19]). The problem of providing location privacy for VANET's is categorised in [10], into classes. The difference between the classes is the goal and the strength of the attacker. In [7], Choy, Jakobsson and Wetzel investigates how to obtain a balance between privacy and audit requirements in vehicular networks using only symmetric primitives.

Many privacy preserving techniques are suggested for on-line transactions (for example in [5,11]). Mainly they are based on mix networks [16,20], which was basically proposed by Chaum in 1981 [6]. A single mix collect messages mixes them and send them towards their destination. A mix networks consits of single mixes, which are linked together. In a mix network, some misbehaving mixes can not break the anonimity of the senders/receivers.

An evident extension of mix networks to the off-line world is the the mix zones, proposed by Beresford et al. in [2,3]. A mix zone is a place where the users of the network are mixed, thus after leaving the mix zone, they can not be distinguished from each other.

The problem of providing location privacy in wireless communication is well studied by Hu and Wang in [12]. They built a transaction-based wireless communication system in which transactions are unlinkable, and give a detailed simulation results. Their solution can provide location privacy for real-time applications as well.

To qualify the operation of the mix zones, the offered anonomity must be measured. The first metric was proposed by Chaum [5], was the size of the anonimity set. It is good metric only if any user leaving the mix zone is the target with the same probability. If the probabilities are different, then entropy based metric should be used. Entropy based metrics were suggested by Díaz et. al [8] and Serjantov *et al.* [23] at the same time.

For the best of our knowledge, the most relevant paper to this work is done by Sampigethaya *et al.* in [21]. In the paper, they study the problem of providing location privacy in VANET in the presence of a global adversary. A location privacy scheme called CARAVAN is also proposed. The main idea of the scheme is that random silent period [13] are used in the communication to avoid continous traceability. The solution is evaluated only in freeway model and in randomly generated manhattan street model.

The change of pseudonyms may also have a detrimental effect, especially on the efficiency of routing and the packet loss ratio. In [22], Schoch *et al.* investigated this problem and proposed a some approaches that can guide system designers to achieve both a given level of privacy protection as well a reasonable level of performance.

5 Conclusion and Future Work

In this paper, we studied the effectiveness of changing pseudonyms to provide location privacy for vehicles in vehicular networks. The approach of changing pseudonyms to make location tracking more difficult was proposed in prior work, but its effectiveness has not been investigated yet. In order to address this problem, we defined a model based on the concept of the mix zone. We assumed that the adversary has some knowledge about the mix zone, and based on this knowledge, she tries to relate the vehicles that exit the mix zone to those that entered it earlier. We also introduced a metric to quantify the level of privacy enjoyed by the vehicles in this model. In addition, we performed extensive simulations to study the behavior of our model in realistic scenarios. In particular, in our simulation, we used a rather complex road map, generated traffic with realistic parameters, and varied the strength of the adversary by varying the number of her monitoring points. Our simulation results provided detailed information about the relationship between the strength of the adversary and the level of privacy achieved by changing pseudonyms.

In this paper, we abstracted away the frequency with which the pseudonyms are changed, and we simply assumed that this frequency is high enough so that every vehicle surely changes pseudonym while in the mix zone. In our future work, we intend to relax this simplifying assumption, and we want to study how the level of privacy depends on the frequency of the pseudonym changes. It seems that changing the pseudonyms frequently has some advantages as frequent changes increase the probability that the pseudonym is changed in the mix zone. On the other hand, the higher the frequency, the larger the cost that the pseudonym changing mechanism induces on the system in terms of management of cryptographic material (keys and certificates related to the pseudonyms). In addition, if for a given frequency, the probability of changing pseudonym in the mix zone is already close to 1, then there is no sense to increase the frequency further as it will no longer increase the level of privacy, while it will still increase the cost. Hence, there seems to be an optimal value for the frequency of the pseudonym change. Unfortunately, this optimal value depends on the characteristics of the mix zone, which is ultimately determined by the observing zone of the adversary, which is not known to the system designer. In our future work, we want to characterize this dependence in more details.

Acknowledgements

This work has partially been supported by the European Commission through the SeVeCom Project (IST-027795), by the Hungarian Scientific Research Fund (T046664), and by the Mobile Innovation Center, Hungary (www.mik.bme.hu).

References

1. Advanced Safety Vehicle Program,
   http://www.ahsra.or.jp/demo2000/eng/demo_e/ahs_e7/iguchi/iguchi.html
2. Beresford, A.R., Stajano, F.: Location privacy in pervasive computing. IEEE Pervasive Computing 3(1), 46–55 (2003)
3. Beresford, A., Stajano, F.: Mix Zones: User privacy in location-aware services. In: Proceedings of First IEEE International Workshop on Pervasive Computing and Communication Security (PerSec) 2004, a workshop in PerCom (2004)
4. Communications for eSafety http://www.comesafety.org/
5. Chaum, D.: The Dining Cryptographers Problem: Unconditional sender and recipient untraceability. Journal of Cryptology 1(1), 65–75 (1988)
6. Chaum, D.: Untraceable electronic mail, return addresses, and digital pseudonyms, Communications of the ACM, vol. 4 (February 981)
7. Choi, J.Y., Jakobsson, M., Wetzel, S.: Balancing Auditability and Privacy in Vehicular Networks. In: Proceedings of International Workshop on QoS and Security for Wireless and Mobile Networks (Q2SWinet 2005), ACM Press, New York (2005)
8. Díaz, C., Seys, S., Claessens, J., Preneel, B.: Towards measuring anonymity. In: Dingledine, R., Syverson, P.F. (eds.) PET 2002. LNCS, vol. 2482, pp. 54–68. Springer, Heidelberg (2003)
9. Doetzer, F.: Privacy issues in vehicular ad hoc networks. In: Workshop on Privacy Enhancing Technologies, Cavtat, Croatia (May 2005)
10. Gerlach, M.: Assessing and Improving Privacy in VANETs. In: ESCAR, Embedded Security in Cars (2006)
11. Gülcü, C., Tsudik, G.: Mixing E-mail With Babel. In: Proceedings of the Network and Distributed Security Symposium - NDSS '96, February 1996, pp. 2–16. IEEE Computer Society Press, Los Alamitos (1996)
12. Hu, Y.C., Wang, H.J.: A Framework for Location Privacy in Wireless Networks. In: Proceedings of the ACM SIGCOMM Asia Workshop 2005, April 2005, ACM, Bejing, China (2005)
13. Huang, L., Matsuura, K., Yamane, H., Sezaki, K.: Enhancing Wireless Location Privacy Using Silent Period. In: IEEE Wireless Communications and Networking Conference (WCNC 2005), IEEE Computer Society Press, Los Alamitos (2005)
14. Hubaux, J.P., Čapkun, S., Luo, J.: The security and privacy of smart vehicles. IEEE Security and Privacy 4(3), 49–55 (2004)

15. Karnadi, F., Mo, Z., Lan, K.: Rapid Generation of Realistic Mobility Models for VANET. In: International Conference on Mobile Computing and Networking (ACM MOBICOMM 2005), ACM Press, New York (2005)
16. Kesdogan, D., Egner, J., Büschkes, R.: Stop-and-Go MIXes: Providing Probabilistic Anonymity in an Open System. In: Aucsmith, D. (ed.) Information Hiding. LNCS, vol. 1525, Springer, Heidelberg (1998)
17. Loca Project, http://www.loca-lab.org
18. Raya, M., Hubaux, J.P.: In: Proc. of Third ACM Workshop on Security of Ad Hoc and Sensor Networks (SASN 2005), Alexandria (November 2005)
19. Raya, M., Hubaux, J.P.: Securing Vehicular Ad Hoc Network (Special Issue on Security of Ad Hoc and Sensor Networks). Journal of Computer Security 15(1), 39–68 (2007)
20. Reiter, M., Rubin, A.: Crowds: Anonymity for Web Transactions. ACM Transactions on Information and System Security, 1 (1998)
21. Sampigethaya, K., Huang, L., Li, M., Poovendran, R., Matsuura, K., Sezaki, K.: Caravan: Providing location privacy for VANET. In: ESCAR 2005. Proc. of 3rd workshop on Embedded Security in Cars, Cologne, Germany (2005)
22. Schoch, E., Kargl, F., Leinmüller, T., Schlott, S., Papadimitratos, P.: Impact of Pseudonym Changes on Geographic Routing in VANETs. In: Buttyán, L., Gligor, V., Westhoff, D. (eds.) ESAS 2006. LNCS, vol. 4357, Springer, Heidelberg (2006)
23. Serjantov, A., Danezis, G.: Towards an information theoretic metric for anonymity. In: Dingledine, R., Syverson, P.F. (eds.) PET 2002. LNCS, vol. 2482, Springer, Heidelberg (2003)
24. SUMO Simulation of Urban MObility, http://sumo.sourceforge.net/
25. Vehicle Safety Communications Project
http://www-nrd.nhtsa.dot.gov/pdf/nrd-12/CAMP3/pages/VSCC.htm

A   Appendix

In this appendix, we show that the decision algorithm of the adversary described in Subsection 2.3 realizes a Bayesian decision. We use the following notations:

- k is an index of a vector. Every port-timeslot pair can be mapped to such an index and k can be mapped back to a port-timeslot pair. Therefore indices and port-timeslot pairs are interchangeable, and in the following discussion, we always use the one which makes the presentation simpler.
- $k \in 1 \ldots M \cdot T$, where M is the number of ports, and T is the length of the attack measured in timeslots.
- $C = [c_k]$ is a vector, where c_k is the number of cars leaving the mix zone at k during the attack.
- N is the number of cars leaving the mix zone before timeslot T (i.e., $N = \sum_{k=1}^{MT} c_k$).
- $p_s(k)$ is the probability of the event that the target vehicle leaves the mix zone at k (port and time) conditioned on the event that it enters the zone at port s at time 0. The attacker exactly knows which port is s. Probability $p_s(k)$ can be computed as: $p_s(k) = q_{sj} f_{sj}(t)$, where port j and timeslot t correspond to index k.

- $p(k)$ is the probability of the event that a vehicle leaves the mix zone at k (port and time). This distribution can be calculated from the input distribution and the transition probabilities: $p(k) = \sum_{s=1}^{M} p_s(k)$.
- $\Pr(k|C)$ is the conditional probability that the target vehicle left the mix zone at time and port defined by k, given that the attacker's observation is C.

We want to determine for which k probability $\Pr(k|C)$ is maximal. Let us denote this k with k^*. The probability $\Pr(k|C)$ can be rewritten, using the Bayes rule:

$$\Pr(k|C) = \frac{\Pr(C|k)p_s(k)}{\Pr(C)}$$

Then k^* can be computed as:

$$k^* = \arg\max_k \frac{\Pr(C|k)p_s(k)}{\Pr(C)} = \arg\max_k \Pr(C|k)p_s(k)$$

$\Pr(C|k)$ has a polynomial distribution with a condition that at least one vehicle (the target of the attacker) must leave the mix zone at k:

$$\Pr(C|k) = \frac{N!}{c_1!\ldots c_{k-1}!(c_k-1)!c_{k+1}!\ldots c_{MT}!}p(k)^{c_k-1} \prod_{j=1, j\neq k}^{MT} p(j)^{c_j}$$

$\Pr(C|k)$ can be multiplied and divided by $\frac{p_k}{c_k}$ to simplify the equation:

$$\Pr(C|k) = \frac{c_k}{p_k}\left(\frac{N!}{c_1!\ldots c_{MT}!}\prod_{j=1}^{MT} p(j)^{c_j}\right)$$

where the bracketed part is a constant, which does not have any effect on the maximization, thus it can be omitted.

$$k^* = \arg\max_k \frac{c_k}{p_k}p_s(k) = \arg\max_k \frac{c_k}{p_k N}p_s(k) = \arg\max_k \frac{\widehat{p_k}}{p_k}p_s(k)$$

where $\widehat{p_k}$ is the empirical distribution of k (i.e., $\widehat{p_k} = c_k/N$). If the number of vehicles in the mix zone is large enough, then $\frac{\widehat{p_k}}{p_k} \approx 1$. Thus correctness of the intuitive algorithm described in Subsection 2.3 holds:

$$k^* = \arg\max_k p_s(k)$$

This means that if many vehicles are travelling in the mix zone, then the attacker must choose the vehicle with the highest $p_s(k)$ probability.

"End-by-Hop" Data Integrity

Stephen Farrell[1] and Christian D. Jensen[2]

[1] Distributed Systems Group
Trinity College, Dublin 2, Ireland
`stephen.farrell@cs.tcd.ie`
[2] Informatics & Mathematical Modelling
Technical University of Denmark
`Christian.Jensen@imm.dtu.dk`

Abstract. Wireless sensor networks have been proposed for various applications, such as environmental monitoring and tactical military applications. For most of these applications sensors, scattered across a large physical area, organize themselves into a network that forwards data back to a central sink. Sensors are typically assumed to be severely constrained with respect to energy consumption, computational power and communication capabilities (especially the data rate and range of the transmitter). Data-centric networking, where forwarding nodes aggregate or filter data en-route to the central sink, have been proposed to reduce the amount of data transported in the network and conserve energy. This means that data-centric networks are significantly different from traditional end-to-end networks, because data are altered on every hop from the source to the sink.

Traditional end-to-end integrity mechanisms ensure that data cannot be modified on the way from the source to the destination. In data-centric networking, however, data is supposed to be altered on every hop from the source to the sink, so new integrity mechanisms must be investigated. In this paper we propose a new "end-by-hop" data integrity service that supports aggregation or filtering in data-centric networks. We also describe a mechanism that could be used to provide this service and provide an initial analysis of the efficiency and security of the mechanism proposed. One of the desirable properties of the proposed mechanism is that it allows the system architect to trade-off the computational load on the sensor nodes against a higher computational load at the sink, which we assume does not have the same severe resource limitations as the sensor nodes.

Keywords: data-integrity service, data-fusion security, end-by-hop security.

1 Introduction

Wireless sensor networks have been proposed for various applications, amongst others: environmental monitoring (air quality, radiation, presence or concentration of particular gasses, hours of sunshine in a location used by farmers or tourism

F. Stajano et al. (Eds.): ESAS 2007, LNCS 4572, pp. 142–155, 2007.

agencies, etc.) and tactical military applications. The integration of recent techno-logical advances in micro-processors, micro-electro-mechanical systems (MEMS) and wireless communications has ostensibly made it both technologically and eco-nomically possible to monitor a large physical area by scattering a high number of relatively cheap sensor nodes over the area, e.g., dropping them from a low flying airplane. In order to achieve the best coverage of the area at the lowest possible cost, sensor nodes have severe constraints on computational power; communica-tion bandwidth and range; and energy consumption. Directed diffusion [1], data aggregation [2,3] and data-centric networking [4,5,6] have been proposed to ad-dress energy conservation and other problems in severely resource constrained sen-sor networks, especially where the bandwidth available between nodes is very lim-ited. Although security has been identified as an important problem in sensor net-works, current proposals are inappropriate for severely resource-constrained net-works. Moreover, it can be shown that many data aggregation functions have poor resilience against faulty data from the senor nodes [7], which makes it important to develop appropriate integrity solutions for data-centric networks.

Data-centric networks are generally organized around a sink node, which ag-gregates the input from the individual sensors and communicates it to the outside world. By imposing an overlay network on the sensor network, e.g., a spanning tree routed in the sink node, intermediate nodes can apply inline aggregation or en-route filtering to significantly reduce the amount of communication in the network and thereby reduce resource consumption by the sensor nodes. It is im-portant to note that, although sensor nodes are assumed to be severely resource constrained, quite complex aggregation or filtering functions may be applied to reduce data communication, because the cost of transmitting data is often orders of magnitude higher than the cost of processing data, i.e., "the cost of running the radio is normally significantly higher than the cost of running the CPU."

Queries for sensor data will be propagated through the network from the sink node, which will also typically collect the final (aggregated) values from its direct neighbours and return it to the outside world. We assume that there is only one such sink node[1] and that this node does not have the same resource limitations on power, computation and storage as the other nodes (sensors) in the data-centric network; otherwise we assign the role of sink node to the first unconstrained host outside the data-centric network.

The following scenario describes one example of this type of networking, which will be used throughout this paper. Assume that we have a sensor network where the sink node s0, asks for the average temperature from its direct neighbour, s1. Node s1 then forwards that request to all the other nodes it knows about directly (its peers/children). Each of those answer and then s1 averages out the answers and gives that to s0. (The children of s1 have done the same of course.) Our problem is how to get some confidence in the integrity of the final answer.

Figure 1 shows the topology of an example like that described above, where s0 sends the initial query to s1, which forwards it to s2 and s3, etc.

---

[1] If more than one potential sink node exists, an election process can select a single root.

```
s0 - s1 - s2 - s4
     |    |
     s3   s5
```

Fig. 1. Data-centric networking example topology

The difficulties in meeting our integrity goal using current mechanisms include:

– Names or addresses are only visible for immediate peers; the other sensor nodes involved in the calculation are not seen by the originator of the query. This increases the difficultly of cryptographic key management.
– The response data (the average temperature) is changing at each node, which makes it difficult to see how standard cryptographic mechanisms, like digital signatures or MACs, may apply in this context.

The "traditional" method of getting end-to-end integrity in this context would have to be along the lines of:

– Each node includes a signature over the inputs to generating its response, i.e. inputs from neighbours and the query received from the sink.
– All signatures are added to the responses, plus the bits needed to reconstruct (possibly partially guessing) the inputs to signing (might not include all bits of measures, just low order bits).

Clearly such a scheme uses far too much bandwidth entirely defeating the purpose of data-centric networking. We therefore need to develop new integrity mechanisms for data-centric networks, which allow inline aggregation of both data and security fields.

The remainder of the paper is organized as follows: Section 2 presents our proposed integrity service for data-centric networks. Section 3 presents a set of mechanisms that implement the service. The proposed service is evaluated in Section 4. We survey related work in Section 5. An outline for future work is presented in Section 6 and Section 7 presents our conclusions.

2   The End-by-Hop Data Integrity Service

In the following we describe a new security service we call **end-by-hop data integrity**, which provides end-to-end integrity while modifying data at every hop. We start by describing the general architecture. This is followed by a presentation of our threat model, which examines possible attacks and identifies the attacks that our solution is designed to prevent.

As outlined above, we assume that sensor nodes respond to a query from an originator located outside the sensor network. As inline aggregation of data means that data will be modified on every hop within the sensor network, the originator needs the ability to verify that the aggregated result from the sensor network is an actual response to the query. This means that the originator should be able to verify that the query has not been altered on the way to the sensor nodes, e.g., that a query for an average temperature from a specific set of sensor nodes has not been changed to a query for a maximum temperature. The originator should also be able to verify that only data from the queried nodes have been included in the aggregated result and also which of the queried nodes, if any, have failed to respond. Finally, the originator should be able to verify that the requested aggregation function has been applied fairly by all nodes on the routes from the queried sensor nodes to the sink.

The end-by-hop data integrity mechanism therefore consists of two "sub"-services, **end-by-hop query integrity** and **end-by-hop response integrity**, defined below:

- Query integrity is a service that allows the originator to verify (maybe offline) that the query was unaltered in each step, and that all responses came from members of a configured set of nodes.
- Response integrity is a service where the originator can verify (again possibly offline) that the response generation function was applied fairly at each node.

In order to limit the communications overhead of providing these services, we require that both services be provided solely via the addition of (nearly) fixed length security fields to each message. The service should be efficient and secure against various spoofing and data modification attacks. However, since the definition of end-by-hop security is (as far as we know) quite new, one cannot expect a full security analysis at this stage. In consequence, one should be careful applying the ideas presented here in real applications until such further analysis is carried out.

In passing we note the following non-goals, which could fairly reasonably have been included as goals, but which we chose to omit for the present: we do not care about the partial order of the responses and we do not require that some nodes are definitely used in the calculation, though we can check which were used, but only after the fact.

3   End-by-Hop Integrity Mechanism

There are two ways that an attacker may manipulate communications in order to successfully violate the integrity of the answer generated by the network: either by changing the query, so that sensors reply to the wrong question or by changing (some of) the replies generated by sensors in the network. We address each of these problems separately in the following.

3.1   Query Integrity

We first demonstrate how to provide basic query integrity, i.e., ensuring that the query is presented properly to each sensor. This mechanism has relatively low computational and communication overhead in the sensor network, but requires some computation on the originating node (s0). We then discuss an improvement to this mechanism, which reduces the computation required on the originating node at the cost of higher communication overhead. Both of these mechanisms allow the originating node to detect whether a malicious node has changed the query, e.g., changing the query for the average temperature to a query for the maximum temperature in an attempt to corrupt the responses from all nodes "after" the malicious node.

Basic Query Integrity. Each sensor is given a Diffie-Hellman (D-H) [8] value (possibly with the public values in an X.509 certificate[2] [9]). Storing these public values in a certificate that should be available to s0 prevents the man-in-the-middle attack normally associated with the Diffie-Hellman key exchange – a potential man-in-the-middle will be unable to impersonate the sensor nodes, but he will still be able to impersonate s0, i.e., to query the sensor network for himself. All of the D-H parameters should be the same for the entire set of sensors; otherwise we would require too much bandwidth.

The query message sent from s0 should contain the query string (e.g. "average temperature" or equivalent) and a nonce. We represent (the encoding of) both of these as q. The query message should also contain the public D-H value (g^x) from s0. The nonce is used because there are probably very few queries so cut-and-paste attacks would be a problem. One also might want to whiten q (e.g., using something like OAEP [10]) to remove structure from the values.

When a node receives a query message containing q and g^x it forwards the unmodified query, including both of these fields, to all of its peer/child nodes. When the node has gotten all the answers (or timed out, which we treat as if that child did not exist), then it calculates its own response message.

Each response message contains a "Query integrity field" (QuIF) which is calculated as follows:

First, the node calculates the D-H shared secret, KK, (shared with s0) using g^x (provided in the query) and the node's own D-H secret. So, $KK = KDF(g^{xy})$ where y is this node's D-H secret and KDF is some key derivation function. This allows the node to calculate the QuIF for its response as follows:

$$QuIF = q^{f(KK)} \cdot \prod_{child} (QuIF_{child}) \bmod p \quad (\text{where } p \text{ is the D-H prime}) .$$

If a node has no peers/children then clearly the QuIF is simply:

$$QuIF = q^{f(KK)} \bmod p .$$

The function $f()$ above is required for good cryptographic hygiene, given that we will also want the KK in order to provide response integrity, but $f(KK)$ must also be as long as p and $f(KK)$ values should be evenly distributed modulo $p - 1$, so simply hashing is not sufficient (as the eventual sum of the $f(KK)$'s may be more easily guessable). One might use a pesudo-random function (PRF) like KDF2 [11].

If all nodes are honest, then the QuIF in the final response message will be some power of q, say $QuIFfinal = q^F$, where F is the sum of the $f(KK)$ values which were used at the various nodes.

---

[2] In an implementation the information in these certificates (e.g. via some location based naming scheme) could also assist the verifier in more efficiently identifying the nodes that would be potentially involved in answering the query.

Our sink node s0 can now validate this since it knows all of the KK values, given that all of the other sensors' public D-H values are in their certificates (and assuming s0 has access to all those certificates). If the validation is successful then all sensors have replied to the unmodified request.

But to validate q^F node s0 has to search among the all the possible sums of the $f(KK)$ which can be quite a large calculation.

If the entire sensor population numbers n, and k sensors were involved in responding to a given query then s0 will have to search a space of size $_nC_k$ [12]. However, given that in general s0 does not know how many nodes were actually involved in the calculation[3] a bigger space needs to be searched (roughly, $\sum_{k=1..e}(_nC_k)$ where e is the maximum number of sensors expected to be involved in processing a query).

If k is small and n is not too large then this should be feasible. For example, with $n = 100$ and $k = 5$, there are "only" 75,287,520 possible combinations. If somewhere between 2 and 5 nodes can be involved in processing the query then there are 79,375,395 combinations possible. While this may seem very large, it only represents searching less than a 28-bit space. If between 2 and 10 nodes might take part in the calculation, then we are dealing with an approximately 42-bit search space which represents quite a computational load!

Improved Query Integrity. There is another trade-off we can make between the computational load on s0 and the number of bits transmitted, basically, we assign an index to each node and then include a field which indicates the indices of the nodes which took part in the query response. Clearly, we cannot have a unique index for each node since that would not scale so we allow for index collisions, which is how we get a trade-off between bits transmitted and the computational load on s0.

We define an INDEX() function where INDEX(KK) could be Hash(KK) modulo A and we add a new A bit field (ANS) to our responses – each node that contributes to the QuIF sets its respective index bit, i.e. INDEX(KK) in the ANS field. S0 then has to manage collisions but has a reduced search space, depending on the size of ANS and the number of nodes. This affects the complexity of s0's search as follows, if I bits of the ANS field are set, then s0 has to check whether each of the nodes which are of index I have contributed to the calculation of the QuIF. If we assume that the INDEX() function uniformly distributes indices amongst the nodes, and that the ANS field is A bits wide, and that there are n nodes as before then each index bit represents n/A nodes on average. With I bits set this means that up to $n \cdot I/A$ nodes may have contributed to the QuIF, so the search space, again if we expect a maximum of e nodes to contribute is: $\sum_{k=1..e}((_{n \cdot I/A})C_k)$. With a 32-bit ANS field, of which say 7 bits are set, then our previously 45-bit search space is reduced to a 23-bit space.

Clearly, however there is a relationship between I, A and e – once e is more than the square-root of A, then the birthday paradox implies that collision

---

[3] This can clearly be improved upon if, as is likely, the query and response messages include some "TTL" or "hop count" field.

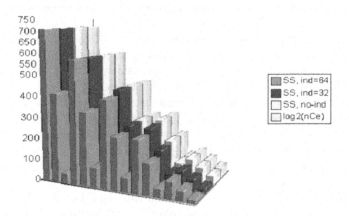

Fig. 2. Exponential increase in workload on s0   (see text for details)

probabilities will increase. In fact, we can estimate that $I = g(A,k)$, where the function $g(A,e)$ can be approximated by $g(A,e) = e - e/\sqrt{A}$.

Figure 2 shows how the search space (SS) for s0 [z-axis in bits] scales with increasing numbers of nodes (n =100,1000,10000) and expected answering-nodes (e =10,30, 50,70,90) [interspersed on the y-axis], for the cases where exactly e nodes answer, where between 2 and e nodes answer but without an ANS field, and the same but with 32 and 64 bit ANS fields. As can be seen, while the ANS field does extend the range of applicability of our scheme, the worst-case load on s0 is still increasing exponentially.

However, s0 can pre-calculate a table of potential F values, and, more importantly, it can re-use its knowledge once the very first query response has been successfully verified. Even if some nodes (e.g., s5 in the example) eventually die, then the processing at s0 is simplified for subsequent responses, because checking for the addition or subtraction of one or two nodes is simple.

3.2 Response Integrity

Having defined a mechanism for query integrity; we wish to extend this mechanism to ensure integrity on the averaged measurements.

We start by defining a "throttling" function, T, which can be applied to measurements to reduce the range of values so that they're more easily searchable (e.g., round() might be a good throttling function for a temperature application). The function to use depends on s0's willingness to do more work in order to get more accurate integrity checking on the measurements.

Further, say that the min and max temperature values seen by sensors are also included in messages (good practice anyway)[4].

---

[4] We ignore the handling of outliers which are not used in the averaging process for now – one could imagine that the throttling function might treat outliers as a special case which could then be handled at s0.

Each node calculates the value of $\text{HMAC}(g(\text{KK}), T(t))$[5] and XOR's that into a second security field (which we call MEASMAC). MEASMAC is a cumulative (XORing) cryptographic checksum from all previous responses.

When s0 gets the final response, and does the QuIF processing, it discovers the KK's that were used but not their ordering, though that's fine, since we're combining using XOR which is order insensitive. Given the KK's, and the min/max it is therefore possible to search the space of throttled measures and their corresponding HMAC's and thus to verify the final measure, at least to within some level of accuracy determined by the throttling function.

Verifying response integrity, given the set of KK's, (of which there are k), requires searching between min and max, with granularity G (i.e., TR = (max − min)$/G$ values, where TR is for throttle range), and checking for each trial HMAC value, whether it, combined with the other $k − 1$ trial values generates the final MEASMAC.

This means that we have k sets of trials each of size TR from which we must select a combination, in other words our worst case involves searching a k^{TR} sized space. The point is that this calculation is mainly dependent on the value of TR which must therefore be kept small, via the definition of a suitable throttling function. In a temperature application the min and max are unlikely to differ by much however, so TR will be small in any case.

In our example with 5 nodes used and temperature ranges between 18 and 26 degrees centigrade with a granularity of 1 degree, then we have, TR=8 and our worst-case search takes 390,625 trials.

Once we have identified the $T(t)$ values which were used in the MEASMAC calculation, then we also need to check that the claimed average temperature fits with this. If k nodes were involved in processing the query, and the throttling function involves rounding with a granularity of G, the test passes if the claimed average (CA) is within (TA−$G/2$, TA+$G/2$), where TA is the throttled average, which is the average calculated based on the KK's and throttled values which led to a correct MEASMAC check.

The security of the response integrity mechanism depends on the fact that nodes cannot "un-mix" each other's MEASMAC values. However, the min and max values are not currently protected so in applications where they are not obvious from context this may allow for some attacks.

In the above, we have assumed that responses are returned along the reverse of the path the query took. We could extend the mechanism so that the set of KK's is derived directly from the MEASMAC, which though more work is still do-able for small values, e.g., with TR= 8, $N = 100$, and k somewhere between 2 and 10, and 7 bits of the 32-bit ANS field set, this is a roughly 29 bit search space (the complexity becoming roughly $\sum_{k=1..e}((n \cdot I/A)C_k \cdot k^{\text{TR}})$.

---

[5] HMAC [13] is the well known secret key based data integrity function. The $g()$ function here is applied for similar reasons to the earlier $f()$ function and could also use the KDF2 function [11], perhaps with a different hash function from $f()$. t is the measured temperature.

4   Evaluation

In this section we present an evaluation of the proposed scheme from the security perspective.

4.1   Threat Model

There are essentially three ways that an attacker may try to control the output of a sensor network: she may try to control the environment, e.g., by artificially heating a temperature sensor; she may try to control the communication between the sink and the sensor nodes, e.g., by adding false nodes to the network; or she may try to control the sensor node itself, e.g., by capturing it, reverse engineering and extracting any key material that may allow her to spoof messages from this node. The integrity service proposed in this paper focuses on the second of these, i.e., protecting the integrity of communication in the data-centric sensor network.

The only way an attacker can interfere with communication in the network, without taking over any individual node, is by jamming all communication or by inserting additional nodes that fabricate, modify or delete messages exchanged between legitimate nodes in the network. Our mechanism must therefore ensure that input returned to the sink corresponds to the query, so that an intermediate node cannot modify the query in order to corrupt the result, e.g., modifying the query for an average temperature to the maximum temperature will change the result returned by the sub-tree and may significantly skew the result. Moreover, the mechanism must ensure that data incorporated into the aggregated result is not modified and that it originates from legitimate sensor nodes (to prevent fabrication).

Finally, although it may be something we would desire, with the current scheme, we cannot prevent an attacker who controls the environment or a dishonest node from skewing the calculation by ignoring some children and/or by not applying the aggregation function fairly. Whether this is a serious vulnerability or not would depend on the application environment. We can however, sometimes detect some such "attacks" though we probably cannot distinguish their occurrence from network failures. Similarly we cannot prevent an attacker who controls the network from deleting messages or partitioning the network in other ways.

4.2   Security Analysis

Given that there is a large space for q^F, it should be hard for an attacker to cause q^F to validate, without presenting the real query to honest nodes.

The basic security analysis required for this mechanism is to estimate the probability that an attacking node can generate a QuIFfinal which passes the test, but where the KK's found by the originator differ from those that were used (or not used!) generating the response.

First we need the probability that a random QuIFfinal (which is $< p$ by definition) will pass our test. Since there are only 2^n potentially valid QuIFfinal values[6], then, so long as $2^n \ll p$, the probability of a random QuIFfinal passing our test should be minimal.

So as currently defined, this mechanism is practically limited to cases where there are perhaps less than one hundred nodes in the network.

Other forms of cheating via manipulation of the QuIF values in responses would all appear to face the hurdle that the cheater cannot know the KK values, (assuming he doesn't know the private D-H values) and therefore is essentially reduced to randomly perturbing QuIFfinal.

Cheating could also be attempted via manipulation of the q or g^x values in the query. However, it is hard to see how this can result in a correct set of KK values resulting, given that we use a reasonable KDF to generate the KK's. (Even without the KDF, it is hard to see how this can benefit the attacker.)

So, we are, it appears, left with the original attack against which we can do nothing – a dishonest node may ignore or not communicate with some peers/children and/or misapply the averaging function or simply invent a measurement. However, as was stated earlier, assuming the first query is processed honestly, the verifier can detect when a previously included node is excluded from the calculation.

5 Related Work

Security is generally regarded as a major concern in wireless sensor networks and is attracting increasing attention [14,15,16], but most of these proposed solutions are general security solutions that are relatively heavyweight and not appropriate for severely resource constrained data-centric networks.

David Wagner [7] examines functions that can be used to aggregate data from sensors that may have been compromised, i.e., where the reporting node may be under the attackers control and attempt to skew the overall result by reporting exaggerated sensor input values. Some aggregation functions are more resilient to this form of attacks and the paper presents a theoretical framework for evaluating data aggregation functions. The paper only considers aggregation at the sink node, and not inline aggregation in the sensor network, which is the object of our investigation. This makes a significant difference, because not all aggregation functions are appropriate for inline aggregation. Consider, for example, a set of 5 sensors that report each of the numbers from 1 to 5 and wish to calculate the median, which is one of the resilient aggregation functions proposed by Wagner. If the underlying sensor network architecture is such that the aggregation is performed pairwise on the sorted list of sensor output, then it is important whether the network architecture is such that the aggregation is performed left-to-right or right-to-left (the medians are respectively 1.9375 or 4.0625,) but neither aggregation results in the correct answer which should be 3. Other, more complex, examples are easily constructed, but the above should

---

[6] Each QuIFfinal value is a combination of some of the n different $f(\text{KK})$'s, and there are 2^n possible combinations of n things.

be sufficient to illustrate that the underlying sensor network architecture may have a profound impact on the result of inline data aggregation.

Ye et al. present "statistical en-route filtering" [17] as a way to use a set of MACs to protect detection events in a sensor network. A core assumption of that work is that there are a number of nodes which all detect the actual event and the main goal is to detect that some subset of those nodes are generating incorrect event information. In contrast, here we are issuing a query which we protect and also allowing for application of a function (e.g. averaging) at each node on the path. The key management models also differ in that Ye et al. consider that asymmetric cryptography is too expensive for sensor nodes, whereas we consider that limited asymmetric operations may be more efficient than distribution of so many symmetric keys. As always, there is no clear winner in this trade-off, since which is better depends on a large number of specific factors. However some of the ideas from Ye could certainly be combined with our approach and such combinations may have merit in some environments.

Boneh et al. [18,19] present an aggregate signature technique which has some similarities to our scheme, but which is aimed at handling the case where multiple parties digitally sign the same message. In our case, the message is potentially being changed at each node and it is unclear whether their scheme can be easily extended to cover this case. Moreover, verification of their aggregate signature scheme requires access to all the original signatures, which defeats the purpose of data-centric networking.

6   Future Work

Clearly additional security analysis is needed as is further work on how the mechanism might be implemented in a real data-centric network. As part of that one would have to decide some details which are currently vague (e.g., the $f()$ function).

The query integrity mechanism here only works since the query is passed around the network unmodified. A more general mechanism might allow for some modifications of the query at each stage.

Work is also needed to extend or replace the response integrity mechanism for cases where functions unlike a simple average are used, for example, if some "outliers" are dropped, or if only a minimum or maximum is calculated. Cases where a sensor network simply reports on presence will also require a modified mechanism. However, once the query integrity mechanism is used, then the originator ends up sharing a secret with each the responding node, and that should be usable to derive the mechanism required.

We are only dealing here with a data integrity service; it is an open question as to whether or not it is also possible to define a useful generic end-by-hop data confidentiality service. However, we may be able to usefully extend our query integrity mechanism to provide a kind of confidentiality for a "presence" type application, say where the query result required is simply the number of nodes which notice the presence of some phenomenon.

This could work as follows, if we change the QuIF calculation so that each node uses $q^{f(\text{KK})}$ as before when it does not detect presence, but uses $q^{f(\text{KK})+1}$ when the phenomenon is present, then QuIFfinal will be $q^{F+\text{pres}}$ where "pres" is the number of nodes which detected presence. This increases the work s0 has to do by about a factor of n, which for small n should be acceptable. At first glance this appears to offer confidentiality (though without integrity) for such a presence application, but since we have not analysed the security of this service, nor whether more general messages could usefully be returned with confidentiality, we simply note the potential for future work here.

Similarly, for the average temperature application, if a result of TA (instead of the true average) were sufficient, then one could drop the average value from the response messages, since the MEASMAC values are sufficient to determine the throttled measurements. Such a protocol offers a similar confidentiality service to that described above.

End-by-hop integrity may also be of use for scenarios where unknown middle boxes are modifying data in transit on the Internet. We have elsewhere [20] analysed some of the security issues with "exotic" networks in a more general context. It may be worth examining whether the mechanisms presented here have broader applicability in other "exotic" contexts.

7   Conclusions

In this paper, we have addressed the problem of integrity in some active networks, in particular, sensor networks using so-called data-centric networking, where aggregation functions or filters may be applied on every intermediate hop between the source and the destination. Data-centric networks invalidate traditional end-to-end integrity services, so new integrity services need to be defined. We have defined the **end-by-hop integrity service**, which we believe is an interesting new security service for what is otherwise a "hard" case for current security technologies. We have also proposed a way to provide that service which we believe will be both practical and secure for some data-centric networks. However, given the limitations involved, we feel that it is likely that this mechanism may be more useful as a motivation to search for better ways to provide the new service.

The proposed integrity scheme has the following interesting properties: the possibility to trade-off computation effort between the sensor nodes and the sink node, the possibility to trade-off sink node computational complexity against bits transmitted and finally the mechanism for simply combining cryptographic values. The trade-off properties are particularly important for sensor networks, where data from thousands of sensor nodes may be processed on a large central server or in a computational grid application.

The proposed scheme, however, only addresses a subset of the security issues in sensor networks and only for a subset of the types of sensor networks and it, or equivalent schemes will have to be combined with other mechanisms in order to for us to provide truly useful security for sensor networks.

Acknowledgements

This work was carried out as part of the Dev-SeNDT project which is funded by Enterprise Ireland via its Commercialisation Fund.

References

1. Intanagonwiwat, C., Govindan, R., Estrin, D.: Directed diffusion: A scalable and robust communication paradigm for sensor networks. In: MobiCom 2000. Proceedings of 6th International Conference on Mobile Computing and Networking, Boston, Massachusetts, pp. 56–67 (2000)
2. Krishnamachari, B., Estrin, D., Wicker, S.: The impact of data aggregation in wireless sensor networks. In: Proceedings of the International Workshop on Distributed Event-Based Systems, Vienna, Austria, pp. 575–578 (2002)
3. Cristescu, R., Beferull-Lozano, B., Vetterli, M.: On network correlated data gathering. In: Proceedings of INFOCOM, Hong Kong (2004)
4. Esler, M., Hightower, J., Anderson, T.E., Boriello, G.: Next century challenges: Data-centric networking for invisible computing. In: MobiCom'99. Proceedings of the 5th International Conference on Mobile Computing and Networking, Seatle, Washington, pp. 256–262 (1999)
5. Heidemann, J.S., Silva, F., Intanagonwiwat, C., Govindan, R., Estrin, D., Ganesan, D.: Building efficient wireless sensor networks with low-level naming. In: SOSP 2001. Proceedings of the 18th ACM Symposium on Operating Systems Principles, Banff, Canada, pp. 146–159. ACM Press, New York (2001)
6. Chatterjea, S., Havinga, P.: A dynamic data aggregation scheme for wireless sensor networks. In: ProRisc 2003. Proceedings of the 14th Annual Workshop on Circuits, Systems and Signal Processing, Veldhoven, The Netherlands (2003)
7. Wagner, D.: Resilient aggregation in sensor networks. In: SASN '04. Proceedings of the 2004 ACM Workshop on Security of Ad Hoc and Sensor Networks, Washington, DC, pp. 78–87. ACM Press, New York (2004)
8. Diffie, W., Hellman, M.E.: New directions in cryptography. IEEE Transactions on Information Theory 22, 644–654 (1976)
9. Rescorla, E.: Diffie-hellman key agreement method. RFC 2631, IETF Network Working Group (1999)
10. Bellare, M., Rogaway, P.: Optimal asymmetric encryption. In: De Santis, A. (ed.) EUROCRYPT '94. LNCS, vol. 950, pp. 92–111. Springer, Heidelberg (1995)
11. Shoup, V.: A proposal for an ISO standard for public key encryption (version 2.1). Input for Committee ISO/IEC JTC 1/SC 27 (2001)
12. Ask Dr. Math FAQ : Permutations and combinations (April 15, 2006) Web-site last visited http://mathforum.org/dr.math/faq/faq.comb.perm.html
13. Krawczyk, H., Bellare, M., Canetti, R.: Hmac: Keyed-hashing for message authentication. RFC 2104, IETF Network Working Group (1997)
14. Perrig, A., Szewczyk, R., Wen, V., Culler, D., Tygar, J.: Spins: Security protocols for sensor networks. In: Proceedings of the 7th International Conference on Mobile Computing and Networking (MobiCom 2001), Rome, Italy, pp. 189–199 (2001)
15. Perrig, A., Stankovic, J., Wagner, D.: Security in wireless sensor networks. Communications of the ACM 47, 53–57 (2004)

16. Slijepcevic, S., Potkonjak, M., Tsiatsis, V., Zimbeck, S., Srivastava, M.B.: On communication security in wireless ad-hoc sensor networks. In: WETICE'02. Proceedings of the 11th IEEE International Workshops on Enabling Technologies: Infrastructure for Collaborative Enterprises, Pittsburgh, Pennsylvania, pp. 139–144. IEEE Computer Society Press, Los Alamitos (2002)

17. Ye, F., Luo, H., Lu, S., Zhang, L.: Statistical en-route detection and filtering of injected false data in sensor networks. In: Proceedings of IEEE INFOCOM 2004, Hong Kong, IEEE Computer Society Press, Los Alamitos (2004)

18. Boneh, D., Gentry, C., Lynn, B., Shacham, H.: A survey of two signature aggregation techniques. RSA's CryptoBytes, vol. 6 (2003)

19. Boneh, D., Gentry, C., Lynn, B., Shacham, H.: Aggregate and verifiably encrypted signatures from bilinear maps. In: Biham, E. (ed.) Advances in Cryptology – EUROCRPYT 2003. LNCS, vol. 2656, Springer, Heidelberg (2003)

20. Farrell, S., Seigneur, J.M., Jensen, C.D.: Security in exotic wireless networks. In: Jerman-Blažič, B., Schneider, W., Klobucar, T. (eds.) Security And Privacy In Advanced Networking Technologies. NATO Science Series: Computer & Systems Sciences, vol. 193, IOS Press, Amsterdam (2004)

Authenticating DSR Using a Novel Multisignature Scheme Based on Cubic LFSR Sequences

Saikat Chakrabarti, Santosh Chandrasekhar, Mukesh Singhal,
and Kenneth L. Calvert

Laboratory for Advanced Networking, Department of Computer Science,
University of Kentucky, Lexington KY 40506
{schak2,schan5,singhal}@cs.uky.edu, calvert@netlab.uky.edu

Abstract. The problem of secure routing in mobile ad hoc networks is long-standing and has been extensively studied by researchers. Recently, techniques of aggregating signatures have been applied to authenticate on demand routing protocols in mobile ad hoc networks. In this paper, we propose an efficient, single round multisignature scheme, CLFSR-M, constructed using cubic (third-order) linear feedback shift register (LFSR) sequences. The scheme, CLFSR-M is derived from a 2-party signature scheme CLFSR-S, formed using a well-known variant of the generalized ElGamal signature scheme. The multisignature has been engineered to produce an efficient technique to authenticate route discovery in the dynamic source routing (DSR) protocol. Our technique supports authentication of cached routes. Delegating special functions to nodes or assuming the existence of a trusted third party to distribute certified public keys is not practical in mobile ad hoc networks. We consider a fully distributed mechanism of public key distribution and present two variations of trust policies, based on PGP, for effective management of individual and aggregate public keys. Finally, we perform a theoretical analysis including correctness and security of CLFSR-M and also present a performance (computation and communication costs, storage overhead) comparison of the proposed scheme with existing ones.

Keywords: secure routing, DSR, multisignatures, generalized El Gamal signatures, LFSR-based PKCs, PGP, small-world graphs.

1 Introduction

Designing secure routing protocols for mobile ad hoc networks is a challenging task. Resource constraints of nodes, limited capacity of the wireless medium, node mobility and the cooperative, self-organized form of the network make it difficult to transfer techniques for securing traditional wired networks to the ad hoc networking environment. The dynamic source routing protocol (DSR) is perhaps the most popular on-demand source routing protocol designed for multi-hop wireless ad hoc networks [1]. DSR is simple and efficient in construction,

F. Stajano et al. (Eds.): ESAS 2007, LNCS 4572, pp. 156–171, 2007.

offers loop-free routing guarantees and load balancing, uses only soft-state, and is robust [1]. However, the original construction of DSR does not consider an adversarial model of the underlying network. Thus, DSR is vulnerable to several forms of attack by malicious nodes such as injection of bogus routing information and formation of feedback loops by colluding adversarial nodes [2,3].

This paper focusses on the following problem: how can a source node wanting to find a route to a destination be assured of the authenticity of the source route advertised in a received routing packet? We would like to guarantee this authenticity without imposing substantial overhead on the nodes that help in discovering routes. We propose an efficient, single round multisignature scheme (aggregate signature on the same message) to authenticate route discovery information in DSR. A number of enhancements and optimizations have been proposed for DSR so far; use of cached routes being one of the most significant ones made. Our scheme also works with *path caching* enabled [4].

Our multisignature scheme is derived from a cubic LFSR-based 2-party signature scheme [5], which uses a well-known variant of the generalized ElGamal signature scheme, EG I.4 [6]. Our scheme is efficient, requiring no prior cooperation to construct the multisignature. The efficiency of the proposed signature schemes can be partially attributed to the use of LFSR sequence-based public key cryptosystems, which employ reduced representations of finite field elements [7]. The security of LFSR-based PKCs is based on the difficulty of solving the discrete logarithm problem in the extension field $\mathbb{F}_{q^n}$ (contains q^n elements). However, all computations involving sequence terms are performed in the base field $\mathbb{F}_q$ (contains q elements). This leads to substantial savings, both in communication and computation overhead, for a desired security level.

We first present the basic idea behind authenticating routes in DSR assuming, for simplicity, all nodes have access to certified public keys of other nodes in the route. Distributing authentic public keys among nodes in a mobile ad hoc network to bootstrap authentication protocols is a challenging task. We discuss solutions using a trusted third party (TTP) to help in distributing certified public keys. However, assuming the existence of a TTP is paradigmatically unsuitable for ad hoc networks. Using the concepts of PGP [8] and previous results of the *small-world* property [9] exhibited in trust graphs in self-organized systems [10,11], we relax the assumption of the TTP and formulate policies for a fully distributed framework for individual and aggregate public key management.

The rest of the paper is organized as follows. We discuss related work in Section 2. In Section 3.1, we describe mathematical preliminaries of PKCs based on cubic LFSR sequences, and provide a short description of DSR. In Section 4, we describe techniques for authenticating route discovery in DSR based on multisignatures. We present a novel multisignature scheme in Section 5. In Section 6, we discuss a fully distributed mechanism of public key management. We provide a theoretical analysis of the proposed multisignature scheme in Section 7. Section 8 concludes the paper.

2   Related Work

The original design of DSR [1] did not incorporate any security mechanism, making it vulnerable to several attacks [2]. Papadimitratos et al. [12] and Hu et al. [13] independently proposed secure on-demand routing protocols, SRP and Ariadne, respectively, to authenticate routes using message authentication codes (MACs). In SRP, intermediate nodes in the route are not authenticated, thus exposing SRP to attacks, including addition and deletion of honest nodes from the route. In Ariadne, route request packets grow in size due to accumulation of MACs. Ariadne also requires loose time synchronization. Kim et al. [3] presented a generic DSR authentication protocol, SRDP, using MACs and aggregate signature schemes of [14,15,16]. SRDP does not consider authentication of routes using cached information. Moreover, the signature-based variants of SRDP have performance drawbacks, discussed in Section 7.3. Bhaskar et al. [17] developed a MAC based aggregate designated verifier signature scheme for authenticating DSR. The MAC-based scheme in [17] cannot authenticate cached routes. Moreover, MAC-based authentication protocols do not offer non-repudiation. Also, in MAC-based schemes, early detection of invalid MACs by intermediate nodes requires additional key setup overhead.

The concept of a multisignature was first proposed by Itakura et al. [18]. Horster et al. [6] proposed a generalized ElGamal signature scheme [19], integrating several ElGamal variants, including Schnorr's signature [20] and the DSA. Micali et al. [14] formalized the concept of multisignatures and proposed a three round multisignature scheme based on the Schnorr variant [20]. Multisignatures are a specialized form of aggregate signatures — Boneh et al. [15] first proposed the concept of a generalized aggregate signature scheme using efficiently computable bilinear maps. Lysyanskaya et al. [16] proposed sequential constructions of aggregate signatures using families of certified trapdoor permutations.

Capkun et al. [10] analyzed PGP trust graphs and showed that such graphs exhibited the small-world phenomenon [9,21]. Kleinberg [21] gave an algorithmic perspective to the small-world phenomenon. Capkun et al. [11] also proposed a PGP-like, self-organized public key management system for ad hoc networks.

Recently, new PKCs have emerged based on LFSR sequences under the Trace-DLP [7] assumption. The first PKC based on LFSR sequences was introduced by Niederreiter [22]. Gong et al. [23,24] and Lenstra et al. [25] independently proposed the GH-PKC and the XTR-PKC, respectively, using cubic LFSR sequences. We omit a discussion on higher order LFSR sequence-based PKCs in this paper, due to space constraints.

3   Background

We present a brief discussion of the mathematics underlying cubic LFSR sequences and PKCs constructed using cubic LFSR sequences. We also provide a short note on DSR, including possible optimizations of DSR.

3.1   Cubic LFSR Sequences and Related Public Key Cryptosystems

We provide a brief discussion of the cryptographic preliminaries needed to under-stand the construction of the proposed signature schemes based on cubic LFSR sequences.

A sequence of elements $\{s_k\} = s_0, s_1, \ldots$ over the finite field $\mathbb{F}_q$ is called a 3rd order homogeneous linear recurring sequence in $\mathbb{F}_q$ if for all $k \geq 0$:

$$s_{k+3} = c_0 s_{k+2} + c_1 s_{k+1} + c_2 s_k \tag{1}$$

where, $c_0, c_1, c_2 \in \mathbb{F}_q$ and s_k denotes the kth term of the sequence $\{s_k\}$. Such sequences can be efficiently generated by a special kind of electronic switching circuit, called LFSR. Consider the following monic irreducible polynomial over $\mathbb{F}_q$: $f(x) = x^3 - ax^2 + bx - 1$, where $a, b \in \mathbb{F}_q$. The sequence $\{s_k\}$ is said to be a cubic LFSR sequence generated by $f(x)$ if we have $c_0 = a$, $c_1 = b$ and $c_2 = 1$ in Equation 1, i.e., for all $k \geq 0$: $s_{k+3} = as_{k+2} - bs_{k+1} + s_k$. The polynomial $f(x)$ is called the *characteristic polynomial* of the sequence $\{s_k\}$ if, given a root α of $f(x)$, for all $k \geq 0$, we have $s_k = \alpha^k + \alpha^{kq} + \alpha^{kq^2}$, where $\alpha \in \mathbb{F}_{q^3}$. The sequence $\{s_k\}$ is called the third-order *characteristic sequence* generated by $f(x)$ (or by α). The initial state (kth state denoted as $\bar{s}_k = \{s_k, s_{k+1}, s_{k+2}\}$) of the characteristic sequence of $f(x)$ is given by $\bar{s}_0 = \{3, a, a^2 - 2b\}$ [7].

Recently, two PKCs, namely, GH-PKC [23] and XTR-PKC [25] were pro-posed based on cubic LFSR sequences [26]. In cubic LFSR-based PKCs [23,25], elements in $\mathbb{F}_{q^3}$ are represented by their corresponding minimal polynomials whose coefficients are chosen from $\mathbb{F}_q$. However, the security of cubic LFSR-based PKCs is based on the difficulty of solving the discrete logarithm problem in $\mathbb{F}_{q^3}$. This leads to substantial savings, both in communication and computa-tional overhead, for a desired security level. In particular, 170-bits of XTR-PKC gives security equivalent to 1024-bits of cryptosystems using traditional repre-sentation of finite fields [25]. The XTR cryptosystem is constructed by choosing:

1. p, a large prime of the order of 170 bits. Set $q = p^2$.
2. Q, a large prime factor of $p^2 - p + 1$ of the order of 160 bits.
3. Characteristic polynomial $f(x) = x^3 - ax^2 + a^p x - 1$ with period Q by ran-domly choosing $a \in \mathbb{F}_q$ and using standard irreducibility testing algorithms.

Let $f_k(x)$ denote the minimal polynomial of α^k where $\alpha \in \mathbb{F}_{q^3}$ is a root of $f(x)$. It can be shown that the polynomial $f_k(x)$ can be represented as [7,23,25]: $f_k(x) = x^3 - s_k x^2 + s_k^p x - 1$ in the XTR-PKC. Thus, the polynomial f_k (we drop the indeterminate x for simplicity of notation) can be represented by $s_k \in \mathbb{F}_q$ in XTR. The sequence terms are computed using the following two sequence operations [24]:

1. OP_1: given an integer k and f_e, compute the $(ke)^{\text{th}}$ state of the LFSR, $\bar{s}_{ke}$.
2. OP_2: given $\bar{s}_k$ and $\bar{s}_e$ (both integers k and e need not be known), compute the $(k + e)^{\text{th}}$ state of the LFSR, $\bar{s}_{k+e}$.

These sequence operations have been efficiently implemented in hardware [27]. We use the sequence operations to create/manipulate sequence terms in the proposed multisignature scheme.

In cubic LFSR-based PKCs, an entity randomly chooses a *long-term private key* SK $= x$ in $\mathbb{Z}_Q^*$ and computes the *long-term public key* PK $= \bar{s}_x = \{s_x, s_{x+1}, s_{x+2}\}$ using the sequence operation $\mathsf{OP}_1(x, f)$. Algorithms for sequence term computations use the following *commutative law* [23] for characteristic sequences: for all integers r and e, the rth term of the characteristic sequence generated by the polynomial $f_e(x)$ equals the $(re)^{\mathrm{th}}$ term of the characteristic sequence generated by the polynomial $f(x)$, i.e., $s_r(f_e) = s_{re}(f) = s_e(f_r)$.

Throughout the paper, we construct our signature schemes using the XTR-PKC for simplicity, although the proposed schemes can be seamlessly built using the GH-PKC and also extended to PKCs based on higher order LFSR sequences, with minor modifications.

3.2 A Short Note on DSR

DSR is composed of two central mechanisms, namely, route discovery and route maintenance. In this paper we focus on DSR's route discovery mechanism. The source initiates route discovery by generating an RREQ (route request) packet and broadcasting it to all its neighbors. The RREQ packet contains a field indicating the destination and a source route field intended to accumulate the desired route. Each node that is not the destination and has not encountered the RREQ packet previously appends its IP address to the source route contained in the packet and re-broadcasts the packet to its own neighbors. RREQ propagation continues until the destination is encountered. When the destination receives the RREQ packet, it generates the route reply (RREP) packet containing the accumulated (source) route and unicasts the RREP to the initiator of the route discovery along the reverse path of the source route.

DSR is an on-demand routing protocol and thus, attempts to discover a route to a destination node only when a source originates a data packet addressed to that node. To avoid initiating route discovery before each data packet is sent, the source needs to cache routes [4]. The RREP packet at all times contains a complete sequence of links leading to the destination. Intermediate nodes forwarding the RREP packets can (optionally) accumulate these complete paths into *path caches* so they can efficiently reply to route requests at a later time. Path caches are simple to implement and also guarantee that all routes are loop-free, since all source routes contained in the RREP are loop-free themselves. This mechanism of caching is one of the most important enhancements made to DSR.

4 Authenticating Route Discovery in DSR

As with most routing protocols, the original construction of DSR did not consider an adversarial model of the underlying network. As a result, DSR is vulnerable to several forms of attacks by malicious nodes, including injection of bogus routing information and formation of feedback loops by colluding adversarial nodes [3]. The classical approach to mitigating such attacks is to use cryptographic tools to authenticate information exchanged during the route discovery process. In this section, we present techniques for authenticating route discovery in DSR (with and without path caching) based on multisignatures.

4.1   First Construction

A first intuition for authenticating route discovery in DSR would be to have each node sign RREQ packets as they are forwarded toward the destination, so that the destination could authenticate the accumulated source route before generating an RREP packet. However, due to flooding of RREQ packets in the DSR route discovery algorithm, several nodes would end up wasting computation and communication resources by signing, verifying and forwarding RREQ packets if these nodes are not included in the eventual route. Also, in this mechanism, if authentication is done by combining signatures on different messages, a sequential aggregate signature must be used; such signatures are usually computationally more expensive than the more specific form of multisignatures. In our technique, we authenticate the source route contained in the RREP packets using an efficient, single round multisignature scheme, requiring no prior cooperation among nodes to construct the signature.

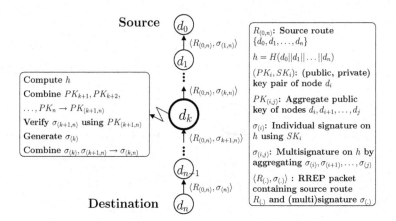

Fig. 1. Propagation and authentication of RREP

We first present the basic idea of authenticating the route discovery process in DSR without considering caching of routes. Let nodes $\{d_0, \ldots, d_k, \ldots, d_n\}$ constitute a source route. An arbitrary node and its IP address are denoted by the same notation, d_k, for simplicity. First, let us assume that an arbitrary node d_k has authentic copies of public keys $PK_{k+1}, \ldots, PK_n$ of all nodes leading to the destination. Fig. 1 shows the propagation of authenticated RREP packets from the destination d_n to the source d_0. Node d_k does the following: (1) combines the public keys to form aggregate public key $PK_{(k+1,n)}$, (2) verifies multisignature $\sigma_{(k+1,n)}$ that it receives from node d_{k+1}, (3) signs the hashed concatenation of the IP addresses contained in source route (all nodes sign this message) to create $\sigma_{(k)}$ if the verification in Step (2) is successful, (4) combines $\sigma_{(k+1,n)}$ and $\sigma_{(k)}$ to form multisignature $\sigma_{(k,n)}$, (5) removes $\sigma_{(k+1,n)}$ from and appends $\sigma_{(k,n)}$ to the RREP packet and (6) sends the RREP packet to the next node d_{k-1}. At the source d_0, successful verification of multisignature $\sigma_{(1,n)}$ under the aggregate public key $PK_{(1,n)}$ establishes the authenticity of all signatures on the source route. Note that signature verification by intermediate nodes facilitates early detection of bogus routes injected by an adversary. The procedures for combining public keys, generation, verification and aggregation of signatures are presented in Section 5.

4.2   Incorporating Path Caching

Now, we extend the above technique to incorporate path caching[1]. Consider the case where source d_0 has already established a route to destination d_n as shown in Fig. 2. All nodes $\{d_0, d_1, \ldots, d_{n-1}, d_n\}$ cache the source route, $R_{(0,n)}$, along with their respective multisignatures $\{\sigma_{(0,n)}, \sigma_{(1,n)}, \ldots, \sigma_{(n-1,n)}, \sigma_{(n)}\}$ (destination caches its own signature $\sigma_{(n)}$). Suppose node d_0' (a new source) now attempts to discover a route to the same destination d_n and the RREQ packet generated by the new source d_0' containing the accumulated route $\{d_0', d_1', \ldots, d_m'\}$ reaches node d_l as shown in Fig. 2.

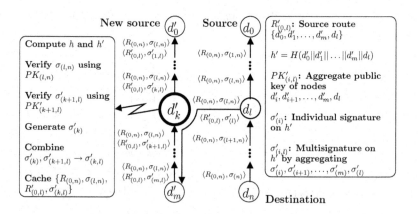

Fig. 2. Propagation and authentication of cached RREP

Node d_l prepares the RREP packet containing: (1) cached information $\langle R_{(0,n)}, \sigma_{(l,n)}\rangle$ and (2) accumulated route, signature pair $\langle R'_{(0,l)} = \{d_0', \ldots, d_k', \ldots d_m', d_l\}, \sigma'_{(l)}\rangle$, where $\sigma'_{(l)}$ is node d_l's own signature on the hashed concatenation of the IP addresses in the accumulated route $h' = H(d_0'||\ldots||d_m'||d_l)$. Node d_l sends

---

[1] We use multisignatures in authenticating cached routes and thus, do not consider using link caches [4].

the RREP packet to node d'_m. Now, consider an arbitrary node d'_k en route to the new source d'_0. Node d'_k does the following: (1) Verifies multisignatures $\sigma_{(l,n)}$ and $\sigma'_{(k+1,l)}$ that it receives from its previous node d'_{k+1} using aggregate public keys $PK_{(l,n)}$ and $PK'_{(k+1,l)}$ respectively; (2) generates it's own signature $\sigma'_{(k)}$ on h'; (3) combines $\sigma'_{(k)}$ and $\sigma'_{(k+1,l)}$ to form multisignature $\sigma'_{(k,l)}$ on h'; (4) caches $\{R_{(0,n)}, \sigma_{(l,n)}, R'_{(0,l)}, \sigma'_{(k,l)}\}$ under the cached entry for route to d_n and (5) sends the RREP packet containing $\langle R_{(0,n)}, \sigma_{(l,n)} \rangle$ and $\langle R'_{(0,l)}, \sigma'_{(k,l)} \rangle$ to node d'_{k-1}. In this fashion, the RREP packet propagates to the source d'_0, which performs the same operations as node d'_k. Successful verification of multisignatures $\sigma_{(l,n)}$, $\sigma'_{(1,l)}$ under the aggregate public keys $PK_{(l,n)}$, $PK'_{(1,l)}$ establishes the authenticity of the route $R'_{(0,l)}$ and the partial route $\{d_{l+1}, \ldots, d_n\}$ contained in $R_{(0,n)}$. Note that the remaining part of $R_{(0,n)}$, i.e., IP addresses $\{d_0, \ldots, d_{l-1}\}$, are not authenticated by nodes. Finally, source d'_0 extracts $\{d_{l+1}, \ldots, d_n\}$ from $R_{(0,n)}$, and appends the extracted route to $R'_{(0,l)}$ to obtain the desired route $\{d'_0, \ldots, d'_m, d_l, \ldots, d_n\}$. Similarly, nodes in the route $R'_{(0,l)}$ may use cached information to reply to future RREQs encountered for destination d_n.

5   Construction of an Efficient and Scalable Multisignature Scheme

In this section, we construct an efficient, single round, multisignature scheme based on cubic LFSR sequences, suitable for authenticating route discovery in DSR.

5.1   A Variant of a Generalized ElGamal Signature Scheme Based on LFSR Sequences

We present the cubic LFSR-based 2-party signature scheme, CLFSR-S [5], with a unique construction that uses the EG I.4 [6] variant of the generalized ElGamal signature scheme. Generation of individual signatures and verification of (multi)signatures in multisignature scheme, CLFSR-M, follow the procedures in CLFSR-S.

The CLFSR-S scheme consists of four phases: initialization, key generation, signature generation and signature verification. During the initialization phase, both entities, i.e., the signer and the verifier, choose and agree on the system public parameters: params $= \langle p, Q, f(x), H \rangle$, where p, Q and $f(x)$ are as described in Section 3.1 and $H : \{0,1\}^* \mapsto \mathbb{Z}_Q$ is a cryptographic hash function. The signer generates its long-term private and public key pair, $(SK, PK) = (x, \bar{s}_x)$. Fig. 3 describes the signature generation and signature verification phases of CLFSR-S scheme. Note that a naive cubic LFSR variant of EG I.4 will generate the signature $\sigma = (f_k, t)$. We perform an additional computation in Step 3 (Fig. 3) of the signature process to compute the term $\bar{s}_{kr}$. The specific format of the individual signature that CLFSR-S generates enables us to efficiently construct the multisignature in a single round, i.e., without any prior cooperation among the nodes participating in the RREQ phase of DSR.

Signature Generation	Signature Verification
1. Randomly choose ephemeral private key $k \in_R \mathbb{Z}_Q^*$ and compute ephemeral public key $\bar{s}_k \leftarrow OP_1(k, f)$. Denote $r = s_k \mod Q$ as an integer. 2. Compute hash of message $h = H(m)$; Solve for t in the following equation: $t \equiv kr - xh \mod Q$. 3. Compute $\bar{s}_{kr} \leftarrow OP_1(\bar{s}_k, r)$. 4. Send the signature $\sigma = (\bar{s}_{kr}, t)$ and the message m to verifier.	1. Compute $h = H(m)$. 2. Compute $A = f_{(th^{-1}+x)} \leftarrow OP_2(th^{-1}, \bar{s}_x)$. 3. Compute $B = f_{(rh^{-1}k)} \leftarrow OP_1(h^{-1}, f_{kr})$. f_{kr} can be directly derived from $\bar{s}_{kr}$. 4. Accept signature if $A = B$, else reject signature.

Fig. 3. The CLFSR-S Signature Scheme

Next, we present an efficient, single round multisignature scheme that uses the individual CLFSR-S signatures to generate a multisignature.

5.2   The Proposed Multisignature Scheme CLFSR-M

The multisignature scheme, CLFSR-M, consists of five phases: initialization, key generation (MS.K), signature generation (MS.G), multisignature verification (MS.V) and multisignature generation (MS.A). During the initialization phase, all nodes choose and agree upon the system public parameters $\mathsf{params} = \langle p, Q, f(x), H \rangle$. The process of key generation consists of: (1) generation of individual long term private public key pair $(SK_l, PK_l) = (x_l, \bar{s}_{x_l})$ of node d_l and (2) the generation of aggregate public key $PK_{(l,n)} = \bar{s}_{x_{(l,n)}} \leftarrow OP_2(\bar{s}_{x_l}, \bar{s}_{x_{(l+1,n)}})$ of nodes $d_l, d_{l+1}, \ldots, d_n$, where $x_{(l,n)} = \sum_{i=l}^{n}(x_i)$.

The signature generation, multisignature verification and multisignature generation phases of CLFSR-M work as follows:

1. Signature generation (MS.G(params, $SK_l, m = d_0||\ldots||d_n) \rightarrow \sigma_{(l)}$): Each node, d_l, participating in the RREP propagation generates an individual signature $\sigma_{(l)} = (\bar{s}_{k_l r_l}, t_l)$ on the hashed concatenation of the IP address in the source route $h = H(m)$ following the CLFSR-S signature generation.
2. Multisignature Verification (MS.V(params, $PK_{(l+1,n)}, \sigma_{(l+1,n)}, m) \rightarrow (Valid, Invalid)$): Each intermediate node (other than the destination), d_l, receives a signed RREP packet containing the multisignature $\sigma_{(l+1,n)} = (t_{(l+1,n)}, \bar{s}_{k_{(l+1,n)}})$, where $t_{(l+1,n)} = \sum_{i=l+1}^{n}(t_i)$ and $k_{(l+1,n)} = \sum_{i=l+1}^{n}(k_i r_i)$. Node d_l verifies $\sigma_{(l+1,n)}$ following the CLFSR-S signature verification procedure, using the aggregate public key $PK_{(l+1,n)} = \bar{s}_{x_{(l+1,n)}}$, where $x_{(l+1,n)} = \sum_{i=l+1}^{n}(x_i)$. Note that for the node d_{n-1} (the last hop before the destination d_n) the signature $\sigma_{(l+1,n)}$ denotes σ_n.
3. Multisignature Generation (MS.A(params, $\sigma_{(l+1,n)}, \sigma_{(l)}) \rightarrow \sigma_{(l,n)}$): If the signature $\sigma_{(l+1,n)}$ passes the verification procedure, MS.V, node d_l, generates the multisignature $\sigma_{(l,n)}$ by computing $t_{(l,n)} = t_{(l+1,n)} + t_l$ and $\bar{s}_{k_{(l,n)}} = \bar{s}_{k_{(l+1,n)}+k_l r_l} \leftarrow OP_2(\bar{s}_{k_l r_l}, \bar{s}_{k_{(l+1,n)}})$. Node d_l finally removes the multisignature $\sigma_{(l+1,n)}$ from and adds the multisignature $\sigma_{(l,n)} = (t_{(l,n)}, \bar{s}_{k_{(l,n)}})$ to the RREP packet before forwarding the RREP to the next hop node d_{l-1}.

The wave of signature generation, multisignature verification and multisignature aggregation continues until the RREP packet containing the multisignature $\sigma_{(1,n)} = (t_{(1,n)}, \bar{s}_{k_{(1,n)}})$, is delivered to the source. If the multisignature $\sigma_{(1,n)}$ passes the verification procedure, MS.V, under the aggregate public key $PK_{(1,n)}$, then individual signatures $\sigma_{(1)}, \ldots, \sigma_{(n)}$ of corresponding nodes $d_1, \ldots, d_n$ in the discovered source route (to the destination d_n) are verified collectively. In the following section, we present a discussion on policy aspects of bootstrapping authentication protocols in ad hoc networks.

6   A Discussion on Distributing Public keys

An authentication protocol is typically composed of two distinct phases — the bootstrapping phase and the authentication phase. In the realm of public key cryptography, entities need to use authentic channels (need not be confidential) to exchange public keys constituting the "bootstrapping material" [28]. Once this exchange has taken place in the bootstrapping phase, entities can authenticate each other by proving the possession of their corresponding private keys.

6.1   Using a Trusted Third Party

A trusted third party (TTP) can be used to distribute certified public keys (the bootstrapping material) and also provide a way to check the validity of certificates via publishing certificate revocation lists. An online TTP works as follows: an arbitrary node d_k wanting to authenticate the source route can request and receive certified copies of public keys $PK_{k+1}, \ldots, PK_n$ of nodes leading to the destination from the TTP. However, an online TTP in an ad hoc network introduces circular dependency between the need for a TTP to perform secure routing and the need to find a secure route to the TTP. However, in such a case, public keys have to be redistributed when network membership changes, i.e., when nodes join or leave the network. To avoid this, an offline TTP can distribute all certified public keys to all nodes when the network is set up. Such an offline TTP may not be viable, since nodes would require to store all certified public keys. Various such solutions of bootstrapping authentication have been proposed for securing ad hoc networks, each having its own disadvantages [29]. In essence, the assumption of a TTP-based public key management policy in an ad hoc networking paradigm is not practical. Delegating specialized functions to a single node or a small subset of nodes [30,31] does not suit the ad hoc networking paradigm. These restrictions motivate us towards a fully distributed public key management policy.

6.2   Towards Fully Distributed Self-organized Bootstrapping

PGP [8] is a policy-based mechanism for public key management and can be used to distribute certified copies of public keys in the absence of a centralized TTP. In PGP, each node generates its own (public, private) key pair and certifies its own public key as well as public keys of other nodes based on certain trust policies. Similarly, in an ad hoc network, when two nodes come within radio-range of each other, they can certify each other's public keys, based on policies. This process of certification creates a *certificate graph* $G = (V, E)$, where $V = \{d_0, d_1, \ldots, d_N\}$ and $E = \{(d_i, d_j) : \forall i, j : 0 \leq i, j \leq N, \exists \sigma_{SK_i}(d_j, PK_j)\}$, where N is the total number of nodes in the network and $\sigma_{SK_i}(d_j, PK_j)$ denotes node d_i's signature on node d_j's public key. When a node d_i wants to verify the authenticity of public key PK_j of node d_j, node d_i tries to find a simple path $d_i \rightsquigarrow d_j = d_i \rightarrow d_{i_0} \rightarrow \ldots d_{i_n} \rightarrow d_j$ in the certificate graph, where $d_{i_k} \rightarrow d_{i_l} \implies (d_{i_k}, d_{i_l}) \in E$. Capkun et al. [10,11] studied PGP certificate graphs and observed that trust graphs in self-organized systems, for example mobile ad hoc networks, naturally exhibit the *small-world* phenomenon. Informally, a graph is said to exhibit the *small-world* property if any two nodes in the network are likely to be connected through a short sequence of intermediate acquaintances. Since the first experimental study by Milgram [9], several network models [21,32] have been proposed to study the problem analytically.

In our public key management model, individual nodes store, manage and distribute certificates themselves in a such a way that the size of the certificate repository at each node is small compared to the total number of certificates in the network, while still maintaining a high probability of finding a trust path from one node to another. We assume routing initiates after convergence of the certificate graph.

Policy Variants

In Policy I, the trust is based on the following. Node d_i completely[2] trusts node d_j implies: (1) node d_i believes that node d_j's public key PK_j is valid and authentic, and (2) node d_i trusts node d_j's decision on signing any other public key PK_k of node d_k, i.e., d_j would be careful not to sign any bogus public key. Thus, the following condition should hold for authenticating the route discovery process: $\forall i, \exists d_i \rightsquigarrow d_j, i < j \leq n$. Informally, this condition means that any node d_i wanting to authenticate the route from itself to the destination $\{d_i, d_{i+1}, \ldots, d_n\}$ needs to find a way to verify the authenticity of all corresponding public keys $\{PK_i, PK_{i+1}, \ldots, PK_n\}$.

In Policy II, the trust policy has an added condition. Node d_i completely trusts node d_j implies: (1), (2) and (3) node d_i trusts node d_j to honestly aggregate and sign other public keys $PK_{j+1}, \ldots, PK_n$ of nodes $d_{j+1}, \ldots, d_n$. Note that in Policy II, the following condition should hold for authenticating the route discovery process: $\forall i, \exists d_i \rightsquigarrow d_{i+1}, 0 \leq i \leq (n-1)$. This means that any node d_i wanting to authenticate the route from itself to the destination $\{d_i, d_{i+1}, \ldots, d_n\}$ needs to look-up a single node in the certificate graph, i.e., to verify the authenticity of one public key PK_{i+1}. Node d_{i+1} would sign the aggregate public public key $PK_{(i+1,n)}$ and deliver $(PK_{(i+1,n)}, \text{Cert}_{(i+1,n)} = \sigma_{SK_{i+1}}(d_{i+1}, \ldots, d_n, PK_{(i+1,n)}))$ to node d_i, where $\text{Cert}_{(i+1,n)}$ denotes the certificate on the aggregate public key $PK_{(i+1,n)}$.

---

[2] For simplicity, we assign trust either a true or false value. We do not model marginal or partial trust.

7   Theoretical Analysis

We present a concise theoretical analysis of correctness, security and performance of the proposed multisignature CLFSR-M.

7.1   Correctness

A multisignature scheme constructed following the procedures described in Section 5.2 is correct if an arbitrary multisignature, $\sigma_{(l+1,n)}$, received by node $d_l \in \{d_0, \ldots, d_{n-1}\}$ from node, d_{l+1}, passes the verification procedure MS.V at node d_l under the aggregate public key $PK_{(l+1,n)}$ provided: (1) Each node $d_i \in d_{l+1}, \ldots, d_n$ chooses and agrees upon the system public parameters params $= \langle p, Q, f(x), H \rangle$ and, honestly executes the key generation algorithm, MS.K(params) $\rightarrow (PK_i, SK_i)$ and the signature generation algorithm, MS.G(params, SK_i, m) $\rightarrow \sigma_{(i)}$, where $m = d_0 || \ldots || d_n$; (2) each node $d_i \in \{d_{l+1}, \ldots, d_{n-1}\}$, honestly executes the multisignature generation algorithm, MS.A(params, $\sigma_{(i+1,n)}, \sigma_{(i)}$) $\rightarrow \sigma_{(i,n)}$.

Proposition 1. *The multisignature scheme* CLFSR-M *follows the correctness property.*

Proof. Consider any arbitrary node $d_l \in \{d_0, \ldots, d_{n-1}\}$. We show that the multisignature, $\sigma_{(l+1,n)}$, of node d_{l+1} passes the verification procedure MS.V(params, $PK_{(l+1,n)}, \sigma_{(l+1,n)}, m$) $\rightarrow (Valid, Invalid)$ executed at d_l under the aggregate public key $PK_{(l+1,n)} = \bar{s}_{x_{(l+1,n)}}$ provided the above mentioned conditions hold.

In the verification of the multisignature $\sigma_{(l+1,n)}$ using the algorithm MS.V, we observe: $A_{(l+1,n)} = f_{v+x_{(l+1,n)}} \leftarrow \mathsf{OP}_2(v, \bar{s}_{x_{(l+1,n)}})$, where, $v = h^{-1} \sum_{i=l+1}^{n}(t_i)$ and $x_{(l+1,n)} = \sum_{i=l+1}^{n}(x_i)$. All nodes use the signing equation: $t_i \equiv k_i r_i - x_i h$ mod Q, where $(l+1) \leq i \leq n$ and $k_{(l+1,n)} = \sum_{i=l+1}^{n}(k_i r_i)$. Thus,

$$A_{(l+1,n)} = f_{\sum_{i=l+1}^{n}(h^{-1}t_i + x_i)} = f_{\sum_{i=l+1}^{n}(h^{-1}k_i r_i)}$$
$$= f_{h^{-1}k_{(l+1,n)}} = \mathsf{OP}_1(h^{-1}, f_{k_{(l+1,n)}}) = B_{(l+1,n)}$$

Thus, the multisignature, $\sigma_{(l+1,n)}$, is valid under $PK_{(l+1,n)}$.

Now, we need to show that it is hard for an adversary to deviate from the key pair and signature generation algorithms and still generate a correct signature. However, this is precisely the issue of forgery which we discuss in the following section.

7.2   Security

The security of CLFSR-M is based on the difficulty of solving the trace discrete logarithm (Tr-DL) problem in $\mathbb{F}_q$ [7,23,24,25]. Informally, the trace function $Tr : \mathbb{F}_{q^3} \mapsto \mathbb{F}_q$ is given as $Tr(\alpha) = \alpha + \alpha^q + \alpha^{q^2}$. The Tr-DL problem and assumption can be defined as follows:

Definition 1 (Tr-DL Problem/Assumption). *Let α be a generator of the multiplicative group $(\mathbb{F}_{q^3})^*$, where q is a large prime or a power of a large prime. The Tr-DL Problem in $\mathbb{F}_q$ can be defined as follows: Given $(q, \alpha \in (\mathbb{F}_{q^3})^*, \beta \in \mathbb{F}_q)$, find an index k such that $\beta = Tr(\alpha^k)$ or determine that there is no such index. Let $\mathcal{A}$ be a probabilistic polynomial time (PPT) algorithm that runs in time t and solves the Tr-DL problem with probability at least ϵ. Define the advantage of the (t, ϵ) Tr-DL solver $\mathcal{A}$ as: $\mathsf{Adv}_{\mathcal{A}}^{TrDL} = Pr[\mathcal{A}(q, \alpha, \beta) = k \mid \alpha \in_R \mathbb{F}_{q^3}, k \in_R \mathbb{Z}_Q, \beta = Tr(\alpha^k)]$. The probability is over the random choices of α, k and the random bits of $\mathcal{A}$.*

Tr-DL Assumption: *The finite field $\mathbb{F}_q$ satisfies the Tr-DL Assumption if $\mathsf{Adv}_{\mathcal{A}}^{TrDL}(\lambda)$ is a negligible function.*

Lemma 1 (Giuliani et al. [7]). *The Tr-DL Problem is equivalent to the DL problem.*

A total break of CLFSR-M occurs if, given a public key $\mathsf{PK}_i = \bar{s}_{x_i}$ of an arbitrary node d_i, the adversary is able to compute the corresponding private key $\mathsf{SK}_i = x_i$. In such a case, any node's signature can be forged. However, given $\bar{s}_x$, finding x is equivalent to solving the DL problem in the extension field $\mathbb{F}_{q^3}$ [24]. Using the following lemmas we show that, assuming a total break has not occurred, if an adversary can successfully forge a CLFSR-M multisignature, then it can successfully forge a signature in the EG I.4 variant of the generalized ElGamal scheme.

Lemma 2 (Chakrabarti et al. [5]). *The 2-party signature scheme CLFSR-S is equivalent to the well-known EG I.4 variant of the Generalized ElGamal scheme.*

Lemma 3. *The 2-party signature scheme CLFSR-S reduces to the proposed multisignature scheme CLFSR-M.*

Proof (Sketch). Suppose there exists a PPT forger $\mathcal{F}$, which given system parameters $\mathsf{params} = \langle p, Q, f(x), H \rangle$, public keys $\bar{s}_{x_0}, \ldots, \bar{s}_{x_n}$ and message m, outputs a forged multigsignature $\sigma_{(0,n)}^F = (t_{(0,n)}^F, \bar{s}_{k_{(0,n)}}^F)$ on $h = H(m)$ with non-negligible probability, i.e., $\sigma_{(0,n)}^F$ passes the verification procedure, MS.V, under the aggregate public key $\bar{s}_{x_{(0,n)}}$.

We show that given access to the PPT forger $\mathcal{F}$, system parameters params, public key $PK = \bar{s}_x$ and message m, an adversary can output a forged signature $\sigma^F = (\bar{s}_{kr}^F, t^F)$ on $h = H(m)$ that passes the verification procedure of CLFSR-S under public key PK. The adversary generates σ^F as follows: (1) picks $x_0, \ldots, x_{n-1} \in_R \mathbb{Z}_Q^*$ and computes $\bar{s}_{x_0}, \ldots, \bar{s}_{x_{n-1}}$, (2) computes $\bar{s}_{x_n} \leftarrow \mathsf{OP}_2(-\sum_{i=0}^{n-1} x_i, \bar{s}_x)$, (3) calls $\mathcal{F}$ with inputs $\mathsf{params}, \bar{s}_{x_0}, \bar{s}_{x_1}, \ldots, \bar{s}_{x_n}$ and m. $\mathcal{F}$ outputs forged multisignature $(t_{(0,n)}^F, \bar{s}_{k_{(0,n)}}^F)$ on $h = H(m)$; and (4) sets $\bar{s}_{kr}^F = \bar{s}_{k_{(0,n)}}^F$ and $t^F = t_{(0,n)}^F$. The signature $\sigma^F = (\bar{s}_{kr}^F, t^F)$ is a forged signature on $h = H(m)$ under public key PK.

Theorem 1. *The well-known EG I.4 variant of the Generalized ElGamal signature scheme reduces to the proposed multisignature scheme CLFSR-M.*

Proof. The proof of the theorem is immediate from Lemmas 2 and 3.

Note that CLFSR-M, though not provably secure, is engineered to be an efficient means to authenticate routes in DSR. In contrast, Micali et al.'s multisignature scheme [14] uses the Schnorr's variant [20] (the only known provably secure variant) and takes three communication rounds. We omit a thorough discussion on provable security; the reader is requested to refer to [33] for an exemplary discussion on the subject. Next, we present a performance comparison of CLFSR-M with existing schemes.

7.3   Performance

Table 1 shows a performance comparison of the proposed multisignature scheme, CLFSR-M with three signature aggregation techniques used to instantiate SRDP [3], namely the multisignature by Micali et al. (ASM) [14], the generalized aggregate signature by Boneh et al. (MBLS) [15] and the sequential aggregate signature by Lysyanskaya et al. (SAS) [16].

Table 1. Performance Comparison. e : modular exponentiation, m : modular multiplication, h : hash operation, p : pairing computation, s : scalar multiplication, n : number of signers, $*$: ephemeral public key propagated during RREQ phase.

	SAS	ASM	MBLS	CLFSR-M
Rounds	2	1	1	1
Generation cost	$e + h$	$e + 2m + h$	$s + h$	$2OP_1 + h + 2m$
Verification cost	$n(h + e)$	$2e + m + h$	$2p + h$	$OP_1 + OP_2 + h + m$
Aggregation cost	–	–	m	OP_2
Signature size (bits)	1024	$320 + (160^*)$	160	500
PK size (bits)	2048	2048	766	680

The original construction of Micali et al's multisignature scheme [14] takes three communication rounds; ASM in SRDP requires two rounds for completion, with prior cooperation (though small: one exponentiation and one modular multiplication) among nodes during the RREQ phase, which might be wasteful if the node is not included in the final route. The proposed multisignature, CLFSR-M, uses extremely fast LFSR sequence operations [25,27] and achieves the best computational efficiency. The public key sizes equivalent to 1024-bit RSA (excluding shared components of the public key) are highest in SAS and ASM, followed by MBLS. CLFSR-M offers the least public key size. Note that in ASM, nodes need to additionally propagate the accumulated ephemeral public keys (160-bits) during the RREQ phase, wasting bandwidth. Signature sizes are lowest for MBLS, followed by ASM and CLFSR-M, while SAS incurs the highest sizes.

8   Conclusions

In this paper, we presented the first LFSR sequence-based multisignature scheme CLFSR-M geared toward authenticating routes in DSR. Our scheme also works with cached routing information. The scheme CLFSR-M scheme is derived from a cubic LFSR sequence-based, 2-party signature scheme, CLFSR-S [5], and uses extremely fast LFSR operations, small public keys (smallest among schemes in [3]) and generates a reasonably small multisignature (500 bits). The security of the scheme, CLFSR-M, is based on the Tr-DL(DL) Problem in $\mathbb{F}_q(\mathbb{F}_{q^3})$. CLFSR-M was constructed using the XTR-PKC for simplicity, although it can be seamlessly constructed using the GH-PKC and can also be extended to PKCs based on higher order LFSR sequences, with minor modifications, depending on the desired security level.

Distributing authentic public keys among nodes in a mobile ad hoc network to bootstrap authentication protocols is a challenging task. Delegating special functions to nodes or assuming the existence of a TTP to distribute certified public keys is paradigmatically unsuitable for ad hoc networks. We consider a fully distributed mechanism of public key distribution and present two variations of trust policies, based on PGP, for effective management of individual and aggregate public keys.

References

1. Johnson, D.B., Maltz, D.A., Hu, Y.C.: The Dynamic Souce Routing Protocol for Mobile Ad Hoc Networks (DSR). Internet draft draft-ietf-manet-dsr-10, IETF MANET Working Group (July 2004)
2. Hu, Y.C., Perrig, A.: A survey of secure wireless ad hoc routing. IEEE Security & Privacy 2(3), 28–39 (2004)
3. Kim, J., Tsudik, G.: SRDP: Securing route discovery in DSR. In: Proceedings of MobiQuitous, pp. 247–260. IEEE Computer Society Press, Los Alamitos (2005)
4. Hu, Y.C., Johnson, D.B.: Caching strategies in on-demand routing protocols for wireless ad hoc networks. In: Proceedings of MOBICOM, pp. 231–242 (2000)
5. Chakrabarti, S., Chandrasekhar, S., Singhal, M., Calvert, K.L.: Authenticating feedback in multicast applications using a novel multisignature scheme based on cubic LFSR sequences. To appear in Proceedings of SSNDS (2007)
6. Horster, P., Petersen, H., Michels, M.: Meta-ElGamal signature schemes. In: ACM Conference on Computer and Communications Security, pp. 96–107 (1994)
7. Giuliani, K.J., Gong, G.: New LFSR-based cryptosystems and the trace discrete log problem (trace-DLP). In: Helleseth, T., Sarwate, D., Song, H.-Y., Yang, K. (eds.) SETA 2004. LNCS, vol. 3486, pp. 298–312. Springer, Heidelberg (2005)
8. Zimmermann, P.: The official PGP user's guide (1995)
9. Milgram, S.: The small world problem. Psychology Today 61(2), 60–67 (1967)
10. Čapkun, S., Buttyán, L., Hubaux, J.P.: Small worlds in security systems: an analysis of the PGP certificate graph. In: Proceedings of NSPW (2002)
11. Čapkun, S., Buttyán, L., Hubaux, J.P.: Self-organized public-key management for mobile ad hoc networks. IEEE Transactions on Mobile Computing 2(1), 52–64 (2003)
12. Papadimitratos, P., Haas, Z.J.: Secure routing for mobile ad hoc networks. In: Proceedings of CNDS (2002)
13. Hu, Y.C., Perrig, A., Johnson, D.B.: Ariadne: A secure on-demand routing protocol for ad hoc networks. Wireless Networks 11(1-2), 21–38 (2005)

14. Micali, S., Ohta, K., Reyzin, L.: Accountable-subgroup multisignatures: extended abstract. In: Proceedings of CCS, pp. 245–254 (2001)
15. Boneh, D., Gentry, C., Lynn, B., Shacham, H.: Aggregate and verifiably encrypted signatures from bilinear maps. In: Biham, E. (ed.) EUROCRPYT 2003. LNCS, vol. 2656, pp. 416–432. Springer, Heidelberg (2003)
16. Lysyanskaya, A., Micali, S., Reyzin, L., Shacham, H.: Sequential aggregate signatures from trapdoor permutations. In: Cachin, C., Camenisch, J.L. (eds.) EURO-CRYPT 2004. LNCS, vol. 3027, pp. 74–90. Springer, Heidelberg (2004)
17. Bhaskar, R., Herranz, J., Laguillaumie, F.: Efficient authentication for reactive routing protocols. In: Proceedings of AINA, pp. 57–61. IEEE Computer Society Press, Los Alamitos (2006)
18. Itakura, K., Nakamura, H., Nakazawa, K.: A public-key cryptosystem suitable for digital multisignatures. NEC Research and Development (1983)
19. ElGamal, T.: A public key cryptosystem and a signature scheme based on discrete logarithms. In: Blakely, G.R., Chaum, D. (eds.) Advances in Cryptology. LNCS, vol. 196, pp. 10–18. Springer, Heidelberg (1985)
20. Schnorr, C.P.: Efficient signature generation by smart cards. Journal of Cryptology 4(3), 161–174 (1991)
21. Kleinberg, J.M.: The small-world phenomenon: an algorithm perspective. In: Proceedings of STOC, pp. 163–170 (2000)
22. Niederreiter, H.: A public-key cryptosystem based on shift register sequences. In: McCurley, K.S., Ziegler, C.D. (eds.) Advances in Cryptology 1981 - 1997. LNCS, vol. 1440, pp. 35–39. Springer, Heidelberg (1999)
23. Gong, G., Harn, L.: Public-key cryptosystems based on cubic finite field extensions. IEEE Transactions on Information Theory 45(7), 2601–2605 (1999)
24. Gong, G., Harn, L., Wu, H.: The GH public-key cryptosystem. In: Vaudenay, S., Youssef, A.M. (eds.) Selected Areas in Cryptography. LNCS, vol. 2259, pp. 284–300. Springer, Heidelberg (2001)
25. Lenstra, A.K., Verheul, E.R.: The XTR Public Key System. In: Bellare, M. (ed.) Advances in Cryptology - CRYPTO 2000. LNCS, vol. 1880, pp. 1–19. Springer, Heidelberg (2000)
26. Golomb, S.W.: Shift Register Sequences. Holden-Day (1967)
27. Peeters, E., Neve, M., Ciet, M.: XTR implementation on reconfigurable hardware. In: Joye, M., Quisquater, J.-J. (eds.) CHES 2004. LNCS, vol. 3156, pp. 386–399. Springer, Heidelberg (2004)
28. Chakrabarti, S., Giruka, V.C., Singhal, M.: Security in Distributed, Grid, and Pervasive Computing, Edited by Prof. Yang Xiao. Auerbach Publications, CRC Press, Boca Raton (2006)
29. Čapkun, S., Hubaux, J.P.: BISS: building secure routing out of an incomplete set of security associations. In: Workshop on Wireless Security, pp. 21–29 (2003)
30. Zhou, L., Haas, Z.J.: Securing ad hoc networks. IEEE Network 13(6), 24–30 (1999)
31. Kong, J., Zerfos, P., Luo, H., Lu, S., Zhang, L.: Providing robust and ubiquitous security support for mobile ad hoc networks. In: Proceedings of ICNP, pp. 251–260. IEEE Computer Society Press, Los Alamitos (2001)
32. Watts, D.J.: Small Worlds: The Dynamics of Networks Between Order and Randomness. Princeton University Press, Princeton (1999)
33. Koblitz, N., Menezes, A.: Another Look at Provable Security. In: Barua, R., Lange, T. (eds.) INDOCRYPT 2006. LNCS, vol. 4329, pp. 148–175. Springer, Heidelberg (2006)

Security for Mobile Low Power Nodes in a Personal Area Network by Means of Trusted Platform Modules

Ulrich Grossmann, Enrik Berkhan, Luciana C. Jatoba, Joerg Ottenbacher,
Wilhelm Stork, and Klaus D. Mueller-Glaser

University of Karlsruhe, Institute of Information Processing Technology,
Engesserstr. 5, 76131 Karlsruhe, Germany
Ulrich.Grossmann@itiv.uni-karlsruhe.de

Abstract. The growing field of ubiquitous applications and the use of resource constrained mobile devices strongly demands for mechanisms to provide the security and privacy of such mobile devices. In this paper we show that especially new teletherapeutic applications are not feasible without strong cryptographic protection of data and platform. Based on the analysis of security requirements, we introduce a mobile low power node that is secured by means of a Trusted Platform Module (TPM). For privacy and security of the communication between the mobile device and a webserver, which is part of the distributed network, we propose a security protocol based on webservice technology that uses the mechanisms of the TPM. Finally, measurements that were done with the secured mobile node are presented. We show that TPMs are well suited for resource constrained mobile devices and are a step towards trusted ubiquitous computing.

Keywords: Teletherapy of pain, remote controlled infusion pump, platform integrity of resource constrained device.

1 Introduction

Resource constrained mobile and embedded systems that are used in an ubiquitous manner (here referred to as mobile devices) are getting more and more popular (e.g. Smartphones or health monitoring devices [1]). These devices are apt to support its users and improve quality of life without being intrusive, so that they can be comfortably worn as part of the clothing or for example like a watch, directly on the body. These devices are limited in size, weight and computational power.

Personal Area Networks (PAN) are used to exchange information between different nodes in the vicinity of a person. For example, one node is used to sense vital parameters and the other node analyses these parameters and gives a direct feedback to the person. These nodes can use the PAN in form of a standalone network to fetch and deliver information.

In other scenarios the local PAN must interact with external nodes or services that are not a part of the local network. According to [2] these networks are

F. Stajano et al. (Eds.): ESAS 2007, LNCS 4572, pp. 172–186, 2007.

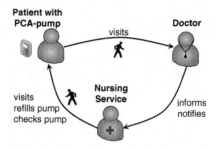

Fig. 1. Workflow of current therapy of pain. The patient visits the physician who is responsible for providing information about the necessary treatment. He informs the nursing service, which is responsible to configure and maintain the infusion pump. If the doctor notifies the nursing service of a reconfiguration, the nursing service must visit the patient and reprogram the pump.

called Personal Networks (PN). One or more nodes are used to connect the local PAN to other networks and provide mechanisms such as routing or protocol translation to make the services of other networks (for example the web server of a service provider) reachable to the local PAN.

This paper resulted from research in the field of telemedicine specifically the field of teletherapy of chronic pain [3]. We aimed to find methods to increase efficiency of the treatment of patients suffering from severe pain by means of mobile drug delivery systems.

These patients use an infusion pump which applies analgesic drugs continuously over an intravenous line in order to reduce pain. Often the infusion pump is designed to provide patient controlled analgesia (PCA) which means that the patient can control the delivery of an extra dose by pressing a specific button, which is possible only once in a predetermined time interval. Figure 1 shows the workflow of the current therapy of pain.

There are several shortcomings in the current treatment of these patients:

- Frequent control visits are necessary to check if there is still enough analgesic left in the reservoir for proper operation of the infusion pump. Mostly it is not possible to forecast the fill level, since it is not known how often the patient ordered an extra dose.
- Tolerance requires reconfiguration. Tolerance is the effect of getting used to a certain analgesic because of its permanent application. If a patient develops a tolerance, the analgesic dose must be increased to get the same level of pain release. Therefore current infusion pumps provide a local interface for the physician to reconfigure the operational parameters.

Because normally the network of clinics distributed in a country is not dense enough, a therapy with PCA pumps requires that the patient travels long distances to visit the physician or the nursing service and vice versa. This makes frequent control visits and reconfigurations of therapy parameters a cost intensive

Fig. 2. Teletherapy system (TTS): Vital sensors, a PCA-pump and a Smartphone are connected via a PAN. The Smartphone connects the PAN to the internet and provides internet access to vital sensors and pump to store data on the webserver. The pump can be configured remotely by physicians or nurses [4].

task for the health system. To improve this situation we suggest a Teletherapy System (TTS) with remote control capability as shown in figure 2.

The security in our TTS is of paramount importance. If an attacker gets unauthorized access to the remote configuration capability of the infusion pump, he could cause life-threatening complications for the patient.

Our Contribution: In this paper we present the concept and implementation of a secure resource constrained mobile network node. The node can be used in ad hoc and sensor networks with strong security requirements, for example in telemedical applications. The security is based on a standard embedded Trusted Platform Module which stores the keys and the platform configuration of the mobile device and performs cryptographic operations. The node uses the Bluetooth Personal Area Network Profile. A Smartphone or Access Point inside the Bluetooth PAN acts as a gateway to provide internet access to all other nodes inside the PAN. To securely authenticate the node, a security protocol which is based on a webservice is presented. After the authentication procedure the node can exchange encrypted data with the webserver of the service provider.

This paper is organized as follows: The first section explains the basic principles in the field of Trusted Platform Modules and Personal Area Networking. In the next section we describe the requirements for the security node and show how our new concept improves the state of the art. Here we focus on the architecture of the mobile node, the usage of TPM's and introduce a webservice based security protocol. After this, we present our implementation of the personal network which consists of the mobile node with TPM integration, the Bluetooth Access Point and the webserver with webservice interface. Finally, power consumption and timing measurements are shown and the results are discussed.

2   Basic Principles

2.1   Trusted Platform Module

The Trusted Platform Module (TPM) is specified by the Trusted Computing Group (TCG) and is a hardware component that is intended to create a trusted environment in networking applications (see figure 3). It provides strong cryptographic mechanisms including key generation, an engine for an asymmetric cryptosystem, a hash engine and mechanisms that provide tamper resistance. One special feature of the TPM is a mechanism for attesting the platform integrity of a system. A TPM uses Platform Configuration Registers (PCR) to store information about the software and hardware configuration of the system. These PCR can be used to confirm the platform integrity to a remote entity.

The interface of the TPM to communicate with the host processor is specified to be a Low Pin Count (LPC) bus which was introduced by Intel in 1998. The LPC bus defines seven wires. Four wires carry addresses and data in multiplexed mode. Three are used as control signals (frame, reset and clock). The bus has a clock rate of 33 MHz.

Some manufacturers of TPM hardware provide versions with serial interfaces which can be used in an embedded system with lower clock rates. Atmel, for example, uses a System Management Bus (SMBus) interface.

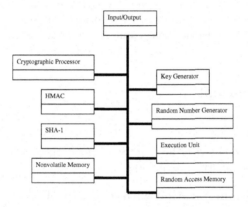

Fig. 3. This figure shows the components of a TPM. The cryptographic processor provides the asymmetric cryptosystem. Keyed-Hash Message Authentication Codes are created by the HMAC engine for data integrity. The engine for Secure Hash Algorithm (SHA-1) is used for hash value creation for platform integrity measurements. Nonvolatile memory holds the Platform Configuration Register (PCR) and the private keys of the TPM which are created by the key generation unit. Furthermore the TPM has several controlling components and random access memory (RAM). The input-output-interface and the components are connected via an internal bus.

2.2   Bluetooth Personal Area Network

Bluetooth is a wireless radio standard which defines communication protocols for low power and low range applications. It operates in the ISM (Industrial, Scientific and Medical) band and therefore its use is free of license costs.

Bluetooth defines several protocols including Host Controller Interface (HCI), Logical Link Control and Adaptation Layer Protocol (L2CAP), Service Discovery Protocol (SDP), Bluetooth Network Encapsulation Protocol (BNEP) and others. BNEP is responsible to encapsulate packets from various networking protocols e.g. the Internet Protocol (IP), which are directly transported over the L2CAP protocol. BNEP is seen from higher layers as an IEEE 802.3 (Ethernet) protocol.

Bluetooth profiles define the usage of these protocols and guarantee the interoperability of different Bluetooth enabled devices.

The Bluetooth Personal Area Networking Profile (PAN) defines a means of enabling Bluetooth devices to participate in a personal area network. Completely unmodified Ethernet payloads can be transmitted using the BNEP protocol to exchange packets between Bluetooth devices. The PAN profile defines different roles for the nodes:

- Network Access Point (NAP). Devices are connected to at least one more network and act as a bridge or router between the PAN and the other network. A NAP enables PAN devices to exchange packets with nodes of external networks.
- Group Ad-Hoc Network (GN). Devices with the capability to act as a router inside the PAN. A GN cannot route or bridge packets to external nodes.
- PAN User (PANU). Device that connects to a NAP, a GN or another PANU and uses the services of the corresponding device.

3   System Concept

3.1   Requirements

In this section we summarize the requirements for our Personal Network as well as the requirements for the mobile nodes:

Bidirectional Communication with central webservice. The mobile nodes send the acquired vital data of a person (sensor node) or other fetched information to a centralized server for storage. On the other hand, the node must have the ability to receive information from the server in order to reconfigure itself or execute commands (actuator node). Therefore the node must be connected (directly or indirectly) to the network of the server.

Mobility and ubiquitous operation. In order to realize mobile devices that can be used in everyday life, it is necessary that these devices are non intrusive to the person who uses them. We need ubiquitous operation wherever possible which demands for high battery lifetime and minimal user interaction. The system must be mobile so the user can carry it without noticing it. This results in constraints in size, form factor and weight. Mobility and ubiquitous operation leads to a resource constrained device which has low computational power and minimum memory to increase battery lifetime and decrease size and weight.

Standardized communication and components. The usage of established communication protocols and wireless technologies should be enforced in order to be open and interoperable to other systems. To keep development costs low, out of the box components and standard hardware should be used whenever possible. Especially in the field of security, standard components have another big advantage. The security of well known and widely used standard components is subject to many investigations and can therefore be considered more secure than proprietary systems.

3.2   Threat Model

To analyze the security requirements we build a threat model with different layers. The higher the layer, the bigger the number of potential attackers. The lower the layer, the higher the costs in time, know-how and equipment for an attacker.

Threats to embedded hardware (Layer 1): An attacker has full access to the hardware of the mobile device and is able to monitor hardwired busses and decode the bus communication on bit level and analyze power consumption. For example he can listen to the bus between microcontroller and crypto accelerator to gain knowledge of decrypted session keys. Also the attacker has the possibility of removing components or connecting additional hardware components to the system in order to bypass security mechanisms.

Threats to embedded software (Layer 2): An attacker only has access to the programming interface of the system which is reachable from outside without great effort. Such a programming interface is desired to easily update the software of the system in order reuse the costly hardware. Without protection, the attacker is able to load malicious software onto the device during maintenance (e.g. at the nursing service) in order to get access without authentication later on. The programming interface also enables an attacker to read keys that may be stored in the nonvolatile memory of the microcontroller. Such keys are typically used for authentication or encryption in pure software solutions.

Threats to near field communication (Layer 3): An attacker has access to the local interface for near field communication, for example the Bluetooth interface. Without protection the attacker is able to impersonate an authorized user and send commands to the device. The number of potential attackers is restricted, because of the limited range of the personal area network.

Threats to internet communication (Layer 4): An attacker has access to the internet communication and is able to eavesdrop and manipulate the data transmission. Without protection it is, for example, possible to change the monitoring data that is send by the device in order to prompt the user to perform a wrong remote configuration.

3.3   Required Protection

It is a great effort in knowledge, equipment and time to threaten the mobile device on layer 1. An attacker has to open the device and manipulate the board or the hardware components to get access to the desired signals and busses. In order to bypass the security mechanisms it is necessary to attach additional components to the system or change hardwired connections. Using a physical sealing of the board further increases the effort for an attacker.

Because of the high cost of such an attack in comparison to harm the patient by directly applying a dangerous dose of analgesics, the protection of the system against threats of layer 1 does not significantly increase the security of this application. Hence, the protection of layers 2, 3 and 4 is sufficient. The requirements are as follows:

Requirements for layer 2
- The secret keys that are used for authentication and encryption must reside in a protected hardware to avoid access by an attacker to the keys in any kind.
- The platform integrity has to be proved before the communication with a remote platform takes place, to avoid an attacker of loading malicious code to the mobile device via the programming interface during the maintenance phase.

Requirements for layer 3 and 4
- Before every data transmission, the authentication of both communication endpoints (mobile device and server) has to be proved.
- Integrity and confidentially must be proved during data transmission.
- All applied mechanisms must be based on strong cryptographic technologies [5].

3.4   State of the Art

Security in embedded, wireless and mobile devices is a very important and active field of research and development. The migration of mobile standalone applications to wireless ad hoc and personal area networking application requires additional security mechanisms [6,7]. Until now, it is e.g. common to use a single personal identification number (PIN) to get access to the local programming interface of an infusion pump. Knowing this three digit PIN enables the user to change the infusion rate to an arbitrary value. It is obvious that such a PIN does not offer sufficient protection in a networked application.

Strong cryptographic algorithms are needed. Asymmetric algorithms, which are based on modular exponentiation with large operands, are hardly suitable for resource constrained microcontrollers, because they need a large amount of memory and computational power. Asymmetric algorithms based on elliptic curve cryptography (ECC) do not use modular exponentiation and therefore are suitable to be implemented in resource constrained microcontrollers [8] or tiny hardware components [9]. These concepts are promising, however aspects of tamper resistance must be additionally considered.

Another approach is the usage of cryptographic coprocessors which can be connected to a microcontroller or can be embedded into the processor itself [10] to perform the time consuming cryptographic operations. Most of the research works focus on encryption of high data rate streams and have no constrains concerning the power consumption.

Modern wireless technologies such as Bluetooth integrate support for authenticated connections and encrypted data transmissions. But apart from known vulnerabilities in the security system of Bluetooth [11] other problems arise:

If the communication of the Bluetooth PAN is secured and one node sends data to a service entity outside the PAN, the packet has do be forwarded by the gateway, for example by the Smartphone. Even though the Smartphone uses an encrypted connection to the server, data from the node is briefly unencrypted because the encryption format has to be transformed. If we take into consideration that there are already numerous viruses and other malicious programs for Smartphones circulating [12], plaintext on the Smartphone is a serious problem and must be prevented.

End-to-end security avoids the problem of plaintext on gateways or similar systems. There are many web applications that use strong end to end security. For example secure websites, secure shells and home banking applications. End to end mechanisms are well understood and provide a high level of security.

3.5   Design Alternatives

The following design alternatives are considered and compared concerning the previously introduced threat layers, availability and costs:

1. Application Specific Integrated Circuit (ASIC). An implementation that uses an ASIC that runs the application software and has cryptographic functions and methods for tamper resistance is able to protect an embedded system against threats of all layers (1-4). However, the development and production of an ASIC is too expensive for applications with low device quantities.
2. Pure Software Solution (e.g. Software ECC). Solutions based on pure software implementations of cryptographic algorithms are able to protect a system against threats of layer 3 and 4. This is due to the fact that the private keys have to be stored in the nonvolatile memory of the microcontroller and therefore can be read by an attacker through the programming interface.
3. Microcontroller and TPM. Low power microcontrollers with integrated TPM alike functionality are not available at present. Therefore the usage of an external TPM that is connected to a low power microcontroller is a cheap and feasible solution with a high level of security (layer 2-4).

3.6   Proposed Architecture

In this section we present our concept of the system architecture for a secure personal network (see figure 4).

We use end-to-end security to protect the communication between the mobile device and the webserver. The TPM is needed on the mobile device to meet the protection requirements as follows:

- Secret keys are created and stored inside the TPM which has mechanisms for tamper resistance. Cryptographic functions that use these keys are run inside the TPM. The TPM protects the keys from being exposed to an attacker.
- The platform configuration is stored inside the TPM during boot time and is used to attest the platform integrity to a remote entity by using the TPM command quote. The attestation protects the system against malicious software on the mobile device.
- The mobile device is authenticated by signing an authentication challenge of the remote entity. The signing is done inside the TPM and cannot be counterfeited.
- The remote entity is authenticated by the use of a password restricted TPM key. The password is stored inside the TPM and cannot be read. The remote entity has to know the password in order to use the key to decrypt the session key. If the session key can be decrypted by the TPM, the remote entity is authenticated. By the use of the Object Independent Authorization Protocol (OIAP) which is a TPM mechanism, it is avoided to transfer the password in plaintext.
- Eavesdropping during data transmission is avoided by symmetric AES encryption on the microcontroller and the use of the session key.

To build the Personal Area Network, the Bluetooth PAN profile is used. The mobile devices act as Bluetooth PANU. Inside the Bluetooth PAN, there is a device that acts as a Bluetooth AP to enable connectivity to the webserver. The Bluetooth module of the mobile device consists of the whole Bluetooth stack that is necessary for PAN operation. Above the BNEP protocol, the TCP/IP layer is also integrated in the Bluetooth module.

The microcontroller is connected to the TPM via a serial SMBus. The communication between the microcontroller and the Bluetooth module is done by means of a Universal Asynchronous Receiver/Transmitter (UART). The software of the microcontroller consists of the following modules:

- The security module is responsible to communicate with the TPM. Therefore a driver for the SMBus and a driver for the TPM are needed. Additionally, for a hybrid encryption mode with a one-time PSK, it holds a module for the AES algorithm.
- The SOAP module consists of utilities to build and parse XML packets in order to invoke the method-calls of the webservice.
- The HTTP module is responsible of exchanging requests and responses with the webserver. The HTTP requests are built and sent via a TCP/IP connection to the server. The response is received and the payload is forwarded to the SOAP module for further processing.

The webserver is reachable from the Bluetooth Access Point via a direct link, for example, an internet connection. The HTTP packets are received over a TCP/IP connection from the mobile device and sent to the SOAP module for further processing. The security module is responsible to guarantee the security requirements such as authentication, platform integrity, data integrity and confidentiality.

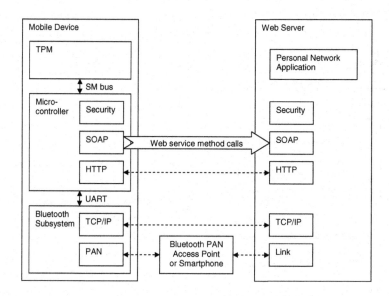

Fig. 4. Diagram of system architecture of secure Personal Network. The system components are the low power mobile device on the left hand side, an access point or Smartphone for external communication and the webserver with the Personal Network application on the right hand side.

3.7   Integrity Measurement and Security Protocol

Integrity Measurement. To use the TPM mechanism for attestation of platform integrity, the platform measurement must be performed before the software on the microcontroller is started. Code for the platform measurement has to reside in Read Only Memory (ROM), so it can be granted that the code is trustworthy. During the platform measurement, the whole program memory of the system is transferred in segments to the TPM and the resulting hash value is directly stored inside of one or more PCR registers. After the platform measurement, the program of the microcontroller is started.

Security Protocol. To establish a secure session between the webserver and the mobile device, we developed a security protocol that is based on a webservice interface (see figure 5). The security protocol is a means to use the TPM mechanisms by a remote entity to create a secure session and transfer encrypted data.

In figure 5 a sequence chart of the session establishment using the security protocol is shown. The connection establishment starts by sending an open request to the server. The server sends an open response and the mobile device performs a quote and sends back the result in form of an identify request. The identity is checked and the mobile device is authenticated. Then an AES key is generated and encrypted and sent to the mobile device. If the mobile device is able to decrypt the AES key with the password protected key inside the TPM, the server is also authenticated. An unbound notification is send to the server

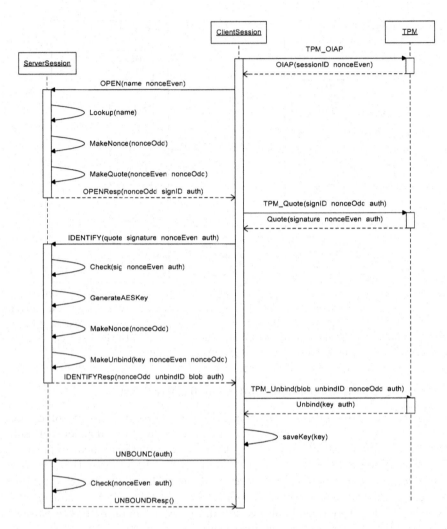

Fig. 5. Sequence chart of session establishment using the proposed security protocol

and notifies the session establishment. After that, data can be exchanged using AES encryption.

4   Implementation and Results

4.1   Implementation

In this section we present the implementation of the secure personal network system and show measurements performed with the mobile device. There we use the low power microcontroller MSP430F1611 from Texas Instruments. It is a

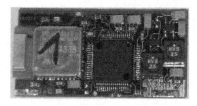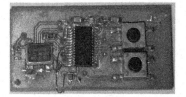

Fig. 6. Implemented low power security node. On the left hand side is the board with the microcontroller and the Bluetooth module. On the right hand side is the daughterboard with the TPM chip. The boards are pluged together with connectors on the backside.

16-bit RISC-CPU with 16 registers. It has 48 KB flash and 10 KB RAM. In our tests, we run the microcontroller at a clock rate of 8 MHz.

The Trusted Platform Module we use is the AT97SC3203S of Atmel and has a serial SMBus interface which is ideal for interfacing a resource constrained microcontroller at a low clock rate. The TPM needs an external 33 MHz clock to drive the internal RISC processor. The TPM is compatible with version 1.2 of the TCG specification for TPMs.

Integrated on the hardware of the mobile device is the Bluetooth module WML-C29 from Cambridge Silicon Radio (CSR). The WML-C29 contains a CSR BlueCore2 chip which has a complete Bluetooth stack integrated and supports the PAN profile up to the TCP/IP layer. There is also an antenna integrated on the WML-C29. In figure 6 the implemented low power node and the TPM board are shown.

In our tests the mobile device communicates over a PAN with the Bluetooth Access Point AXIS 9010 of Axis Communications which is a LINUX based standalone system that acts as a NAP according to the PAN profile. The AXIS 90100 is connected to the internet via a Local Area Network (LAN).

On the server side we use the Apache Tomcat webserver which is a part of the open source Jakarta project of the Apache Software Foundation. In order to offer a webservice interface, the Apache Webservice Project AXIS is used. Apache AXIS is an implementation of SOAP which is used to invoke webservice methods by means of XML. Apache AXIS offers modules to process incoming calls and redirect the call to the corresponding java method of the webservice implementation.

4.2   Measurements

To test our implementation and to evaluate the usage of a TPM in a resource constrained system, we added components to the mobile hardware to measure the power consumption of the TPM in different states of operation. In figure 7 we show the results for the states SHA-1 (calculation of the platform configuration), quote (signing of PCA for attestation of platform integrity) and unbind (decryption of the one time PSK).

As shown in figure 7, the boot process of the microcontroller is done after the measurement of the platform configuration (SHA-1). After this, the connection

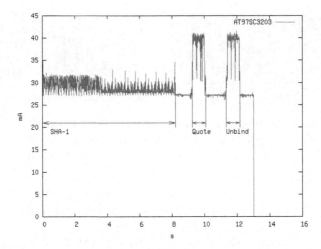

Fig. 7. Current measurement of the TPM. The first section shows the consumption while the hash engine was running. The second and third section show high power consumption because of the asymmetric cryptographic operation. After the third section the TPM is send to standby mode.

Table 1. Timing information and power consumption for several TPM commands according to transfer time of the command, execution time and transfer time of the answer

Command	Transfer time Command	Execution time	Transfer time answer	Power consumption
SHA1	6910 ms	1030 ms	7.81 ms	29.0 mA
Quote	11.7 ms	801 ms	46.9 ms	38.1 mA
Unbind	44.6 ms	801 ms	9.77 ms	38.2 mA

request is send to the server and the session is established at the end of decrypting the session key for AES. Hence the authenticated session is established in less than 3 seconds.

Some other timing information is found in table 1. The transfer time of the hash command is more than 5 seconds. That is due to the fact, that the hash for the PCR is calculated over the whole flash memory of the MSP. So the 48 KB of data has to be transferred to the TPM over the slow SMBus.

5   Conclusion

In this paper, we have introduced a concept and implementation of a secure Personal Network which consists of mobile low power nodes that are secured by means of a Trusted Platform Modules.

We showed that especially in the field of teletherapeutic application it is of great importance to protect the whole system by strong cryptographic mechanisms. Analyses of security requirements showed that end-to-end security is a strong method to guaranty the security and privacy of the teletherapeutic system (TTS). Therefore our new approach is to use TPMs which were originally developed to be used in personal computers and devices that have enough computational power to do asymmetric encryption without cryptographic coprocessors. We developed a concept for the integration of a TPM into our resource constrained mobile device and designed a security protocol which uses the mechanisms of a TPM to meet the security requirements of the personal network.

The integration of TPM chips into resource constrained microcontroller based platforms is possible since some manufacturer of TPMs introduced serial interfaces to their chips. In our research, we used an Atmel TPM which has a two wire serial SMBus interface and integrated it in our resource constrained mobile node. This node is suitable for use in mobile infusion pumps, which are used in current pain therapy, and allow the secure remote control of such pumps. The mobile node is also suitable for securing vital sensors.

The measurements done with the new secure mobile node showed that the power consumption is low (compared to the power consumption of normal operation) and therefore the usage of TPMs does not significantly lower the battery lifetime of a mobile system. Timing measurements showed that some operations such as platform configuration measurements take relatively long (several seconds). Such measurements of the platform configuration are only done during boot time and therefore do not pose a drawback for the operation of the device.

We can conclude that TPMs are well suited for resource constrained mobile devices and in our opinion their use is a step towards trusted ubiquitous computing.

References

1. PHMon: Personal Health Monitoring System, http://www.phmon.de/englisch
2. Niemegeers, I.G., de Groot, S.M.H.: Research Issues in Ad-Hoc Distributed Personal Networking. Wireless Personal Communications 26(2-3), 149–167 (2003)
3. TCS: Teletherapy of Cronical Pain, http://www.itiv.org/tcs
4. Grossmann, U., Schiessl, C., Jatobá, L., Ottenbacher, J., W., S., Mueller-Glaser, K.: Securely control Infusion Pumps via Internet for efficient Remote Therapy of Pain. In: IFMBE Proceedings of the World Congress on Medical Physics and Biomedical Engineering, Seoul, vol. 14 (2006)
5. Zhuge, J., Yao, R.: Security mechanisms for wireless home network. Global Telecommunications Conference 3, 1527–1531 (2003)
6. Miller, S.: Facing the challenge of wireless security. Computer 34(7), 16–18 (2001)
7. Ravi, S., Raghunathan, A., Chakradhar, S.: Embedding security in wireless embedded systems. In: VLSI Design, 2003. Proceedings. 16th International Conference on (2003), pp. 269–270 (2003)

8. Kumar, S., Girimondo, M., Weimerskirch, A., Paar, C., Patel, A., Wander, A.: Embedded end-to-end wireless security with ECDH key exchange. In: Circuits and Systems, 2003. MWSCAS '03. Proceedings of the 46th IEEE International Midwest Symposium, vol. 2, pp. 786–789 (2003)
9. Batina, L., Mentens, N., Sakiyama, K., Preneel, B., Verbauwhede, I.: Low-Cost Elliptic Curve Cryptography for Wireless Sensor Networks. In: Buttyán, L., Gligor, V., Westhoff, D. (eds.) Security and Privacy in Ad-Hoc and Sensor Networks. LNCS, vol. 4357, pp. 6–17. Springer, Heidelberg (2006)
10. Smyth, N., McLoone, M., McCanny, J.: Reconfigurable cryptographic RISC microprocessor. In: VLSI Design, Automation and Test (VLSI-TSA-DAT). 2005 IEEE VLSI-TSA International Symposium on (2005), pp. 29 – 32 (2005)
11. Hager, C., Midkiff, S.: An analysis of Bluetooth security vulnerabilities. Wireless Communications and Networking, 2003. WCNC 2003. 2003 IEEE 3, 1825–1831 (2003)
12. Töyssy, S., Helenius, M.: About malicious software in smartphones. Journal in Computer Virology 2(2), 109–119 (2006)

ALGSICS — Combining Physics and Cryptography to Enhance Security and Privacy in RFID Systems

Neil Bird[1], Claudine Conrado[1], Jorge Guajardo[1], Stefan Maubach[2,*],
Geert-Jan Schrijen[1], Boris Skoric[1], Anton M.H. Tombeur[1], Peter Thueringer[3],
and Pim Tuyls[1]

[1] Philips Research Europe, Eindhoven, The Netherlands
{neil.bird,claudine.conrado,jorge.guajardo,geert.jan.schrijen,
boris.skoric,a.m.h.tombeur,pim.tuyls}@philips.com
[2] IMAPP, Radboud University Nijmegen, Nijmegen, The Netherlands
s.maubach@science.ru.nl
[3] NXP, Gratkorn, Austria
peter.thueringer@nxp.com

Abstract. In this paper, we introduce several new mechanisms that are cheap to implement or integrate into RFID tags and that at the same time enhance their security and privacy properties. Our aim is to provide solutions that make use of existing (or expected) functionality on the tag or that are inherently cheap and thus, enhance the privacy friendliness of the technology "almost" for free. Our proposals, for example, make use of environmental information (presence of light temperature, humidity, etc.) to disable or enable the RFID tag. A second possibility that we explore is the use of delays in revealing a secret key used to later establish a secure communication channel. We also introduce the idea of a "sticky tag," which can be used to re-enable a disabled (or killed) tag whenever the user considers it to be safe. We discuss the security and describe usage scenarios for all solutions. Finally, we review previous works that use physical principles to provide security and privacy in RFID systems.

Keywords: RFID, privacy, cheap solutions, sensors, physics and crypto.

1 Introduction

The pervasiveness of RFID tags, their ability to carry more information than bar codes, their expected low cost (below US$0.10), and their lack of need for line of sight communication pose interesting challenges to those interested in their widespread adoption. Such challenges include both privacy and security concerns. On the privacy front, we can identify concerns on the part of consumers who will be carrying tagged objects. In particular, the wireless communication capabilities of RFID tags and their simple functionality (when queried they simply reply with a unique identifier) could make it easier to track people based on tag identifiers as well as to find out consumer preferences clandestinely. Similarly,

---

* Work performed while at Philips Research Laboratories, The Netherlands.

F. Stajano et al. (Eds.): ESAS 2007, LNCS 4572, pp. 187–202, 2007.
© Springer-Verlag Berlin Heidelberg 2007

companies and defense organizations will also be more vulnerable to espionage as it will be much easier to gather information on the competition or the enemy and much harder to detect such spying activities. On the security front, there is the authentication problem, i.e., how a legitimate party can assess whether an RFID tag associated with an object (and thus the object) is authentic or not. The ability to authenticate legitimate tags has direct implications on industry's ability to decrease the counterfeit market, which in 2004 was expected to surpass the 500 billion USD per year mark [1].

Based on the solutions that are known today, we propose to divide security and privacy solutions for RFID into two groups: algorithmic solutions and solutions that either combine cryptography and physical principles, or that simply take advantage of a physical process. By algorithmic solutions, we mean solutions based on cryptographic mechanisms. Examples include: basic access control through passwords, minimalistic cryptography [2] and lightweight protocols [3], solutions based on symmetric-key cryptography (e.g. [4,5]), hash functions (e.g. [6]), and elliptic curve based solutions [7,8]. However, at the present moment, solutions based on traditional public-key cryptography, symmetric-key cryptography, and hash functions are out of the question for the cheapest of RFID tags. Notice that if RFID tags are to be widely deployed (as bar codes are) then they also need to be in the same price range as a bar code, which only requires ink to be printed on a given item and thus, has cost close to zero. In the search for cheaper solutions, researchers have turned away from algorithmic approaches. Thus, ideas have been developed such as the `kill` command, the blocker tag [9,10] and similar blocking/proxy mechanisms [11,12]. More engineering oriented approaches have also been introduced such as the IBM clipped tags [13], distance bounding protocols [14], or techniques that take advantage of noise in the communication channel to camouflage the reader-tag communication [15,16]. We will refer to all such approaches as *algsics* methods.

It is clear that the major advantages of tagging objects with RFID tags, as Juels [17] points out, are the abilities to uniquely identify objects and to automate tasks that previously had to be performed by a human. This will result in clear advantages to manufacturers of products or service providers. However, one may ask what is the general public case for tagging everyday objects? RFID tags also have the potential to enable new applications (only limited by the reader's imagination) such as smart refrigerators that are able to tell when a product's life has expired or when you have run out of milk, washing machines that simply need to be started and know based on clothing information what wash cycle it should run, intelligent posters that allow a consumer to know in which cinemas and at what times a movie is playing, and finally, as a an enabling technology in smart homes for the elderly and the cognitively impaired [17]. However, the possibilities offered by the wide deployment of RFID technology will only become true if the privacy of individuals is properly protected.

CONTRIBUTIONS. In this paper, we propose several additional mechanisms to enhance privacy and security of RFID tags. Our aim is to provide privacy solutions which make use of existing (or expected) functionality on the tag or that are inherently cheap and thus, enhance the privacy friendliness of the technology "almost" for free. Some of our proposals make use of environmental information to disable or enable the RFID tag. Although the combination of sensors with RFID tags is not new [18,19], the realization that such environmental information can be used to enhance privacy is new and to the authors' knowledge has not been proposed before. A second possibility that we explore is the use of delays in revealing a secret key used to later establish a secure communication channel. We would like to point out that we do not claim that all the solutions presented in this paper will constitute stand-alone solutions to the privacy (or security) problems in RFID. Rather, we believe that these solutions will enhance other security and privacy solutions. It is possible that such methodology will in the end be the way towards securing RFID. The remainder of this contribution is organized as follows. In Sect. 2, we introduce solutions which make use of sensor information to enhance consumer privacy. Section 3 describes a new RFID proxy mechanism that we call a sticky tag. Sticky tags allow the implementation of the `kill` command without its disadvantages by re-enabling the tag wherever and whenever the user considers it safe to do so. In Sect. 4, we explain how we can use time delays in the messages exchanged between the tag and the reader to enhance security. Section 5 summarizes related work proposing algsics solutions. Finally, we end with some conclusions in Sect. 6.

2   Physics at the Service of Privacy

In this section, we describe solutions that enhance the privacy of users carrying objects with associated RFID tags. We assume that guidelines for RFID privacy have been followed, such as placing the tag on the outside of the object and that this position has been clearly identified. This also allows consumers to have the option of removing the tag if desired. We also assume the integration of sensors in the RFID tag functionality. This assumption gives rise to several questions. The first question we ask is if this approach is feasible at all from a technical point of view and if such a sensor-RFID tag can be implemented in a battery-free manner. The answer to these two questions is positive as [18,20,19] provide evidence of the feasibility of this approach. The second question regards price. How much such a sensor-RFID tag costs will in the end dictate whether such a solution will experience widespread adoption or not. To be successfully adopted at the item level, we require a price in the range of US$0.05 per tag [21]. The experience of [18] seems to indicate that today it is possible to build RFID tags including sensor functionality under a US$1 but far from the US$0.05 mark. In fact, some are already available, albeit only battery powered ones [22]. In the end, we expect that the continued decrease in silicon prices as well as consumer and customer requirements for additional functionality will enable the integration of sensor functionality into cheap RFID tags. In the following, we describe several scenarios which take advantage of embedded sensor functionality in an RFID tag to make the technology more privacy friendly. The basic idea in all the solutions is to use environmental information as an on/off switch. By environmental information, we mean data from temperature, light presence (or absence), or humidity readings of the environment surrounding the sensor-RFID tag. Depending on the setting and the application, a certain sensor might be more appropriate than another. Then, whenever the chosen environmental information attains a certain value (or range of values) or the user "creates" the right environmental conditions, the RFID tag is able to transmit data to an interrogating reader. Otherwise, the tag functions as if it was completely disabled. In the next sections, we describe usage scenarios for particular sensors and we discuss advantages and disadvantages of such solutions.

2.1 Tag Privacy Protection Via Light Controlled Tag Activation

IDEA. The idea is to control access to the powering circuit of the RFID tag via a fully integrated light-sensitive diode which can detect the presence of a laser-beam, e.g., from a laser pointer. This allows for the presence of a secure light-controlled ON/OFF switch on the tag. When the tag is powered by a reader and a laser-beam is pointed at the light-sensor, a digital ON code is written into the RFID's non-volatile memory. This ON code can, by means of an active switch (e.g., a MOS-transistor), be used to enable the power-supply voltage to parts of the RFID-chip, or enable other circuits to the rest of the chip, in such a way that the chip becomes fully functional. Even when the tag is taken out of the reader field, this ON state remains stored in memory. The tag can also be set in its OFF mode under similar conditions. When the tag is powered by a reader and a laser beam is pointed again to the light-sensor, an OFF bit will be written in non-volatile memory and the power-supply voltage will be disabled from the rest of the tag. In that case, the tag is not functional anymore until it is switched ON again by means of the laser beam. Even though such a switch provides the desired functionality of access control to the tag, it suffers from the drawback that a laser beam needs to be pointed to the tag. Thus, this could be considered as undermining one of RFID's main advantages: no line of sight communication. As an alternative, it is also possible to make an RFID tag that will only function if enough environmental light is present. In this case, the user can protect his tags from being read by an unauthorized party simply by covering the tag such that no light can reach its photo detector or by keeping the tags in the dark. Notice that in many situations, this would not be an unnatural thing to assume (just think of a grocery bag, a wallet, or a purse). Alternatively, an RFID tag could be part of a label that can be closed or opened (covered/uncovered) such that light to the tag is blocked or passed, respectively. This way the user is in control of the readout of his tags and can choose when and where his tags may be read. No special reader is required for reading out the RFID tag. The silicon-area required for the light-sensitive diode, including control circuits, can be very small [23]. This results in a cheap protection method that can be, if necessary, combined with other existing privacy enhancing technologies.

DISCUSSION. A consumer carrying items with such a modified RFID tag disables the tag at the point of sale terminal and re-enables it again once he/she is in a safe environment, e.g., at home. Thus, future ambient intelligent applications are still supported and the user's privacy not affected. Another example application of such a solution is in the tagging of bank notes. By turning off the RFID interface in his/her bank notes via their light-enabled switch, a user very simply avoids tracking. Another attack that is prevented is that in which a thief targets passers-by who are carrying 500 Euro notes in their wallets [24] by simply reading their tags. On the other hand, any person or organization desiring to verify the authenticity of the bank note can do so upon obtaining the bank note as a form of payment for a service or product. Notice that the light enabled switch does not support all the properties put forward by Juels and Pappu in [24]. In particular, it would only allow law enforcement agencies (or any authorized entity) to trace bank notes after detaining a potential suspect and not in an unobtrusive manner as suggested in [24]. Finally, a potential attacker, intending to track someone via the RFID tags that his victim is carrying, would be required to point a light source at each consumer tag that needs to be enabled without this activity being detected by the victim.

2.2 Tag Privacy Protection Via Moisture Dependent Contact and Other Sensors

IDEA. Inclusion of RFID tags in clothing has been proposed as a means to support activities such as supply chain and retailer product management. However, including RFID tags in clothing raises privacy concerns to those that wear such garments (see for example [25]). To enhance the privacy of users in this situation, a modified tag is proposed. The tag operates normally prior to sale. At the point of sale, the tag is *disabled*, e.g. by burning a ROM component or wire, which can be done by applying a large amount of power to the tag at the point of sale reader/terminal. Notice that we do not completely kill the tag but rather disable its RF interface. Once in the disabled state, the tag can still function but only if enough conducting moisture is present. This can be done by means of a switch (put in a strategic location such as the tag's antenna) that can only make electric contact if conducting liquid is present. Therefore, the tag is effectively disabled in the street (as long as it stays dry) and can be finally re-enabled when the washing machine pumps water onto the clothes. One may worry that tag read-out is hampered by large volumes of water absorbing RF radiation. However, studies have shown that this is not a problem. In particular, it is well known that at low frequencies (in the 10 to 20 MHz range) water is transparent to an RF signal [26, pages 2-6–2-7]. At higher frequencies, the attenuation is significant and it is highly frequency dependent. For example, the study in [27] shows that the attenuation of the signal traveling a distance of 6 cm varies between 7 dB and 23.5 dB for frequencies between 100 MHz and 950 MHz. Notice, however, that there are solutions starting to appear that can perform well in the presence of water and metals at high frequencies as shown in [28]. Finally, for the particular case of an RFID-tag operating in the 13.56 MHz band, a weakening of the signal by 10 dB is deemed acceptable. It can be shown experimentally that at frequencies around 10 MHz the RF signal penetrates 25 cm into salty liquid, which is more than sufficient for the washing machine example.

DISCUSSION. In addition to supporting activities such as supply chain and retailer product management, RFID tags associated with clothing items could also support other applications such as smart washing machines. Smart washing machines could be equipped with an RFID reader, which allows the machine to access clothing information. Therefore, the machine could autonomously select a washing program based on that information or it could advise the user to remove an item that needs a different washing program via an alarm. A second example of a sensor used to enhance privacy is a temperature sensor for a smart refrigerator application. In this setting, RFID tags could be allowed to be read only in certain temperature ranges. Thus, when the groceries are in the refrigerator at a certain temperature range, the RFID tags associated with the groceries would be readable and otherwise not. Such an RFID tag would enable applications as diverse as : checking whether a product has been at the correct temperature during the whole supply-chain or placing an automatic order when the user has run out of certain food items. On the other hand, one can argue that whenever the temperature outside was also in the range of the refrigerator temperature, the RFID tag would be allowed to transmit and thus, the user would be traceable. However, the ability that an attacker has to trace someone would be highly dependent on weather conditions and not on the attacker's choice. This diminishes the attacker's tracing abilities or forces him to change environmental conditions around his target. In this case, security is also highly dependent on how close the attacker can get to his target and stay there for extended periods of time. Clearly the closer the attacker is to his target, the easier it is for him to be discovered but also the more successful he will be in cheating the system. Finally, notice that a single sensor will probably not be applicable to all scenarios, with the possible exception of the light sensor. For example, a humidity sensor might be suitable for clothing but not for electronic items, and similarly temperature sensors might work well with food but not with clothing. Light sensors, on the other hand, seem to allow a wide range of applications.

3   Sticky Tags and Privacy

Current privacy preserving solutions for RFID are such that they either add cost to the tag by including additional hardware to perform cryptographic functions or require the modification of current tag specifications to perform additional operations. On the other hand, the most widely available (standardized) solution for privacy concerns is the `kill` command that permanently disables the tag. This solves the privacy problem but it gives up the advantages that RFID tags can provide in other applications. Thus, the idea proposed in this section can be seen as middle ground between the two extremes of rendering tags completely useless with the `kill` command or having additional costs added to current RFID tags. It can also be seen as yet another instantiation (with different properties and characteristics) of a privacy sentinel [29] or watchdog tag [11].

IDEA. The basic idea is to allow the `kill` command to completely disable the RF functionality of the RFID tag but to allow access to the information in the tag via a second interface, which requires proximity to the tag. This second interface could take different forms. The simplest instantiation of the second interface would be a contact-based interface. In this case, proximity means "as close as it is physically possible," i.e. touching the disabled tag. We emphasize that adding a contact interface to an RFID tag is not new. However, to the authors' knowledge the idea that a second interface can be used in combination with a second (more powerful) tag to "resurrect" the functionality of the killed tag and guarantee privacy (and security) for the user is novel. Notice that the resurrecting functionality is different from the resurrecting duckling security policy of Stajano and Anderson [30], where a node in an ad-hoc network establishes a secure channel after being "resurrected" by an adjacent node. A second possibility is a modified antenna system which upon receiving the `kill` command changes its configuration. For example, the read-range could be limited by the `kill` command to 1 mm. By a modified antenna system, we mean both an antenna which changes its range (for example, via clipped tags as in [13]) or simply a system consisting of two antennas. The first antenna has a normal range and it gets disabled upon the tag receiving the `kill` command whereas the second antenna has a very short range and it is not affected by the `kill` command. Notice that this instantiation might succumb to relay attacks. The second interface can then be used by another device, presumably a more powerful RFID tag both in terms of computational power and security, to access the data in the original RFID tag and communicate in a secure manner with RFID readers. We will refer to this device in what follows as a *sticky tag* to illustrate the fact that we expect such devices to be implemented as a sticky label that adheres to objects whose original RFID tags have been killed. "Sticking" our new more powerful tag on the less powerful tag has the effect of "resurrecting" the tag. Figure ?? depicts an illustration of the system. In particular, a standard reader powers up both antennas, the sticky tag's antenna and the original RFID tag's antenna. Since the RFID tag's antenna has been disabled, only if the sticky tag is present will the reader obtain a response from the RFID tag. Notice that the sticky tag acts as a bridge between the disabled RFID tag and the RFID reader. As such, the sticky tag, when queried, forwards the information residing in the original RFID tag to the reader. Also the sticky tag must not have an identifier (e.g. EPC) of its own.

   In addition, the sticky tags do not necessarily have to be more powerful devices. A sticky tag could simply be a much cheaper device without memory or functionality other than reviving the killed RF interface of the original tag. This instantiation would have the advantage of extremely low cost. Finally, an added advantage of sticky tags is that they could be used to resurrect RFID tags with a defective RF interface.

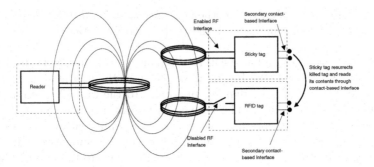

Fig. 1. Sticky tag in the presence of a reader with a secondary contact-based interface

DISCUSSION. As usual, at check-out the RFID tag is disabled. However, by attaching a sticky tag to the killed tag now the user is able to take advantage of the information stored in the killed tag just as if the tag in the object had never been killed. This has the added advantage that the identifier is transmitted to the readers in a secure manner (if the sticky tag is equipped with cryptographic functionality) or in a more secure environment, since it is the user that decides where and when to resurrect the killed tag. The sticky tag is also envisioned to be re-usable, i.e., users could have a bag of such sticky tags and attach them to objects whose RFID tags have been killed. Once the object's usable life has expired, the user could simply detach the tag and store it for future use after discarding the object. The manufacturer who would also like to check an object's information once the object is in the recycling phase, could similarly resurrect the originally embedded RFID tag by using a sticky tag as well. A final usage case is the scenario in which a user returns a product to the shop because of regular maintenance, repair, or malfunction. In this case, the shop can use a sticky tag to read the product information available in the original tag associated with the object. Admittedly, a main issue with the sticky tags is usability. Can we expect that users will tag their groceries so that they can make use of their smart refrigerator? Notice that owning a smart appliance implies that the user has an interest in using the intelligence features in the refrigerator, otherwise he would not have bought it in the first place. In addition, attaching a sticky tag both at home and at the repair shop scenarios does not need to be a cumbersome activity. It could be similar to the customary practice of detaching anti-theft tags at clothing stores once an item has been sold or to adding a pricing tag to an item as it had been done for years (and in some places it is still done) before the widespread adoption of bar codes. On the other hand, a main advantage of the sticky tags is that they are an opt-in solution. By default, we are safeguarding individual's privacy and if they desire they can regain many of the advantages that RFID offers. Sticky tags would be best suited to objects that are meant for home use once they have bought (e.g., groceries, TVs, DVD players, etc.). Similarly, using sticky tags for clothing for example, would imply that the user needs to remember to detach the sticky tag from his clothing before going out. Otherwise, he could risk traceability. This seems a burden not likely to be accepted by most people.

4   Time-Released Secrets and RFID

IDEA. This solution tries to hinder the ability of a reader randomly placed in the street to read or identify a tag when a person passes by. This achieved by implementing an actual physical time delay functionality in the RFID tag. This time delay forces the reading of sensitive data to require more time when the tag is in an unprotected environment than when it is in a protected setting. In this case, the tag itself acts as the agent that releases the secret at a given time in the future. The user or user's devices (e.g. smart home appliances) are the party requesting access to the secret-key information. The unprotected environment may be, for instance, the user's path from shop to home. In this case, the chances that an unauthorized reader is able to obtain any information from the tag are decreased thanks to the time delay between a reader requesting information (powering up the tag) and the time when the tag actually responds. On the other hand, when the tag is in a protected environment, e.g. the shop or the user's home, the tag responds without delay, thus not hindering trusted applications. Notice that the delay can be used to send the tag identification number, product information stored on the tag, or a key used to encrypt the previously mentioned data. One can think of many different configurations for the delay. For example, the delay could occur before any actual data is transmitted from the tag to the reader (after which the message would be transmitted normally) or there could be a permanent delay introduced between the bits (bytes, or any other part) of a message being transmitted. In the latter case, a one-time switch can be used to permanently change a fast-readable tag into a slow-readable tag. In what follows, we describe a particular implementation of the above idea.

An RFID built to support these delays could contain three areas of ROM. The first area stores the EPC and product information PI in Erasable ROM (E-ROM), which is fast-readable. The second area stores the symmetric encryption of the EPC and the PI, $\mathtt{Enc}_K(EPC\|PI)$, which is also fast-readable, while the third area stores the encryption key K, which is slowly-readable. Before purchase, the shop can quickly read the EPC and the PI from the E-ROM. When the product is sold, this fast reading path is destroyed or blocked, e.g. by erasing the E-ROM. Thus in an unprotected environment only the value $\mathtt{Enc}_K(EPC\|PI)$ can be read fast by any reader. Notice that this could potentially allow the tracking of the tag via the persistent identifier, $\mathtt{Enc}_K(EPC\|PI)$, but it does not reveal anything about the EPC or the PI, themselves. Finally, in the users home, a trusted device can slowly read the key K, quickly read the encrypted value $\mathtt{Enc}_K(EPC\|PI)$, and store the pairs $(\mathtt{Enc}_K(EPC\|PI), K)$ in a product database. When product information is needed, the home devices can use the quickly sent value $\mathtt{Enc}_K(EPC\|PI)$ as an identifier to search the database for the key K which can in turn be used to decrypt $\mathtt{Enc}_K(EPC\|PI)$ to give the EPC and the PI. A variation of the above scheme that does not

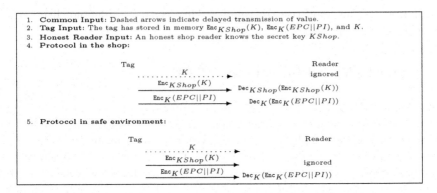

1. **Common Input:** Dashed arrows indicate delayed transmission of value.
2. **Tag Input:** The tag has stored in memory $Enc_{KShop}(K)$, $Enc_K(EPC||PI)$, and K.
3. **Honest Reader Input:** An honest shop reader knows the secret key $KShop$.
4. **Protocol in the shop:**

    Tag   Reader

             K ignored

    $Enc_{KShop}(K)$

                        $Dec_{KShop}(Enc_{KShop}(K))$

    $Enc_K(EPC||PI)$

                        $Dec_K(Enc_K(EPC||PI))$

5. **Protocol in safe environment:**

    Tag   Reader

             K

    $Enc_{KShop}(K)$

                        ignored

    $Enc_K(EPC||PI)$

                  $Dec_K(Enc_K(EPC||PI))$

Fig. 2. Delayed tag identification without physical switch

require a switch is shown in Fig. 2. The advantage here is that the $EPC||PI$ value is never sent in the clear (even in the shop). In addition, there is no need for erasing or destroying the fast-reading path as in the previous system. The tags' tracking problem can be solved if the tags are assumed to have more capabilities, namely, a random number generator and the capability to evaluate hash values. This, however, requires hardware to support a hash function or a dedicated encryption module (as opposed to just memory). Finally, another simple variant would have the tag send the EPC and/or the PI at normal speed at the shop and with a delay after the product is sold.

DISCUSSION. The protocols presented here seem to be well suited for many applications. However, we would like to point out that in any version of the protocol, an attacker is successful if he is able to keep the attacked tags in its reader field long enough to obtain the secret key K. In particular, if the tag is stationary for long periods of time, then the attacker can seriously compromise the privacy of the user. Clearly, then security and usability can be traded off against each other. The longer it takes for the tag to release the next bit of its secret key, the longer the attacker will have to be present in the surrounding of the tag and thus, the less likely that he will obtain the whole secret information. On the other hand, the longer it takes for the tag to release the secret key, the longer that the legitimate user will have to wait when he wants to access the tag's encrypted information at home[1]. Given this limitation, delays appear to be well suited for objects that will not be carried outside the safe environment of the user very often (e.g., food, TVs, home electronics, etc.). On the other hand, tags incorporated into clothing would be less likely to be a privacy problem if using different privacy enhancing solutions such as those based on sensors. We end by noticing that the assumption that the attacker tends to be stationary and thus unable to query tags for extended periods of time is not new in the RFID setting (see for example [2]).

---

[1] This is only true the first time that the tag is queried at home.

Remark 1. The idea of using a delay to enhance security is not new in cryptography. In particular, May [31] introduces timed-release cryptography as a new primitive. The solution that we present here can be seen as a timed-release system in a different time scale and with different granularity as the system of [31]. In the context of RFID security, Juels [2] seems to be the first to use delays to limit the ability of an attacker to perform successive queries to a tag by using a hardware-based throttling mechanism for his pseudonyms scheme. However,schemes such as the ones presented in this section and the ability to turn on and off the delays were not discussed.

5   Related Work

In this section, we survey other *algsics* methodologies found in the literature. They are organized according to the ideas in which they are based.

PRIVACY SENTINEL AND BLOCKER TAGS. The term "privacy sentinel" was introduced by Sarma in [29]. However, the concept of a proxy device that manages the communication of the RFID tag with the external world was originally introduced by Floerkemeier et al. [11] while the blocker tag was originally introduced by Juels et al. [9] (see also [10]). In what follows, we will use the term privacy sentinel and watchdog tag interchangeable. Similar approaches have also been introduced in [12,32,33]. The idea is to provide users with a more powerful trusted device (the privacy sentinel device) that takes care of their privacy, manages their privacy preferences and could, for example, be integrated into a user's cell phone. The watchdog tag's (as it is called in [11]) main purpose is to manage the communication between the reader and the tags that the user is carrying. In addition, the watchdog tag could show warnings to the user, prompt him for authorization, and log all data transfers. Reference [12] extends the watchdog tag concept to include key management, authentication operations, and tag simulation (i e. the privacy sentinel is able to mimic the operations of the less powerful tags that is managing). Juels et al. [32] consider the problems of tag relabeling, acquisition and ownership transfer. A somewhat different but related approach is the idea of the blocker tag [9] which protects tags from unauthorized reading by interfering with the normal singulation protocol used to identify tags by a reader. Singulation is based on a binary tree algorithm. At each step in the algorithm the reader requests all those tags with their next bit in their identifier equal to one (for the sake of argument) to reply and all those with a zero to stay quite. Eventually, the reader requests all bits and is also able to singulate the desired tag. The blocker tag interferes with this algorithm by always responding with all identifiers effectively simulating all tags or those tags designated within a given range of identifiers. The blocker tag is expected to be cheap and be of the same type as a regular RFID tag.

CHANNEL DISTURBANCES. Recently, [16,15] have taken advantage of the noise present (or artificially generated) in the communication channel between reader and tag to enhance the security of their communication. Reference [16] takes advantage of the noise in the channel to allow readers and tags to share a secret without a *passive* adversary being able to learn it. Readers and tags perform a protocol where information reconciliation and privacy amplification take place through the use of universal hash functions. The scheme in [15] is somewhat different. It assumes the existence of *noisy tags* owned by the system which inject noise into the communication channel. The noisy tags also share a secret key with the reader, which is used to pseudo-randomly generate noise. Whenever the tag sends its secret key to the reader, an eavesdropper will see a signal that is the sum of the signal corresponding to the tag's secret key and the noise injected by the noisy tags. On the other hand, the reader is able to replicate the noisy tags' noise and it is able to subtract the noise signal from the received signal, thus recovering the tag's secret key. A similar approach to [15] is presented in [34]. The difference is that the authors do not assume the presence of a noisy tag but rather assume that the reader and tag can synchronize their communications. Both tag and reader send a pseudo-random sequence to each other, whenever their bits are different an eavesdropper will not know which bit was sent by the tag and which bit by the reader. On the other hand, both the tag and the reader are able to obtain each others keys.

DISTANCE BOUNDING PROTOCOLS. Cryptographically secure distance bounding protocols date back to 1993 as introduced in [35]. However, [36] seems to be the first to suggest a protocol specifically suited to the RFID setting. Notice that in the context of RFID protocols proximity implies trust. Fishkin et al. [36] find that looking at the signal noise (in particular to the Fano factor, which is used to approximate signal noise) and at the actual signal strength received by an RFID tag correlates fairly well with the tag distance from the reader. They can use this correlation to decide whether the energy received from the reader antenna can be considered to be in the far field or in the near field. Then, based on this decision, the RFID tag could have a policy of responding to the interrogating reader or not. This distance bounding protocol is combined in [36] with the idea of tiered revelation and authentication in which the tag reveals more and more information according to the level of authentication used by the reader. Reference [36] also noticed that the tiered level can also be associated with the amount of energy emitted by the reader. Thus, for example, a reader that requests more information will also be required to power the tag for a longer period of time while using a longer key size. The work in [37] proposes a new distance bounding protocol based on ultra-wideband pulse communication where the verifier is the reader and the prover the RFID tag. Thus, it considers the reverse problem, i.e., the reader wants to verify that it is talking to an honest tag. The protocol makes use of a keyed hash function or symmetric-key primitive to generate a sequence of pseudo-random bits which upon a challenge from the verifier are returned by the prover. Only an honest prover can generate the correct sequence as he also knows the secret key used to generate the sequence.

CHANGING-TAG SYSTEMS. By changing-tag systems, we mean systems in which the tag or tags change physically. Examples are the works presented in [38,13] as well as [39]. The work in [38] is interesting in that they suggest to physically split the IDs of RFID tags. In particular, their approach envisions splitting global RFID tag identifiers into a class ID (related to the class of objects) and a pure ID (which identifies the specific object, lot number, serial number, etc.). The idea is then for the user to be able to physically remove the class ID from the object and at a later stage attach a second tag with a different global ID, which might be unique in the user environment but not globally. The authors in [38] also notice that the same effect (changing IDs) can be achieved by using re-writable memory in an RFID tag. Reference [39] considers systems in which an object is associated with multiple RFID tags. Then, chaffing and winnowing in the sense of [40] can be used to disguise the true identity of the object. Notice that Weis [21] was the first to notice that chaffing and winnowing can be used in the RFID context but he assumed that the readers would be the ones generating the chaff. In [13], the authors propose to physically disconnect the antenna and the chip in an RFID tag. In addition to allowing for visual confirmation (on the part of the consumer) that the tag communication capabilities have been disabled, it allows for this functionality to be "pasted" back on if the user desires to resurrect the RFID tag functionality once he/she is in a safe environment.

TAG SWITCHES. The work in [41] explores the idea of physically deactivating a tag via a physical bit-dependent switch. If the bit is set to one, the RFID tag answers as usual to a reader query whereas if the bit is set to zero, then the tag is deactivated until the user activates it again. The idea is based on the assumption that only someone with physical access (or close proximity) to the tag can activate it again. Thus, consumer privacy is safeguarded and at the same time, tag functionality is preserved for privacy-friendly environments. The author describes three possible implementations of the physically changeable bit (PCB). The first implementation consists in physically (dis)connecting the antenna from the chip, much in the same way as the clipped tags in [13]. Other methods include: including electrically erasable ROM memory in the tag, writing or erasing the PCB depending on user wishes, and using "magnetic bits" in the tags to represent (and set or unset) the PCB bits. In this category, we also include the `kill` command, which works by completely disabling the tag if the tag is presented with the correct password. Although not application friendly, the `kill` command is a rather effective mechanism to safeguard individuals' privacy.

6   Concluding Remarks

In this paper, we have discussed and introduced solutions that show how the physics present in RFID systems can be leveraged to enhance security and privacy solutions at a low cost. We believe that this approach is promising in the sense that the cheapest RFID tags are constrained devices which will not allow (due to pricing requirements) the implementation of expensive cryptographic primitives. We point out, as it has been done also in previous works, that the security guarantees provided by *algsics* methods are not the same as those provided by crypto protocols using sophisticated primitives (for example, most algsics solutions provide security in a weak model against passive adversaries). However, it is also true that in many cases such guarantees might be enough. For example, it might not be feasible to implement an active attack without being discovered. Finally, the future might show that algsics solutions turn out to be effective additional countermeasures against attacks. In other words, when combined with other more sophisticated methods, the overall security (or privacy) guarantees of the system are enhanced.

References

1. Staake, T., Thiesse, F., Fleisch, E.: Extending the EPC Network — The Potential of RFID in Anti-Counterfeiting. In: Haddad, H., Liebrock, L.M., Wainwright, A.O. (eds.) SAC 2005, March 13-17, 2005, ACM Press, New York (2005)
2. Juels, A.: Minimalist Cryptography for Low-Cost RFID Tags. In: Blundo, C., Cimato, S. (eds.) SCN 2004. LNCS, vol. 3352, pp. 149–164. Springer, Heidelberg (2005)
3. Juels, A., Weis, S.: Authenticating Pervasive Devices with Human Protocols. In: Shoup, V. (ed.) CRYPTO 2005. LNCS, vol. 3621, pp. 293–308. Springer, Heidelberg (2005)
4. Feldhofer, M., Dominikus, S., Wolkerstorfer, J.: Strong Authentication for RFID Systems Using the AES Algorithm. In: Joye, M., Quisquater, J.-J. (eds.) CHES 2004. LNCS, vol. 3156, pp. 357–370. Springer, Heidelberg (2004)
5. Dominikus, S., Oswald, E., Feldhofer, M.: Symmetric Authentication for RFID Systems in Practice. Printed handout of Workshop on RFID and Light-Weight Crypto, pp. 25–31. ECRYPT Network of Excellence (July 13-15, 2005)
6. Weis, S.A., Sarma, S.E., Rivest, R.L., Engels, D.W.: Security and privacy aspects of low-cost radio frequency identification systems. In: Hutter, D., Müller, G., Stephan, W., Ullmann, M. (eds.) SPC 2003. LNCS, vol. 2802, pp. 201–212. Springer, Heidelberg (2004)
7. Tuyls, P., Batina, L.: RFID-tags for Anti-Counterfeiting. In: Pointcheval, D. (ed.) CT-RSA 2006. LNCS, vol. 3860, pp. 115–131. Springer, Heidelberg (2006)
8. Batina, L., Guajardo, J., Kerins, T., Mentens, N., Tuyls, P., Verbauwhede, I.: Public-Key Cryptography for RFID-Tags. In: PerCom 2007 Workshops. IEEE Conference on Pervasive Computing and Communications Workshops, New York, March 19-23, 2007, IEEE Computer Society, Los Alamitos (2007)
9. Juels, A., Rivest, R.L., Szydlo, M.: The blocker tag: selective blocking of RFID tags for consumer privacy. In: Jajodia, S., Atluri, V., Jaeger, T. (eds.) CCS 2003. ACM Conference on Computer and Communications Security, October 27-30, 2003, pp. 103–111. ACM Press, New York (2003)
10. Juels, A., Brainard, J.G.: Soft blocking: flexible blocker tags on the cheap. In: Atluri, V., Syverson, P.F., di Vimercati, S.D.C. (eds.) WPES 2004. ACM Workshop on Privacy in the Electronic Society, October 28, 2004, pp. 1–7. ACM Press, New York (2004)

11. Floerkemeier, C., Schneider, R., Langheinrich, M.: Scanning with a purpose – supporting the fair information principles in RFID protocols. In: Murakami, H., Nakashima, H., Tokuda, H., Yasumura, M. (eds.) UCS 2004. LNCS, vol. 3598, pp. 214–231. Springer, Heidelberg (2005)

12. Rieback, M., Crispo, B., Tanenbaum, A.: RFID guardian: A battery-powered mobile device for RFID privacy management. In: Boyd, C., González Nieto, J.M. (eds.) Information Security and Privacy. LNCS, vol. 3574, pp. 184–194. Springer, Heidelberg (2005)

13. Karjoth, G., Moskowitz, P.: Disabling RFID tags with visible confirmation: Clipped tags are silenced. In: WPES. Workshop on Privacy in the Electronic Society, Alexandria, Virginia, November 2005, ACM Press, New York (2005)

14. Munilla, J., Ortiz, A., Peinado, A.: Distance bounding protocols with void-challenges for RFID. Printed handout of Workshop on RFID Security – RFIDSec 06, pp. 15–26. ECRYPT Network of Excellence (July 2006)

15. Castelluccia, C., Avoine, G.: Noisy tags: A pretty good key exchange protocol for RFID tags. In: Domingo-Ferrer, J., Posegga, J., Schreckling, D. (eds.) CARDIS 2006. LNCS, vol. 3928, pp. 289–299. Springer, Heidelberg (2006)

16. Chabanne, H., Fumaroli, G.: Noisy Cryptographic Protocols for Low-Cost RFID Tags. IEEE Transactions on Information Theory 52(8), 3562–3566 (2006)

17. Juels, A.: RFID Security and Privacy: A Research Survey. IEEE Journal on Selected Areas in Communications 24(2), 381–394 (2006), Extended version available from `http://www.rsasecurity.com/rsalabs/node.asp?id=2029`

18. Philipose, M., Smith, J., Jiang, B., Mamishev, A.: Battery-Free Wireless Identification and Sensing. IEEE Pervasive Computing 4(1), 37–45 (2005)

19. Opasjumruskit, K., Thanthipwan, T., Sathusen, O., Sirinamarattana, P., Gadmanee, P., Pootarapan, E., Wongkomet, N., Thanachayanont, A., Thamsirianunt, M.: Self-powered wireless temperature sensors exploit RFID technology. IEEE Pervasive Computing 5(1), 54–61 (2006)

20. Kitayoshi, H., Sawaya, K.: Long range passive rfid-tag for sensor networks. In: IEEE 62nd Vehicular Technology Conference — VTC-2005, September 25-28, 2005, pp. 2696–2700. IEEE Computer Society, Los Alamitos (2005)

21. Weis, S.: Security and privacy in radio-frequency identification devices. Master thesis, May 2003, Massachusetts Institute of Technology (MIT), Cambridge, Massachusetts (2003)

22. Swedberg, C.: DHL Expects to Launch Sensor Tag Service by Midyear. RFID Journal (January 19th, 2007) Available at `http://www.rfidjournal.com/article/articleprint/2986/-1/1/`

23. Radovanovic, S., Annema, A., Nauta, B.: High-speed lateral polysilicon photodiode in standard CMOS technology. In: ESSDERC'03. 33rd European Solid-State Circuits Conference, September 16-18, 2003, IEEE Computer Society, Los Alamitos (2003)

24. Juels, A., Pappu, R.: Squealing Euros: Privacy Protection in RFID-Enabled Banknotes. In: Wright, R.N. (ed.) Financial Cryptography. LNCS, vol. 2742, pp. 103–121. Springer, Heidelberg (2003)

25. Batista, E.: Step Back' for Wireless ID Tech? Wired News (April 8th, 2003), Available at `http://www.wired.com/news/wireless/0,1382,58385,00.html`

26. Karygiannis, T., Eydt, B., Barber, G., Bunn, L., Phillips, T.: Draft Special Publication 800-98, Guidance for Securing Radio Frequency Identification (RFID) Systems. National Institute for Standards and Technology, Gaithersburg, MD, USA. (September 2006) Available for download at `http://csrc.nist.gov/`

27. Chan, Y., Meng, M.Q.H., Wu, K.L., Wang, X.: Experimental Study of Radiation Efficiency from an Ingested Source inside a Human Body Model. In: IEEE Annual International Conference of the Engineering in Medicine and Bilogy Society — IEEE-EMBS (September 1st-4th, 2005), pp. 7754–7757 (2005)

28. KU Information & Telecommunication Technology Center. The University of Kansas: UHF KU-RFID Tag (2006) Available at
http://www.rfidalliancelab.org/publications/ittc_press_release.shtml

29. Sarma, S.: Some issues related to rfid and security. Introductory Talk – RFIDSec 06 (July 2006) Available at
http://events.iaik.tugraz.at/RFIDSec06/Program/index.htm

30. Stajano, F., Anderson, R.J.: The Resurrecting Duckling: Security Issues for Ad-hoc Wireless Networks. In: Malcolm, J.A., Christianson, B., Crispo, B., Roe, M. (eds.) Security Protocols. LNCS, vol. 1796, pp. 19–21. Springer, Heidelberg (2000)

31. May, T.C.: Timed-release crypto. Posting to the Cypherpunks Mailing List (February 10th, 1993) Available at
http://cypherpunks.venona.com/date/1993/02/msg00129.html

32. Juels, A., Syverson, P., Bailey, D.: High-Power Proxies for Enhancing RFID Privacy and Utility. In: Danezis, G., Martin, D. (eds.) PET 2005. LNCS, vol. 3856, pp. 210–226. Springer, Heidelberg (2006)

33. Soppera, A., Burbridge, T.: Off by default - RAT: RFID acceptor tag. Printed handout of Workshop on RFID Security – RFIDSec 06, pp. 151–166. ECRYPT Network of Excellence (July 2006)

34. Haselsteiner, E., Breitfuss, K.: Security in near field communication (NFC). Printed handout of Workshop on RFID Security – RFIDSec 06, pp. 151–166. ECRYPT Network of Excellence (July 2006)

35. Brands, S., Chaum, D.: Distance-bounding protocols (extended abstract). In: Helleseth, T. (ed.) EUROCRYPT '93. LNCS, vol. 765, pp. 344–359. Springer, Heidelberg (1994)

36. Fishkin, K.P., Roy, S., Jiang, B.: Some Methods for Privacy in RFID Communication. In: Castelluccia, C., Hartenstein, H., Paar, C., Westhoff, D. (eds.) ESAS 2004. LNCS, vol. 3313, pp. 42–53. Springer, Heidelberg (2005)

37. Hancke, G., Kuhn, M.: An RFID distance bounding protocol. In: Conference on Security and Privacy for Emerging Areas in Communication Networks – SecureComm 2005, September 2005, pp. 67–73. IEEE Computer Society, Los Alamitos (2005)

38. Inoue, S., Yasuura, H.: RFID privacy using user-controllable uniqueness. RFID Privacy Workshop (November 2003)

39. Bolotnyy, L., Robins, G.: Multi-tag radio frequency identification systems. In: Workshop on Automatic Identification Advanced Technologies — AutoID, 345 E. 47th St, New York, October, 2005, NY 10017, pp. 83–88 (2005)

40. Rivest, R.L.: Chaffing and Winnowing: Confidentiality without Encryption. CryptoBytes 4(1), 12–17 (1998)

41. Zou, C.C.: PCB: Physically Changeable Bit for Preserving Privacy in Low-End RFID Tags. RFID White Paper Library, RFID Journal (May 2006)

Detecting Node Compromise in Hybrid Wireless Sensor Networks Using Attestation Techniques

Christoph Krauß, Frederic Stumpf*, and Claudia Eckert

Department of Computer Science
Darmstadt University of Technology
Darmstadt, Germany
{krauss,stumpf,eckert}@sec.informatik.tu-darmstadt.de

Abstract. Node compromise is a serious threat in wireless sensor networks. Particular in networks which are organized in clusters, nodes acting as cluster heads for many cluster nodes are a valuable target for an adversary. We present two efficient hardware-based attestation protocols for detecting compromised cluster heads. Cluster heads are equipped with a Trusted Platform Module and possess much more resources than the majority of cluster nodes which are very constrained in their capabilities. A cluster node can verify the trustworthiness of a cluster head using the Trusted Platform Module as a trust anchor and therefore validate whether the system integrity of a cluster head has not been tampered with. The first protocol provides a broadcast attestation, i.e., allowing a cluster head to attest its system integrity to multiple cluster nodes simultaneously, while the second protocol is able to carry out a direct attestation between a single cluster node (or the sink) and one cluster head. In contrast to timing-based software approaches,the attestation can be performed even if nodes are multiple hops away from each other.

Keywords: Sensor Network, Security, Trusted Computing, Attestation.

1 Introduction

Wireless sensor networks (WSNs) [1] provide a technological basis for many different security-critical applications, such as military surveillance, critical infrastructure protection and surveillance. WSNs can be deployed in unattended and even hostile environments for monitoring the physical world. The monitored environment is covered by hundreds or even thousands of sensor nodes with embedded sensing, computation, and wireless communication capabilities. If sensor nodes are not specially protected, an adversary can easily compromise them, recover information (e.g. keying material) stored on the nodes, and subvert them to act as authorized nodes in the network to perform insider attacks.

One approach to detect compromised nodes is based on attestation techniques, where sensor nodes must prove that their system has not been modified

---

* The author is supported by the German Research Foundation (DFG) under grant EC 163/4-1, project *TrustCaps*.

F. Stajano et al. (Eds.): ESAS 2007, LNCS 4572, pp. 203–217, 2007.

by an adversary. Attestation techniques that have already been proposed for WSNs [2,3,4] are software-based and rely on relatively accurate time measurement. These techniques are unsuitable for attestation along multiple hops and when static interferences delay message transmissions, which prevents an exact time measurement. One promising approach for overcoming the shortcomings of software-based attestation is using the Trusted Platform Module (TPM) as specified by the Trusted Computing Group (TCG) [5] as the trust anchor for attestation protocols. The trust anchor is responsible for providing assurance of delivered attestation values. The TPM provides such a hardware-based trust anchor. It also offers certain cryptographic functions which provide the foundation for attesting the configuration of the local platform to a remote platform. Due to the large scale and desired low-cost of WSNs, it is not feasible to integrate a TPM into each individual node. Fortunately, many WSNs are organized in clusters where a minority of nodes perform some special functions. These nodes may act as cluster heads (CH), performing special duties, such as data aggregation or key management for a number of cluster nodes (CN).

Since CHs are a valuable target for an adversary, it might be reasonable to equip them with a TPM in scenarios where a high level of security is desired. CNs and the sink should be able to verify whether a CH is still trustworthy, even if it is multiple hops away. Since CNs are very limited in their resources, attestation protocols must be very lightweight, i.e., requiring only few, small messages and cheap operations (such as symmetric encryption).

In this paper, we propose two efficient TPM-based attestation protocols for hybrid WSNs organized in clusters. Networks consist of low-cost CNs and more expensive TPM-equipped CHs. The first protocol allows a number of CNs to simultaneously validate the trustworthiness of a CH in regular intervals, while the second protocol enables an individual CN (or the sink) to verify the trustworthiness of a CH at any time. Both protocols do not require expensive public key cryptography on the CNs and the exchanged messages are very short. Due to the unreliable, multihop communication, we can only prove the trustworthiness of the CHs, but not untrustworthiness. In addition, these protocols are not limited to cluster-based scenarios. For example the attestation protocols can be used in WSNs where many (mobile) TPM-equipped sinks exist, which are deployed in insecure locations. The network operator can verify if the data received from these sinks is still trustworthy.

2   Background on TCG-Mechanisms

The core of the TCG specifications [5] is the TPM, which is basically a smartcard, that serves as a trust anchor for trust establishment. The TPM offers protected storage for cryptographic keys and hardware enhanced calculation engines for random number generation, key-calculation and hash computation. Although the TPM chip was not specified as necessarily being tamper-resistant, many hardware vendors offer security mechanisms for preventing tampering and the unauthorized extraction of protected keys, such as active security sensors.

The TPM can generate and store cryptographic keys, both symmetric and asymmetric, and perform asymmetric cryptographic operations. The asymmetric keys can either be marked as migratable or non-migratable, which is specified when the key is generated. Non-migratable keys are always protected by the TPM and must not leave its protected storage.

The TPM also offers so-called Platform Configuration Registers (PCRs), which are used to store platform-dependant configuration values. These registers are initialized on power up and are used to store software integrity values. Software components (BIOS, bootloader, operating system, applications) are measured by the TPM before execution and the corresponding hash-value is then written to a specific PCR by extending the previous value:

$$Extend(PCR_N, value) = SHA1(PCR_N||value) \qquad (1)$$

SHA1 refers to the cryptographic hash function used by the TPM and $||$ denotes a concatenation. The trust anchor for a so-called trust-chain is the *Core Root of Trust Measurement* (CRTM), which resides in the BIOS and is first executed when a platform is powered up. The CRTM then measures itself and the BIOS, and hands over control to the next software component in the trust-chain. For every measured component an event is created and stored in the Stored Measurement Log (SML). The PCR values can then be used together with the SML to attest the platform's state to a remote entity. To assure that these values are authentic, they are signed with a non-migratable key, the Attestation Identity Key (AIK). The remote platform can verify the signature and compare these values with reference values to see if the system integrity is trustworthy.

The TPM also offers a concept called *sealing*, which allows a data block to be bound to a specific platform configuration. A sealed message is created by selecting a range of platform configuration registers, a non-migratable key, and the data block which should be sealed. The TPM is then able to decrypt and transfer the sealed data block, only if its current platform configuration matches the platform configuration from when the sealing was executed. Sealing provides the assurance that protected messages are only recoverable when the platform is in a known system state.

3   Attestation Techniques

In this section we compare different attestation techniques and evaluate their applicability for WSNs.

3.1   TPM-Based Attestation

Existing attestation protocols [6,7] are based on the TPM's ability to report the system configuration to a remote party. These approaches are mainly developed for non-resource constrained computer systems and requires each communication partner to perform public key cryptography. The complete system configuration, as denoted in the PCRs of the attesting entity, must be transmitted to the verifying entity. The verifying entity evaluates the trustworthiness of the attested entity by comparing the received SML and PCR values with given reference values. Since the verifying entity receives the current platform configuration directly, we refer to this as *explicit attestation*. However, in hybrid WSNs most sensor nodes do not possess enough resources to perform public key cryptography and the transmission of large messages increases the energy consumption significantly. This causes explicit attestation to be inapplicable in WSNs.

To perform an attestation in WSNs, computation intensive operations must be transferred to nodes which posses sufficient computational power, and resource constrained sensor nodes need only to perform minimal verification computations. The sealing concept of the TPM enables an attestation without directly transferring the platform configuration (PCR values and SML). We refer to this as *implicit attestation*. This approach minimizes the amount of transmitted data and does not require public key cryptography on resource constrained nodes. Sealing provides the functionality to bind data to a certain platform configuration. The TPM releases, i.e., decrypts, this data only if the current platform configuration is valid. The disadvantage of this approach is that software updates change the values inside the PCRs. Since this results in inaccessible sealed data, this approach is not very applicable in non-resource constrained computer systems, where software configurations change very often through legitimate system updates. Fortunately, the software configuration of sensor nodes may not change during the whole lifetime of a WSN. Therefore, the attested entity is only able to decrypt a sealed data structure if the current platform configuration matches its initial platform configuration. Our protocols smartly exploit this property to enable a lightweight attestation of the trustworthiness of the attested entity.

3.2   Software-Based Attestation

The main disadvantage of TPM-based attestation is that the platform configuration only reflects the initial load-time configuration. Therefore, memory modifications during the runtime can not be detected, e.g., buffer-overflows. To overcome this shortcoming, attestation software may measure the memory and report the values to a remote party. In this case, the attestation software forms the trust anchor which must be protected against tampering. In [2,3,4], approaches based on measuring the execution time of an optimal attestation routine is introduced. The routine cannot be optimized further, i.e., the execution time cannot be made faster, which prevents an adversary from injecting malicious code without detection. However, the success of this approach relies critically on the optimality of the attestation routine and on minimal time fluctuations of the expected responses. Particularly in WSNs with multihop verification and external influences, time intervals for responses can vary. In these cases the attestation would fail, even though a sensor node is in a trustworthy system state.

In scenarios where attestation along multiple hops is required or external inter-ferences prevent an exact time measurement, timing-based software attestation techniques are not applicable.

4   Setting and Notation

In this section we explain the setting and formulate the assumptions which are of concern for the protocols we propose.

4.1   Setting

We are considering a hybrid WSN, which is deployed in an unattended, hostile environment. The network consists of low-cost nodes and more expensive TPM-equipped nodes. TPM-equipped nodes act as cluster heads (CHs) for a number of low-cost cluster nodes (CNs), performing operations such as data aggregation, key management and so on.

We assume an adversary who tries to compromise a CH to access stored in-formation, e.g., keying material, and misuse the node to perform insider attacks, e.g., injecting false reports to cause false alarms. Therefore, the adversary can try to read out data or re-program the node to behave according to the purposes of the adversary. Furthermore, due to wireless communication, the adversary can eavesdrop on all traffic, inject packets, or replay old packets.

CNs are very limited in their storage, computational, communication, and en-ergy resources. However, they have enough space to store a few bytes of keying information and are able to perform some basic operations, such as comput-ing hash functions, symmetric encryption, etc., but they are not able to perform public key cryptography. These nodes might be comparable to the Berkeley Mica Motes [8]. CHs are assumed to possess much more computing power, memory capacity, and energy resources, e.g., comparable to the resources of the Stargate platform [9]. The TPM, integrated in the CHs, is used to protect keys and other security related data. We do not require any modification of the TPM, such as adding support for symmetric encryption with external data. Since present TPMs only support internal symmetric encryption, some data must be stored temporarily in the Random Access Memory (RAM) of a CH for further pro-cessing. We assume that access to this temporarily stored data is not possible. As soon as future TPMs support symmetric encryption with external data this assumption can be revoked. To subvert a CH, an adversary must re-program and reboot the node to either modify the system so that access to the RAM is possible or to access the security related data directly. After a reboot with a modified system, the platform configuration is changed and the access to sealed data is no longer possible. Thus, this data is neither accessible directly to the ad-versary nor loaded into the RAM. To achieve the binding of cryptographic keys to a specific platform configuration, which subsequently prevents rebooting in a compromised system configuration, we assume that we have a reduced measure-ment architecture, such as IBM's IMA [10], that extends the trust chain specified by the TCG up to the firmware and therefore includes integrity measurement of the kernel and operating system of the CH.

Sensor nodes (CHs and CNs) can be deployed randomly, e.g., via aerial scattering. That means the immediate neighboring nodes of any sensor node are not known in advance. The sensed data is sent via multihop communication to the *sink*. The sink is assumed not to be constrained in its resources and cannot be compromised. It possesses all keying material shared with the sensor nodes.

4.2   Notation

CHs are denoted as $CH_i, i = 1, \ldots, a$ and the CNs are denoted as $CN_j, j = 1, \ldots, b$, where $b \gg a$.

$E(m, e)$ denotes the *encryption* of data m using an encryption function E and encryption key e. *Encrypted data* m using the key e is denoted with $\{m\}_e$. The *decryption* of $\{m\}_e$ using a decryption function D and the decryption key d is denoted with $D(\{m\}_e, d)$.

Applying a cryptographic *hash function* h on data m is denoted with $h(m)$. A one-way *hash chain* [11] stored on CH_i is denoted with $C^{CH_i} = c_0^{CH_i}, \ldots, c_n^{CH_i}$. The hash chain is a sequence of hash values of some fixed length l generated by a hash function $h : \{0,1\}^l \rightarrow \{0,1\}^l$ by applying the hash function h successively on a seed value $c_0^{CH_i}$ so that $c_{v+1}^{CH_i} = h(c_v^{CH_i})$, with $v = 0, 1, \ldots, n - 1$.

A specific state of a CH_i is referred to as *platform configuration* $P_{CH_i} := (PCR_0, \ldots, PCR_p)$ and is stored in the appropriate PCRs of the TPM. Data m can be cryptographically bound to a certain platform configuration P_{CH_i} by using the TPM_Seal command. Using the TPM_Unseal command, the TPM releases, i.e., decrypts m only if the platform configuration has not been modified. This concept allows an implicit attestation to be performed without a direct validation of the PCRs by a CN. Since we are abstracting the TPM_Seal and TPM_Unseal commands, we denote our commands with Seal and Unseal. Given an non-migratable asymmetric key pair (e_{CH_i}, d_{CH_i}) we denote the *sealing* of data m for the platform configuration P_{CH_i} with $\{m\}_{P_{CH_i}}^{e_{CH_i}} = \text{Seal}(P_{CH_i}, e_{CH_i}, m)$. To *unseal* data m it is necessary that the current platform configuration P'_{CH_i} is equal to P_{CH_i}: $m = \text{Unseal}(P'_{CH_i} = P_{CH_i}, d_{CH_i}, \{m\}_{P_{CH_i}}^{e_{CH_i}})$.

5   Attestation Protocols

In this section we describe our two proposed protocols which enable a CN to verify the platform configuration of a CH. These protocols represent some basic primitives which can be used in conjunction or in more complex protocols. Our proposed protocols enable only CNs to verify the platform configuration of CHs. To verify the trustworthiness of received data from CNs, a CH has to perform additional mechanisms like redundancy checks or voting schemes.

We have adapted the sealing technique provided by the TPM to realize the implicit attestation (see Section 2). In the initialization phase the platform configuration of a CH is trustworthy. Data needed to perform a successful attestation is sealed in this phase to this platform configuration. Access to this sealed data is only possible if the CH is in the initial specified platform configuration. Compromising a CH results in a different platform configuration where access to this data is not possible. Thus, a successful attestation is no longer possible.

The first proposed protocol enables a broadcast attestation, where a CH broadcasts its platform configuration to its CNs in periodic intervals. This enables CNs to verify the platform configuration of the CH simultaneously. The second protocol enables a single CN (or the sink), to either individually verify the platform configuration of a CH using a challenge response protocol or to send data to a CH and receive a confirmation that the data has been received correctly and that the CH is trustworthy.

5.1   Periodic Broadcast Attestation Protocol (PBAP)

In some scenarios, many CNs perform measurements in parallel and in regular intervals. For example, a couple of CNs monitor the temperature in a specific region of the WSN. The measurement is performed every 10 minutes to see the change over time. Therefore, the CNs report their measurement nearly in parallel in specific time intervals to their CH. If each CN performs an individual attestation of the CH, this results in an avoidable overhead. It might be desirable that all CNs are able to nearly simultaneously verify if their CH is still trustworthy using an efficient mechanism.

The PBAP adapts the idea of μTESLA [12] to use one-way hash chains for authentication and extends it to enable attestation in hybrid WSNs. The sealing function of the TPM is used to bind a one-way hash chain to the platform configuration of a CH. A CH releases the values of the hash chain in periodic intervals, which can be verified by its CNs. The proof of trustworthiness of a CH is only possible while its platform configuration has not been modified.

The protocol is divided into two phases. In the *initialization* phase the CHs and the CNs are preconfigured before deployment. In the *attestation* phase, CHs periodically broadcasts an attestation message. This phase normally lasts for the whole lifetime of the CHs.

Initialization. Before CH_i is deployed, it is preconfigured with a non-migratable public key pair (e_{CH_i}, d_{CH_i}) and a hash chain C^{CH_i}. The seed value $c_0^{CH_i}$ of the hash chain is generated on CH_i using the TPM's physical random number generator and used by the CPU to perform the additional computations. CH_i is assumed to possess only one valid platform configuration, denoted as P_{CH_i}. After CH_i is powered up, a measurement about each component (BIOS, bootloader, operating system, applications) is performed, and the related values are stored in the corresponding PCR registers. Each value of the hash chain C^{CH_i} is sealed to this platform configuration P_{CH_i}: $\{c_0^{CH_i}\}_{P_{CH_i}}^{e_{CH_i}}, \ldots, \{c_n^{CH_i}\}_{P_{CH_i}}^{e_{CH_i}} = $ $\mathtt{Seal}(P_{CH_i}, e_{CH_i}, c_0^{CH_i}), \ldots, \mathtt{Seal}(P_{CH_i}, e_{CH_i}, c_n^{CH_i})$.

Each CN_j which interacts with CH_i is configured with the last value $c_n^{CH_i}$ of the hash chain C^{CH_i}. Since the number of CHs is very small compared to the number of CHs, the CNs could be preprogrammed with the values of all CHs.

After deployment, the CNs can only keep the values for its CH and another certain number of CHs in their vicinity to save memory.

Attestation. CH_i and the associated CNs (denoted as CN_*) are loosely time synchronized. The time is divided into intervals I_λ, $\lambda = 1, \ldots, n$. At the beginning of each interval, CH_i sends a broadcast attestation message to the CNs. The attestation messages consist of the values of the hash chain released in reversed order of the generation and the identifier I_λ of the current interval. If the platform configuration of CH_i has not been modified, it can unseal the values of the hash chain C^{CH_i}. In the first interval I_1, CH_i unseals the hash value $c_{n-1}^{CH_i}$ and transmits it together with the interval identifier. In the second interval $c_{n-2}^{CH_i}$ is unsealed and transmitted and so on. CN_* check if the interval I_1 stated within the message matches their local interval counter I_1' within a certain error range. If they match, CN_* verify whether $h(c_{n-1}^{CH_i}) = c_n^{CH_i}$. If the equation holds, CH_i is considered trustworthy and the value $c_n^{CH_i}$ is overwritten with the value $c_{n-1}^{CH_i}$. In the next interval CH_i releases $c_{n-2}^{CH_i}$ and so on, which are similarly checked. The protocol is shown in Figure 1 and repeated from $\lambda = 1$ to n.

Interval	Node(s)	Message	Action
I_λ	CH_i		$\texttt{Unseal}(P_{CH_i}, d_{CH_i}, \{c_{n-\lambda}^{CH_i}\}_{P_{CH_i}}^{e_{CH_i}}) = c_{n-\lambda}^{CH_i}$
I_λ	$CH_i \to CN_* : c_{n-\lambda}^{CH_i}, I_\lambda$		
I_λ	CN_*		$I_\lambda \stackrel{?}{=} I_\lambda'$
I_λ	CN_*		if $h(c_{n-\lambda}^{CH_i}) \stackrel{?}{=} c_{n-\lambda+1}^{CH_i}$, state of CH_i is valid
I_λ	CN_*		overwrite $c_{n-\lambda+1}$ with $c_{n-\lambda}$
$\ldots$	$\ldots$	$\ldots$	$\ldots$

Fig. 1. Periodic Broadcast Attestation Protocol

Due to unreliable communication, a CN could miss some messages. Thus, CNs should not immediately declare a CH as being untrustworthy but wait for a certain threshold of time. If a CN receives messages again, it can resynchronize by applying the hashfunction multiple times.

5.2   Individual Attestation Protocol (IAP)

Using the IAP, a CN (or the sink) can individually verify the platform configuration of a CH. Alternatively a CN can send data to a CH and receive a confirmation that the data has been received correctly and that the CH is trustworthy. A CN needs only to perform symmetric operations and two short messages need to be exchanged. The messages are very small, because no long public key primitives, e.g., keys, signatures need to be transmitted. Since transmitting messages is the most cost intensive factor in WSNs [13], this is of particular interest, especially if the sink wants to verify the platform configuration of a CH. In this case, messages are transferred along several hops.

The protocol we propose is again divided in *initialization* phase and *attestation* phase. The initialization phase is performed only once after deployment of the sensor nodes while the attestation phase can be performed every time a CN (or the sink) wants to verify the platform configuration of a CH.

Initialization. Each CN_j establishes a shared, symmetric key K_{CN_j,CH_i} with its CH_i. Therefore, existing (non TPM-based) techniques, e.g., [14], might be used. However, we recommend using the key establishment protocol presented in [15], as it also assumes a hybrid WSN with TPM-equipped CHs and resource constraint CNs. This approach has the advantage that key generation within a TPM is inherently more secure than key generation on off-the-shelf embedded WSN platforms. As in [14], we assume that this short period of time to establish pairwise keys is secure and nodes cannot be compromised. The keys K_{CN_j,CH_i} are sealed on CH_i to its valid platform configuration P_{CH_i}. Thus, CH_i can access these keys only if it is in its valid state.

To enable the sink to perform the attestation with CH_i, a shared symmetric key K_{Sink,CH_i} is preconfigured on CH_i before deployment and sealed likewise.

Attestation. Figure 2 shows how CN_j can verify the platform configuration of CH_i. First, CN_j sends a challenge to CH_i. The challenge consists of an encrypted block containing a *Nonce* and the identifier ID_{CN_j} of CN_j, and additionally ID_{CN_j} in cleartext. K_{CN_j,CH_i} is used for encryption. After receiving the challenge, CH_i unseals K_{CN_j,CH_i} related to ID_{CN_j}. This is only possible if the platform configuration P_{CH_i} is valid. Using this key, CH_i decrypts the encrypted block and verifies if the decrypted identifier is equal to the identifier received in cleartext. If they match, CH_i knows that this message originates from CN_j, encrypts the *Nonce'* using K_{CN_j,CH_i}, and sends it back.[1] Otherwise, CH_i aborts. CH_i then deletes K_{CN_j,CH_i} from the RAM. CN_j decrypts the received response message and checks if the decrypted *Nonce"* matches the *Nonce* it has sent in the first step. If they match, CH_i is declared trustworthy and CN_j can send data to CH_i. This data is encrypted using K_{CN_j,CH_i}. The attestation of CH_i by the sink is performed analog, using the key K_{Sink,CH_i}.

Alternatively, data can be transmitted directly within the challenge. This might be preferable in scenarios where an immediate receipt of data is important or where CNs send data very infrequently to a CH. Therefore, the protocol is modified in steps 1 and 2b. Figure 3 shows the modifications. In step 1' CN_j sends the data to CH_i within the encrypted block. CH_i can only decrypt this message in step 2b' if its platform configuration is valid and access the data. All other steps remain the same as shown in figure 2. Thus, if CN_j receives the message in step 2e and the checks in steps 3a and 3b succeed, CN_j can be assured that CH_i has successfully received the data and is still trustworthy.

---

[1] However, the trustworthiness of CN_j cannot be assumed, because the node could be potentially compromised and the key is not protected by a TPM.

1. $CN_j \rightarrow CH_i : ID_{CN_j}, \{Nonce, ID_{CN_j}\}_{K_{CN_j,CH_i}}$

2a. CH_i $\text{Unseal}(P_{CH_i}, d_{CH_i}, \{K_{CN_j,CH_i}\}^{e_{CH_i}}_{P_{CH_i}}) = K_{CN_j,CH_i}$

2b. CH_i $D(\{Nonce, ID_{CN_j}\}_{K_{CN_j,CH_i}}, K_{CN_j,CH_i}) = (ID'_{CN_j}, Nonce')$

2c. CH_i check $ID'_{CN_j} \overset{?}{=} ID_{CN_j}$

2d. CH_i $E(\{Nonce', ID_{CH_i}\}, K_{CN_j,CH_i}) = \{Nonce', ID_{CH_i}\}_{K_{CN_j,CH_i}}$

2e. $CH_i \rightarrow CN_j : ID_{CH_i}, \{Nonce', ID_{CH_i}\}_{K_{CN_j,CH_i}}$

2f. CH_i delete K_{CN_j,CH_i} from RAM

3a. CN_j $D(\{Nonce', ID_{CH_i}\}_{K_{CN_j,CH_i}}, K_{CN_j,CH_i}) = (Nonce'', ID'_{CH_i})$

3b. CN_j if $Nonce'' \overset{?}{=} Nonce$, state of CH_i is valid

Fig. 2. Individual Attestation Protocol

1'. $CN_j \rightarrow CH_i : ID_{CN_j}, \{Nonce, ID_{CN_j}, data\}_{K_{CN_j,CH_i}}$

2b'. CH_i $D(\{Nonce, ID_{CN_j}, data\}_{K_{CN_j,CH_i}}, K_{CN_j,CH_i}) = (ID'_{CN_j}, Nonce', data)$

Fig. 3. Modified Individual Attestation Protocol

6 Analysis

In this section, we first discuss the security of the two proposed attestation protocols. Then we evaluate their performance.

6.1 Security Discussion

The goal of both protocols is that CNs can prove the trustworthiness of CHs. If an adversary compromises a CH, he cannot successfully deceive the CNs or the sink to perform insider attacks. We distinguish between two types of possible attacks: (1) attacking a CH directly, and (2) en-route attacks if the communication involves multiple hops. Due to the unreliable multihop communication, we can only prove the trustworthiness of CHs. But untrustworthiness could not be proven since either communication errors can result in modified attestation messages or malicious en-route nodes can modify forwarded messages to defame a CH. Therefore, a valid attestation makes no statement about the trustworthiness of a used route. In addition, an invalid attestation could be caused either by a compromised CH or by a compromised en-route CN.

Security of the PBAP. To compromise a CH and forge a trustworthy platform configuration, an adversary needs access to the hash chain. Therefore, he has to either perform the unseal command under a compromised platform configuration, or try to access the key used to seal the hash chain with physical attacks. As described in Section 2 the TPM is basically a smartcard and offers high security mechanisms for preventing unauthorized extraction of protected keys. This makes it extremely difficult for an adversary to retrieve the necessary keys to decrypt the sealed hash chain. Additionally, access to the sealed hash chain is only possible if the platform configuration has not been modified. This prevents the unauthorized extraction of the values of the hash chain in a compromised system environment. Even if an adversary could access the RAM of a sensor node, he can not retrieve other hash values, because for each attestation only the actual hash value is unsealed and loaded into the RAM.

However, our approach can not handle runtime attacks caused by buffer overflows, since we report the platform configuration measured in the initialization phase, i.e., when the software is first executed. Such attacks would result in a (malicious) modified system configuration, but the platform configuration stored in the PCRs is still the valid configuration.

If the attestation is performed between nodes which are multiple hops away, an adversary might also try to perform a man-in-the middle attack by compromising an en-route CN. The adversary can try to spoof, alter or replay attestation messages, or perform a selective forwarding attack [16]. Spoofing is not possible, because PBAP is not an authentication protocol. It gives an assertion about the trustworthiness of the specific CH and not which node has relayed the message. Altering attestation messages is possible and results in an unsuccessful attestation. To cope with that, a CN should possess an additional mechanism which enables the CN to reach its CH using a different communication path or change to a different CH. The CN can then use an alternative path and perform the IAP with the CH to make a clear statement, whether the route, or the node has been compromised. If the CH is compromised, a CN could, for example, switch to another CH where the communication paths and the new CH may not have been compromised. Replay attacks or an attack where an adversary first blocks the forwarding of legitimate hash values to collect them, then compromises a CH and finally releases these hash values are not possible, because hash values are only valid for a specific interval, which is validated by each CN. Since the PBAP is performed in cleartext an adversary can distinguish between attestation and data messages and therefore perform a selective forwarding attack by forwarding attestation messages, but blocking data messages. Such attacks are a general problem in WSNs and show that the PBAP is not resistant against all attacks in a multihop scenario with malicious en-route CNs.

Security of the IAP. The security of the IAP relies on the sealing of the symmetric keys to the valid platform configuration analogue to the sealing of the hash chain described above. Thus, an adversary compromising a CH cannot access the necessary keys to perform a successful attestation.

If the attestation messages are forwarded along multiple hops, an adversary can try to perform a man-in-the-middle attack. Since the IAP includes an authentication protocol, spoofing is not possible. A CH detects the modification of the first attestation message (see Figure 2) by an en-route adversary, since the included identifier does not match the identifier sent in cleartext. If the adversary alters the response sent to a CN, the latter cannot distinguish if either the attestation has failed or if the message has been altered by the adversary. Replay attacks are not possible, because a new Nonce is used in each message. Since attestation messages and data messages have the same form (identifier plus encrypted data block), an adversary cannot distinguish between them to perform a sophisticated selective forwarding attack. If the modified IAP is used, where data is sent in the first step, an adversary might be able to distinguish between this message and the response message (step 2e) because of the different lengths of the messages. To cope with that, the message sent in step 2e could be padded to the same length.

Thus, if an attestation fails, a CN should first try to perform a new attestation of the same CH using another communication path, if possible. If this is not possible or the attestation fails again, either the CH or a node on the communication path is compromised. The CN should then select a new CH, since messages sent to the old one might be susceptible to attacks.

Furthermore, in contrast to WSNs where CHs are not equipped with a TPM, a single compromise of a CH does not result in the compromise of all shared keys stored on this node. Even using the TPM in only a few sensor nodes results in a higher resiliency to node compromise.

6.2   Performance Analysis

Efficiency is crucial for security protocols for WSNs because of the scarce resources. Protocols should not introduce a high storage overhead and should not significantly increase energy consumption. Since we assume that CHs possess sufficient ressources, we perform our analysis only for the CNs. First, we analyse the additional storage requirements. Next, we estimate the additional energy consumption by evaluating the computational and communication overhead.

Storage Requirements. For the PBAP, a CN must store one hash value and the identifier for the corresponding CH. Depending on the network configuration, it might also store hash values (and identifiers) for other CHs in its vicinity. Let L_N, and L_H denote the length of a *node identifier* and a *hash value* respectively. Let the number of CHs for which a CN stores values be v. Thus, the storage requirements SR_{PBAP} for a CN are:

$$SR_{PBAP} = v * (L_N + L_H) \tag{2}$$

For example, suppose a CN stores values for 5 CHs. The length of each hash value is 64 bits and the length of a node identifier is 10 bits. This results in a total of 46.25 bytes.

For the IAP, a CN must store one symmetric key for each CH with which it wants to perform an attestation. Let this number be denoted by w and the length of a key denoted by L_K. Thus, the storage requirements SR_{IAP} for a CN are:

$$SR_{IAP} = w * L_K \tag{3}$$

For example, suppose a CN stores keys for 5 CHs. The length of each key is 64 bits. This results in a total of 40 bytes.

The Berkeley Mica2 Mote [8] offers 4KB of SRAM. Therefore, the storage requirements are suitable for current sensor nodes, even if both protocols are used in conjunction.

Energy Consumption. The PBAP requires a CN to receive one attestation message and to perform one hash computation at each time interval. An attestation message consists of a hash value and an identifier of the interval, e.g., a counter. Although computing hash values only marginally increases energy consumption [12], we consider the computational overhead, since a hash computation is performed in each time interval.

We use $e_1 = e_{1s} + e_{1r}$ to denote the energy consumed in sending and receiving one byte, and e_2 to denote the energy for one hash computation. In addition to the notation used above, let L_T denote the length needed for the interval identifier. The total number of intervals in the whole lifetime of the network is denoted with t. This results in an additional energy consumption:

$$E_{PBAP} = t * ((L_T + L_H) * e_{1r} + e_2) \qquad (4)$$

For example, suppose the lifetime of the network is one year and broadcast messages are sent every 10 minutes. Therefore, a 16 bit counter is sufficient for numbering each interval. We use the results presented in [13] to quantify $e_{1s} = 16.25\ \mu J$ for sending, $e_{1r} = 12.5\ \mu J$ for receiving, and $e_1 = 28.75\ \mu J$ for sending and receiving one byte using Berkeley Mica2 Motes. The energy consumed for performing one hash computation using RC5 [17] block cipher is $e_2 = 15\ \mu J$. This results in a total energy consumption of 7358.4 mJ. The Mica2 Motes are powered with two 1.5 V AA batteries in series connection. We assume a total capacity of 2750 mAh using standard AA batteries which results in 29700 J. Thus, the ratio of energy consumed in one year by the PBAP is about 0.025% of the total available energy which is neglibly small.

The IAP requires a CN to generate and send a challenge[2], and the verification of the response (see Figure 2, steps 1, 2e, 3a and 3b). The challenge requires one Nonce generation, one encryption and one transmission, while the response verification requires the receipt of one message, one decryption and one comparison of two values. As in [12], the Nonce is generated using a Message Authentication Code (MAC) as pseudo-random number generator with a generator key $K_{CN_j}^{rand}$. The energy consumed therefor using RC5 for MAC generation is $e_2 = 15\ \mu J$. The encryption cost using RC5 are also 15 μJ. We neglect the energy cost for the comparison of two values since they are negligibly small. Thus, the additional energy consumption is:

$$E_{IAP} = 3 * e_2 + e_{1s} * (2 * L_N + L_H) + e_{1r} * L_H \qquad (5)$$

---

[2] We do not consider the case where data is sent within the challenge, because we estimate only the additional overhead introduced by our protocol.

Assuming the values from above, this results in a total energy consumption on a CN for one individual attestation of about 315 μJ which is $1.06 * 10^{-4}$ % of the total available energy.

7   Related Work

In the context of attestation in WSNs, a number of software-based approaches have been presented [2,3,4] which rely on optimal program code and exact time measurements. These approaches enable software-based attestation by introducing an optimal program verification process that verifies the memory of a sensor node by calculating hash values of randomly selected memory regions. However, these approaches are not applicable in multihop WSNs, since they require, on the one hand, an authenticated communication channel between the verifier and the attestor, and on the other hand, rely on minimal time fluctuations (compare Section 3). In [18] a similar approach is presented which relies on code obfuscation techniques and time measurement. Proposed hardware-based approaches [10,6] are based on public-key cryptography and require extensive computational power, as well as the transmission of large messages, making these approaches not usable in WSNs. In [15] the advantages of using a TPM in hybrid WSNs are first identified. A framework for key establishment, distribution, and management is presented. The approach shows that a TPM can dramatically improve the security of WSNs. However, attestation techniques offered by the TPM are not considered.

8   Conclusions and Future Work

In this paper we argue that timing-based software attestation techniques are not applicable in multihop WSNs. We therefore introduce another approach which exploits the property of a hardware-based trust anchor to enable attestation in multihop WSNs. In this context, we present two attestation protocols for hybrid WSNs, where the network consists of resource constrained CNs and CHs with more resources equipped with a TPM chip that acts as a trust anchor. Both protocols allow CNs to verify whether the platform configuration of a CH is trustworthy or not, even if they are multiple hops away. The PBAP runs in fixed time intervals, allowing multiple nodes to verify the trustworthiness simultaneously, while the IAP enables a direct attestation. We shown that both the overhead for storage and the energy consumption are negligible.

We are currently working on the implementation of our proposed architecture using both hardware TPM and a TPM emulator. Furthermore, we are investigating how a CN should react if a multihop attestation, either based on a compromised node on the route or a compromised CH fails. To achieve this, an efficient algorithm must be developed that either selects a new route to the existing CH or chooses a new CH. Another part of our future work will be the choice of optimal parameters for CHs and CNs, taking the cost benefit aspects into account.

References

1. Akyildiz, I., Su, W., Sankarasubramaniam, Y., Cayirci, E.: A survey on sensor networks. IEEE Comm. Mag. 40(8), 102–114 (2002)
2. Seshadri, A., Perrig, A., Doorn, L.v., Khosla, P.: SWATT: SoftWare-based ATTestation for Embedded Devices. In: IEEE Symp. on Sec. and Priv., IEEE Computer Society Press, Los Alamitos (2004)
3. Seshadri, A., Luk, M., Shi, E., Perrig, A., Doorn, L.v., Khosla, P.: Pioneer: verifying code integrity and enforcing untampered code execution on legacy systems. In: SOSP '05: Proceedings of the twentieth ACM symposium on Operating systems principles, Brighton, United Kingdom, pp. 1–16. ACM Press, New York (2005)
4. Seshadri, A., Luk, M., Perrig, A., van Doorn, L., Khosla, P.: SCUBA: Secure Code Update By Attestation in Sensor Networks. In: WiSe '06: Proceedings of the 5th ACM workshop on Wireless security, Los Angeles, California, ACM Press, New York (2006)
5. Trusted Computing Group: Trusted Platform Module (TPM) specifications, Technical report (2006) https://www.trustedcomputinggroup.org/specs/TPM
6. Stumpf, F., Tafreschi, O., Röder, P., Eckert, C.: A Robust Integrity Reporting Protocol for Remote Attestation. In: WATC'06. Proceedings of the Second Workshop on Advances in Trusted Computing (2006)
7. Shi, E., Perrig, A., Van Doorn, L.: BIND: A Fine-Grained Attestation Service for Secure Distributed Systems. In: SP '05. Proceedings of the 2005 IEEE Symposium on Security and Privacy, pp. 154–168. IEEE Computer Society Press, Los Alamitos (2005)
8. Crossbow Technology: Mica2 datasheet http://www.xbow.com/Products/Product_pdf_files/Wireless_pdf/MICA2_Datasheet.pdf
9. Crossbow Technology: Stargate datasheet http://www.xbow.com/Products/Product_pdf_files/Wireless_pdf/Stargate_Datasheet.pdf
10. Sailer, R., Zhang, X., Jaeger, T., Doorn, L.v.: Design and Implementation of a TCG-based Integrity Measurement Architecture. In: 13th USENIX Security Symposium, IBM T. J. Watson Research Center (August 2004)
11. Lamport, L.: Password authentication with insecure communication. Commun. ACM 24(11), 770–772 (1981)
12. Perrig, A., Szewczyk, R., Tygar, J.D., Wen, V., Culler, D.E.: SPINS: security protocols for sensor networks. Wirel. Netw. 8(5), 521–534 (2002)
13. Ye, F., Luo, H., Lu, S., Zhang, L.: Statistical en-route filtering of injected false data in sensor networks. In: Proceedings IEEE INFOCOM., IEEE Computer Society Press, Los Alamitos (2004)
14. Zhu, S., Setia, S., Jajodia, S.: LEAP: efficient security mechanisms for large-scale distributed sensor networks. In: CCS '03. Proceedings of the 10th ACM conference on Computer and communications security, ACM Press, New York (2003)
15. Ganeriwal, S., Ravi, S., Raghunathan, A.: Trusted platform based key establishment and management for sensor networks (Under review)
16. Karlof, C., Wagner, D.: Secure routing in wireless sensor networks: attacks and countermeasures. In: Proceedings of the First IEEE International Workshop on Sensor Network Protocols and Applications, pp. 113–127. IEEE Computer Society Press, Los Alamitos (2003)
17. Rivest, R.L.: The RC5 Encryption Algorithm. In: Proceedings of the 1994 Leuven Workshop on Fast Software Encryption, pp. 86–96. Springer, Heidelberg (1995)
18. Shaneck, M., Mahadevan, K., Kher, V., Kim, Y.: Remote software-based attestation for wireless sensors. In: Molva, R., Tsudik, G., Westhoff, D. (eds.) ESAS 2005. LNCS, vol. 3813, Springer, Heidelberg (2005)

Direct Anonymous Attestation (DAA): Ensuring Privacy with Corrupt Administrators[*][**]

Ben Smyth[1], Mark Ryan[1], and Liqun Chen[2]

[1] School of Computer Science,
University of Birmingham, UK
{B.A.Smyth,M.D.Ryan}@cs.bham.ac.uk
[2] HP Laboratories,
Bristol, UK
liqun.chen@hp.com

Abstract. The Direct Anonymous Attestation (DAA) scheme provides a means for remotely authenticating a trusted platform whilst preserving the user's privacy. The protocol has been adopted by the Trusted Computing Group (TCG) in the latest version of its Trusted Platform Module (TPM) specification. In this paper we show DAA places an unnecessarily large burden on the TPM host. We demonstrate how corrupt administrators can exploit this weakness to violate privacy. The paper provides a fix for the vulnerability. Further privacy issues concerning linkability are identified and a framework for their resolution is developed. In addition an optimisation to reduce the number of messages exchanged is proposed.

Keywords: cryptographic protocol, trusted computing, privacy, anonymity.

1   Introduction

1.1   Trusted Computing

Trusted computing is a mechanism by which a server can obtain cryptographically-strong guarantees about the state of a remote platform. Such guarantees can include information about the platform's configuration, the software it is running, the identity of its users and its geographical location. Once in possession of such information the server can make an informed decision as to whether to trust the platform. At the core of the architecture is a hardware device called a Trusted Platform Module (TPM). This chip provides the cryptographic guarantee that the reported data is indeed correct.

Applications for trusted computing include *ad hoc* networks, grid computing and corporate digital rights management (DRM). A mobile *ad hoc* network consists of a number of mobile nodes. Unlike traditional network topologies, *ad hoc*

---

[*] An extended version of this paper can be found at http://www.cs.bham.ac.uk/~bas/
[**] This research was funded by the Engineering and Physical Sciences Research Council (EPSRC) under the WINES initiative as part of the UbiVal project.

F. Stajano et al. (Eds.): ESAS 2007, LNCS 4572, pp. 218–231, 2007.
© Springer-Verlag Berlin Heidelberg 2007

networks do not rely upon a fixed infrastructure. Instead, hosts rely upon each other to become and remain connected. Such technology could be deployed to support a campus network. However nodes may cheat: a selfish user may refuse to forward messages from others, thus becoming a 'freeloader.' Trusted computing can force each node to act in a fair manner. In the Grid Computing application, the resources of a large number of systems are used to tackle computationally expensive problems. The *M4 Message Breaking Project* is an example, and has recently deciphered two of the three previously unsolved German ciphers used during World War II. All Grid Computing projects share a similar impediment. The client may abuse the system by running modified software or may simply return fictitious values. Trusted computing addresses this problem by providing a guarantee that the client is running the legitimate program in the correct manner. In the corporate DRM setting, organisations can be assured that machines are running only authorised software which is capable of enforcing strict policies for the control of documents and electronic mail. Restrictions may prevent printing sensitive corporate data, or forwarding it to external sources.

1.2   Privacy Concerns with Trusted Computing

The aforementioned grid computing example relies upon the ability of a trusted platform to provide a remote attestation. In a similar scenario a situation could exist where the user demands that their identity be protected. The server must therefore only learn that a platform is trusted and not which particular one. Cryptographers and privacy advocates have voiced concerns. The Trusted Computing Group (TCG) has addressed the issue.

   The concept of privacy has been widely debated and several taxonomies have been formally proposed [1,2,3]. For the purposes of this document a privacy preserving protocol is one that satisfies anonymity and unlinkability, the definitions of which have been adopted from Pfitzmann & Köhntopp [2]. *Anonymity* is the state of not being identifiable within a set of agents with the same attributes. The set of agents consists of all those who might cause an action and anonymity becomes stronger as the size of the set increases. Reiter & Rubin [3] liken the notion to "blending into a crowd." In the presence of a large crowd, each member of which is equally likely to have performed an action, it is impossible to establish from whom the action originated. *Unlinkability* (also called *relationship anonymity*) specifies that given two or more items originating from the same agent it is not possible to link them. As a counterexample, two documents bearing the handwritten signature of an individual allow the items to be linked. Unlinkability only has meaning once anonymity has been achieved, since actions can always be linked if the identity of the agent is known. Of course, privacy is only achievable in a communications protocol if the channel supports anonymity [3,4].

1.3   Addressing Privacy Concerns

The solution first adopted by the TCG [5] required a trusted third party, namely a *privacy certification authority* (privacy CA). Each TPM has an embedded RSA key pair called an Endorsement Key (EK) which the privacy CA is assumed to know. In order to attest the TPM generates a second RSA key pair called an Attestation Identity Key (AIK). It sends the AIK, signed by EK, to the privacy CA who checks its validity and issues a certificate for the AIK. The host/TPM is now able to authenticate itself with respect to the certificate. This approach permits two possibilities for the detection of rogue TPMs: firstly the privacy CA should maintain a list of EKs known to be rogue and reject requests from them, secondly if a privacy CA receives too many requests from a particular EK it may reject them. The number of permitted requests should be subject to a risk management exercise and goes beyond the scope of this paper. This solution is problematic since the privacy CA must take part in every transaction which makes use of a new AIK, and thus must provide high availability whilst remaining secure. Furthermore privacy requirements may be violated if the privacy CA and verifier collude.

The Direct Anonymous Attestation (DAA) [6] scheme draws upon techniques developed for group signatures, identity escrow and credential systems. The protocol allows the remote authentication of a trusted platform whilst preserving the privacy of the system's user. It eliminates the need for a trusted third party and has been adopted by the TCG in the current TPM specification [7]. The approach can be seen as a group signature scheme without the ability to revoke anonymity, with an additional mechanism to detect rogue members. In broad terms the *host* contacts an *issuer* and requests membership to a group. If the issuer wishes to accept the request, it grants the host/TPM an *attestation identity credential*. The terms *credential* and *certificate* will be used interchangeably hereafter to mean attestation identity credential. The host is now able to anonymously authenticate itself as a group member to a *verifier* with respect to the certificate. The platform need only contact the issuer once, if the host chooses to use a single DAA key associated with this issuer, alleviating the previously discussed bottleneck.

1.4   Contribution

This paper shows a weakness of the DAA protocol which allows an adversarial issuer and verifier to collude in order to violate the user's privacy. Subsequently, the paper describes how the vulnerability can be fixed. Further privacy issues with regards verifier-linkability are identified and a framework for their resolution is developed. In addition, an optimisation to the protocol is proposed. The paper presents the DAA protocol in an accessible format which we believe is easier to understand than the original paper.

Structure of paper. The remainder of this paper is structured as follows. Section 2 introduces the mathematical and cryptographic primitives used by this work. The DAA protocol is explained in Section 3. In Section 4 an informal security analysis of the protocol is conducted, as a result of which a vulnerability is discovered and subsequently corrected. In Section 5 the privacy problems concerning verifier-linkability are identified and a solution is presented. In Section 6 optimisations are proposed to reduce the number of messages exchanged and to improve the efficiency of rogue tagging. An appraisal of the work is presented in Section 7 and future research is considered in Section 8. Finally for completion, the DAA protocol is provided in its entirety, including the security fixes discussed, in the appendices (the appendices can be found in the extended version of this paper).

2   Preliminaries

2.1   Protocols to Prove Knowledge

Various protocols which prove knowledge of and relations among discrete logarithms are used by DAA. These protocols will be described using the notation introduced by Camenisch & Stadler [8]. The example below has been adapted from Camenisch *et al.* [6]:

$$PK\{(\alpha, \beta, \gamma) : y = g^\alpha h^\beta \wedge \tilde{y} = \tilde{g}^\alpha \tilde{h}^\gamma \wedge \alpha \in [u, v]\}$$

It denotes a *"zero knowledge Proof of Knowledge of integers* α, β, γ *such that* $y = g^\alpha h^\beta$ *and* $\tilde{y} = \tilde{g}^\alpha \tilde{h}^\gamma$ *holds, where* $\alpha \in [u, v]$.*"* The values $y, g, h, \tilde{y}, \tilde{g}$ and $\tilde{h}$ are elements of some groups $G = \langle g \rangle = \langle h \rangle$ and $\tilde{G} = \langle \tilde{g} \rangle = \langle \tilde{h} \rangle$. Greek letters are used for quantities of the knowledge that is being proved and values kept secret by the prover, while all other values are known to the verifier.

The Fiat-Shamir heuristic [9] allows an interactive zero knowledge scheme to be converted into a signature scheme. A signature acquired in this way is termed a *Signature Proof of Knowledge* and is denoted, for example, as $SPK\{(\alpha) : y = g^\alpha\}(m)$.

3   High Level Overview

This section describes the DAA protocol at a high level. For simplicity in presentation, when the TPM is said to have sent or received a value, the message should be assumed to have been delivered by way of the host. The scheme requires that each issuer and verifier has a unique name, termed a basename, denoted bsn_I and bsn_V respectively.

The TPM is a small chip with limited resources. DAA therefore aims to minimise the operations that it must perform. This is achieved by outsourcing computation to the host whilst maintaining security. A corrupt host should not of course be able to authenticate without the TPM. However, privacy properties need only be guaranteed if the host is not corrupt. Since a corrupted host can always reveal its identity as it controls all external communication. The low level distinction between computation conducted by the host and TPM are described in the appendices (see the extended version of this paper).

The protocol is initiated when a host wishes to obtain a credential. This is known as the join protocol and is shown in Figure 1. The TPM creates a secret f value and a blinding factor v'. It then constructs the blind message

$U := blind(f, v')$ and $N_I := \zeta_I^f$, where $\zeta_I := (hash(1\|bsn_I))^{(\Gamma-1)/\rho} \pmod{\Gamma}$ and Γ, ρ are components of the issuer's public key. The U and N_I values are submitted to the issuer I. The issuer creates a random nonce value n_e, encrypts it with the public key PK_{EK} of the host's TPM and returns the encrypted value. The TPM decrypts the message, revealing n_e, and returns $hash(U\|n_e)$. The issuer confirms that the hash is correctly formed and is convinced that it is communicating with a valid host/TPM. The issuer checks whether the N_I value stems from a rogue TPM or if it has been seen previously (the issuer might chose to reissue the credential in this case). Rogue tagging will be detailed later. The issuer generates a nonce n_i and sends it to the host. The host/TPM constructs a signature proof of knowledge that the messages U and N_I are correctly formed. The issuer verifies the proof and generates a blind signature on the message U. It returns the signature along with a proof that a covert channel, which could violate privacy, has not been used (for more detail see the appendices of the extended version of this paper). The host verifies the signature and proof and the TPM unblinds the signature revealing a secret credential v (the signed f).

Once the host has obtained an anonymous attestation credential from the issuer it is able to produce a signature proof of knowledge of attestation on a message. This is known as the sign/verify protocol and is shown in Figure 2. Intuitively if a verifier is presented with such a proof it is convinced that it is communicating with a trusted platform and the message is genuine. The message m may be either a public part of an Attestation Identity Key (AIK) produced by the TPM or an arbitrary message. If m is an AIK, the key can later be used to sign PCR data or to certify a non-migratable key. Where m is arbitrary its purpose is application dependent. It may for example be a session key. To distinguish between these two modes of operation a variable b is defined. When $b = 0$ the message was generated by the TPM and when $b = 1$ the message was input to the TPM. The process of convincing a verifier that a host has obtained attestation will now be more precisely described. The host engages in communication with the verifier, during which the verifier requires the host to demonstrate that it is indeed a trusted platform. The host and verifier negotiate whether the verifier is able to link transactions and the verifier sends nonce n_v to the host. The host/TPM produce a signature proof of knowledge of attestation on the message $(n_t\|n_v\|b\|m)$, where n_t is a nonce defined by the TPM and m is a message. In addition the host computes $N_V := \zeta^f$, where $\zeta := (hash(1\|bsn_V))^{(\Gamma-1)/\rho}$ $\pmod{\Gamma}$ or ζ is chosen randomly. The value N_V allows for rogue tagging. In addition, if ζ is not random the N_V value can be used to link different transaction made by the same TPM while not identifying it, and possibly to reject a N_V where it has appeared too often.

3.1   Rogue Tagging

The DAA protocol is designed so that a known rogue TPM can be prevented from obtaining certification or making a successful claim of attestation to a verifier. A rogue TPM is defined as one that has been compromised in such a way that its secret f value has been extracted. Once a rogue TPM is discovered,

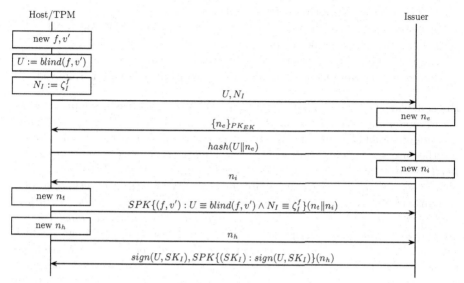

Fig. 1. Join Protocol

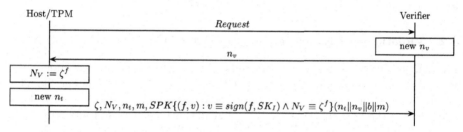

Fig. 2. Sign/Verify Protocol

the secret f values are distributed to all potential issuers/verifiers who add the value to their rogue list. On receipt of N_I and N_V values the issuer/verifier can check if the originating TPM is rogue by ensuring the N_I, N_V value is not equal to $\zeta^{\tilde{f}} \pmod{\Gamma}$ for all values $\tilde{f}$ that are known to stem from rogue TPMs. This check can be done efficiently since the rogue list can be expected to be short and the exponents are relatively small [6].

4 Security Analysis

4.1 DAA Security Properties

The objective of DAA is to provide a mechanism for the remote authentication of a trusted platform whilst preserving the privacy of the system's user. The DAA protocol [6] defines the following security properties:

1. Only a trusted platform is able to authenticate.
2. Privacy of non-corrupt host is guaranteed by the sign/verify protocol:
   (a) Interactions are anonymous.
   (b) Linkability (of transactions) is controlled by the user.
3. Privacy is restored to a corrupted host if malicious software is removed.

Brickell, Camenisch & Chen [6] have shown DAA to be secure in the provable security model under the decisional Diffie-Hellman and strong RSA assumption in the random oracle model. Such proofs are an important part of protocol analysis, but they are insufficient. Showing that breaking the scheme is *"essentially as difficult as solving a well-known and supposedly difficult problem"* [10] is a limited view of security and fails to anticipate the majority of attacks on cryptographic systems [11,12]. Koblitz & Menezes [12] argue that *"throughout the history of public-key cryptography almost all of the effective attacks on the most popular systems have not* [been solving difficult problems (for example integer factorisation)], *but rather by finding a weakness in the protocol."* Koblitz & Menezes go on to suggest that *"formalistic proofs* [are] *so turgid that other specialists don't even read* [them]. *As a result, proof-checking* [is] *a largely unmet security objective, leaving* [protocols] *vulnerable to attack."* This forms the motivation for an informal security analysis of the DAA scheme.

4.2   Violation of Privacy in the Presence of Corrupt Administrators

It is now shown that a colluding issuer and verifier can conspire to break anonymity when linkable transactions are used, violating security properties 2a and 2b. The verifier and issuer conspire to use the same basename, i.e. $bsn_V = bsn_I$. This will result in the host computing $\zeta = \zeta_I$. Recall that $\zeta_I = (hash(1\|bsn_I))^{(\Gamma-1)/\rho}$ (mod Γ) and $\zeta = (hash(1\|bsn_V))^{(\Gamma-1)/\rho}$ (mod Γ). The issuer learnt the identity of a host and which N_I value the host used during the join protocol. The verifier receives N_V during the execution of the sign protocol. The host identity is revealed, since $N_I = N_V = \zeta_I^{f_0+f_1 2^{l_f}} = \zeta^{f_0+f_1 2^{l_f}}$ (mod Γ) and the issuer is able to link the hosts identity with N_I.

The privacy violation relies upon the assumption that an issuer and verifier share the same basename (i.e. $bsn_I = bsn_V$). For example, this assumption holds in the following scenario. An online service provider could act as an issuer during the registration process and a verifier during service usage. This use case is in fact presented[1] by Camenisch et al. in earlier work on the idemix (identity mixer) system [13,14] which forms the basis of the DAA protocol. Under these conditions the issuer and verifier are the same entity and thus it makes logical sense for them to share a single basename. In fact, not doing so could cause confusion. Requiring the user to distinguish between bsn_I and bsn_V values places unnecessary burden on the user and will inevitably lead to their incorrect use. Furthermore, putting in place a procedure for obtaining a unique basename would ultimately require a worldwide governing body. At best this is undesirable since interaction with

---

[1] See http://www.zurich.ibm.com/security/idemix/idemix-slides.pdf (slide 10).

an authority reintroduces the bottleneck DAA aims to avoid. At worst, such a body is infeasible. It is simply not economic to setup an organisation for the sole purpose of issuing basenames. In addition such a body is likely to charge for its services.

4.3   Fix

The values ζ_I and ζ need not be computed in such a similar manner. It is therefore proposed that the join protocol uses $\zeta_I := (hash(0\|bsn_V))^{(\Gamma-1)/\rho} \pmod{\Gamma}$ and the sign/verify protocol uses $\zeta := (hash(1\|bsn_V))^{(\Gamma-1)/\rho} \pmod{\Gamma}$. The collusion between issuer and verifier to break privacy is no longer possible, regardless of whether $bsn_V = bsn_I$. Basenames may now be selected from a single name space as the distinction between issuer and verifier is no longer required.

4.4   Revised DAA Protocol

The appendices, of the extended version of this paper, present the complete DAA protocol. The presentation attempts to provide clarity to the reader, incorporates the security fix (Section 4.3) and includes the observation made by Camenisch & Groth [15] for increased efficiency [16]. We believe our presentation is in a more accessible format which is easier to understand than the original paper. To avoid over-complication the optimisations described in Section 6.1 and the construction/use of basenames (Section 5) are not shown; making these changes is trivial.

5   Overcoming Problems with DAA Basenames

The DAA protocol provides user controlled linkability (security property 2b, Section 4.1). More precisely two modes of operation are defined: verifier-linkable and verifier-unlinkable. Verifier-linkability is controlled by the construction of $N_V := \zeta^f$, where ζ is either derived from a basename or selected randomly (see Section 3). The former construction allows linkability, whereas the latter prevents it. By design DAA therefore provides provisions to link transactions which use the same basename. There are three types of linkable transactions:

1. **Single application linkability.** A verifier providing a single application is able to link transactions.
2. **Cross application linkability.** A verifier providing multiple applications which share the same basename is able to link transactions between different applications.
3. **Cross verifier linkability.** Different verifiers offering several applications which share the same basename are able to link transactions.

These forms of linkability are shown under various operating conditions in Figure 3. We note that cross issuer linkability - that is linkability between applications with different issuers - is not possible. Since the construction of N_V

contains the TPM's secret f value, which in turn incorporates the issuer's public key. Different issuers must use different public keys, thus cross issuer linkability is not possible.

The DAA protocol does not define the security requirements of basenames nor does it specify how basenames should be implemented. This presents two potential problems:

1. **Security properties.** In order to ensure the user controlled linkability, the user must be assured as to which verifier(s) will use a basename and for what application(s). DAA does not provide adequate provisions for this. Thus the host may inadvertently allow linkability between verifiers and/or applications, violating user controlled linkability.
2. **Implementation.** The protocol does not specify how to implement user controlled linkability. A naïve solution is that the host maintains a list of basenames associated with its communicating partners, including DAA issuers and a DAA verifiers, who have been associated with a basename. However, if a DAA key is used for a long time and for many different applications, which is the DAA scheme designed for, maintaining such a list is infeasible for most ordinary users.

Subsection 5.1 defines a technique which will resolve these two issues and Section 5.2 will discuss its use in practice.

5.1   Constructing a Basename

The host must be able to uniquely identify with whom a basename should be used and for what application. It is therefore proposed that the basename is constructed from application, verifier and issuer specific data. An example of such information is shown in Table 1. The host is then able to check a basename prior to its use, thus preserving user controlled linkability.

The construction of the basename may be undertaken by either the verifier or the host. Alternatively it could be created through negotiation. This decision is left to application developers. When the host is responsible for construction,

Table 1. Information to be used for computing a basename

Application	DAA operation	Issuer/verifier data	Date	Other
1. Specification	1. DAA key issuing	1. Issuer identity	1. Start date	1. Random data
2. URL	2. PCR signing	2. Issuer public key	2. Expiry date	string*
3. User ID	3. AIK signing	3. Verifier identity	3. Other	2. Policy
4. Password	4. External input	4. Verifier public key		3. Terms &
5. Shared key	signing	5. Auth request		conditions
6. Other	5. System input	6. Auth algorithm		4. Other
	signing	7. Other		
	6. Other			

* This item is listed in the table for completion. The data string must be freshly created by the host and it should only be used for the construction of random basenames.

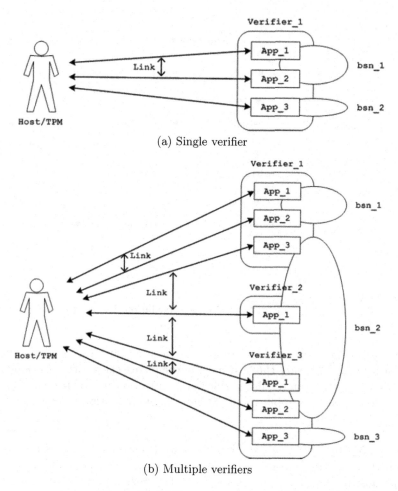

(a) Single verifier

(b) Multiple verifiers

Fig. 3. Linkability in various scenarios

it may be pre-programmed in the host's software, or determined by the user at run-time for example.

5.2   Using a Basename

The host will be required to maintain the information used for constructing basenames as shown in Table 1 and a blacklist of basenames which the host does not want to be used any more. When a new basename is required, the host (and the verifier) will create it based on the particular application. When an existing basename is given it is selected from the list and the host checks that it matches the application specification. The host's blacklist will then be consulted to ensure that the basename has not previously been blacklisted. If desired the verifier will be asked to authenticate to the host. This process is presented in Figure 4.

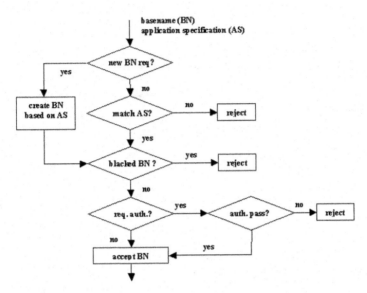

Fig. 4. The proposed solution

Motivating authentication of the verifier. To ensure that a user's affiliations are not learnt by an adversary the host must authenticate the verifier. Although the DAA protocol does not require verifier authentication it is expected that this will be the case in real applications. Standard authentication techniques can be used.

Manageability of basename list. The framework makes basenames more manageable. Basenames are constructed from application specific data and prior to use the host may authenticate the verifier. This means that the host need not maintain a complete list of basenames, since checks can be made to ensure that the basename is suitable for use with a specific application/verifier. This will ensure the list is relatively short. The host need only keep a blacklist if it wishes to avoid certain basenames. Expired basenames can be removed from either list.

6   Optimisations

6.1   Reduction in Messages

An optimisation of the join protocol, which reduces the number of messages exchanged from seven to four, is shown in Figure 5. A formal analysis of the optimisation is beyond the scope of this paper, but an informal discussion is given. The optimisation allows the host to learn n_i earlier than the original protocol. Since this value provides the host with no advantage the protocol is believed to remain secure. The three subsequent messages are all passed from the host to the issuer in succession, it therefore makes no difference to the security

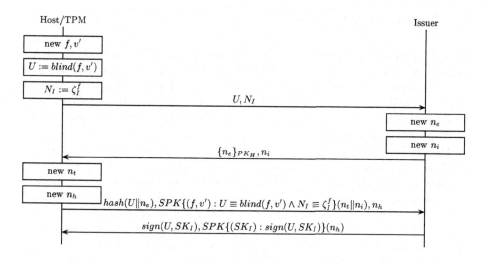

Fig. 5. Optimised Join Protocol

of the protocol to concatenate these messages into a single message. It is claimed the optimisation reduces the number of messages whilst maintaining security.

6.2   Rogue Tagging

The rogue tagging checks can be optimised. Since ζ_I is a constant in the join protocol the issuer is able to precompute $\zeta_I^{\tilde{f}_0 + \tilde{f}_1 2^{l_f}}$ (mod Γ) for all $(\tilde{f}_0, \tilde{f}_1)$ on the rogue list. This technique can also be applied to the join protocol when ζ is fixed. In the case where ζ is random Brickell, Camenisch & Chen [6] propose that a considerable speedup can be achieved using the batch verification techniques defined by Bellare, Garay & Rabin [17,18].

7   Conclusion

In this paper a weakness of the Direct Anonymous Attestation protocol is presented. The weakness allows an issuer and verifier to collude to violate the privacy of the host. The vulnerability is fixed by making a minor alteration to the scheme. It is noted that the modification only affects the host part of the protocol (i.e. no modifications need be made to the hardware TPM). The fix is believed to be safe. Proving this formally is the topic of current research. Further privacy issues surround verifier-linkability. The DAA protocol provides inadequate provisions to enable the host to identify with whom, and for which application, a basename may be used. This may result in a privacy violation. The problem is resolved by the development of a framework which facilitates the correct construction/use of basenames. In addition, optimisations to reduce the number of messages exchanged and to improve the efficiency of rogue tagging are presented.

8 Further Work

This paper used informal techniques to identify an inadequacy of the DAA scheme. Such methods are not complete and thus formal verification techniques must be applied to give assurance that the protocol is indeed secure. The applied pi calculus is a formalism suitable for modelling DAA which allows us to verify properties using automatic tools. The verification of the scheme remains the topic of future research.

The strength of a security system is inversely proportional to its complexity. DAA provides a esoteric solution to a seemingly simply problem. This work has discovered a vulnerability in its design. Inevitably, implementation will result in intrinsic weaknesses. Further research should aim to establish simpler solutions, ultimately producing systems with greater security and efficiency.

Cryptographers can create secure systems which deliver provably strong security properties. Society, however, is unwilling to accept such systems. Chaum introduced digital cash in the 1980s offering powerful properties including anonymity and unlinkability. Digital cash attracted little attention and was essentially rejected by society over concerns of *"taxation* [evasion] *and money laundering, instability of the exchange rate, disturbance of the money supply, and the possibility of a Black Monday in cyberspace"* [19]. DAA addresses society's concerns using linkability, an impurity which appears undesirable, but is demanded by the real world. Further research should look to enable a more fine-grained approach to the level of privacy provided to the user. Revocable unlinkability could for example be provided. This would provide absolute privacy in normal operation but would allow linkability to be revoked by the collaboration of the issuer and n verifiers.

References

1. Pfitzmann, A., Köhntopp, M.: Anonymity, unobservability, and pseudeonymity a proposal for terminology. In: International workshop on Designing privacy enhancing technologies, pp. 1–9. Springer, Heidelberg (2001)
2. Pfitzmann, A., Köhntopp, M.: Anonymity, unlinkability, unobservability, pseudonymity, and identity management a consolidated proposal for terminology. version 0.26. Technical report, Department of Computer Science, Technische Universität Dresden (2005)
3. Reiter, M.K., Rubin, A.D.: Crowds: anonymity for web transactions. ACM Transactions on Information and System Security (TISSEC) 1(1), 66–92 (1998)
4. Reed, M.G., Syverson, P.F., Goldschlag, D.M.: Anonymous connections and onion routing. Selected Areas in Communications 16(4), 482–494 (1998)
5. TCG: Trusted Computing Platform Alliance (TCPA) Main Specification Version 1.1b. Technical report, Trusted Computing Group, Previously published by the Trusted Computing Platform Alliance (2002)
6. Brickell, E., Camenisch, J., Chen, L.: Direct anonymous attestation. In: CCS '04: 11th ACM conference on Computer and communications security, New York, United States of America, pp. 132–145. ACM Press, New York (2004)

7. TCG: TCG TPM Specification Version 1.2 Revision 85. Technical report, Trusted Computing Group (2005)
8. Camenisch, J., Stadler, M.: Efficient group signature schemes for large groups (extended abstract). In: Kaliski Jr., B.S. (ed.) CRYPTO 1997. LNCS, vol. 1294, pp. 410–424. Springer, Heidelberg (1997)
9. Fiat, A., Shamir, A.: How to prove yourself: practical solutions to identification and signature problems. In: Odlyzko, A.M. (ed.) CRYPTO 1986. LNCS, vol. 263, pp. 186–194. Springer, Heidelberg (1987)
10. Menezes, A.J., van Oorschot, P.C., Vanstone, S.A.: Handbook of Applied Cryptography. 5 edn. CRC Press (2001)
11. Meadows, C.: Formal methods for cryptographic protocol analysis: emerging issues and trends. Selected Areas in Communications 21(1), 44–54 (2003)
12. Koblitz, N., Menezes, A.J.: Another look at "provable security". Cryptology ePrint Archive, Report 2004/152 (2004)
13. Camenisch, J., Lysyanskaya, A.: An efficient system for non-transferable anonymous credentials with optional anonymity revocation. In: Pfitzmann, B. (ed.) EUROCRYPT 2001. LNCS, vol. 2045, pp. 93–118. Springer, Heidelberg (2001)
14. Camenisch, J., Herreweghen, E.V.: Design and implementation of the idemix anonymous credential system. In: CCS '02: Proceedings of the 9th ACM conference on Computer and communications security, pp. 21–30. ACM Press, New York (2002)
15. Camenisch, J., Groth, J.: Group signatures: better efficiency and new theoretical aspects. In: Blundo, C., Cimato, S. (eds.) SCN 2004. LNCS, vol. 3352, pp. 120–133. Springer, Heidelberg (2005)
16. Brickell, E., Camenisch, J., Chen, L.: The DAA Scheme in Context. In: Mitchell, C.(eds.) Trusted Computing. The Institute of Electrical Engineers (IEE) (2005)
17. Bellare, M., Garay, J.A., Rabin, T.: Fast batch verification for modular exponentiation and digital signatures. In: Nyberg, K. (ed.) EUROCRYPT 1998. LNCS, vol. 1403, pp. 236–250. Springer, Heidelberg (1998)
18. Bellare, M., Garay, J.A., Rabin, T.: Fast batch verification for modular exponentiation and digital signatures. Cryptology ePrint Archive, Report 1998/007, Full version (1998)
19. Tanaka, T.: Possible economic consequences of digital cash. In: INET '96. Proceedings of the 6th Annual Internet Society Conference, ISOC (1996)
20. Brickell, E., Camenisch, J., Chen, L.: Direct anonymous attestation. Cryptology ePrint Archive, Report 2004/205, Full version of ACM CCS '04 paper (February 2004)
21. Brickell, E., Camenisch, J., Chen, L.: Direct anonymous attestation. Technical report, HP Labs (HPL-2004-93) (June 2004)

New Strategies for Revocation
in Ad-Hoc Networks

Tyler Moore, Jolyon Clulow, Shishir Nagaraja, and Ross Anderson

Computer Laboratory, University of Cambridge
15 JJ Thomson Avenue, Cambridge CB3 0FD, United Kingdom
firstname.lastname@cl.cam.ac.uk

Abstract. Responding to misbehavior in ad-hoc and sensor networks is difficult. We propose new techniques for deciding when to remove nodes in a decentralized manner. Rather than blackballing nodes that misbehave, a more efficient approach turns out to be *reelection* – requiring nodes to secure a majority or plurality of approval from their neighbors at regular intervals. This can be implemented in a standard model of voting in which the nodes form a club, or in a lightweight scheme where each node periodically broadcasts a 'buddy list' of neighbors it trusts. This allows much greater flexibility of trust strategies than a predetermined voting mechanism. We then consider an even more radical strategy still – *suicide attacks* – in which a node on perceiving another node to be misbehaving simply declares both of them to be dead. Other nodes thereafter ignore them both. Suicide attacks, found in a number of contexts in nature from bees to helper T-cells, turn out to be more efficient still for an interesting range of system parameters.

Keywords: credential revocation, sensor networks, key management.

1 Introduction

The last ten years have seen the invention and deployment of a range of systems which organize themselves out of a collection of nodes in order to perform some task. Peer-to-peer systems emerged in the late 1990s, first as a means of resisting censorship on the Internet [1] and then as a mechanism for file-sharing. Communications technologies such as WiFi, Bluetooth and Homeplug support short-range networking of disparate devices in home and office environments, and may allow larger networks to be assembled opportunistically. Sensor networks then came along – networks assembled from large numbers of low-cost nodes that could be scattered into an area of interest to perform some task such as surveillance or environmental monitoring. We describe such communications strategies generically as 'ad-hoc networking'.

One consequence for these new technologies is that management by central authority is being discarded in favor of decentralized mechanisms to improve efficiency and robustness. Here, tasks are distributed amongst member nodes which cooperate to provide services and reach decisions. Another key feature

F. Stajano et al. (Eds.): ESAS 2007, LNCS 4572, pp. 232–246, 2007.

of wireless ad-hoc networks is their support for mobile devices. Devices move while remaining connected to the network, breaking links with old neighbors and establishing fresh links with new devices. Finally, resource constraints limit the tools available to the protocol designer: at most a minority of nodes have the capability to create digital signatures or store large amounts of data; symmetric cryptography is preferred for establishing and maintaining key material.

There are various threats to ad-hoc networks, of which the most interesting and important is probably *node subversion*. A node in a military sensor network may be reverse-engineered by the enemy, and replaced by a malicious node that knows its key material and can thus impersonate it. A participant in a peer-to-peer network may be forced to hand over his keys to an enforcement agency. Subverted nodes can perform a number of attacks on the network, for example, decrypting messages, injecting false data and manipulating decentralized operations such as voting. Thus they must be identified and removed quickly.

In this paper, we seek to address this revocation problem. We are primarily concerned with ad-hoc networks where a minority of nodes can be subverted, and with mechanisms whereby a subverted node can be efficiently removed. Existing strategies using certificate revocation lists and certification authorities are inappropriate for the requirements of these new systems. Instead, we propose lightweight revocation mechanisms suited to decentralized and mobile networks.

In Section 2, we review existing work. We then propose new distributed mechanisms for deciding when to remove bad nodes: reelection in Section 3 where nodes cast positive votes rather than negative ones, and suicide attacks in Section 4 where a node unilaterally decides to remove a bad node at the expense of its own participation on the network. In Section 5, we compare the performance and security of each scheme before concluding in Section 6.

2   Background

2.1   System Model

There are four basic events in the life cycle of an ad-hoc network: *pre-deployment*, *initialization*, *operation* and *revocation*. In pre-deployment, the network owner (if one exists) programs nodes with key material. For instance, symmetric keys are often pre-loaded onto sensor nodes [2,3,4,5]. Nodes are then deployed and initialized; during this phase they establish keys with their neighbors. When nodes are mobile, this is a continuing process rather than one-off. At any stage, one or more nodes may find another misbehaving, and this may prompt a decision to remove the bad node from the system.

Good nodes adhere to their programmed strategy including algorithms for routing and revocation. The attacker can compromise a small minority of nodes. A bad node can communicate with any other node, good or bad. Bad nodes may have access to the keys of all other bad nodes, whom they can therefore impersonate if they wish. They do not execute the authorized software and thus do not necessarily follow protocols to identify misbehavior, revoke other bad nodes, vote honestly or delete keys shared with revoked nodes.

We consider the two main threat models in the literature. Under the *conservative* model, a global, active adversary is present from the start of deployment; networks thus require a pre-deployment phase where nodes are assigned keys. Under the *relaxed* threat model, the opponent can monitor at most a small minority of communications during the initialization phase [6,7]. This means that no, or fewer, keys need to be pre-loaded; instead, nodes set up link keys with neighbors immediately after deployment. In each case, however, the focus is on the ease and cost of security maintenance after deployment.

Another important threat is the *Sybil attack* [8,9], in which an opponent denies service by causing large numbers of malicious nodes to join the network. A Sybil variant is node replication [10], where many copies of a subverted node are introduced. These stratagems have been used to attack peer-to-peer systems. We focus on networks in which the Sybil attack can be contained, perhaps by having a cost of entry, or perhaps by using initially trustworthy nodes whose subversion requires a finite effort of reverse engineering.

2.2   Dealing with Bad Nodes

Three stages are required to revoke a bad node: detecting misbehavior, deciding whether to revoke, and implementing punishment. While each stage is important, in this paper we focus on the decision whether to revoke an accused node.

Deciding when to remove a node is complicated by two factors. First, detection mechanisms rarely produce evidence that is universally non-repudiable. When such mechanisms do exist (e.g., geographic packet leashes [11] for detecting wormholes and node replication detection in sensor networks [9]), they require extensive use of costly signed messages. Furthermore, situations where a bad node is forced into self-incrimination are limited. It can be hard to get hanging evidence against a node that drops occasional messages because messages vanish for many reasons unconnected with malice. More typically, evidence is gathered which is non-repudiable to a single party. For example, a message authentication code (MAC) generated with a key shared between two nodes guarantees authenticity to the other node. Detection mechanisms of this type include temporal packet leashes [11], Sybil attack [8] detection by querying for possessed keys [9] and distance-bounding protocols [12,13,14]. Still other mechanisms rely on evidence that is entirely repudiable (e.g., the wireless monitoring scheme Watchdog [15] where nodes promiscuously listen to their neighbors' routing actions). Repudiable evidence enables bad nodes to falsely accuse good nodes. Hence, it would be foolish to design a simple decision mechanism that revokes any node accused of misbehavior following a single unsubstantiated claim of impropriety.

The second factor hindering the design of decision mechanisms is that untrusted nodes, not central authorities, are often in the best position to detect misbehavior. If node A accuses node B of making inconsistent statements about its location and B denies making them, a trusted base station can only determine one of them is misbehaving. Hence a distributed decision mechanism is required, and existing proposals for collective decision-making have been voting-based. Threshold voting is a natural choice to implement revocation as it conceptually distributes the decision-making process while taking into account the observations of others. Once the number of votes cast exceeds the specified threshold, then the target node is deemed to be malicious and revoked from the network. Any such *blackballing* scheme must deal with a number of key issues: which nodes are eligible to vote, how individual votes are verified, how votes are tallied and how the outcome of a vote is verified. (In the absence of global non-repudiation, the Byzantine generals problem means that, in general, we need a majority of $\frac{2}{3} + \epsilon$ rather than $\frac{1}{2} + \epsilon$ of good nodes; we are concerned in this paper with applications in which the proportion of wrongdoers is much less than $\frac{1}{3}$.)

Once a decision is reached, the bad node is punished. Typically, bad nodes are kept from interacting with good nodes by instructing every node to delete all keys shared with the bad node [2,3,6]. Alternatively, nodes could be implicitly removed by routing around the bad node [15] or by maintaining a blacklist.

2.3 Existing Decision Mechanisms

In [3], Chan, Perrig and Song propose a distributed revocation mechanism for sensor networks using the random pairwise key-predistribution scheme, where nodes sharing a pre-assigned pairwise key can vote to remove a node. Their scheme is extended and generalized in [16]. Here, each node B that shares a pairwise key with A is assigned to the set of *participants of* A, V_A. While the average number of voting members v is significantly larger than the number of neighbors in direct communication range, tying voting eligibility to key predistribution avoids the difficulties in accurately determining neighbors post-deployment.

Every node A is assigned a unique revocation secret rev_A, which is divided into secret shares and given to every $B \in V_A$ along with an authentication value for the revocation secret, $h^2(\mathrm{rev}_A)$. Nodes vote for another's removal by revealing their share. If enough shares are revealed, then rev_A can be reconstructed and the hash $h(\mathrm{rev}_A)$ is broadcast throughout the network. Every node $B \in V_A$ deletes its key shared with A upon verifying the broadcast. Only nodes eligible to vote against a revoked node are loaded with the authentication value for the revocation secret. Any path keys established between a non-voting node and a revoked node are not removed since the non-voting node cannot verify the revocation secret. Thus, authentication values for revocation secrets should be loaded onto every node; [17] describes an efficient $1 + v \log n$ solution.

One problem with voting by revealing secret shares is that cast votes are permanent; a slow trickle of votes against a node over its lifetime is equivalent to a burst in a short period. To avoid stale votes, Chan et al. create T revocation sessions each with a unique revocation secret $\mathrm{rev}_{A,i}, i \in \{1, \ldots, T\}$ and associated shares $\mathrm{rev}_{A,i,B}$; thus a revealed share only counts as a vote for a single period i.

To recap, each node A is loaded with information to do the following:

1. **Vote against each node $B \in V_A$:** Secret share $\mathrm{rev}_{B,i,A} \forall B \in V_A, i \in \{1, \ldots, T\}$) (storage cost vT)
2. **Prove to all $B \in V_A$ that vote is valid:** $\log v$ path-authentication values for each vote $\mathrm{rev}_{B,i,A}$ (storage cost $vT \log v$)

3. **Verify votes from others:** Merkle tree roots $\forall B \in V_A, i \in \{1, \ldots, T\}$ (storage cost vT)
4. **Verify revocation secrets:** Authentication values for each revocation secrets $h^2(\mathrm{rev}_{B,i})\forall B \in N, i \in \{i, \ldots, T\}$ (storage cost nT)

However, voting schemes are slow, expensive and prone to manipulation. They are often susceptible to false accusations, collusive attackers and Sybil attacks; they can result in a delayed attack response between a node starting to misbehave and a revocation order being issued; they do not cope well with node mobility and churn; they may require that at least some nodes can do public-key cryptography; and they impose high storage and communications overhead.

In Sections 3 & 4, we propose new decision mechanisms with the aim of improving security and performance. We use Chan et al.'s blackballing decision mechanism as a basis for comparison.

3   Reelection

Existing proposals for decision and punishment require action by the honest members of the network to remove misbehaving nodes. For example, all nodes must follow the voting, blacklisting and key removal procedures to prevent a malicious node from rejoining the network. This represents a significant computational and communications burden shared by all honest nodes and shirked by malicious ones. In contrast, we propose a mechanism that turns the computational liability on its head by requiring additional effort for honest nodes to continue participating on the network but no effort to remove malicious devices.

We propose a system where a node, on joining the network and periodically thereafter, must demonstrate that it is still authorized to be on the network. Revocation becomes preventing a bad node from renewing its membership. Conceptually, this corresponds to a voting scheme with positive votes instead of negative ones: good nodes reelect each other to the club once in each time period.

We first present a robust protocol for remaining on the network using threshold-secret-sharing mechanisms. Since threshold schemes can be too expensive for peanut processors, we then propose a lightweight reelection mechanism using hash operations exclusively.

3.1   Reelection for Semi-capable Devices

We define a *network access token* $\mathrm{access}_{A,i}$ that allows node A onto the network during time period $i \in \{1, \ldots, T\}$. A must present the token $\mathrm{access}_{A,i}$ to its neighbors to continue interacting with them. Tokens are created using a hash chain where $\mathrm{access}_{A,i-1} = h(\mathrm{access}_{A,i})$, for $i = 1, \ldots, T$. The end-of-chain authentication value $\mathrm{access}_{A,0}$ is distributed to every voting member $B \in V_A$, which can authenticate $\mathrm{access}_{A,i}$ for time period i by verifying that $\mathrm{access}_{A,0} = h^{(i)}(\mathrm{access}_{A,i})$.

Each token $\mathrm{access}_{A,i}$ is divided into v shares using a (k,v) threshold-secret-sharing scheme. The shares are distributed to the voting members $B \in V_A$. In particular, B is assigned shares $\text{access}_{A,i,B}$ for each $i = 1, \ldots, T$. Responsibility for reconstructing tokens rests with A, which asks its voting members for their shares. So B casting $\text{access}_{A,i,B}$ is an affirmation of A's honesty rather than a claim of impropriety. Hence, the threshold of votes k may be larger than for black-balling, as more positive votes are required than negative ones. Note that if the voting members are those pre-assigned a pairwise key (as in Chan et al.'s black-balling scheme),then nodes should delete any voting shares for non-neighbors following neighbor discovery. Alternatively, we could reduce the average number of voting members v by choosing the voting set upon deployment.

Nodes must store additional information to verify transmitted votes and tokens. To verify received votes, node A can store a hash of each share $h(\text{access}_{A,i,B})$ for each $B \in V_A$ and $i = 1, \ldots, T$. To authenticate reconstructed tokens, the owner creates a hash tree where the leaf pre-images are the end-of-chain authentication values $\text{access}_{A,0}$ for each $A \in N$. Each node A stores the tree's root-authentication value, its own end-of-chain authentication value $\text{access}_{A,0}$ and the $\log n$ path-authentication values required to authenticate $\text{access}_{A,0}$.

Here is the reelection protocol for a node during time period i:

1. $A \longrightarrow * : A, i$
2. $B \longrightarrow A : A, B, \text{access}_{A,i,B}$
3. $A \longrightarrow * : A, i, \text{access}_{A,i}, \text{access}_{A,0}, \text{path-authentication values}$
4. $\quad * : \quad$ verify $h^{(i)}(\text{access}_{A,i}) = \text{access}_{A,0}$, verify $\text{access}_{A,0}$

A asks each neighbor B for its share $\text{access}_{A,i,B}$ (step 1). If k voting neighbors cooperate (step 2), then A can reconstruct $\text{access}_{A,i}$, which is then broadcast to A's neighbors (step 3). The neighbors verify $h^{(i)}(\text{access}_{A,i}) = \text{access}_{A,0}$ (step 4).

If node B wishes to vote against A, then it simply deletes the stored shares $\text{access}_{A,i,B}, i = 1, \ldots, T$. Once all of the node's neighbors minus k have done so, A can no longer reconstruct tokens. Revocation is final and absolute: even if the adversary subsequently compromises all neighbor nodes, it cannot reconstruct the tokens. The basic method can be trivially modified to temporarily punish A by deleting a subset of the tokens for a number of time periods.

Nodes must wait to delete a revealed neighbor's share until the following round; otherwise an attacker could ask for a neighbor's share so that the intended node does not observe the response. Also, note that step 1 is optional; any node loaded with secret shares for a node A can reveal the share without being asked. Dropping this broadcast step means that nodes must continuously listen for neighbors revealing their shares.

To recap, each a node A is loaded with information to do the following:

1. **Token share for each node $B \in V_A$:** Secret share $\text{access}_{B,i,A} \forall B \in V_A$, $i \in \{1, \ldots, T\}$ (storage cost vT)
2. **No need to prove token shares to $B \in V_A$:** (storage cost 0)
3. **Verify received shares:** Hash values of all token shares for A (storage cost vT)
4. **Prove to all that token is valid:** Root-authentication value and path-authentication values (storage cost $1 + \log n$)

3.2   Lightweight Reelection with Buddy Lists

Reconstructing secret shares can be too demanding for devices with peanut processors. In addition, the effort involved in pre-assigning, swapping and storing vT shares per node may be unattractive in some applications. Also, in some applications we might want to use diverse strategies: risk-averse nodes might shun a neighbor as soon as one of its other neighbors had done so, while more relaxed nodes might continue to do business with any node that was still supported by two of its neighbors. In some applications, one might want a diverse population of risk-averse and risk-loving nodes, so that the network performed well in normal times but still performed acceptably under serious attack. It therefore makes sense to disentangle the voting mechanism as far as possible from the strategy.

We therefore consider a lightweight reelection mechanism that is general enough to support diverse strategies. The central idea is that nodes periodically transmit a *buddy list* of approved neighbors across their local neighborhoods. Since many node neighbors overlap, they can cross-reference received lists to determine whether enough nodes have also approved their buddies. If so, they continue to interact with the nodes during the next time period. The definition of 'enough' is made independently of the protocol mechanism described here.

Approved buddy lists are authenticated using Guy Fawkes-style [18] hash chains: upon deployment, node A distributes a key authentication value $K_{A,0} = h^{(T)}(\text{seed}, A)$ to its neighbors. Buddy lists are signed with a session authentication key $K_{A,i} = h^{(T-i)}(\text{seed}, A)$ during time period i, and $K_{A,i}$ is not revealed until the start of period $i+1$. Here is the protocol:

1. $A \longrightarrow * : k_{i-1}, \text{access}_{A,i}(\text{buddies}) = \langle A, i, \text{buddies}, \text{HMAC}_{K_i}(A, i, \text{buddies}) \rangle$
2. $\quad * : \quad$ Verify $\text{access}_{A,i-1}(\text{buddies})$, delete offending neighbor's keys

Each node A broadcasts a list of approved neighbors $\text{access}_{A,i}(\text{buddies})$, where buddies is a set of approved node identifiers. Notably, no pre-assigned storage or topological information is required, yet buddy lists work even under the conservative threat model. They also support extremely general strategies for maintaining a network's trusted membership. Nodes' risk aversion could change over time, according to news from other nodes, or as part of an evolutionary game; one could even implement dynamic games similar to Conway's game of 'Life'. Separating trust strategies from the underlying protocol, and implementing it using lightweight and purely local mechanisms, is the strength of this option.

4   Suicide Attacks

Doing revocation by blackballing has turned out to be complex and costly. Matters were improved by a move to reelection, whereby each node had to persuade a quorum of its neighbors to support its continued membership at regular intervals, and still further by the buddy-list mechanism. Here we introduce a radical, even simpler and in some ways even cheaper method: suicide.

Decisions are much simpler if a single node can decide. Should a node believe another has misbehaved, then it can carry out punishment. The trouble with this approach is that a malicious node can falsely accuse legitimate ones; the solution is to make punishment costly. If a node determines another node has cheated, there is no more convincing way to let its neighbors know than to be prepared to die to certify the fact. (The many echoes in pre-modern human societies range from ancient feuds, through medieval trial by combat, to the duels of eighteenth-century Europe.) We discussed suicide as a strategy in [19]; here we describe implementations and ways to mitigate abuse. We present three cases in order of increasing complexity: where a central trusted authority is available; using limited asymmetric cryptography without access to a trusted authority; and using only conventional cryptography without access to a trusted authority.

4.1   Suicide Using a Central Authority

The simplest way to implement suicide attacks is using a central authority such as a base station. Upon detecting a node M engaging in some illegal activity, node A sends a *suicide note* suicide$_{A,M}$ with the identities of both A and M to the base station authenticated by the pairwise unique key shared between the node and the base station. The base station S confirms that node A is entitled to revoke node M and informs the other nodes in the network by sending either individually authenticated messages or a single TESLA-authenticated message [20]. Note that the decision mechanism remains distributed: it is the nodes, not the authority, who decide when to revoke each other since nodes are better positioned to detect misbehavior than far-away base stations.

4.2   Distributed Suicide Using Signatures

Nodes may not have access to a trusted base station; instead node A broadcasts a signed note suicide$_{A,M}$ with the identities of both A and M. The other nodes in the network verify the signature and, if correct, revoke both A and M by deleting all keys shared with them and/or adding both identities to a blacklist.

Public key cryptography works when nodes are sufficiently capable. The owner generates a new public-private key pair for each node and signs the public key. The key pair, certificate and owner's public key are stored on the node. When a node issues a suicide note, it broadcasts its public key certificate along with the suicide note for other nodes to verify the public key and suicide note.

In constrained devices, one-time signatures using only pseudo-random functions may be substituted [21]. Each node is pre-loaded with a single private signing key and the associated public key: this key might be certified by the network owner, or a hash of the key might be the device's name, depending on the deployment model and computational constraints. Nodes verifying a signed suicide note must be able to authenticate the public key. Thus the owner constructs a hash tree with the public keys as leaves suitably ordered to tie a node's identity to its position in the tree. Each node stores the root-authentication value and the $\log n$ path-authentication values required to verify their own public key. The path-authentication values are subsequently broadcast along with the signed suicide note.

4.3 Flypaper and Trolling Attacks

One challenge for a decentralized suicide scheme is ensuring that multiple nodes do not issue suicide notes for a single misbehaving node. In a *flypaper attack*, a malicious node in a fixed location presents widely observable misbehavior to attract many simultaneous suicides. A base station S can trivially resolve multiple suicide offers for the same node by accepting just one of them:

1. A :   detects M misbehaving
2. $A \longrightarrow S : A, M, \text{HMAC}_{K_{AS}}(\text{suicide}_{A,M})$
3. S :   verify signature, wait for duplicates
4. $S \longrightarrow B : A, M, \text{HMAC}_{K_{SB}}(\text{suicide}_{A,M}) \ \forall B \in N$
5. $*$:   verifies signature, deletes keys shared with A, M, adds to blacklist

In a decentralized scheme, where each node must be able to reach a decision independently, two precautions can mitigate a flypaper attack. First, a node can wait a random back-off period ($0 \leq t_{\text{r}} < t_{\text{max}}$) before transmitting an offer. If it observes another suicide note for the same node while waiting for its own timer to expire, the node abandons its offer in favor of the already-published one. If its timer does expire, the node transmits a suicide message. Larger values of t_{max} lower the probability of a collision at the expense of slower revocation. This back-off can significantly reduce the number of simultaneous transmissions; however, duplicate offers are still possible if a second timer expires before the first transmitted suicide message is received by the second node.

To address this possibility, a tie-breaking mechanism is required. If loose time synchronization exists in the network, nodes can append a timestamp to their signed suicide message. Nodes then wait long enough for all offers to be broadcast (t_{bcast}) and honor the suicide note with the earliest timestamp. Alternatively, time synchronization can be avoided by using a using a random number transmitted along with each suicide message. However, using time stamps to resolve conflicts is more efficient since earlier offers are likely to propagate faster. One consequence when using one-time signatures is that we must now store Q key pairs per node, or generate signing keys on the fly from a secret (using a modified hash chain or stream cipher encryption of a secret). Here is the distributed protocol for two nodes A and B detecting M misbehaving:

1a. A :   detect M misbehaving; start random timer t_r
1b. B :   detect M misbehaving; start random timer $t_{r'}$
2. A :   Timer t_r expires (assuming $t_r < t_{r'}$)
3. $A \longrightarrow * : A, M, t_A, \{\text{suicide}_{A,M}, t_A\}_{K_A^{-1}}$
4. $*$:   waits t_{bcast} for earlier offers, verifies signature, deletes keys shared
           with A, M and adds them to blacklist

Trolling is where a node presents itself in several locations, either re-using identities (node replication) or presenting different ones (Sybil). This could be done with the aid of collusive malicious nodes that present the same misbehaving identity in multiple locations. Alternatively, a powerful transmitter or flying over the area achieves the same effect. We have assumed in this paper that other mechanisms exist for detecting and preventing Sybil and node-replication attacks. However, our multiple-offer resolution mechanism addresses trolling with re-used identities even when node replication detection is not available, provided the network is connected and a long enough time-out is used to allow multiple offers notes to traverse the network.

If the adversary is capable of partitioning the network, then a single malicious node can kill multiple good nodes either by issuing different suicide notes in each partition, or by misbehaving in different partitions with the aim of prompting multiple suicide notes. The number of honest nodes affected is proportional to the number of partitions. A potential countermeasure is *resurrection*: once the network is reconnected, several suicide attacks on a single node can be converted into the resurrection of all but the first sacrificed node along with revoking the replicated node. In this case, suicide notes would have to be stored, and a blacklist operated in preference to deleting keys. (Note that if revocation is reversible, then all the mechanisms compared in this paper become more complex.)

4.4 Extensions: Probabilistic Suicide and Suicide Pacts

Suicide may not be well suited to detection mechanisms that identify malicious nodes with less than high confidence. Yet the basic mechanism can be extended to cope with uncertainty. Suppose a node detects behavior that is probably malicious, and can assign a probability to this (e.g., bad with $p = 0.7$).

One solution is for a node to maintain a running total for each node it can observe. When the total exceeds a specified threshold (e.g., $\sum p_i \geq 1$), a suicide attack is triggered. A stateless alternative is for the node to attack with probability p. One limitation of these approaches is that each node operates in isolation, gaining no benefit from the collective knowledge of its neighbors.

We can modify the suicide offers to include probability p as offer$_{A,M}, t_A, p,$ $\{$offer$_{A,M}, t_A, p\}_{K_A^{-1}}$. Thus revocation decisions can be made on collective knowledge of uncertain observations, and the nodes participating in this decision might be thought of as having entered into a *suicide pact* against the suspect. Deciding which member of the pact has to carry out the suicide attack should reflect the probability claimed in the suicide offer, whether based on a weighted, verifiable coin toss, or simple probabilistic attack in the second round of the protocol.

5 Analysis and Comparison

5.1 Storage and Communication Costs

A comparison of the storage costs is presented in Table 1. Each column represents the tasks discussed in Sections 2.3 & 3.1.

Reelection is more efficient than blackballing in terms of storage: access shares ('positive votes') need only be verified by one node, and only one node (the target node) need store the authentication information for the recovered token. Thus, storage costs for reelection are $O(vT + \log n)$, compared to $O(vT + v \log n)$ for

Table 1. Node storage costs for alternative schemes

Node storage for	1.	2.	3.	4.
Blackballing	vT	$v \log Tv$	vT	$1 + v \log n$
Reelection	vT	0	vT	$1 + \log n$
Suicide (sym.)	$O(Q)$	$Q \log nQ$	0	1
Suicide (asym.)	1	1	1	1

blackballing. However, reelection arguably may require more, shorter time periods (and hence larger values for T) since a revoked node does not immediately lose access to the network but only at the end of the current time period. As with blackballing, we can also reduce v using a weakened threat model.

Both blackballing and reelection increase storage well beyond the initial costs of key distribution. This is not easily borne, particularly for large networks of constrained devices. In contrast, suicide using one-time signatures is not affected by the number of keys that are pre-assigned. Here, a node only needs the ability to transmit a very small number (Q) of offers. But the size of each public and private key for one-time signatures can be very large, requiring two hash values per signed bit. Suicide using asymmetric cryptography requires far less storage as nodes keep only their own private and public keys (small when elliptic curve cryptography is used) as well as the owner's public key and certificate.

Table 2 shows the respective communication costs associated with each scheme. Reelection is unique in that there is a fixed cost per session when a nodes asks for and receives its access shares. This requires a node to broadcast a request to its immediate neighbors, while the k shares can be returned as unicast messages. The reconstructed token is also broadcast. However, communication costs do not increase as nodes get revoked. In contrast, the communication costs of blackballing increase with the number of votes cast. $k + 1$ locally broadcast votes are required to remove a node, where each vote comprises the vote and $\log v$ path-authentication values. These messages may need to be forwarded by other nodes since we are not guaranteed that all voting members are within communication range of each other. The final revocation order must be broadcast across the network (along with $\log n$ path authentication values) to ensure that everyone revokes the malicious node. Since votes are only valid in a given session, it is possible for up to k votes to be cast each session without revoking a node. Thus, blackballing is more efficient than reelection under low rates of misbehavior; reelection fares better when more attackers are present.

Asymmetric suicide is noted for its low communication costs (only one network-wide broadcast), though these energy savings are offset by increased computational expense due to the use of signatures when compared to symmetric-key-based schemes. Of course, voting schemes using asymmetric cryptography faces even higher costs since signatures are required for every vote.

Suicide using one-time signatures can face high communication costs, particularly if the public key must be transmitted along with the signature instead of being pre-loaded onto devices. In fact, recent work has demonstrated that one-time-signature schemes perform only slightly better than elliptic curve

Table 2. Communication costs for alternative schemes

	# sessions	Setup per session	Comm. per rev.	Min accrued comm. without revocation	Max comm. without rev.
Blackballing	T	0	$k+1$ broadcasts	0	kT
Reelection	T	k unicasts +2 broadcasts	0	$2kT$ unicasts +T broadcasts	$2kT$ unicasts +T broadcasts
Suicide (both)	1	0	1 broadcast	0	0

algorithms when considering both the communication and computational overhead [22]. Thus, the limited asymmetric cryptographic operations needed by suicide may be preferable to the higher complexity and storage requirements imposed by one-time signature schemes.

Suicide does offer other advantages over any voting-based scheme, however. Suicide does not suffer from the problem of stale votes nor a delay before the revoked node is removed from the network. It also requires fewer, less restrictive assumptions. Specifically, suicide places no restrictions on node mobility for normal or compromised nodes. It also places no topological restrictions, such as requiring nodes to have a minimum number of neighbors.

On the other hand, suicide does require good nodes to value the social welfare of the network over individual utility. This condition is reasonable whenever the nodes are deployed by a single entity (e.g., a sensor network deployed on a battlefield) but may be less so when nodes are individually controlled (e.g., a peer-to-peer file-sharing system) [23].

5.2   Denial-of-Service Attacks

Suicide enables precision denial-of-service attacks since adversaries can remove any node. Network topology differences increase the importance of some nodes due to their location or number of neighbors. Even unsophisticated attackers can wreak havoc by taking out high-value nodes with low-value-node suicides.

But suicide is arguably less susceptible to DoS attacks than threshold voting schemes. Threshold voting schemes become totally vulnerable once the attacker gains sufficient numerical advantage (exceeding the threshold) in a region. Here the adversary can vote out all good nodes in the area. This is a particular concern when devices are mobile as an attacker can use the minimum number of compromised devices, moving them around the network and ejecting good nodes unchallenged. Suicide, by contrast, bounds the maximum amount of damage a set of malicious nodes can do but means that twice as many nodes are removed from the network – one good node for every bad node.

5.3   Quantifying Suicide Abuse

While protections against flypaper and trolling attacks ensure only one good node is sacrificed per bad node, reconciling several suicide notes due to these

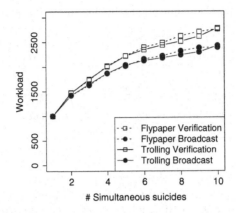

Fig. 1. Workload versus simultaneous suicides

attacks triggers increased communication and computational complexity. An attacker may still attempt flypaper or trolling attacks aiming to consume resources (e.g., battery life or network capacity) by forcing multiple offers to be resolved.

We quantify the increased workload due to these attacks compared to the transmission of a single suicide note. We use simulation since this analysis probabilistically depends on the topology of the network as well as the random back-off period. We consider three scenarios of increasing complexity: normal operation where only a single suicide note is issued; a simple collision where two suicide notes are issued simultaneously; and a trolling attack where misbehavior is presented to nodes across the network simultaneously in the absence of node replication detection to trigger multiple suicide offers. We compute two quantifiable measures: the number of broadcasts attributed to all suicide offers and the number of signature verifications attributed to all suicide offers.

We simulated a wireless network comprised of 1000 nodes uniformly distributed over a plane, where the communication radius of nodes ensures an average of 60 immediate neighbors in communication range. We averaged our results using 10 iterations on a network sample. Each suicide note is embedded with a timestamp. A node re-broadcasts a received suicide note to its immediate neighbors if it is either the first one received, or has the earliest timestamp. In this way, suicide notes are propagated throughout the network until the one with the earliest timestamp completely dominates the network.

When one suicide note is broadcast, every node in the network broadcasts and verifies once. Two simultaneous suicide notes increases the workload by approximately 50%, a manageable rise. But what is the effect of additional simultaneous suicides? Figure 1 plots workload (number of broadcasts and verifications) during trolling and flypaper attacks as a function of the number of simultaneously issued suicide notes. As expected, the computational and communication burden increases. Notably, the function is mostly marginally decreasing, so that most additional suicides increase the workload less than previous ones. At most, resource consumption attacks increase system workload by a small multiple; thus we conclude they are not as dangerous a threat as originally feared.

6 Conclusions

A major challenge for ad-hoc networks is how to remove nodes that are observed to be behaving badly. Existing threshold voting proposals for node revocation enfranchise too many of the wrong nodes, undermining their efficiency and security. They are susceptible to manipulation, particularly if nodes are mobile.

So we switched from voting against bad nodes to a protocol where good nodes reelect each other to the club at regular intervals. Reelection reduces storage costs by shifting the responsibility of verifying votes from a node's neighbors to the node itself. This is a significant improvement, but simple reelection remains infeasible for severely constrained devices. We then proposed a lightweight reelection mechanism requiring no pre-assigned storage and using just hash operations: each node broadcasts a buddy list of trusted neighboring nodes locally at each time period. This can support a much wider range of membership strategies and is significantly cheaper. However (like the other mechanisms we have discussed) it still has some communications costs, and it may be less effective where there are many mobile nodes or an uneven network topology.

We then showed that the most effective way of doing revocation in general ad-hoc networks is the suicide attack. A node observing another node behaving badly simply broadcasts a signed message declaring both of them to be dead. This is cheap; it scales well; it is not affected much by mobility; and it works across interesting parameter ranges. Such strategies are well known in nature, from bees attacking an intruder to the operation of helper T-cells in the immune system. They even find an echo in some human societies, such as the dueling culture of the eighteenth century and the US Wild West. We believe that suicide attacks are attractive for a wide range of distributed system applications.

References

1. Anderson, R.: The eternity service. In: First International Conference on the Theory and Applications of Cryptology (PRAGOCRYPT) (1996)
2. Eschenauer, L., Gligor, V.D.: A key-management scheme for distributed sensor networks. In: 9th ACM Conference on Computer and Communications Security (CCS), ACM, pp. 41–47. ACM Press, New York (2002)
3. Chan, H., Perrig, A., Song, D.X.: Random key predistribution schemes for sensor networks. In: IEEE Symposium on Security and Privacy (S&P), pp. 197–213. IEEE Computer Society Press, Los Alamitos (2003)
4. Du, W., Deng, J., Han, Y.S., Varshney, P.K.: A pairwise key pre-distribution scheme for wireless sensor networks. In: 10th ACM CCS, pp. 42–51. ACM, New York (2003)
5. Liu, D., Ning, P.: Establishing pairwise keys in distributed sensor networks. In: 10th ACM CCS, pp. 52–61. ACM Press, New York (2003)

6. Zhu, S., Setia, S., Jajodia, S.: LEAP: efficient security mechanisms for large-scale distributed sensor networks. In: 10th ACM CCS, pp. 62–72. ACM Press, New York (2003)

7. Anderson, R.J., Chan, H., Perrig, A.: Key infection: Smart trust for smart dust. In: 12th IEEE International Conference on Network Protocols, IEEE Computer Society, pp. 206–215. IEEE Computer Society Press, Los Alamitos (2004)

8. Douceur, J.R.: The Sybil attack. In: Druschel, P., Kaashoek, M.F., Rowstron, A. (eds.) IPTPS 2002. LNCS, vol. 2429, pp. 251–260. Springer, Heidelberg (2002)

9. Newsome, J., Shi, E., Song, D.X., Perrig, A.: The Sybil attack in sensor networks: analysis and defenses. In: 3rd International Symposium on Information Processing in Sensor Networks, pp. 259–268. ACM Press, New York (2004)

10. Parno, B., Perrig, A., Gligor, V.D.: Distributed detection of node replication attacks in sensor networks. In: IEEE S&P, IEEE Computer Society, pp. 49–63. IEEE Computer Society Press, Los Alamitos (2005)

11. Hu, Y.C., Perrig, A., Johnson, D.B.: Packet leashes: A defense against wormhole attacks in wireless networks. In: 22nd IEEE INFOCOM, IEEE Computer Society Press, Los Alamitos (2003)

12. Brands, S., Chaum, D.: Distance-bounding protocols (extended abstract). In: Helleseth, T. (ed.) EUROCRYPT 1993. LNCS, vol. 765, pp. 344–359. Springer, Heidelberg (1994)

13. Hancke, G.P., Kuhn, M.G.: An RFID distance bounding protocol. In: IEEE Secure Comm., pp. 67–73. IEEE Computer Society Press, Los Alamitos (2005)

14. Capkun, S., Buttyan, L., Hubaux, J.P.: SECTOR: secure tracking of node encounters in multi-hop wireless networks. In: 1st ACM Workshop on Security of ad hoc and Sensor Networks, pp. 21–32. ACM Press, New York (2003)

15. Marti, S., Giuli, T.J., Lai, K., Baker, M.: Mitigating routing misbehavior in mobile ad hoc networks. In: 6th International Conference on Mobile Computing and Networking, pp. 255–265. ACM Press, New York (2000)

16. Chan, H., Gligor, V.D., Perrig, A., Muralidharan, G.: On the distribution and revocation of cryptographic keys in sensor networks. IEEE Transactions on Dependable Secure Computing 2(3), 233–247 (2005)

17. Moore, T., Clulow, J.: Secure path-key revocation for symmetric key predistribution schemes in sensor networks. In: 22nd IFIP TC-11 International Information Security Conference 2007 (to appear)

18. Anderson, R., Bergadano, F., Crispo, B., Lee, J.H., Manifavas, C., Needham, R.: A new family of authentication protocols. ACM SIGOPS Operating Systems Review (OSR) 32(4), 9–20 (1998)

19. Clulow, J., Moore, T.: Suicide for the common good: a new strategy for credential revocation in self-organizing systems. ACM SIGOPS OSR 40(3), 18–21 (2006)

20. Perrig, A., Canetti, R., Tygar, J.D., Song, D.X.: Ecient authentication and signing of multicast streams over lossy channels. In: IEEE S&P, pp. 56–73. IEEE Computer Society Press, Los Alamitos (2000)

21. Merkle, R.C.: A certified digital signature. In: Brassard, G. (ed.) CRYPTO 1989. LNCS, vol. 435, pp. 218–238. Springer, Heidelberg (1990)

22. Seys, S., Preneel, B.: Power consumption evaluation of efficient digital signature schemes for low power devices. In: IEEE International Conference on Wireless And Mobile Computing, Networking And Communications, pp. 79–86. IEEE Computer Society Press, Los Alamitos (2005)

23. Danezis, G., Anderson, R.: The economics of resisting censorship. IEEE Security& Privacy 3(1), 45–50 (2005)

Author Index

Lecture Notes in Computer Science

For information about Vols. 1–4469

please contact your bookseller or Springer

Vol. 4513: M. Fischetti, D.P. Williamson (Eds.), Integer Programming and Combinatorial Optimization. IX, 500 pages. 2007.

Vol. 4511: C. Conati, K. McCoy, G. Paliouras (Eds.), User Modeling 2007. XVI, 497 pages. 2007. (Sublibrary LNAI).

Vol. 4510: P. Van Hentenryck, L. Wolsey (Eds.), Integration of AI and OR Techniques in Constraint Programming for Combinatorial Optimization Problems. X, 391 pages. 2007.

Vol. 4509: Z. Kobti, D. Wu (Eds.), Advances in Artificial Intelligence. XII, 552 pages. 2007. (Sublibrary LNAI).

Vol. 4508: M.-Y. Kao, X.-Y. Li (Eds.), Algorithmic Aspects in Information and Management. VIII, 428 pages. 2007.

Vol. 4507: F. Sandoval, A. Prieto, J. Cabestany, M. Graña (Eds.), Computational and Ambient Intelligence. XXVI, 1167 pages. 2007.

Vol. 4506: D. Zeng, I. Gotham, K. Komatsu, C. Lynch, M. Thurmond, D. Madigan, B. Lober, J. Kvach, H. Chen (Eds.), Intelligence and Security Informatics: Biosurveillance. XI, 234 pages. 2007.

Vol. 4505: G. Dong, X. Lin, W. Wang, Y. Yang, J.X. Yu (Eds.), Advances in Data and Web Management. XXII, 896 pages. 2007.

Vol. 4504: J. Huang, R. Kowalczyk, Z. Maamar, D. Martin, I. Müller, S. Stoutenburg, K.P. Sycara (Eds.), Service-Oriented Computing: Agents, Semantics, and Engineering. X, 175 pages. 2007.

Vol. 4501: J. Marques-Silva, K.A. Sakallah (Eds.), Theory and Applications of Satisfiability Testing – SAT 2007. XI, 384 pages. 2007.

Vol. 4500: N. Streitz, A. Kameas, I. Mavrommati (Eds.), The Disappearing Computer. XVIII, 304 pages. 2007.

Vol. 4499: Y.Q. Shi (Ed.), Transactions on Data Hiding and Multimedia Security II. IX, 117 pages. 2007.

Vol. 4497: S.B. Cooper, B. Löwe, A. Sorbi (Eds.), Computation and Logic in the Real World. XVIII, 826 pages. 2007.

Vol. 4496: N.T. Nguyen, A. Grzech, R.J. Howlett, L.C. Jain (Eds.), Agent and Multi-Agent Systems: Technologies and Applications. XXI, 1046 pages. 2007. (Sublibrary LNAI).

Vol. 4495: J. Krogstie, A. Opdahl, G. Sindre (Eds.), Advanced Information Systems Engineering. XVI, 606 pages. 2007.

Vol. 4494: H. Jin, O.F. Rana, Y. Pan, V.K. Prasanna (Eds.), Algorithms and Architectures for Parallel Processing. XIV, 508 pages. 2007.

Vol. 4493: D. Liu, S. Fei, Z. Hou, H. Zhang, C. Sun (Eds.), Advances in Neural Networks – ISNN 2007, Part III. XXVI, 1215 pages. 2007.

Vol. 4492: D. Liu, S. Fei, Z. Hou, H. Zhang, C. Sun (Eds.), Advances in Neural Networks – ISNN 2007, Part II. XXVII, 1321 pages. 2007.

Vol. 4491: D. Liu, S. Fei, Z.-G. Hou, H. Zhang, C. Sun (Eds.), Advances in Neural Networks – ISNN 2007, Part I. LIV, 1365 pages. 2007.

Vol. 4490: Y. Shi, G.D. van Albada, J. Dongarra, P.M.A. Sloot (Eds.), Computational Science – ICCS 2007, Part IV. XXXVII, 1211 pages. 2007.

Vol. 4489: Y. Shi, G.D. van Albada, J. Dongarra, P.M.A. Sloot (Eds.), Computational Science – ICCS 2007, Part III. XXXVII, 1257 pages. 2007.

Vol. 4488: Y. Shi, G.D. van Albada, J. Dongarra, P.M.A. Sloot (Eds.), Computational Science – ICCS 2007, Part II. XXXV, 1251 pages. 2007.

Vol. 4487: Y. Shi, G.D. van Albada, J. Dongarra, P.M.A. Sloot (Eds.), Computational Science – ICCS 2007, Part I. LXXXI, 1275 pages. 2007.

Vol. 4486: M. Bernardo, J. Hillston (Eds.), Formal Methods for Performance Evaluation. VII, 469 pages. 2007.

Vol. 4485: F. Sgallari, A. Murli, N. Paragios (Eds.), Scale Space and Variational Methods in Computer Vision. XV, 931 pages. 2007.

Vol. 4484: J.-Y. Cai, S.B. Cooper, H. Zhu (Eds.), Theory and Applications of Models of Computation. XIII, 772 pages. 2007.

Vol. 4483: C. Baral, G. Brewka, J. Schlipf (Eds.), Logic Programming and Nonmonotonic Reasoning. IX, 327 pages. 2007. (Sublibrary LNAI).

Vol. 4482: A. An, J. Stefanowski, S. Ramanna, C.J. Butz, W. Pedrycz, G. Wang (Eds.), Rough Sets, Fuzzy Sets, Data Mining and Granular Computing. XIV, 585 pages. 2007. (Sublibrary LNAI).

Vol. 4481: J. Yao, P. Lingras, W.-Z. Wu, M. Szczuka, N.J. Cercone, D. Ślęzak (Eds.), Rough Sets and Knowledge Technology. XIV, 576 pages. 2007. (Sublibrary LNAI).

Vol. 4480: A. LaMarca, M. Langheinrich, K.N. Truong (Eds.), Pervasive Computing. XIII, 369 pages. 2007.

Vol. 4479: I.F. Akyildiz, R. Sivakumar, E. Ekici, J.C.d. Oliveira, J. McNair (Eds.), NETWORKING 2007. Ad Hoc and Sensor Networks, Wireless Networks, Next Generation Internet. XXVII, 1252 pages. 2007.

Vol. 4478: J. Martí, J.M. Benedí, A.M. Mendonça, J. Serrat (Eds.), Pattern Recognition and Image Analysis, Part II. XXVII, 657 pages. 2007.

Vol. 4477: J. Martí, J.M. Benedí, A.M. Mendonça, J. Serrat (Eds.), Pattern Recognition and Image Analysis, Part I. XXVII, 625 pages. 2007.

Vol. 4476: V. Gorodetsky, C. Zhang, V.A. Skormin, L. Cao (Eds.), Autonomous Intelligent Systems: Multi-Agents and Data Mining. XIII, 323 pages. 2007. (Sublibrary LNAI).

Vol. 4475: P. Crescenzi, G. Prencipe, G. Pucci (Eds.), Fun with Algorithms. X, 273 pages. 2007.

Vol. 4474: G. Prencipe, S. Zaks (Eds.), Structural Information and Communication Complexity. XI, 342 pages. 2007.

Vol. 4472: M. Haindl, J. Kittler, F. Roli (Eds.), Multiple Classifier Systems. XI, 524 pages. 2007.

Vol. 4471: P. Cesar, K. Chorianopoulos, J.F. Jensen (Eds.), Interactive TV: a Shared Experience. XIII, 236 pages. 2007.

Vol. 4470: Q. Wang, D. Pfahl, D.M. Raffo (Eds.), Software Process Dynamics and Agility. XI, 346 pages. 2007.